Under the editorship of

C. GILBERT WRENN

Professor of Educational Psychology
University of Minnesota

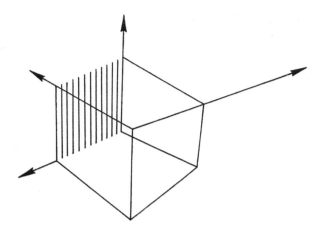

Perspectives on the

C. GRATTON KEMP
The Ohio State University

Group Process

A Foundation for Counseling with Groups

HOUGHTON MIFFLIN COMPANY · BOSTON

Editor's Introduction

A familiar but intriguing analogy attributed to Dr. George McKinley warrants a paraphrase here. If we condense the two billion years during which there has been life on earth to one calendar year, the events of the aeons unroll in a more comprehensible fashion. On January 1 there was a single-cell form of life; on July 1 invertebrate animals made their appearance; in August and September huge reptiles roamed the earth, and by October 1 they were gone; early in October mammals evolved; by December 25 there were walking ape men; six or seven minutes before midnight on December 31 primitive man made his appearance; *twenty-five seconds before midnight on December 31 men began living together in groups for the first time.*

From this analogy, the appalling youthfulness of our opportunity to learn how individuals in groups interact with each other — to say nothing of the recency of our attempts to improve the quality of this interaction — is readily apparent. It is most apparent on a large scale in the clash of nationalisms and on a small scale in marriage conflicts. Less apparent is the great reduction of human efficiency in many small group settings because of friction, lack of direction, and diffusiveness of effort.

An awareness of the recency of our opportunity for the study of groups does not prepare us for the fact that there is available a rather considerable body of literature on group behavior — the result of work in sociology, psychology, and education. It sometimes appears, however, that the left hand knoweth not what the right hand doeth, for many students in one field are poorly read in the others. For this reason it is helpful indeed that this book of readings is truly interdisciplinary in nature. The fifty-three selections that comprise the book have been chosen almost equally from books and journals, with twenty-three having their research or scholarly source in education, seventeen in psychology, eleven in sociology, and two in philosophy. Of equal significance is the fact that this volume introduces the reader to some of the most scholarly and reliable literature in the total field, regardless of the source of discipline. As I have reread the page proofs, I have become impressed anew with how much I have learned from being exposed to some of the best of these writers.

The editor's introductions to and summaries of each part contribute in no small fashion to the total value of the book. Dr. Kemp knows his subject and has written a series of thoughtful, integrative discussions of The Group, The Group Process, Leadership, and the Group Member. This book is designed to provide the understanding of these dimensions of group activity that must undergird any attempt to engage in group development, group counseling, or group therapy.

"Counseling," a term most commonly used to describe a face-to-face relationship of two people, is based upon an understanding of the individual's attributes and dynamics. Until recently "the group" was something to be endured, manipulated, or apologized for. Now we know that a knowledge of the group's characteristics and dynamics is essential to any intelligent attempt to provide individual growth through group membership. "Group counseling" also has its basic disciplines and literature, for which this book provides an introduction.

This is a far cry from the group guidance and group work of the decades prior to 1950. As a consequence of the publication of a book such as this the future will see less professional malpractice with groups.

C. GILBERT WRENN

Preface

The decisions which determine our future are made in small groups. This has always been true to some degree. But never before has its importance been so widely recognized nor has the possibility of its improvement and increasing significance been so widely accepted.

This possibility arises from the breadth and depth of an increasing body of knowledge. The study of small groups has moved in succession from one level to another: from an analysis of the nature of the group, to observation of the process, to analysis of the functioning of leaders, to the study of the behavior of individuals in the group, and to the slowly dawning recognition and acceptance of the interdependence of the members and the responsibility of each to contribute to the welfare of the whole.

The present urgency for expanding and deepening our understanding of groups necessitates an interdisciplinary approach in which concepts old and new are focused in the expectancy that where the disciplines meet new insights may emerge. If this increasing emphasis is to be most constructive, consideration should be given not only to the horizontal dimension of definition, process, and skills but also to the vertical dimension, or its *raison d'être* — its roots in human nature, relevant basic principles from pertinent disciplines, and its possibilities for human development.

The particular contribution of this book is its devotion to both emphases, the horizontal and the vertical. There is not only a presentation of the kinds and types of groups, methods, problems, needed skills, and evaluational processes but also of the foundational principles drawn from several disciplines which undergird and clarify the horizontal dimension.

There are several premises which provide a consistent basis for understanding of the content: (1) the potential limits of the group are based on the potentialities and limitations of man himself; (2) the possibility for realization of potential limits is directly related to the insights gained from psychology, sociology, education, religion, and other disciplines; (3) different types of leadership result in different outcomes; (4) ability to participate constructively and adequately in a group is an extended developmental process; (5) group process enhances the possibilities for change in the perceptions and self-concepts of the members.

The book is planned especially for college students and teachers who are interested and involved in human relationships as they develop in groups. However, industrial groups, church groups, and all youth groups will find the theory enlightening and will gain ideas and insights which will improve their own efficiency in working with groups. Teachers and counselors will find clarification of the functioning of groups and of their own roles as leaders. They will appreciate the research evidence concerning various problems.

vii

Many persons indirectly and directly have contributed to the writing of this book. Students in both elementary and high schools and adult groups have shared ideas with me in several types of settings. College students through analysis and evaluation of the group climate and process have aided in the clarification of the significant content in the training of group leaders. I am also indebted to others who have contributed directly, especially to the critical acumen and patience of the editor, Dr. C. Gilbert Wrenn, and to my wife, Agnes Lackie Kemp, for her encouragement, suggestions, and critical reading of the entire manuscript. Special thanks are also due to the publishers and authors of the fifty-three selections for their permission to reprint their materials. I wish to express my appreciation to all who have shared in the task.

C. GRATTON KEMP

The Ohio State University
Columbus, Ohio

Contents

EDITOR'S INTRODUCTION   v

PREFACE   vii

PART ONE: Issues in the Group Process   3

PART TWO: The Group   19

SECTION A. DEFINITIONS OF THE GROUP

  1. Definitions of the Group — *Cecil A. Gibb*   23

SECTION B. FOUNDATIONS OF THE GROUP

  2. Individuality in Modern Culture — *Reinhold Niebuhr*   30
  3. A Tentative Formulation of a General Law of
     Interpersonal Relationships — *Carl R. Rogers*   33

SECTION C. TYPES AND LEVELS OF GROUPS

  4. Group Guidance: Content and Process — *Leo Goldman*   41
  5. Socio and Psyche Group Process: Integrative
     Concepts — *Hubert Stanley Coffey*   46

SECTION D. GROUP PATTERNS

  6. The Authoritarian Group — *L. Thomas Hopkins*   56
  7. The Democratic Group — *L. Thomas Hopkins*   58
  8. The Group-Centered Group — *Thomas Gordon*   61

SECTION E. VALUES OF THE GROUP

  9. Developing Potentialities Through Class Groups —
     Leland P. Bradford   68
  10. Group Experience: The Democratic Way —
     Bernice Baxter and *Rosalind Cassidy*   76

SUMMARY, QUESTIONS, AND SUGGESTED READINGS   79

PART THREE: The Group Process   83

SECTION A. CHARACTERISTICS OF THE GROUP PROCESS
11. The Causal Relation of Person and Act — *Solomon E. Asch*   86
12. What Is Group Process? — *L. Thomas Hopkins*   91

SECTION B. SPECIAL PROBLEMS IN INTERACTION
13. Group Size as a Factor in Success of Academic
    Discussion Groups — *James A. Schellenberg*   96
14. The "Small Group": An Atom the School
    Can't Split — *Charles A. Tonsor*   102
15. The Silent Period in Group Process — *D. Patrick Hughes*   106

SECTION C. GROUP DECISION AND SOCIAL CHANGE
16. Difficulties Encountered in Group Decision-Making —
    Kenneth F. Herrold, Joel Davitz, David Fox, Irving Lorge   110
17. Social Engineering in Educational Change:
    An Outline of Method — *David H. Jenkins*   114

SECTION D. PROBLEM SOLVING
18. Theoretical Analysis of the Factors Uniquely Affecting Group
    Solutions — *Harold H. Kelley* and *John W. Thibout*   122
19. Group Forces Affecting Learning — *Leland P. Bradford*   135

SECTION E. GROUP COUNSELING
20. Multiple Counseling: Why? When? How? —
    E. Wayne Wright   142
21. Counseling Within a Group Setting — *Merle M. Ohlsen*   150
22. Group-Centered Counseling — *Nicholas Hobbs*   156

SECTION F. EVALUATION
23. Group Self-Evaluation — *David H. Jenkins*   163
24. A Closer Look at the Role of Group Observer —
    National Training Laboratory in Group Development   171

SUMMARY, QUESTIONS, AND SUGGESTED READINGS   181

PART FOUR: Leadership   187

SECTION A. THE LEADER
25. Definition of the Leader — *Cecil A. Gibb*   190
26. Qualities of the Leader — *Murray Ross* and *Charles E. Hendry*   197

Section B. Theories of Leadership

27. The Trait Theory — A. W. *Gouldner*   203
28. The Situationist Theory — A. W. *Gouldner*   206
29. The Interaction Theory — *Helen Hall Jennings*   211

Section C. Psychological Foundations of Leadership

30. Foundations of Authoritarian and Democratic
   Leadership — L. *Thomas Hopkins*   216
31. Foundations of Group-Centered Leadership —
   C. *Gratton Kemp*   219
32. Differing Assumptions in Authoritarian, Democratic,
   and Group-Centered Leadership — C. *Gratton Kemp*   222

Section D. Leadership Functioning

33. Distinctions in Leadership Functioning — C. *Gratton Kemp*   229
34. The Functioning of the Group-Centered Leader —
   Thomas Gordon   232

Section E. Problems of Leadership

35. Making Better Decisions — C. *Gratton Kemp*   245
36. Changing the Group "Climate" — L. *Thomas Hopkins*   248
37. Maintaining a Creative Difference — *Nathaniel Cantor*   251

Section F. Evaluation

38. Evaluation Through the Study of the Leader's
   Behavior — *Andrew W. Halpin*   261
39. Evaluation Through the Leaderless Group Discussion —
   Bernard M. Bass   267
40. Evaluation Through Self-Evaluation — *Thomas Gordon*   272

Summary, Questions, and Suggested Readings   276

PART FIVE: The Group Member   279

Section A. Becoming a Member

41. The Internal Dialogue of the Self — *Reinhold Niebuhr*   282
42. Perception and Its Function — *Arthur W. Combs*
   and *Donald Snygg*   286
43. Self-Actualizing People: Psychological Health — A. H. *Maslow*   290

SECTION B. INTERPERSONAL RELATIONSHIPS OF GROUP MEMBERS

44. Measurement of Self-Oriented Needs in Discussion Groups
— *Nicholas T. Fouriezos, Max L. Hutt,* and *Harold Guetzkow*   296
45. Self-Esteem, Group Interaction, and Group Influence on
Performance — *Ezra Stotland* and *Nickolas B. Cottrell*   306

SECTION C. PERFORMANCE OF GROUP MEMBERS

46. Functional Roles of Group Members —
Kenneth D. Benne and *Paul Sheats*   319
47. What Does Each Member Contribute? — *L. Thomas Hopkins*   324

SECTION D. THE PROCESS OF CHANGE IN GROUP MEMBERS

48. Conduct, Knowledge, and Acceptance of New Values —
Kurt Lewin and *Paul Grabbe*   329
49. Changes in Self-Concepts in Relation to Perceptions
of Others — *Dorothy M. Kipnis*   336

SECTION E. ASSISTING MEMBERS

50. Some Factors of Resistance Which Affect Group
Participation — *Hazel Osborn*   351
51. Understanding the Behavior of "Problem Members" in Groups
— *Horace Mann–Lincoln Institute School of Experimentation*   354

SECTION F. EVALUATION

52. Evaluating the Performance of Individuals as Members
of Small Groups — *Launor F. Carter*   361
53. A Group Studies Itself — *Alice Miel*   366

SUMMARY, QUESTIONS, AND SUGGESTED READINGS   378

INDEX   383

PERSPECTIVES ON THE GROUP PROCESS

A Foundation for Counseling with Groups

PART ONE

Issues in Group Process

Groups are indigenous to all civilizations. Such names as tribe, clan, family, and gang have a long history. Although new lands have been discovered, new governments established, new industries organized, and new cultures have emerged through the efforts of groups, it is only in comparatively recent times that orderly attempts have been made to understand groups and their functionings.

HISTORICAL DEVELOPMENTS

Two great historical developments have characterized interpersonal relationships: the philosophy of authority with its mechanical explanation of nature and man and the philosophy of experience with its organic explanation of nature and man.

The philosophy of authority, the earlier development, is one in which "authority becomes the all-pervasive measure of the social order—the basis for the upbringing of children in home and school, and for the administration of business and industry as well as public affairs."[1] Basic to this philosophy are the following assumptions: (1) that the leader has the knowledge, makes the plans, and directs the members of the group, whether they are citizens, employees, students, colleagues, or members of his family; (2) that knowledge is gained from a study of the past; and (3) that theoretical formulations depend upon reason and faith.

The later development, the philosophy of experience, sometimes known as the "Great Tradition" or the "Democratic Way," is one in which "each of the multitude of individuals that constitute modern societies can make his own life statement and yet not encroach upon the others around him, and in which each individual is encouraged to develop his capacities to their

[1] Harold Rugg, *Foundations for American Education* (Yonkers-on-Hudson, New York: World Book Co., 1947), p. 36.

3

uttermost limits, but without blighting those of his neighbors."[2] According to this philosophy, sometimes called organicism, nature and man are explained by the concept of the "field," with emerging forces and needs satisfied by the integrated energy of the whole organism. Distributive leadership, cooperative planning, and democratic action emerged with the development of this philosophy.

The transition toward this understanding of nature and man was initiated by Galileo, Newton, and Descartes. Its early development was further advanced by Hobbes, Locke, Berkeley, Hume, and others. As late as the middle of the nineteenth century, however, the world was still viewed in terms of the mechanical concepts of action and reaction. Organicism or the field concept awaited later developments.

By the close of the nineteenth century the concept of man as dynamic, acting and acting upon, was widely accepted. Also by 1890 the acquiring of knowledge by direct observation rather than by authority and by use of the scientific method was established. More and more, the rights and privileges of the individual were recognized. Each man, regardless of his status, was increasingly respected for his own ideas. Decisions were reached through the use of empirical evidence that was pertinent to the situation, and the recognition of the significance of the contribution of each informed citizen to the welfare of the body politic became an established principle.

The widespread nature of this change can be indicated by a brief consideration of the contributions of the leading minds of this unusual century. The first step which made it possible for physicists to give up mechanical explanations and grasp the magnetic field as a "field of force" came through Faraday's experimental discovery of induced currents (1831) and Oersted's studies of the deflection of the magnetic needle (1820). Einstein considered these "the two most important pillars of support for the theory of the electric and magnetic field." This step was followed by Maxwell's formulation of the equations which stated the structure of the electromagnetic field (1873) and Hertz's proof of the existence of electromagnetic waves and his demonstration of evidence that their velocity equalled that of light (1885–1890).

Insights from other disciplines also advanced understanding of the field concept. Auguste Comte, Herbert Spencer, and Lester Frank Ward pioneered the study of society which came to be known as sociology. Charles Darwin's *Origin of Species* provided the clue that, after 1870, started many of the physiologists, psychologists, philosophers, and social scientists on the search for concepts underlying the new industrial-democratic culture. Sir Francis Galton's *Inquiries into Human Faculty and Its Development,* which furthered the Darwinian concept of variation and described the mental faculties of individual man, had wide influence on both sides of the Atlantic. Claude Bernard engaged in his pioneer investigations of the organismic role of the endocrine glands; Charles Peirce and Chauncey Wright developed the "operational" psychology of meaning. These advances led to an increasing emphasis on the accumulation of empirical data as the principal means of gaining dependable evidence and of understanding relationships.

[2] *Ibid.,* p. 38.

Implications for Group Process

Such an epoch of change provided the conditions for a new kind of group, a cooperative planning group in which each individual shared in the making of decisions which were agreed upon for action through a consensus. Since knowledge was now the result of observation and experiment, and since all knowledge was continually subjected to critical analysis provided through the scientific method, respect for the authoritarian leader gradually decreased.

From the 1890's to the 1940's these two contrasting viewpoints regarding man and the universe were clarified, the one *mechanistic* and *authoritarian*, the other *organic* and *cooperative*. These two views of experience are, of course, still expressed in contrasting types of interpersonal relationships among members of both primary and secondary groups.

The two views are in opposition ideationally and operationally. The disagreement focuses on whether or not the continued refinement of authoritarian human relations will result in a better life for all members of society. Those who believe it will disagree on which individuals should assume such authority, but they are united in support of the policy of central authoritarian control.

Those who hold the opposing view consider cooperative human relations to be the basic climate in which to resolve or solve problems of living among themselves and between themselves and people of other societies. They believe that the cooperative process respects individuality, develops intelligence, and promotes creativity. They also believe that it matures personality to the point where thoughtful deliberative human action becomes the accepted pattern in interpersonal relationships. The point of view which will finally prevail depends upon the decisions of both kinds of groups everywhere.

Many significant decisions will be reached in large formal groups, but many also will be made in small groups. These small groups are a natural part of our living in homes, schools, industries, churches, hospitals, and other social organizations. Decisions of these groups determine the quality of our personal and national life and our influence abroad.

The concern of this text is with these small groups, especially those which exist in schools and universities. They are diverse in size, methods, and interests. They range from the informal play group to the structured content group, whose main objective is planning and problem solving, and the therapy group, whose chief interest is the assistance of persons who need help in understanding themselves and their problems.

SOME UNRESOLVED ISSUES

Group members continue to place emphasis on one kind of truth, the objective truth of science, and to give little consideration to the recognition and acceptance of the explanation which is true for the person who gives it, although it may be scientifically false.

Many groups encourage an intellectualism which is characterized by passivity, desensitization, and withdrawal from commitment to responsibility.

Others foster an approach which leads to commitment and involvement in the group relationship, growth in sensitivity, and the development of a sense of responsibility for group members and the quality of the group climate. Many group members remain ego-centered in that they lack the interest and apparently the ability to improve interpersonal understanding by resolving incongruences in interpersonal perceptions.

These issues are given consideration in the following pages, which will (1) examine man's potentialities and capacities for cooperation; (2) present recent insights from philosophy and psychology which provide a new perspective for the understanding of interpersonal relationships and of the personality characteristics conducive to the enhancement of the group process; and (3) discuss the limitations of the present dimensions of group living and present tentative suggestions for attaining a significant and necessary depth in group experience.

The Basis of Group Relationship

Western society has based its progress on individual competitiveness and the use of reason. This is our heritage from Malthus,[3] Herbert Spencer,[4] and Darwin,[5] whose principles were consistent with the thinking and the conditions of a new country with an open frontier.

As a consequence, survival of the fittest came to be regarded as the norm of life and Darwinism to be the biological justification for competition. The Lynds discovered this doctrine to be part of the behavioral equipment and overt beliefs of the people of Middletown.[6] In the words of a typical businessman, "You can't make the world all planned and soft. The strongest and best survive—that's the law of nature after all—always has been and always will be."

This view of the natural selectionists has been severely attacked. The attack was begun by Darwin himself in the *Descent of Man*, published in 1871, and followed by Prince Peter Kropotkin in *Evolution*. Further observation and study gradually established the recognition that the social relationship is characteristic of all living organisims. Wheeler pointed out that "most animals and plants live in associations, herds, colonies or societies."[7] Successive experiments have demonstrated in insect and animal life what has since become known as "the social appetite."

Today it is widely accepted that cooperation is the most important factor in the development and well-being of animal groups. According to Allee, ". . . If cooperation had not been the stronger force, the more complicated

[3] Thomas Robert Malthus, *An Essay on the Principle of Population* (London: Reeves and Turner, 1872).

[4] Herbert Spencer, *Education: Intellectual, Moral and Physical* (London: Watts and Co., 1905).

[5] Charles R. Darwin, *The Origin of Species by Means of Natural Selection* (New York: Modern Library, Inc., 1896).

[6] Robert S. Lynd and Helen Merrell Lynd, *Middletown in Transition* (New York: Harcourt, Brace & Co., 1937), p. 407.

[7] W. H. Wheeler, *The Social Life of Insects* (New York: Harcourt, Brace and Co., 1922).

animals, whether orthoptera or vertebrates, could not have evolved."[8] Evolution is dependent upon cooperation. The individual in large measure derives his well-being from participation in a group.

The basis of the group is not only that man is social but that, at any given moment of time, he can stand "outside" himself and the world and make a judgment. Moreover, because of that judgment it is possible that he may become selfish, tyrannical, egotistical, cruel, and destructive. On the other hand, he may become committed to ideals and goals which are unselfish and constructive.

This freedom of decision and action is commonly accepted by religious leaders, sociologists, and others. The crucial question is no longer rugged individualism versus cooperation in the group but rather, What should be the basis of interpersonal relationships within the group as a whole and the character of the members who compose it?

Psychology has in recent years had much to say concerning this. Experimental evidence indicates the possibility now that men may be conditioned by other men to develop any number of predetermined characteristics.[9] For this purpose it has been hypothesized "that the social reinforcement type of influence is more effective than physical devices because the subject is less likely to respond to [the latter]."[10] Here, then, is a contrasting basis for group work. The group becomes a setting for the manipulation, by an authority, of the members who compose it. The members, unaware of what is happening to them, would be conditioned to accept and work toward predetermined goals. Are groups to be used for conditioning individuals toward ends of which they are ignorant, or are they to be used for the development of the individual's understanding of himself?

Either position must confront at least three challenges: (1) Is the goal not merely scientifically possible but practically attainable? (2) Will it produce a society which will ensure optimum conditions for individual development? (3) Does it provide the environment which has the best possibility for enabling man to fulfill his destiny in accordance with his nature?

Concerning the Nature of Man. In meeting these challenges there must be a fuller, more penetrating study of the nature of man. To proceed on the assumption that he is an intelligent, sophisticated animal is to ensure the attainment of disappointing results. The following injunction by Mowrer is worth further examination:

> Man cannot be fully understood either within the bounds of natural necessity or rational prudence. Long ago we were reminded that man does not live by bread alone and it is none too early for us to turn to the identification and better understanding of this something more.[11]

   [8] Walter C. Allee, *The Social Life of Animals* (New York: W. W. Norton & Company, Inc., 1938).
   [9] B. F. Skinner, "Freedom and the Control of Men," *American Scholar*, LXVI (Winter, 1955), 47–65.
   [10] B. F. Skinner, *Walden Two* (New York: The Macmillan Company, 1948), p. 218.
   [11] O. H. Mowrer, "Some Philosophical Problems in Psychological Counseling," *Journal of Counseling Psychology*, IV (1957), 110.

Let us take Mowrer's advice and briefly consider "this something more" with reference to the controversial claims that man can be conditioned to develop predetermined characteristics.

Those who would condition man to accept and work for the goals that have been formulated for him by others plan to do so in a manner that will ensure a pleasant experience as judged by those who condition. They assume that the use of this procedure will guarantee the avoidance of any opposition or rejection, but they fail to recognize that man's difficulty in bringing his various impulses into harmony is not the result of his resistance to authority but because of his innate freedom. Freedom should not be identified with reason; rather, it must be recognized that freedom rises above reason. The freedom of man is not contained within the mind's urge toward coherence and synthesis.

Skinner and his associates apparently made no allowance for the fact that man is free to violate both the necessities of nature and the logical systems of reason. Their principle of interpretation does not do justice to man's spirit, to his ability to stand apart and judge his feelings, thoughts, and behavior, or to the organic unity between this ability and his intellectual and natural self.

On the other hand, those who place emphasis on the possibility that man can become fully mature and society completely democratic, creative, and productive place too much confidence in man's capacity and willingness to be guided by reason.

John Dewey was convinced that through disinterested intelligence a group could free itself or rise above the biases, prejudices, and closed-mindedness of its individual members through "organized cooperative inquiry." What he failed to consider was that man, regardless of his good intentions, cannot be sufficiently open-minded, objective, or secure in dealing with conflicts of interest to achieve the goals of disinterested intelligence.

Instead of recognizing the limited character of their decisions, groups of all kinds, using "free cooperative inquiry,"[12] pretend to achieve more complete impartiality than is possible for human justice. Both Dewey and Whitehead, rather than accept the sobering fact that the potentiality for evil is inherent in human nature, believe that injustices are the result of a "cultural lag"[13] and that the evil of the times is the result of the inertia of intelligence. But human egotism is more than man's natural impulse to preserve his own existence. Injustices do not necessarily disappear with the overcoming of the cultural lag.

The recognition of these unique capacities of man to judge himself and to disregard the dictates of reason casts severe doubts on the possibility of improving his state through conditioning. Rogers concludes that

> Science cannot come into being without a personal choice of the values we
> wish to achieve. And these values we choose to implement will forever be

[12] John Dewey, "Intelligence in the Modern World" in *John Dewey's Philosophy*, edited by Joseph Ratner (New York: Modern Library, Inc., 1939), p. 381.

[13] Alfred North Whitehead, *Adventures of Ideas*, chap. 5 (New York: The Macmillan Company, 1933).

outside of the science which implements them; the goals we select, the purposes we wish to follow must always be outside of the science which achieves them. To me this has the encouraging meaning that the human person, with his capacity for subjective choice, can and will always exist, separate from and prior to any of his scientific undertakings. Unless as individuals we choose to relinquish our capacity for subjective choice, we will always remain free persons, not simply pawns of a self-created behavioral science.[14]

Since individuals and groups have demonstrated that they will cherish their freedom to evaluate and to choose, the group leader should realize that there is always the possibility that cooperative decisions will be impregnated with selfish concerns in both planning and implementation. On the other hand, the group members may succeed in reaching and implementing decisions which are comparatively unselfish and free of destructive prejudices. Unless the leader learns to live with the fact that the improper use of human freedom may cause certain ambiguities, he may attempt to force the planning and decision-making into rigid patterns in order to increase his own security.

The degree to which we can hope to realize our potentialities through group life is directly related to the degree to which we can and are willing to accept our uniqueness.

Determinants of Group Functioning

Groups form for many purposes. Broadly stated, the members relate to one another for the satisfaction of some recognized need. One set of needs may be the planning of some future event, the finding of some solution to a current problem, or the evaluation of some past undertaking in order to discover better methods for future operations. Groups with one or more of the above purposes are involved primarily with thinking rather than with feeling. They have been characterized by Coffey as socio-process groups, and their discussions have been generally referred to as group guidance.

Groups meet also for the satisfaction of other needs. One of these needs may be the individual member's clarification of his personal attitudes and values and a greater understanding of the values and attitudes of other members. The outcome is not a plan to be put into action in the community but rather the resolving of personal and group conflicts, improved understanding, acceptance of oneself and others, and perhaps the setting of levels of aspiration by individuals or by the group. Groups meeting for this purpose are more deeply involved on the emotional level than on the intellectual level. They may be thought of as psyche-process groups, and their discussions are often spoken of as group psychotherapy or group counseling.

For the most significant and useful group experience the whole person must be fully involved. Beyond this, for each member to be mutually helpful, he must be interested, willing, and active in helping every other member to participate. Mutual interest and acceptance, combined with the sense of respon-

[14] Carl R. Rogers, *On Becoming a Person* (Boston: Houghton Mifflin Company, 1961), pp. 400–401.

sibility for helping one another, reduces resistance to new ideas and feelings. There is less need for the immediate acceptance, rejection, or distortion of a communication from another member.

If some basic change in an individual is expected, it is well to consider how such a change affects him: (1) it alters his perception of his world; (2) it modifies his valences and values, which include his attractions and aversions to groups and group members, and (3) it alters his disposition toward and individual control over his physical and social movements.[15]

The achievement of this kind of involvement is a challenge to a group leader. It helps us to realize why tragedy purifies the emotions. Too frequently we assume that intellectual or intellectualized understanding will alter values and purposes. Beck's statement is more accurate: "We cannot know without the intellect; we do not know until we experience with the emotions."[16]

Indications of the immaturity and inability of the leader and members to improve the quality of decisions through group process is evident in the following illustration. A school committee is meeting to consider the problem of homework. Present are Mr. Smith, the principal; Miss Johnson, English teacher and head of the department; Miss Frost, another English teacher; Mr. Russell, a social studies teacher; Miss Hadley, mathematics; and Mr. Roberts, physical sciences.

1. PRINCIPAL: Parents are complaining again about homework. One man called to say his son worked four hours last night. Another feels she is doing the teaching for the teachers. Miss Johnson, what happened when this problem was brought up at P.T.A.?

2. MISS JOHNSON: Many parents felt the school expects too much homework. Some thought this was a lazy way of teaching. Others thought it unfair to have to help children do math problems because methods of working are different now. However, some parents thought that more homework was needed, that the students were not working in school. I'm glad to report these parents were few in number.

3. MISS HADLEY: The trouble with such a meeting is that the few parents with complaints speak so loudly that it looks as though the whole P.T.A. agrees. Many parents do not seem to care how their children get along. When you try to get their cooperation, you get all kinds of excuses. If we want to lower our standards, all we need to do is to eliminate homework.

4. MR. RUSSELL: It's easy enough to talk about eliminating homework. In schools where children have a fine home background, perhaps work can be finished in school. But when you have children with backgrounds like ours, it's impossible to keep standards up without study at home.

5. MISS JOHNSON: Every time we talk about homework, someone mentions standards. High educational standards can be maintained without loading students down with extra homework at night. Good teaching makes children want to read so much that reading can become a pleasure and not homework.

[15] Kurt Lewin and Paul Grabbe, "Conduct, Knowledge, and Acceptance of New Values," *The Journal of Social Issues*, I (August, 1945), 56–64.

[16] Samuel J. Beck, "Emotional Experience as a Necessary Constituent in Knowing," in *Feelings and Emotions*, edited by Martin L. Reymert (New York: McGraw-Hill Book Co., Inc., 1950), p. 106.

6. MR. ROBERTS: The confusion gets worse when there is a lack of basic policy on the part of the school administration.

7. PRINCIPAL: We want everyone to express his ideas. Miss Frost, what do you think?

8. MISS FROST: Part of the answer may depend upon the subject studied.

9. PRINCIPAL: Now that we have expressed our opinions, I think we should vote on a final decision.

10. MISS HADLEY: I don't think we will solve anything by voting. We must get at the real issue of educational standards.

11. PRINCIPAL: Perhaps we should appoint a subcommittee to study the situation and report back to us.

12. MISS JOHNSON: Don't you think, Mr. Smith, we have most of the facts we need now? I think we can come to a decision very soon.

13. PRINCIPAL: Perhaps, after all, we are pretty much in agreement. I'm sure you'll all agree that the best solution is for each teacher to make every effort to lessen the homework requirements as much as possible. You will, I am sure, also keep the high educational standards our school has always been noted for. If you wish, I'll tell the parents, at the next P.T.A. meeting, of our decision.

We note in this situation a high degree of emotional involvement with several ego-centered responses (nos. 2, 4, 5, 11, 12, and 13). In response number 2, Miss Johnson tries to put Miss Hadley, the math teacher, in her place. In number 4, Mr. Russell comes to the rescue of Miss Hadley. In number 5, Miss Johnson quietly congratulates herself. In number 11, the principal has become threatened. In Number 12, Miss Johnson tries to manipulate him. In Number 13, still threatened, the principal assumes a consensus.

There are indications of attempts to reject or escape from the problem. In response number 3, Miss Hadley seeks an easy way out. In response number 6, Mr. Roberts tries to place the responsibility with the school administration. In response number 8, Miss Frost distorts and narrows the problem. Of the total of thirteen responses, only number 10 appears to be an actual problem-centered response.

There is also an appalling lack of understanding of the principles and procedures of group process. There is no understanding of goals or boundaries within which the group should operate. There are no apparent methods for working as a group, and no attention is given to the process problems.

In the following illustration of a group situation it can be seen that some progress has been made in working effectively as a group. The driver of the school bus complained that the fifteen eighth-graders were generally disorderly, shouting to one another, pushing, changing seats, and shooting rubber bands. The principal considered this a matter for group guidance. He turned the problem over to the counselor with the suggestion that he use his own judgment in clearing up the matter and added that any more disorder would lead to serious consequences for those involved.

The counselor considered the problem, then asked himself whether the students might be expected to have useful ideas for its solution. Was it possible to accept their ideas and work with them to reach the best possible decision? Had the principal given him the necessary freedom to decide the matter through the group process? Having satisfactorily answered these questions for himself in the affirmative, he met with the students.

He explained the reason for calling them together and the conditions under which they were meeting. He then asked for suggestions for a solution.

MARY: A few started it and the rest joined in.

BESS: It was the same few each time.

MARVIN: I don't know why everyone had to be called in, when only a few were to blame.

TOM: I think that the few should be punished, and that Mr. Arnold should report them.

MR. ARNOLD: But you are making it my problem. I am here to help, but it is the problem of us all.

TED: The driver could hand in the names of the few to the principal.

MR. ARNOLD: You are assuming it is the driver's problem; is it?

DICK: I think we just want to put the blame on someone else; it's not his problem.

JIM: Those who didn't behave should be made to walk.

SUE: Who would make them walk?

FRANK: We have to take care of ourselves; it's up to each one of us.

BILL: I'm not in favor of that. A lot of us may be able to do this, but some of us can't.

MR. ARNOLD (*reflecting*): You feel the idea wouldn't work because some of us can't take care of ourselves.

Long pause.

MR. ARNOLD: Learning self-control is not easy, and each of us has had different kinds of experience in taking care of himself. Some of us know that we are strong enough to control ourselves, but others haven't tried or have tried and found that we were still unable. Suppose each of us considers whether he is strong enough to control himself on the bus. You can answer only for yourself. Only you know how you feel about it.

Another pause.

MR. ARNOLD: Do you think you are strong enough to control yourself?

Some heads nodded, and some hands went up.

ERIC: As I see it, those who can take care of themselves are O.K. Why not ask those who can't to sit at the front of the bus where the driver can watch them?

MR. ARNOLD: But you are making it the driver's problem. I think it is our problem. We have to work out something together; it's the problem of each of us and all of us together.

Silence.

MARY: Why can't those of us who have had experience and know that we can control ourselves help the others?

JIM: How could we do it?

BOB: A lot depends on whom you are with. If you are with someone who controls himself, it's a lot easier.

BILL: Then, let those of us who have no difficulty be with those who find it pretty hard.

The group accepted this plan.

Let us consider the operational principles in this situation which illustrate some determinants in group functioning.

1. Progression is from individual, ego-centered to group, problem-centered behavior.

2. Thoughts are focused on the problem. Ego-centered behavior is minimal.

3. Responsibility for decision centered in the group.

4. Emphasis was on responsibility for helping one another and for group action.

5. The leader clarified, stimulated, and accepted differences and kept the issue in focus.

6. There was continuous clarification of boundaries.

7. Analysis, synthesis, and evaluation were engaged in by the members as well as by the leader.

8. Agreement was reached without pressure, which increased the possibility of a "true" consensus.

Approaching the analysis of these two situations from the standpoint of personality dynamics, there appear to be widely divergent attitudes. In the first situation, the staff meeting was used chiefly for ego-centered, competitive personality struggles. In the second situation, the intention was to cooperate in finding a solution; expressed egocentricity was minimal.

In the first situation, the principal apparently had little confidence in the group's interest in working out a solution. He expected bickerings and was defensive. He did not give the group leadership in establishing boundaries and setting goals. In the second situation, the counselor established boundaries and goals; he expected the group to focus on the problem, assume responsibility, and reach a satisfactory decision.

In the faculty meeting the members avoided any reorganization of their value systems by distortion, rejection, and aggression. Their thinking and their imaginative processes were oriented only to the past. The students, on the other hand, assisted by the counselor, confronted the situation as it was. They remained open to ideas, and their orientation to past, present, and future events enabled them to relate past events to the present and to make realistic plans for the future.

New Insights into Interpersonal Relationships. Now let us turn to a consideration of two contributions of existential psychology.

The first insight is the recognition of a new kind of truth. In most discussions concerning truth, reflection is directed to the truth as an object to which the discussant is related. This subject-object relationship is recognized as only one kind of truth, however. Occasionally we catch a glimmer of the realization that *there is a kind of truth which may be false for everyone except he who expresses it.* When, instead of emphasizing this subject-object relationship, the question of the truth is raised subjectively, reflection is directed to the relationship between the individual and his belief. If what he says follows logically from his perception of the matter, then it is considered true for him, even if his criteria and referents are objectively false.[17]

[17] Søren Kierkegaard, "Concluding Unscientific Postscript," in *A Kierkegaard Anthology,* edited by Robert Bretall (Princeton, N.J.: Princeton University Press, 1951), pp. 210–211.

Using the situation of the eighth-graders on the bus as an illustration, the counselor's response, "But you are making it my problem. I am here to help, but it is the problem of us all," was no doubt true from his point of view. To the boys and girls, however, apparently conditioned by the traditional form of discipline, it was not true, but in recognizing that it was true from his point of view, they were gradually led to a deeper understanding of the counselor and also of themselves. Yet the counselor's perception of the truth did not minimize the significance of the subject-object relationship, for both counselor and students knew that if the disturbance continued, serious consequences would result.

A second insight also is derived from the writings of Kierkegaard: *the need for commitment.* Kierkegaard was convinced that the very increase of truth (subject-object relationship) may increase insecurity unless we are committed to relating to the truth in our own experience.[18] If we are to understand the person we observe, we cannot be separate from him. The group leader must commit himself to becoming a real participant in the relationship with successive members of the group if he hopes to discern what is taking place with clarity and understanding. This is contradictory to the traditional position, which states that "the less we are involved in a given situation, the more clearly we can observe the truth."

Not only must the group leader commit himself to "drink of the same cup," but the member also must be committed to enter into the meaning of the leader's feelings, thoughts, and words.

A group leader frequently listens to a member discussing a problem at length, knowing that his theoretical and academic profuseness is of questionable value and may, in fact, be a defense against the recognition of the need for a commitment to the truth. Many would agree that such a situation presents "the necessity for arousing anxiety in the patient," but Rollo May, who points out that this approach may be inadequate, considers the following to be the more fundamental principle: "The patient must find or discover some point in his existence where he can commit himself before he can permit himself even to see the truth of what he is doing."[19]

These two principles of "truth in relationship" and "commitment" must exist to produce the necessary quality of interpersonal functioning for the generation of the curative forces in group process.

Needed Depth in Group Process

Interpersonal relationships which lead to growth and development are characterized by two qualities, productive imagination and the use of symbols. The quality of the group process bears a direct relation to them.

Productive Imagination. Education utilizes the imagination. The goal, ideal, or image always precedes and accompanies the desire and the struggle.

[18] *Ibid.*

[19] Rollo May, Ernest Angel, and Henri F. Ellenberger (eds.), *Existence, A New Dimension in Psychiatry and Psychology* (New York: Basic Books, Inc., 1958), p. 28.

Images which embrace our purposes and convictions motivate our actions.

Not all of our imaginings serve such useful and practical ends. Some of them do not encourage growth toward maturity and may even hinder our progress in relationships with ourselves and with others. Such impractical and obstructive imagination falls into two categories: (1) that which is given over to phantasy and is too far removed from the possible to be useful and (2) that which reproduces the past for the purpose of enjoyment. The latter, known as "reproductive imagination,"[20] has been described by Jung[21] as a focusing upon the past and its manifest content and is considered by him to be thoroughly intelligible and, for certain types of temperaments, sufficiently satisfying to make any further efforts toward deeper understanding unnecessary.

Another kind of imagination displays its peculiar power not by imitative images but by the creation of new images or new relationships between old images. This kind of imagination Kroner has named "productive"[22] and Jung has described as "purposive."

Productive imagination is undoubtedly a creative dynamic in the group process. It has three unique functions:

1. It submits the material of sense perception to our understanding and is an important element in the attempt to understand another from his frame of reference. Kant in his *Critique of Pure Reason* introduces productive imagination into the field of objective knowledge as a necessary link between sensation and understanding.

2. It encompasses the group member's purposes and goals and represents the concrete life of his convictions. The desired accomplishment of each member and the group is the language of the imagination.

3. It unifies sensation and reason and aids in the development of the quality of group interaction which we frequently try to explain by the statement, "the group as a whole is more than the sum of its parts." It enhances the group's quality of cohesiveness, planning, and decision-making. Through imagination each member views the future goal.

Symbols in Group Process. The most profound insights into human relationships are expressed through symbols. The "true" symbol has the following characteristics: (1) it points beyond itself to something else; (2) it participates in that to which it points; (3) it opens up levels of reality which are otherwise closed; (4) it opens up hidden depths of our being; (5) it cannot be produced intentionally; (6) it dies when it no longer produces a response in the group in which it originally found expression.[23] The true symbol has an objective referent and great possibilities of opening up hidden depths of meaning within ourselves. Although signs, which refer only to the concrete, the knowable, and the measurable are useful at times, they may be at other times frustratingly inadequate.

---

[20] Richard Kroner, *The Religious Function of Imagination* (New Haven, Conn.: Yale University Press, 1941), p. 5.

[21] C. C. Jung, *Psychological Types* (New York: Harcourt, Brace and Co., 1923), p. 577.

[22] *Op. cit.*, p. 6.

[23] Paul Tillich, *Dynamics of Faith* (New York: Harper & Brothers, 1958), pp. 42–43.

Some educators and counselors, of course, are aware of this. In fact, as Francis Horn concludes, the task of educators of our time is "to help young people establish a life solidly constructed upon these enduring values: truth, beauty, integrity and love."[24] But although Horn recognizes the need for symbols to give depth and meaning to life, he is apparently unaware of the nature of the task and the specific problems involved. His emphasis on the necessity and importance of teaching students how to achieve greater adaptability to the changing environment illustrates the dilemma in which we are placed. What is called "adjustment" will merely strengthen the process meanings (understanding of methods) already attained.

This task of helping young people, as suggested by Horn, necessitates the clarification of (1) the meaning of the symbol and (2) the conditions conducive to its development.

Illustrative of the inadequacy in understanding the meaning of the symbol is the popular idea that the key to the city given to an honored guest is a symbol, and the giving of it, a symbolic act. The key is not a true symbol since its referent, the city, is knowable or capable of being known. Correctly understood, the key is a sign. Similarly, the "wings" worn by the pilot are not a symbol of the air service, but a sign that distinguishes the personnel of the service.

The use of sign for symbol, however, is only one source of the difficulty. The reverse is also involved in the lack of clarity on this point: the treatment of a symbol as if it were a sign. For example, suppose we treat Plato's symbol of the cave as a sign. Using a Freudian analysis, Jung[25] says that we should naturally come to the conclusion that the cave represents the uterus and assume that Plato was stuck in the primeval levels of "infantile sexuality."

Another fault with this interpretation is that it lacks the assumption that a symbol refers to something beyond what is stated. Without this recognition and its use we would remain ignorant that Plato created from his philosophical knowledge, understanding, and intuition the whole problem of the theory of cognition (thinking, imagination, and memory). If the symbol is defined as having no external referent, then its possibilities for generating deeper insights and understanding are greatly reduced. This occurs in situations such as that in which the "wings" of the pilot are assumed to be a symbol of the air force.

With the characteristics of the true symbol in mind, let us look at the symbol frequently referred to in individual and group counseling, that of love. The love relationship points to something beyond our accomplishment. We cannot comprehend it fully or think that we have discovered it in its entirety. As we enter into the love relationship we become aware of other levels of understanding and new meanings.

These meanings, however, cannot be produced through thought; they come from an unknown source. Our recognition of this fact causes a tension, and we suspect that they may disappear in the same manner as they

24 H. Francis Horn, "Education for What?" *Teachers College Record*, LXII (March, 1961), 481.
25 *Loc. cit.*

appeared. In fact, they do disappear when they cease to function in our daily lives, when they no longer cause us to be related dynamically to the world of reality. Disappearance of the symbol is hastened by societal and individual change rather than direct action. Just as love does not come through longing, it does not necessarily die because of scientific or practical criticism.

It is this very ambiguity that increases the desire to define the symbol, to give it boundaries, to make it concrete, knowable, and attainable. Such attempts bring release and therefore deceive us into believing that we have captured the essence of the symbol when actually we have forfeited the possibility of its leading to increasingly creative meanings. When this forfeiture occurs the symbol becomes a sign and process (method) is emphasized. Thus we define improvement in terms of a refinement of methods, and we limit the possibilities of accomplishment.

To live or interpret life in terms of signs is to remove from experience the meaning and significance of freedom, peace, justice, and love. If signs and processes rule our lives, it is conceivable that freedom would mean the license to do what we can get away with; peace, the absence of conflict; justice, penalty in proportion to the infraction; truth, what works to the individual's advantage; and love, physical attractiveness and dependency.

In such a predicament group process would be reduced to each individual's use of the experience solely for the advancement of his own purposes, and its value as a means of constructive development would be greatly minimized.

Conclusions

The improvement of the quality of group process has raised expectations for the solving of problems and improvement of relationships. It is recognized that psychological safety and acceptance facilitate a higher quality of group productivity. Mutual interest and involvement in the subject being discussed and individual acceptance of responsibility for influencing the quality of interpersonal understanding are essential. Individual growth is enhanced by the recognition of a new kind of truth, "truth in relationship," the encouragement of the development of productive imagination, and the utilization of symbolic thought.

PART TWO

The Group

The assumption that group interaction is a spontaneous exchange of ideas unrelated to the individual's social, religious, and family backgrounds yields only a superficial, partial understanding. In reality, the complexity of group structure and performance necessitates the study of the group from several perspectives. In Part Two the group is described in terms of definitions, foundations, types and levels, group patterns, and, finally, values.

The concept of the group is so complex that a single definition is unlikely to give proper emphasis to all the dynamic interrelationships which constitute it. Each of such disciplines as sociology, psychology, religion, philosophy, and anthropology has its own concept, and each concept is slightly different since it is colored by its particular orientation. There are, however, certain common elements. All agree that there must be interaction and modification at some level as the result of participation in the relationship, and that this interaction is enhanced if the members of the group have a common problem and if the combined effort may be expected to satisfy some of the needs of the participants.

Their chief points of difference are concerned with the source of motivation, with the quality of individual change, and with the product. The readings included in Section A emphasize both the common elements and the points of difference in the varying approaches.

Section B focuses attention on the principles upon which group structure, interaction, and outcomes are predicted. To illustrate these principles, material has been selected from those disciplines which have been directly interested in the study of man and his behavior: religion, sociology, and psychology. From religion come insights into the metaphysical nature of man; from sociology, concepts concerning the formation and operation of groups; from psychology, principles regarding human behavior in groups. The readings from these disciplines should add breadth to one's understanding of the basic factors in group functioning.

The readings in Section C describe the many types and levels of groups.

19

Groups are generally classified as group work, group guidance, group counseling, or group therapy. Their least common denominators are that they contain two or more persons in a group setting in which each hopes to benefit. Their chief differences lie in the number of members, the leader and his functioning, and the expected outcomes.

Another more narrowly conceived classification focuses strictly on the purpose of the group. Under this classification we have socio-process and psyche-process groups. The former includes recreation groups, study groups, group work, and group guidance. The latter includes group counseling, group therapy, and group psychotherapy.

These titles not only illustrate the diverse purposes in group functioning but also hint at the great differences in preparation required for leadership. Working with groups is a highly specialized form of leadership necessitating appropriate training and experience. The titles also suggest broad levels of functioning. Group work, for example is generally conceived as a different level of functioning from group counseling, which requires a leader with different capabilities.

Another distinction of special interest to the teacher and counselor is that of the different methods a leader may use in functioning with any one group. Teachers and counselors should be familiar with their levels of operation in relation to the needs and purposes of the group. A too common approach is one in which the leader plans the content and conducts the group in such a manner that the majority of his ideas and plans are accepted, or teaches in the classroom the facts and relationships which he has previously planned.

A deeper level is approached when the importance of the concepts for the life of the community is discussed.

Less frequently, a third level is attempted when each member is encouraged and helped to consider the relevance of the concepts for his own personal life. A rare but important level may be reached by groups whose members become interested in and desirous of assisting one another toward better insights and self-realization.

The third and fourth levels are necessary for the optimum development of each group member, but the quality of character required of both members and leader, together with the necessary capability, makes the attainment of these ideals difficult.

The subject of Section D, the pattern of operation of the group, is related directly to the beliefs of the members, and especially the leader, concerning human relations. The forms of interrelationships have been categorized for purposes of description and discussion into four types of patterns: laissez-faire, authoritarian, democratic, and group-centered. Each of these patterns has its own particular assumptions regarding leadership, interaction, and outcomes.

In laissez-faire groups there is complete permissiveness. There is no guidance or control by the leader, who remains passive and uninvolved. The assumption is that the members are capable of planning, initiating, and bringing to a successful conclusion any undertaking.

In authoritarian or aggregate groups the members are controlled by the leader, who plans in advance the content, method, and outcomes and presents them to the members for acceptance and action. The assumptions are that his greater capability and understanding justifies this method, that the rewards he offers will ensure the required motivation for action, and that learning (personality change) results from his ideas.

In the democratic or organic group the leader and members work cooperatively throughout the process: in selection, initiation, discussion, and decision-making. The assumptions are that the members are capable and motivated and that, with the leader's assistance, they can perform more efficiently and secure better outcomes than would be possible without his direction.

The group-centered method is one in which the members select the subject for discussion, carry it through, make decisions, develop conclusions, and implement the outcomes. The leader refrains from questioning and evaluating; his role is rather to reflect, to clarify, and to establish and maintain a psychological climate of acceptance and understanding. The assumption is that if the leader in such a manner can help the members to make maximum use of their potentialities, they will progress in the constructive solving of problems, in the gaining of insights, and in the application of these insights to their personal lives.

From the above descriptions, it is apparent that each pattern of group organization is unique. The pattern determines in large measure the quality of the group experience and its usefulness to both leader and members.

As the readings in Section E point out, groups differ greatly in the degree to which they assist their members toward maturity. Certain groups, for example, have a retrogressive effect on man's development. These are groups whose leaders indulge in the manipulation of the members for their personal benefit. The dynamics of such groups expresses itself in hierarchial settings; in groups based on social, intellectual, and economic status; and in religious, racial, and cultural discrimination. The assumption here is that the characteristics of man — his intellectual ability, color, religion, social or economic class — are a valid basis for differentiation. The effect on the individual of relationships based on such an assumption is often over-competitiveness, isolation, loss of self-esteem and individuality, and a decrease in the ability to make decisions. Other kinds of groups may materially assist man to understand himself and his environment, to become more productive, to cooperate in building a better community, to raise his levels of aspiration, and to search for deeper spiritual values.

The group whose members have worked together for a period of time is generally superior to the individual in the planning of creative approaches to reach a desired goal or in the analysis of a problem. In this situation each member is helped to gain more insight into his own personality and to make the appropriate adjustments.

No two members of a group derive the same benefits. The value of the group to the individual will depend in large measure upon the degree of prevailing acceptance, the quality of the interaction, the individual's self-perception and interest in other group members, and the process utilized.

PART TWO · THE GROUP

Section A

DEFINITIONS OF THE GROUP

An adequate definition must include at least the size, the quality of interaction, and the potential for change within the group.

Of course, there are variations in emphasis within the different purposes of groups. In solving a problem which includes consideration of alternatives, a small group of three to five persons would be expected to be more efficient than a large group of fifteen to twenty. However, in planning a program or project in which there are several "open ends," the larger number with more ideas could be expected to produce more creative results. In group therapy, using what Coffey has termed the "psyche process," a few persons (six to eight) could engage more readily than a large number in the kind of interaction necessary to obtain therapeutic results.

Dynamics frequently overlooked are the willingness of each member to listen, to try to understand, to consider a statement from another on the basis of its merits, and to draw conclusions based upon the evidence presented rather than solely on pre-formed values. Such willingness is especially necessary for optimum effectiveness in group counseling, group therapy, and group psychotherapy, in which personality change is one of the goals.

These few variations in emphases are indicative of the complexity of the group when its specific function is considered.

The reading selected for this section, "Definitions of the Group," by Cecil A. Gibb, provides working definitions and considers several problems in the understanding of the nature of the group.

1

Definitions of the Group

Cecil A. Gibb

. . . .

The term *group* is so well known that none of us would ordinarily turn to a dictionary to discover its meaning. But any person who asks a class of students to define and give examples of groups will discover that the term by no means has an unequivocal connotation. On the one hand, the word is used to refer to varied relations between objects, while on the other it embraces organizations of such different levels of complexity that it seems incredible that a common set of concepts and methods of study would be applicable to them. In consideration of this first source of confusion, one may point to at least three types of relation frequently denoted by the term "group."

1. Objects (or persons) which are, in some sense, together, for example, together in a certain place or together in the mind of the observer, are frequently said to be grouped or to constitute a group. In this chapter, however, such togetherness will be named an *aggregate* or a *collection*, and it will be differentiated from a *group*. Units of an aggregate are characterized by complete independence of one another. It is true, of course, that the aggregate would disappear if all the units were taken away, but no unit of the aggregate is changed by its nearness to other units. Also, as Asch points out,[1] "their order is of no consequence." Whether any human aggregates actually exist may, of course, be doubted. There is evidence to suggest that mere awareness of the presence of others changes individual behavior in many ways, thus implying an interaction among the units which negates the term "aggregate" or "collection." In any case, aggregations are of little or no importance to the social scientist, since they exclude the facts of interrelation.

2. A group might also be defined as a collection of units having qualities in common. Some aggregates may be homogeneous in some respect and through the perception of this homogeneity they will constitute classes. A heterogeneous pile of objects on a bargain counter may, perhaps, be used to illustrate an aggregate. A similar pile of magazines on a nearby counter,

From Cecil A. Gibb, "Leadership," Chapter 24 in Gardner Lindzey (ed.), *Handbook of Social Psychology*, Vol. 2, 1954. Addison-Wesley, Reading, Massachusetts. pp. 877–880. Reprinted with the permission of the publisher.

[1] S. E. Asch, *Social Psychology*. (New York: Prentice-Hall, Inc., 1952), p. 259.

however, is different, in that every unit here is a member of a class of things. In this case every unit embodies, in some particular manner, the nature of the class in question. While every book belongs to the aggregate we call a pile, it also belongs to the class of things called magazines. The particular pile is a sample of this class of things. Social groups conforming to this concept would be collections of individuals who are perceived to have common characteristics. For example, those who earn more than some arbitrary number of dollars per year may be said to constitute an economic class; those who are accepted into certain prescribed company may be said to form a social class; men who wear Homburg hats constitute a class. "One can say of this type of group also, that it excludes the fact of interaction; the members are what they are with no living relation between them, with no contact or even proximity."[2] For these reasons the class also has little interest for the psychologist concerned with organization and leadership. Without interaction neither of these phenomena can appear.

3. There is a third type of relation between objects (including persons) for which the term *group* is more properly used. A group is characterized by the interaction of its members, in such a way that each unit is changed by its group membership and each would be likely to undergo a change as a result of changes in the group. In this case there is a dependence of each member upon the entire group, and the relation between any two members is a function of the relation between other members. An aggregate of persons thus becomes a human group when interaction occurs among the units comprising it.

While the concept of interaction between members may serve to differentiate the group from the aggregate, it is not, by itself, a satisfactory definition of the group. We shall do well to examine briefly some of the attempts which have been made at definition. Sociologists and social psychologists have frequently tried to reduce to a minimum the criteria of a functional group.

Group definition in terms of interdependence of members has been offered by Kurt Lewin[3] and others. For Lewin, interdependence of members was the criterion of a group, as it was of any unitary whole. He pointed out that many social scientists define groups in terms of similarity of members, and that this was, in fact, the case, whether the primary emphasis was upon similarity of attitudes, or equality of goal, or equality of an enemy, or a feeling of loyalty. It was admitted, of course, that those similarities could be found in association with, and might be the cause of, a certain interdependence of the persons who show them. Krech and Crutchfield have accepted this Lewinian point of view and define the group as follows:

A group does not merely mean individuals characterized by some similar property. Thus, for example, a collection of Republicans or farmers or Negroes or blind men is not a group. These collections may be called classes

---

[2] *Ibid.*, p. 260.
[3] K. Lewin, "Field Theory and Experiment in Social Psychology: Concepts and Methods," *American Journal of Sociology*, XLIV (1939), 868–896.

of people. The term group, on the other hand, refers to two or more people who bear an explicit *psychological relationship to one another.* This means that for each member of the group the other members must exist in some more or less immediate psychological way so that their behavior and their characteristics influence him.[4]

On the other hand, Gillin and Gillin,[5] while they accept the criterion of interdependence or interaction, are inclined to equate this with holding interests or having purposes in common. They point to the function of common interests in motivating the "social relations" which characterize a social group. For these authors the group becomes manifest through the behavior which the members exhibit toward each other and toward the outside world. A group exists when *basic group responses* have been established, and this state would seem to be reflected in the development of what Cooley called *we-feeling.*

Definition of the Group as an Instrument of Satisfaction of Individual Needs. R. B. Cattell[6] has suggested that the definition of a group in terms of "internal interaction" of individuals seems less fundamental than to define it in terms of goals. "Our definition of a group is: 'an aggregate of organisms in which the existence of all is utilized for the satisfaction of some needs of each.'" This is probably the most basic and broadest definition of the group yet put forward. It embraces groups of all kinds, both primary and secondary.

For our purposes, this definition may be restricted and rephrased as follows: *The term functional group refers to two or more organisms interacting, in the pursuit of a common goal, in such a way that the existence of many is utilized for the satisfaction of some needs of each.* In this form the definition of a functional group clearly characterizes it as referring to that type of relation between objects in which each unit (member) is changed by its group membership. In this form there is no direct conflict with the Lewinian type of definition.

Specific mention is made here of common purposes or goals, since there can be little question that some common goals are a necessary condition for the existence of a functional group, and that these goals must be such as to give satisfaction to needs of the individual members who participate in the group. Interaction between members is made part of the definition rather than left as an implied consequence of group formation. It is impossible to conceive of a functional group without interaction and interdependence of members. Organization or *structure-in-interaction,* on the other hand, is not required as a defining characteristic of the concept of "functional group," however generally groups reveal structure in interaction. Nevertheless, the almost inevitable development of organization should not be overlooked.

[4] D. Krech and R. S. Crutchfield, *Theory and Problems of Social Psychology* (New York: McGraw-Hill Book Co., Inc., 1948), p. 18.

[5] J. L. Gillin and J. P. Gillin, *Introduction to Sociology* (New York: The Macmillan Company, 1946).

[6] R. B. Cattell, "New Concepts for Measuring Leadership in Terms of Group Syntality," *Human Relations,* IV (1951), 161–184.

Znaniecki has pointed to the emergence of group institutions as one of the basic processes of group formation. Of this he writes:

> In the beginning of the process of group formation those activities which make it a cultural product are experienced as spontaneous performances of voluntarily cooperating individuals. But as the group is formed and its makers become its members, such activities are normatively standardized and systematized until they come to be regarded as group institutions, the whole system of which constitutes the dynamic organization of the group. The function of each member consists in his obligatory active participation in group institutions; functions vary for the different categories of members.[7]

This definition has the virtue of handling with ease some situations which have presented difficulty to earlier schemes. For example, one may be asked how, in terms of definition, it is possible to handle four persons playing a tennis doubles match. Is this one functional group or two? It is possible to say that all have a common purpose to reach a definitive end of their struggle. On the other hand, it is clear that here there are, at the same time, one group and two. There can be no doubt that there is interaction among all four and all are utilized in the satisfaction of some needs of each. However, both quantitatively and qualitatively the interaction between partners differs from that between opponents. Here, at least, lies a basis for differentiation of the groups which will be dependent upon the purpose for which the groups are being studied or defined. But the possibility, provided by our definition, of differentiation in terms of goal adds greatly to one's comfort in dealing with the situation.

The problem of unitary versus segmentary groups which is raised here is not of purely academic interest. Stice has drawn the writer's attention to just such a problem in the study of air crews in which, for some purposes, it seems profitable to consider an entire crew as a single group, while, for other purposes, the crew is to be seen as a number of segmentary groups, e.g., as a flight team, a bombing team, a defensive team, and so on. As is usual in real-life situations, this question is complicated by the fact that these teams overlap in membership and a crew in action may be seen as a number of segmentary groups which are constantly forming and reforming as the external situation changes. Similar problems are common in the industrial setting. The now-famous Bank-Wiring Observation Room of the Hawthorne Western Electric Plant may best be regarded as a unitary group for the study of some of its behavior, but it can only be fully understood when the clique (segmentary group) formation within it has been observed and examined.

Of the air-crew segmentary groups or teams Stice, in a personal communication, writes: "They are groups that interact with other members of the aggregation certainly, and their members may at other times — or even simultaneously but for other purposes — be a part of others of these overlapping groups. As far as definition and experimental treatment are concerned, the

---

[7] F. Znaniecki, "Social Groups as Products of Participating Individuals," *American Journal of Sociology,* XLIV (1939), 799–811.

advantage here is that once a goal has been established the group can be reasonably well defined, and its organization and customs can be described with some reliability."

Group as a Quantitative Concept. One final characteristic of our definition of a functional group is that it is basically a quantitative concept, since interaction or interdependence is a quantitative variable. Furthermore, investment of individual energies in the group is not an all-or-nothing phenomenon, however difficult it may be to measure this variable with currently available techniques. French[8] and others have pointed out that definition in terms of interdependence implies other relationships also. For example, for French identification of members with the group is implied and this, in turn, is a quantitative variable affording a valuable index to degree of group development or group unity. Further, Cooley's "we-feeling" is a quantitative concept, since estimates of its strength may be obtained. In like fashion, many other indices of group quality or strength have been developed. . . .

Organization. Some writers emphasize the fact that the emergence of leadership is synonymous with differentiation of individual roles within the group. And a group in which the members are differentiated as to their responsibilities for the task of approaching the group goal is commonly called an *organization*. Znaniecki[9] has pointed out that it may frequently be difficult to determine whether any particular collection of organisms constitutes a group and that it may also be difficult at times to determine whether a particular group can be regarded as an organization. This is especially true of work with traditionless laboratory groups. In these groups the emergence of structure or organization can be observed, as can the relations of influence or leadership among the members. It is questionable, however, to refer to these groups as organizations, although they might be regarded as incipient organizations. This is the position of Stogdill, who writes:

> A group may or may not have leaders. If it does have leaders, it is an organization, for at least some of the members are thereby differentiated from the others as to responsibility, or role expectation in relation to some common purpose. The members of a group may or may not have mutual responsibilities for a common task. If the members do have differentiated responsibilities in relation to common goals then the group is an organization — a particular kind of group. The continued presence of leaders and of responsibility differentiations in relation to group goals are indicative of organization. It may not always be easy to determine the exact point at which a group emerges into an organization.[10]

Despite the advantages Stogdill sees in discussing leadership only as a facet of organization, this represents an unnecessary restriction on the concept of

[8] J. R. P. French, *"Organized and Unorganized Groups Under Fear and Frustration,"* Vol. 20, Part 5 in *University of Iowa Studies in Child Welfare*, 1944.

[9] F. Znaniecki, "Social Organization and Institutions," in G. Gurvitch and W. E. Moore, *Twentieth Century Sociology* (New York: Philosophical Library, 1945), pp. 172–217.

[10] R. M. Stogdill, "Leadership, Membership, and Organization," *Psychological Bulletin*, XLVII (1950), 3.

leadership and has no operational advantage in research. If it is recognized that groups vary with respect to a factor or dimension of organization, measurements of organization may be made and related to observations of leader behavior. It has long been claimed, as Sherif has said so clearly,[11] that all groups are characterized to some degree by hierarchical structure or organization. As Znaniecki[12] indicates, however, this can be realized only in a lasting "social group" or "association." In laboratory groups no persistent structure may be present during the early hours of common action but, with respect to any particular task, there is differentiation of roles or "structure" which may be regarded, as suggested above, as incipient organization. Organization, of course, may take many more complex forms than the differentiation of an influence hierarchy. But there can be no real objection to talking about organization leadership rather than group leadership if one so desires, and this is frequently done.

· · · ·

[11] M. Sherif, *An Outline of Social Psychology* (New York: Harper & Brothers, 1948).
[12] F. Znaniecki, *op. cit.* (1945).

Section B

FOUNDATIONS OF THE GROUP

The interaction which is the basis of the group arises out of the beliefs of the members, individually and as a whole. These beliefs are the result of the communal, religious, and historical experience of individuals. Even more specifically, experiences in the home or primary group are influential in building the beliefs which are the foundations of the group structure.

Ideas, attitudes, and behaviors in today's primary groups differ significantly from those of less than fifty years ago. They are different because "times have changed." Research and study in the major disciplines have greatly improved and have increased our understanding of man and his society. These insights, which have been refined, described, and applied to the life of man, are the foundations of our group relationships.

The beliefs held by group members and implicit in group functioning are those which concern man, society, and personal development.

Is man different from other animals in degree only or is he unique? Will he work for the benefit of others without expecting reward? Will he respect another's way of life, however dissimilar from his own? These questions are broadly concerned with the nature of man, which is ably discussed by Reinhold Niebuhr in excerpts from his book, The Nature and Destiny of Man.

Can man advance beyond his self-centeredness to become truly interested in others and interested in the betterment of their condition? Can he reach the degree of understanding and acceptance necessary to the achievement of a group harmony which releases the creative potential of all? One possibility for the attainment of such a goal is discussed by Carl Rogers in "A Tentative Formulation of a General Law of Interpersonal Relationships."

Although other disciplines contain meanings pertinent to an understanding of the bases of groups, the disciplines selected may be considered among the most important. They indicate the complexity of the various interrelated roots of group behavior. They also challenge us to reach higher levels of maturity in our interpersonal relationships.

2

Individuality in Modern Culture

Reinhold Niebuhr

Individuality is a fruit of both nature and spirit. It is the product of nature because the basis of selfhood lies in the particularity of the body. The self is most obviously separated from other selves by the simple fact that it is grounded in a physical organism which maintains its discrete existence and has its particular and dated history. Yet nature rises only gradually to the reality of individuality. In the inorganic world substances or forces are integrated and disintegrated so as to produce capriciously "unique" events (the upheaval of a particular mountain, for instance, and its gradual corrosion) but no unique or irreproducible unities. The inorganic world is thus subject to recurrences which can be charted with mathematical exactitude; hence the intimate relation between physics and mathematics.

In the organic world nature rises to the particularity of organisms, characterized by an interdependent and indestructible unity. The plant lives as a unity and its death means the destruction of that particular unity, its component elements sinking back into the inorganic world. On a still higher level animal life achieves a higher measure of discrete particularity, through an organism with a specific centre of unified interdependence, a central nervous system. Through this nervous system the animal achieves a higher degree of separation from its environment; yet its actions are governed by instincts which bind the individual animal to the general characteristics of the species. Variations in colour, size and, possibly, temper are capricious rather than significant and are subject to predictable recurrences. In animal life it is the species rather than the individual which is really unique. The particular animal merely expresses through endless repetition the special life-strategy of the species.

Genuine individuality, embodying both discreteness and uniqueness, is a characteristic of human life. It must consequently be regarded as the product of spirit as well as of nature. Nature supplies particularity but the freedom of the spirit is the cause of real individuality. Man, unlike animal existence, not only has a centre but he has a centre beyond himself. Man is the only animal which can make itself its own object. This capacity for self-transcend-ence which distinguishes spirit in man from soul (which he shares with animal existence), is the basis of discrete individuality, for this self-conscious-ness involves consciousness of the world as "the other." The animal knows its particular needs and the particular objects in its environment which satisfy those needs. Its consciousness therefore does not transcend the natural process in which it is involved. Animal consciousness is merely the expression of a central organic unity of an organism in relation to its immediate environment. Human consciousness involves the sharp distinction between the self and the totality of the world. Self-knowledge is thus the basis of discrete individuality.

Human capacity for self-transcendence is also the basis of human freedom and thereby of the uniqueness of the individual. Human consciousness not only transcends natural process but it transcends itself. It thereby gains the possibility for those endless variations and elaborations of human capacities which characterize human existence. Every impulse of nature in man can be modified, extended, repressed and combined with other impulses in count-less variations. In consequence no human individual is like another, no matter how similar their heredity and environment. To a certain degree man is free to reject one environment for another. If he dislikes the spiritual environment of the twentieth century he may consciously choose to live by the patterns of the thirteenth century. If he finds his physical environment uncongenial he has the capacity to modify it. The pride of modern man has sometimes tempted him to forget that there are limits of creatureliness which he cannot transcend and that there are inexorable forces of nature which he cannot defy. It is nevertheless important to remember that human spirituality is sharply distinguished from animal existence by the measure of human freedom and the consequent degree of discrete and unique individuality in man.

Human individuality, being a product of spirit as well as of nature, is subject to development. Primitive man is inserted with comparative friction-less harmony into the "primeval we" of group life.[1] He emerges from this group consciousness only gradually as an individual. But what emerges is an original endowment, present from the beginning. The uniqueness of this special endowment is proved not only by the fact that it develops in human life only but by the character of primitive existence. The primitive com-munity is forced to establish certain common usages and methods of restrain-ing natural impulse whereas animal existence, having no freedom, faces no problem of achieving unity. The lack of social freedom in a primitive community is a testimony of the inchoate freedom of primitive man. This freedom makes for a wide variety of the expression of impulses. Since the primitive community lacks the intelligence to achieve unity within variety it must insist upon uniformity, enforcing standards which may have emerged at first by pure historical caprice but which are gradually submitted to crude pragmatic tests of usefulness.[2]   . . . .

---

[1] Cf. *inter alia*, Fritz Kunkel, *Charakter, Einzelmensch und Gruppe.*

[2] Efforts to explain the emergence of "mind," that is of human freedom, in purely sociological terms are self-contradictory, sometimes to an amusing degree. Thus Professor

. . . The self knows the world, insofar as it knows the world, because it stands outside both itself and the world, which means that it cannot understand itself except as it is understood from beyond itself and the world.

This essential homelessness of the human spirit is the ground of all religion; for the self which stands outside itself and the world cannot find the meaning of life in itself or the world. It cannot identify meaning with causality in nature; for its freedom is obviously something different from the necessary causal links of nature. Nor can it identify the principle of meaning with rationality, since it transcends its own rational processes, so that it may, for instance, ask the question whether there is a relevance between its rational forms and the recurrences and forms of nature. It is this capacity of freedom which finally prompts great cultures and philosophies to transcend rationalism and to seek for the meaning of life in an unconditioned ground of existence. But from the standpoint of human thought this unconditioned ground of existence, this God, can be defined only negatively. . . .

· · · ·

. . . The conviction that man stands too completely outside of both nature and reason to understand himself in terms of either without misunderstanding himself belongs to general revelation in the sense that any astute analysis of the human situation must lead to it. But if man lacks a further revelation of the divine he will also misunderstand himself when he seeks to escape the conditions of nature and reason. He will end by seeking absorption in a divine reality which is at once all and nothing. To understand himself truly means to begin with a faith that he is understood from beyond himself, that he is known and loved of God and must find himself in terms of obedience to the divine will. This relation of the divine to the human will makes it possible for man to relate himself to God without pretending to be God; and to accept his distance from God as a created thing, without believing that the evil of his nature is caused by this finiteness. Man's finite existence in the body and in history can be essentially affirmed, as naturalism wants to affirm it. Yet the uniqueness of man's spirit can be appreciated even more than idealism appreciates it, though always preserving a proper distinction between the human and divine. Also the unity of spirit and body can be emphasized in terms of its relation to a Creator and Redeemer who created both mind and body. . . .

· · · ·

George H. Mead, who elaborates a social behaviourist viewpoint, widely held in America, reasons in his *Mind, Self and Society*: "[Our view] must be clearly distinguished from the partially social view of mind. According to this view, mind can get expression only within or in terms of an organized social group, yet it is nevertheless in some sense a native endowment, a congenital or hereditary biological attribute of the individual organism. . . . According to this latter view the social process presupposes and is the product of the social process. The advantage of our view is that it enables us to give a detailed account of, and actually to explain the genesis of mind" (p. 224). This viewpoint, which has nothing to commend it but rigorous consistency, sacrifices its consistency when Professor Mead explains in a footnote: "Hence it is only in human society, only within the peculiarly complex context of social relations and interactions which the human central nervous system makes psychologically possible, that minds arise or can arise; and thus also human beings are evidently the only biological organisms which are or can be self-conscious or possessed of selves" (p. 235).

. . . Man is not divided against himself so that the essential man can be extricated from the nonessential. Man contradicts himself within the terms of his true essence. His essence is free self-determination. His sin is the wrong use of his freedom and its consequent destruction.

Man is an individual but he is not self-sufficing. The law of his nature is love, a harmonious relation of life to life in obedience to the divine centre and source of his life. This law is violated when man seeks to make himself the centre and source of his own life. His sin is therefore spiritual and not carnal, though the infection of rebellion spreads from the spirit to the body and disturbs its harmonies also. Man, in other words, is a sinner not because he is one limited individual within a whole but rather because he is betrayed by his very ability to survey the whole to imagine himself the whole.

. . . .

. . . He stands at the juncture of nature and spirit. The freedom of his spirit causes him to break the harmonies of nature and the pride of his spirit prevents him from establishing a new harmony. The freedom of his spirit enables him to use the forces and processes of nature creatively; but his failure to observe the limits of his finite existence causes him to defy the forms and restraints of both nature and reason. Human self-consciousness is a high tower looking upon a large and inclusive world. It vainly imagines that it is the large world which it beholds and not a narrow tower insecurely erected amidst the shifting sands of the world.

3

A Tentative Formulation of a General Law of Interpersonal Relationships

Carl R. Rogers

During a recent summer I gave some thought to a theoretical problem which had tantalized me: Would it be possible to formulate, in one hypothesis, the elements which make any relationship either growth-facilitating or the reverse. I worked out a short document for myself, and had occasion to try it out on a workshop group and some industrial executives with whom I

From Carl R. Rogers, *On Becoming a Person*, chap. 18 (Boston: Houghton Mifflin Company, 1961), pp. 338–346. Reprinted with the permission of the publisher.

was conferring. It seemed to be of interest to all, but most stimulating to the industrial leaders who discussed it pro and con in terms of such problems as: supervisor-supervisee relationships; labor-management relationships; executive training; interpersonal relations among top management.

I regard this as a highly tentative document, and am not at all sure of its adequacy. I include it because many who have read it have found it provocative, and because publication of it may inspire research studies which would begin to test its validity.

I have many times asked myself how our learnings in the field of psychotherapy apply to human relationships in general. During recent years I have thought much about this issue and attempted to state a theory of interpersonal relationships as a part of the larger structure of theory in client-centered therapy.[1] This present document undertakes to spell out, in a somewhat different way, one of the aspects of that theory. It endeavors to look at a perceived underlying orderliness in all human relationships, an order which determines whether the relationship will make for the growth, enhancement, openness, and development of both individuals or whether it will make for inhibition of psychological growth, for defensiveness and blockage in both parties.

THE CONCEPT OF CONGRUENCE

Fundamental to much of what I wish to say is the term "congruence." This construct has been developed to cover a group of phenomena which seem important to therapy and to all interpersonal interaction. I would like to try to define it.

Congruence is the term we have used to indicate an accurate matching of experiencing and awareness. It may be still further extended to cover a matching of experience, awareness, and communication. Perhaps the simplest example is an infant. If he is experiencing hunger at the physiological and visceral level, then his awareness appears to match this experience, and his communication is also congruent with his experience. He is hungry and dissatisfied, and this is true of him at all levels. He is at this moment integrated or unified in being hungry. On the other hand if he is satiated and content this too is a unified congruence, similar at the visceral level, the level of awareness and the level of communication. He is one unified person all the way through, whether we tap his experience at the visceral level, the level of his awareness, or the level of communication. Probably one of the reasons why most people respond to infants is that they are so completely genuine, integrated or congruent. If an infant expresses affection or anger or contentment or fear there is no doubt in our minds that he *is* this experience, all the way through. He is transparently fearful or loving or hungry or whatever.

[1] Carl R. Rogers, "A Theory of Therapy, Personality and Interpersonal Relationships," in S. Koch (ed.), *Psychology: A Study of a Science* (New York: McGraw-Hill Book Co., Inc., 1959), Vol. III, Sec. IV; pp. 184–256.

For an example of incongruence we must turn to someone beyond the stage of infancy. To pick an easily recognizable example, take the man who becomes angrily involved in a group discussion. His face flushes, his tone communicates anger, he shakes his finger at his opponent. Yet when a friend says, "Well, let's not get angry about this," he replies, with evident sincerity and surprise, "I'm not angry! I don't have any *feeling* about this at all! I was just pointing out the logical facts." The other men in the group break out in laughter at this statement.

What is happening here? It seems clear that at a physiological level he is experiencing anger. This is not matched by his awareness. Consciously he is *not* experiencing anger, nor is he communicating this (so far as he is consciously aware). There is a real incongruence between experience and awareness, and between experience and communication.

Another point to be noted here is that his communication is actually ambiguous and unclear. In its words it is a setting forth of logic and fact. In its tone, and in the accompanying gestures, it is carrying a very different message — "I am angry at you." I believe this ambiguity or contradictoriness of communication is always present when a person who is at that moment incongruent endeavors to communicate.

Still another facet of the concept of incongruence is illustrated by this example. The individual himself is not a sound judge of his own degree of congruence. Thus the laughter of the group indicates a clear consensual judgment that the man is *experiencing* anger, whether or not he thinks so. Yet in his own awareness this is not true. In other words it appears that the degree of congruence cannot be evaluated by the person himself at that moment. We may make progress in learning to measure it from an external frame of reference. We have also learned much about incongruence from the person's own ability to recognize incongruence in himself in the past. Thus if the man of our example were in therapy, he might look back on this incident in the acceptant safety of the therapeutic hour and say, "I realize now I was terribly angry at him, even though at the time I thought I was not." He has, we say, come to recognize that his defensiveness at that moment kept him from being aware of his anger.

One more example will portray another aspect of incongruence. Mrs. Brown, who has been stifling yawns and looking at her watch for hours, says to her hostess on departing, "I enjoyed this evening so much. It was a delightful party." Here the incongruence is not between experience and awareness. Mrs. Brown is well aware that she is bored. The incongruence is between awareness and communication. Thus it might be noted that when there is an incongruence between experience and awareness, it is usually spoken of as defensiveness, or denial to awareness. When the incongruence is between awareness and communication it is usually thought of as falseness or deceit.

There is an important corollary of the construct of congruence which is not at all obvious. It may be stated in this way. If an individual is at this moment entirely congruent, his actual physiological experience being accurately represented in his awareness, and his communication being accurately congruent with his awareness, then his communication could never contain an expression of an external fact. If he was congruent he could not say, "That rock is hard"; "He is stupid"; "You are bad"; or "She is intelligent." The reason for this is that we never *experience* such "facts." Accurate awareness of *experience* would always be expressed as feelings, perceptions, meanings from an internal frame of reference. I never *know* that he is stupid or you are bad. I can only perceive that you seem this way to me. Likewise, strictly speaking I do not *know* that the rock is hard, even though I may be very sure that I *experience* it as hard if I fall down on it. (And even then I can permit the physicist to perceive it as a very permeable mass of high-speed atoms and molecules.) If the person is thoroughly congruent then it is clear that all of his communication would necessarily be put in a context of personal perception. This has very important implications.

As an aside it might be mentioned that for a person always to speak from a context of personal perception does not necessarily imply congruence, since any mode of expression *may* be used as a type of defensiveness. Thus the person in a moment of congruence would necessarily communicate his perceptions and feelings as being these, and not as being *facts* about another person or the outside world. The reverse does not necessarily hold, however.

Perhaps I have said enough to indicate that this concept of congruence is a somewhat complex concept with a number of characteristics and implications. It is not easily defined in operational terms, though some studies have been completed and others are in process which do provide crude operational indicators of what is being experienced, as distinct from the awareness of that experience. It is believed that further refinements are possible.

To conclude our definition of this construct in a much more common-sense way, I believe all of us tend to recognize congruence or incongruence in individuals with whom we deal. With some individuals we realize that in most areas this person not only consciously means exactly what he says, but that his deepest feelings also match what he is expressing, whether it is anger or competitiveness or affection or cooperativeness. We feel that "we know exactly where he stands." With another individual we recognize that what he is saying is almost certainly a front, a façade. We wonder what he *really* feels. We wonder if *he* knows what he feels. We tend to be wary and cautious with such an individual.

Obviously then, different individuals differ in their degree of congruence, and the same individual differs at different moments in degree of congruence, depending on what he is experiencing and whether he can accept this experience in his awareness, or must defend himself against it.

RELATING CONGRUENCE TO COMMUNICATION IN INTERPERSONAL RELATIONSHIPS

Perhaps the significance of this concept for interpersonal interaction can be recognized if we make a few statements about a hypothetical Smith and Jones.

1. Any communication of Smith to Jones is marked by some degree of congruence in Smith. This is obvious from the above.

2. The greater the congruence of experience, awareness, and communication in Smith, the more it is likely that Jones will experience it as a *clear* communication. I believe this has been adequately covered. If all the cues from speech, tone and gesture are unified because they spring from a congruence and unity in Smith, then there is much less likelihood that these cues will have an ambiguous or unclear meaning to Jones.

3. Consequently, the more clear the communication from Smith, the more Jones responds with clarity. This is simply saying that even though Jones might be quite *in*congruent in his experiencing of the topic under discussion, nevertheless his response will have *more* clarity and congruence in it than if he had experienced Smith's communication as ambiguous.

4. The more that Smith is congruent in the topic about which they are communicating, the less he has to defend himself against in this area, and the more able he is to listen accurately to Jones' response. Putting it in other terms, Smith has expressed what he genuinely feels. He is therefore more free to listen. The less he is presenting a façade to be defended, the more he can listen accurately to what Jones is communicating.

5. But to this degree, then, Jones feels empathically understood. He feels that in so far as he has expressed himself (and whether this is defensively or congruently), Smith has understood him pretty much as he sees himself, and as he perceives the topic under consideration.

6. For Jones to feel understood is for him to experience positive regard for Smith. To feel that one is understood is to feel that one has made some kind of a positive difference in the experience of another, in this case, of Smith.

7. But to the degree that Jones (a) experiences Smith as congruent or integrated in this relationship; (b) experiences Smith as having positive regard for him; (c) experiences Smith as being empathically understanding; to that degree the conditions of a therapeutic relationship are established. I have tried in another paper[2] to describe the conditions which our experience has led us to believe are necessary and sufficient for therapy, and will not repeat that description here.

8. To the extent that Jones is experiencing these characteristics of a therapeutic relationship, he finds himself experiencing fewer barriers to communication. Hence he tends to communicate himself more as he is, more congruently. Little by little his defensiveness decreases.

9. Having communicated himself more freely, with less of defensiveness, Jones is now more able to listen accurately, without a need for defensive distortion, to Smith's further communication. This is a repetition of step 4, but now in terms of Jones.

10. To the degree that Jones is able to listen, Smith now feels empathically understood (as in step 5 for Jones); experiences Jones' positive regard (a parallel to step 6); and finds himself experiencing the relationship as therapeutic (in a way parallel to step 7). Thus Smith and Jones have to some degree become reciprocally therapeutic for each other.

11. This means that to some degree the process of therapy occurs in each

[2] Carl R. Rogers, "The Necessary and Sufficient Conditions of Therapeutic Personality Change," *Journal of Consulting Psychology*, XXI, 95–103.

and that the outcomes of therapy will to that same degree occur in each; change in personality in the direction of greater unity and integration; less conflict and more energy utilizable for effective living; change in behavior in the direction of greater maturity.

12. The limiting element in this chain of events appears to be the introduction of threatening material. Thus if Jones in step 3 includes in his more congruent response new material which is outside of the realm of Smith's congruence, touching an area in which Smith is *incongruent*, then Smith may not be able to listen accurately, he defends himself against hearing what Jones is communicating, he responds with communication which is ambiguous, and the whole process described in these steps begins to occur in reverse.

A TENTATIVE STATEMENT OF A GENERAL LAW

Taking all of the above into account, it seems possible to state it far more parsimoniously as a generalized principle. Here is such an attempt.

Assuming (a) a minimal willingness on the part of two people to be in contact; (b) an ability and minimal willingness on the part of each to receive communication from the other; and (c) assuming the contact to continue over a period of time; then the following relationship is hypothesized to hold true.

> The greater the congruence of experience, awareness and communication on the part of one individual, the more the ensuing relationship will involve: a tendency toward reciprocal communication with a quality of increasing congruence; a tendency toward more mutually accurate understanding of the communications; improved psychological adjustment and functioning in both parties; mutual satisfaction in the relationship.
>
> Conversely the greater the communicated *incongruence* of experience and awareness, the more the ensuing relationship will involve: further communication with the same quality; disintegration of accurate understanding; less adequate psychological adjustment and functioning in both parties; and mutual dissatisfaction in the relationship.

With probably even greater formal accuracy this general law could be stated in a way which recognizes that it is the perception of the *receiver* of communication which is crucial. Thus the hypothesized law could be put in these terms, assuming the same pre-conditions as before as to willingness to be in contact, etc.

> The more that Y experiences the communication of X as a congruence of experience, awareness, and communication, the more the ensuing relationship will involve: (etc, as stated above.)

Stated in this way this "law" becomes an hypothesis which it should be possible to put to test, since Y's *perception* of X's communication should not be too difficult to measure.

The Existential Choice

Very tentatively indeed I would like to set forth one further aspect of this whole matter, an aspect which is frequently very real in the therapeutic relationship, and also in other relationships, though perhaps less sharply noted.

In the actual relationship both the client and the therapist are frequently faced with the existential choice, "Do I dare to communicate the full degree of congruence which I feel? Do I dare match my experience, and my awareness of that experience, with my communication? Do I dare to communicate myself as I am or must my communication be somewhat less than or different from this?" The sharpness of this issue lies in the often vividly foreseen possibility of threat or rejection. To communicate one's full awareness of the relevant experience is a risk in interpersonal relationships. It seems to me that it is the taking or not taking of this risk which determines whether a given relationship becomes more and more mutually therapeutic or whether it leads in a disintegrative direction.

To put it another way. I cannot choose whether my awareness will be congruent with my experience. This is answered by my need for defense, and of this I am not aware. But there is a continuing existential choice as to whether my communication will be congruent with the awareness I *do* have of what I am experiencing. In this moment-by-moment choice in a relationship may lie the answer as to whether the movement is in one direction or the other in terms of this hypothesized law.

PART TWO · THE GROUP

Section C

TYPES AND LEVELS OF GROUPS

Although emphasis is usually placed on the differences among groups and group processes rather than on their similarities — the very use of the terms group work, group counseling, multiple counseling, group therapy, and instructional groups indicates this — it is important also to recognize the common elements. Both differences and similarities may be observed in the group work of teachers. Social studies and mathematics teachers, for example, teach a different content, but they also have certain concerns in common. Each teacher tries to create a good learning climate. Each endeavors to strengthen egos, clarify issues, proclaim values, and set levels of aspiration. And each has the responsibility for assisting the student to succeed as a learner by helping him to succeed as a person.

The attainment of a better comprehension of some of the operational differences among groups, however, may be good preparation for understanding their philosophical similarities. The readings which follow clarify some of the existing differences.

Leo Goldman, in his article, "Group Guidance: Content and Process," differentiates among several types and levels of groups and provides useful illustrations. In "Socio and Psyche Group Process: Integrative Concepts," Hubert S. Coffey discusses the levels of group process, with special emphasis on the characterization and description of these two types of groups.

4

Group Guidance: Content and Process

Leo Goldman

. . . From the counselor's point of view, enriched understanding of his counselees should result from the opportunity to see how each of them functions in the group setting. For these and other anticipated values, counselors in many settings, but especially in schools, looked to group methods for valuable contributions to a total guidance and counseling program.

Despite these presumed advantages, group methods of guidance and counseling seem to have experienced many failures, perhaps most notably in schools. Repeatedly one hears of group activities that were tried and abandoned: homeroom guidance, occupations units in classes, and special guidance and counseling groups. The reasons given for failure are many: lack of interest or ability on the part of teachers, inadequate supervision of group leaders, too large groups, and others. Some have reached the conclusion that group methods are just not suitable for the attainment of guidance goals. Yet there are several books which contain guidelines for effective work with groups and at least some evidence that group methods are useful.[1]

Why then have there been so many unhappy experiences with group methods of guidance and counseling? In the observation of the writer, there seems to have been in many instances a lack of understanding of the roles of *content* and *process*.[2] The crux of the position being taken here is that too many group guidance activities have been guidance only in their contents; the process has often not been suitable.

CONTENT AND PROCESS

Figure 1 shows the two dimensions: content across the rows and process down the columns. In each instance, the total range is divided for con-

From Leo Goldman, "Group Guidance: Content and Process," *Personnel and Guidance Journal*, XL (February, 1962), 518–522. Reprinted with the permission of publisher and author.

[1] Margaret E. Bennett, *Guidance in Groups* (New York: McGraw-Hill Book Co., Inc., 1955); Gertrude Forrester, *Methods of Vocational Guidance* (Boston: D. C. Heath & Company, 1951); Robert Hoppock, *Group Guidance* (New York: McGraw-Hill Book Co., Inc., 1949); and Jane Warters, *Group Guidance* (New York: McGraw-Hill Book Co., Inc., 1960).

[2] Leo Goldman, "Counseling: Content and Process," *Personnel and Guidance Journal*, XXIII (1954), 82–85.

Figure 1
INTERACTION OF CONTENT AND PROCESS IN GROUP GUIDANCE,
GROUP COUNSELING, AND GROUP THERAPY

	Process		
	Level I Leader plans topics Lecture and recitation Facts and skills emphasized Units in regular classes	*Level II* Leader and group members collaborate in planning topics Discussions, projects, panels, visits Attitudes and opinions emphasized Separate guidance groups meet on schedule	*Level III* Topics originate with group members Free discussion, role-playing Feelings and needs emphasized Groups organized as needed, meet as needed
Content			
Type A Usual school subject-matter: mathematics, English, etc.	1	4	7
Type B School-related topics: the world of work, choosing a college, how to study, etc.	2	5	8
Type C Non-school topics: dating behavior, parent-child relations, handling frustrations, etc.	3	6	9

venience of discussion into three parts, but this is arbitrary. Each dimension should be seen as a continuum which could with equal logic be divided into two parts or ten.

Content. Going down the rows, we move from the usual academic subjects — mathematics, literature, and all the others which are universally accepted as school curricular content — to topics at the other extreme which are in many places considered to be off-limits, topics such as dating behavior or parent-child relations. Between the extremes are the school-related topics such as educational and vocational opportunities, which, though not academic subjects, are usually accepted as belonging somewhere in the school's total curriculum.

Process. Moving from left to right we go from the more traditional, teacher-directed methods to those which give pupils more responsibility for planning and conducting classroom activities. Also as we go across the columns, there is decreasing emphasis on cognitive elements and increasing emphasis first on attitudes and opinions, and later on deeper feelings. The manner of forming the groups is also seen to differ. Finally, perhaps the best indicator of differences among these processes is the kind of evaluative questions one asks. At Level I, the questions are likely to be: How much does he know? How much skill has he developed? At Level II, the questions are more likely to be these: Does he have well-developed and well-substantiated opinions? Have his attitudes changed or developed? And at Level III the questions would be: How does he behave in relation to peers or parents? How realistic a degree of self-acceptance does he have? It seems clear that Levels II and III contain more of the elements of guidance and counseling, while Level I has more of those which are appropriate to instruction.

INTERACTION OF CONTENT AND PROCESS

To illustrate the interaction of the two dimensions, we will see how three different group leaders might handle the same guidance topic: choosing a high school course of study.

1. Mr. Jones includes a unit on choosing a high school course of study in his eighth grade English classes. He decides early in the school year which week he will devote to this unit. He introduces the topic one day, pointing out its importance and asking questions to see how much thinking the pupils have already done. Then he assigns some readings in a series of guidance publications. During the next few class meetings he makes sure that the class understands what each of the courses of study consists of — academic, general, commercial, and vocational — and for what kinds of occupations each is suitable. He urges the boys and girls to be realistic in their choices. In particular he points out that pupils sometimes make poor choices because they are too concerned with prestige or doing what their friends do. (This approach would seem to fit most closely the content process interaction of cell 2, a combination of Type B content with a Level I process.)

2. Mr. Smith meets each eighth-grade class one period each week to discuss various guidance topics. The problem of selecting a high school course of study almost always comes up naturally in each group as they discuss their future plans. At that point Mr. Smith helps the class to decide what information they need and how they will go about collecting it. The specific methods vary somewhat from class to class, but generally the pupils divide among themselves a variety of readings, visits, and interviews in order to learn about the courses of study they are thinking about. Then they bring their various findings to class and discuss both the facts and their opinions about the advantages and disadvantages of different courses for different people. Usually each one tells about his own preferences and the reasons for them, and the others comment or raise questions. Mr. Smith tries to get each pupil to think about his educational plans in the light of his previous school history, his parents' values, and other factors. He will often raise thought-provoking ques-

tions and will sometimes correct inaccurate information. (This approach seems to be a combination of Type B content and a Level II process and therefore would be a cell 5 interaction.)

3. Mr. Brown sets up groups for multiple counseling whenever he recognizes common needs among several of his counselees. He has just organized a group of youngsters who are indecisive or conflicted about their high school course of study. They have worked out a schedule to meet twice a week for as many weeks as necessary. During the meetings Mr. Brown encourages each pupil to describe his own problem to the group and to explore it in some depth. Some of the youngsters tell about parental pressures, and others describe their feelings of inadequacy. Sometimes two or three find that they have very similar problems. Together they try to understand the factors that are operating and then try out on each other suggestions for dealing with their problems. Sometimes a boy or girl finds reassurance just in the knowledge that someone else faces a very similar problem. Mr. Brown makes occasional interpretations and reflections, and sometimes he suggests that they role-play a problem situation or a solution that someone has proposed. When the pupils or Mr. Brown feel that information is needed regarding the courses of study or related occupations, they decide how to obtain the information. The group disbands whenever it appears to the pupils and Mr. Brown that their purposes have been fulfilled. (This approach would seem to belong in cell 8 or 9, since it involves Type B or perhaps C content, with a Level III process.)

FROM TEACHING TO GUIDANCE ACTIVITY

The illustrations used show how three different kinds of process might be applied to one of the common group guidance topics. Similar illustrations could be developed for other topics such as dating behavior, study habits, or career planning.

The thesis here is that for a group activity to move from the teaching of a school subject to a guidance activity requires changes both of content and process. Referring to Figure 1, the movement is diagonally from upper-left to lower-right. In cell 1 would be found the kind of classroom that is probably typical at the college level and that decreases in frequency of occurrence as one moves backward through secondary and elementary schools. At the other extreme, in cell 9, is the kind of activity that is usually referred to as group therapy. Somewhere around cell 5 is what the writer would call group guidance; in cells 6 and 8 are the activities that he would identify with the label group counseling or multiple counseling. Others prefer to define these terms differently and would therefore place them differently among the cells.

In the writer's observations, group guidance and group counseling have in many instances gone awry in schools because they have been cell 2 and 3 kinds of operations, such as those conducted by Mr. Jones in the first of the three illustrations. The group leaders have usually been classroom teachers, many of them without any special training in guidance, who spend only a fraction of their time in this so-called guidance activity, be it in a homeroom, a unit of an academic subject, or a once-a-week "guidance" or "occupations" class. It should not surprise us, then, that they use much the same approach in their guidance activities as in the classroom: assigning readings in textbooks, asking pupils to recite in the class, doing much explaining, advising, and exhorting, and even giving grades at the end of a unit or course. Imagine, a grade in "Guidance"!

Even well-trained guidance counselors often find it difficult to depart from Level I in their group guidance work. They too have had their group leadership experience as teachers in subject-matter classrooms. Unfortunately, they receive little preparation for group guidance activities in most counselor-education programs; supervised practice in group guidance or group counseling is almost unheard of. It is understandable, then, that even professional, full-time counselors find it difficult to shift to Level II and III approaches.

What seems to happen in many schools, then, is that "group guidance" becomes merely another academic subject. Yet counselors, teachers, and administrators sometimes expect Level II or III outcomes, such as more realistic planning, changes of attitude, and even changes of observed behavior. When these outcomes are not obtained, too often "group guidance" is denounced as the culprit.

Teaching at Levels II and III

To complete the analysis of Figure 1, we should note that not all teachers use Level I methods exclusively. There are English teachers who use a novel or play to help pupils to understand their own motivations and problems. There are home economics teachers who use a variety of methods to sharpen and develop children's understandings of the roles of various family members. There are social studies teachers who stimulate youngsters to explore opinions, attitudes, and prejudices regarding political and economic matters. One might say that all these teachers are performing guidance kinds of functions. The writer would prefer to regard these rather as a variety of teaching — an excellent variety indeed. The term Guidance, with a capital G, might better be reserved for those activities which are guidance both in content and process.

The purpose here is not to segregate teaching from guidance but simply to maintain a meaningful distinction between the *major* functions of teachers and of guidance specialists in today's schools. Admittedly, the distinction is not perfect, since good teachers sometimes operate at Levels II and III, and good guidance workers sometimes operate at Level I. When one compares the work of teachers as a whole with that of guidance workers as a whole, however, the distinction has validity and serves a useful purpose.

Summary and Conclusions

Group methods in guidance are differentiated from teaching both in their contents and in the processes by which the contents are handled. Too often guidance groups seem to differ from subject-matter classes only in their contents. This may be one of the major reasons for the failure of so many homeroom and other group guidance enterprises. It seems clear that group guidance, group counseling, and group therapy, as these terms are used here, require special training, including supervised practice. Even with such training, it seems doubtful that many classroom teachers will be able to make the transition from the processes which are appropriate to teaching to those which are more appropriate to guidance. Instead it would appear to be necessary that group guidance and group counseling be done only by those who do not concurrently have normal classroom teaching responsibilities.

5

Socio and Psyche Group Process: Integrative Concepts

Hubert Stanley Coffey

The articles in Part I have presented the basic assumptions and some of the distinctive characteristics of the fields of informal education, social group work, and group psychotherapy. In their different ways they have emphasized what seemed to the writers the particular *raison d'être* of the professional field represented. They have described historical as well as systematic reasons which have determined the development of each field. These "histories" have stated the limitations and the boundaries of the field, as well as indicated the horizons. The limits are sometimes stated in terms of the objectives of the professional field, sometimes in terms of the professional preparation, and sometimes in terms of the setting in which the function is to be performed. A study of the content of the three fields would tend to create the impression of rather distinct areas to be pursued by persons with quite distinct types of preparation. But further analysis will also indicate certain similarities, certain convergent trends. When the emphasis is placed on the process of interaction in the group and upon the conditions under which optimal learning takes place, then the adult educator, the group therapist and the social group worker can be seen to share in many ways a similar approach to group process, even though they may differ as to objectives and content.

From Hubert Stanley Coffey, "Socio and Psyche Group Process: Integrative Concepts," *Journal of Social Issues*, VIII (Spring, 1952), 65–74. Reprinted with the permission of publisher and author.

Knowles and Bradford feel that it is no longer possible to think of adult education in terms of content areas as exemplified by the traditional curriculum. They say that "The modern situation requires an adult educator who is more than a teacher of individuals or a manager of groups. Whether the goals be individual or group or both he must be able to develop group cohesiveness, group standards for achievement, and other elements of group effectiveness for producing change." Frank points out quite clearly how permissiveness, stimulation, support, verbalization, and reality testing and practice, as generic aspects of all psychotherapy, are functions performed naturally in a group situation. Yet, it is difficult to imagine any functioning group, whether a therapy group or an adult education group, which does not have these characteristics if it is to accomplish what it sets out to do. Although Coyle shows a sense of uneasiness in delimiting lines of professional competence and defined function in social group work, she clearly recognizes the overlapping aspects among the fields of group work, group therapy and group relations in education. She says, "Although at points they rest on certain differences in emphasis or on somewhat different conceptions of individual or group dynamics, they have much in common in that they are all engaged in refining our social skills."

DISTINCTIONS BASED ON HISTORICAL DEVELOPMENT

In each of the three definitional papers there was an attempt to go beyond the occasion of historical accident, and to find some systematic characterization which we might use to shed light upon both the similarities and differences among the three groups. Each author tried to describe the elements that seem to be intrinsic to his field. But, as is often true, and perhaps inevitable at this stage of development, what is assumed to be a distinctive aspect of the field is simply an expression of a particular structure originally designed to meet a particular social need. Thus, when adult educators saw the need for a more dynamic approach in their field, it was natural that they would turn to the blossoming area of group dynamics; hence, the central focus on group cohesion as a condition for effective problem solving. The development of group therapy, which Frank points out resulted from the convergence of many historical forces, made it necessary to search for a central organizing concept of group interaction which would distinguish it from individual psychotherapy on the one hand, and social action, on the other. The dimensions of support and stimulation, empirically noted as a necessary condition for group therapy, seemed to offer a relevant theoretical focus. The social group worker has always thought in terms of group process, and the emergence of this concept has been accompanied by a search for what might be an intrinsically valid expression of it. Often, however, it was expressed somewhat sloganistically as a process different from individual case work, or as a process operating within a particular setting, such as organized recreation. As fields develop, however, and as their implications for meeting human needs become more comprehensive, the fields themselves press against the comfortable structure of an earlier day. Not only do the fields find that their province of action can no longer be governed in the traditional way, but their encroachment on surrounding fields becomes inevitable and necessary.

This growth, while in general more dynamic in meeting human needs, may be fraught with frustrations for the professional worker who would like to maintain the neat orderliness of definition. Moreover, it may very well seduce the more unreflecting into serving in capacities for which they are not professionally prepared. Such expansions and such overlappings which characterize the area of applied group dynamics, in the most general sense of that term, as well as all professions today, have their elements of danger as well as their elements of promise. Without some conceptual framework in which the relations of these fields can be seen, there is likely to be an uneasy advance and withdrawal in which tidiness is invoked as the central value by some, while others may rationalize any practice on the basis of creativity and functionalism. Neither of these attitudes is an answer to our problem, but both may be a result of our own inability to conceptualize what is involved in these professional relationships.

CONFUSIONS RESULTING FROM LACK OF THEORY

It is evident that this is a real problem, and not one dreamed up in the academic grove, when we view certain situations in which a real confusion about the boundaries exists. For example: A staff interested in becoming more acquainted with group procedures along group dynamics lines requested assistance from a skilled leader. After four or five sessions, frustrations and anxiety had reached a saturation point and they requested that the sessions be terminated. The leader had seen the group almost entirely as a "therapy group," and had assumed a completely non-directive role. His function, as he saw it, was to deal exclusively with individual dynamics in relation to group process. The need for any cognitive structure (that is, content and direction) was not apparent to him.

Another example: A group interested in developing greater sensitivity to the group process as a part of their training objective experienced a session in which each person described his own needs, frustrations, blocks, etc. This was a session charged with personal reminiscence, confessional, and much interpersonal strife. For some it was a time to lay their masochistic souls bare, for others it was a period of aggressive projection. The situation in which this session occurred, the lack of fundamental commitment to the process, and the limitations of time, made this an abortive venture in group therapy. The outcome at best was the acquisition of an "experience"; at its worst it was a laying open of wounds which could be healed only by the defenses of denial, hostility or uneasy forgetting.

Another example: A leader, with a penchant for the "dynamic," pressures a group into self-evaluation through the devious route of group observation, before the group has had sufficient time to work together in problem-solving activities so as to understand or experience any apparent process difficulties. Eager to get started on the work objective, the group has been stopped and dissolved by a process of individual confessional.

Numerous instances like these could be cited by many of us. The intentions of the leaders and the aims of the groups are so worthy in most cases as to make the failure and the confusions more disastrous. In the field of human relations, especially as we think of it in its application to group dynamics, nothing is more needed than a careful appraisal of what group process means in relation to the specific kind of situations where it is used as a concept. The group therapist may be sure that the underlying dynamics of unconscious motivation are the significant aspects of all group interaction, but if he imposes his interpretations on a social action group he is likely to lead the group down the path of frustration to its dissolution. Moreover, if his approach proves attractive to the "dynamically oriented" adult educator or social group worker and his methods, valid in their own setting, are appropriated and applied to situations where they are not appropriate, the consequent difficulties are likely to lead to a wholesale rejection of the methods, including their use in situations where they have proved to be fruitful. Many methods which are creative in their own right, if taken up impulsively and misapplied, may be widely condemned. What is essentially a gain in professional development of a field may be seen as a perversion because of its misapplication. Yet in the field of human relations and group process we need the contribution of those who come to their work, whatever their professional orientation, with an imaginative and sensitive approach; for, these are the people who are likely to bring the richest insights. If we can develop a conceptual framework which shows the relationship of the different professional orientations, then we can utilize these creative contributions in meeting professional needs rather than creating crises which lead to withdrawal into professional encapsulation.

The answer cannot be found in trying to build walls around fields, but rather in seeing what the process is and then determining the appropriate relation of each field to this process. Especially is this so when our fields are related by some generic process as is the case with the three fields we are discussing. For, every idea, as Dewey has said, places some part of a stable world in peril; and it means that no wall can ever be built which will survive the growth demands of the individual or of society. In our case it means that we need to have some conceptual framework by which to evaluate our different activities and our particular emphases. For, some plausible schema by which to relate our separate activities provides the security to make the creative departures so necessary if a field is to retain its vitality. Artificial restrictions based solely upon tradition or rigid orthodoxy are likely to be stultifying, whereas a theoretical expression of relationships is likely not only to provide usable boundaries but also to emphasize growing horizons. To revert to the metaphor, when we know what we are doing, on the basis of some meaningful concepts, then — if we want to scale the wall — we can determine what equipment we need.

SOCIO AND PSYCHE GROUP DIFFERENTIATION

One of the most fruitful differentiations in the field of group process has come from the distinction which Jennings makes between psyche and socio groups.[1] For Jennings, the psyche group might be typified by the boys' gang,

[1] H. H. Jennings, *Leadership and Isolation*, Second Edition (New York: Longmans, Green & Co., 1950).

or the preadolescent girls' clique. The socio group, on the other hand, might be illustrated by the committee which is seeking to deal with the problem of juvenile delinquency in a community. Socio and psyche groups differ in a number of respects.

In the psyche group there is no visualized goal, while in the socio group that is an essential characteristic. In the psyche group there is an informal structure, with little in the way of rules or regulations, and if there are any, they are likely to be transient: the ritual of today is thrown out of the window tomorrow. The members of a psyche group are usually voluntary and the group has a high degree of homogeneity. In the socio group there are both voluntary members and those who are involuntary in the sense that they may be there less by their own inclinations than as representatives of some other organization. Usually the socio group is more heterogeneous with respect to age, status, vocation, etc. The purpose of the psyche group, although it is rarely made explicit, is to satisfy the emotional needs of the group members, whereas the purpose of the socio group is to reach the visualized goal of the group. It will be readily seen that these groups do not present a true dichotomy, but rather separate ends of a continuum of group process. They rarely exist in pure forms, for most groups are a mixture of these two elements.

This leads us to consider that what has been described by Jennings as an entity is actually a process, and that it would be fruitful to think of the *psyche group process* and the *socio group process*. Moreover, it is not strange that we illustrate the psyche group process by reference to preadolescent gangs or cliques, for it is in these groups that the important issues of child development with respect to peer group status, social skills, and personal security are worked out. That is not to say, of course, that the psyche group process is important at no other age. For in numerous situations, in the family, in recreational groups, under informal conditions, we see the psyche group process at work.

Likewise, it is not strange that our example of the socio group process should be drawn from the task-oriented activity of a work committee of adults, for it is this kind of group which demonstrates that the problems of communities by their very nature demand solution by groups. Again, that is not to say that the socio group aspect is limited to adult activities. We can see, for example, the energies of teenagers turned to accomplishing community objectives, or the loose and chaotic nature of organization in a group of boys of Cub Scout age being mobilized for community action in such activities as paper drives, traffic regulation, etc.

Integration of Processes — Group Dynamics

The theoretical differentiation between the psyche group and the socio group processes can be represented in the . . . diagrammatic schema [shown in Figure 1].

Although it is a gross oversimplification, I believe one could characterize the work of the late Kurt Lewin in the field of group dynamics in terms of the socio and psyche group processes as follows: Lewin saw the importance

Figure 1

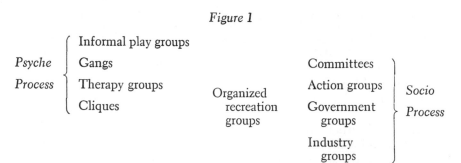

of incorporating into the socio group aspects of the problem-solving group the rich store of potential involvement, motivation, and ego fulfillment characteristic of the psyche group process. The focus of group dynamics has been to study, through experimentation and observation, those forces which make for greater group productivity. And in every instance the goal of group productivity has led inevitably to finding ways and means for greater emotional investments of the individual in the socio-process of problem solving. The problem census, evaluation and feedback, and role playing — all can be seen as ways of bringing the psyche group process into close interrelation with the socio group process.

Now, in problem solving groups the socio group process is the process which is dominant. It is the one which can be described in terms of decision making, goal setting and action research. The focus of these groups is always toward the socio group goal. Yet underlying the whole movement toward the goal, forming a solid foundation for this clear melodic line, are the harmonies of psyche group involvements. The greater their inclusion, i.e., the more ways and means we provide for their constructive incorporation in the movement toward the socio group goal, the more active and productive the group will be.

Psyche Process Focus of Therapy Groups

There are also circumstances when the psyche group process becomes the appropriate focus of attention. The psyche group process can be thought of as including those projections, perceptions of self and others, aggressions, submissions, loves, hostilities, dependencies, etc., which are the raw basic assumptions in all human relations. In some groups these become the principal area for work. Therapy groups are excellent examples of groups in which the focus of attention is the psyche group process. In the immediate face to face relationships in the therapy group, the psyche group process becomes the central concern, for here support and stimulation do not further a visualized group task, but rather serve to create the freedom of expression which, in turn, fosters spontaneity of interaction and reminiscence. These become the data of analysis and interpretation with which the therapist works. It is interesting to note that the content of discussion is most likely to be concerned with past or contemporary psyche group associations, family relation, sibling rivalries, authority problems. It is just these psyche group processes with which the patient struggles in the therapy group, for in his daily life he has not been able to deal with them without occasioning incapacitating anxiety. The therapist is a person in whom these processes do not occasion the same degree of anxiety, and who — in his understanding of his own anxieties — can help the patient understand *his*. *Therapy* groups never have group goals, in the socio group sense.

Frank, in his article, points out how necessary are the aspects of support, stimulation and reality testing in a therapy group. Although these conditions are necessary to the accomplishment of therapy objectives, they are not, to my mind, the definitive aspect of group therapy. Frank pictures vividly how these conditions develop, and how vital these dimensions of the therapy group are to the process of therapy, but I think you could find that each of these dimensions is important to the problem-solving group as well, especially where a high level of cooperation and thinking are required. What makes a therapy group a therapy group, in *my* estimation, is the particular focus of attention: in therapy groups the focus of attention is almost exclusively upon the psyche group process, with only the most minimal attention to other matters.

When these foci are confused, or when there is an attempt to place a heavy emphasis on psyche group and socio group processes simultaneously, the strain on the group process is frequently such as to lead to the dissolution of the group. An example of this is worth noting: in a well known psychiatric retreat, an attempt was made to give the therapy groups the task of choosing representatives in a self-government scheme and to use the group for the discussion of some of these problems. This task became an impossible burden to the therapy groups, although the responsibilities in the usual sense were not onerous. It so confused the orientation of the groups that they set up all kinds of individual ambivalence. The social task could be used as a protective screen behind which to hide what, under other conditions, would be the usual psyche process. Likewise, those who used the group primarily for psyche group goals were resistant to participation on a socio group level. As will be seen, when the focus is on the psyche group process, the informal structure prevails and the maximum opportunity for projectivity and sensitivity at the emotive interpersonal level is provided. When the focus is on the socio group process the direction is in terms of a visualizable task.

THEORETICAL FRAMEWORK AS SOURCE OF DISTINCTIONS

There are no neat ways of classifying all groups in this schema. No attempt has been made to indicate that in many loosely knit, spontaneous groups there may be a psyche group emphasis at one time, and a socio group emphasis at another. A longitudinal dimension could be introduced which would show the primacy of the psyche group at the earlier ages as well as the later ages. Furthermore, in the life of every person, there are periods in which there are sharp differentiations between memberships which are primarily psyche group oriented and those which are socio group directed. The training group, where the objectives of learning are both content and process centered, may actually be an illustration of a group where socio and psyche group processes overlap.

If we can think of adult education groups as somewhat similar to leadership training groups, then, if I understand Knowles and Bradford correctly, what they are pleading for in their exposition of adult education is the incorporation of more psyche group process so that the goals and methods of such groups become more immediately relevant to the needs and aspirations of the learner.

Even if we cannot achieve precision in locating groups along the continuum, we can use the framework as one which helps us clarify the distinctions, remembering that a general conceptual framework serves to provide working hypotheses, rather than rigid categories. For, using the term socio and psyche groups as a classificatory reference may lead to what Whitehead has described as the fallacy of misplaced concreteness; or, at times the emphasis on one aspect rather than the other may seem to place a value connotation on one or the other. While in one type of activity the need for a greater psyche emphasis may be seen, just the reverse may be true in other activities.

It is not strange that much of the social group workers' activities have been within the youth-serving organizations. For here the transition from a more psyche process-centered group to a more task-oriented group is under way. There is nothing inherently precious about the psyche group process. The demands of citizenship and maturity require that within every individual these processes become sufficiently structured so that the person can become a team member and can assume social responsibility.

It is my opinion that a group cannot completely escape the danger of being either too rigidly intellectual or too loosely therapeutic. All groups have in common some therapeutic aspect, for the very social nature of man makes the group a potential source of his self-esteem and ego gratifications. If we cannot neatly divide the areas of the educator, the social group worker, and the group therapist, we can at least try to understand the generic processes common to all and keep in mind the appropriate emphasis each should have.

I should not want to equate all adult education with problem-solving, but also allow for the inclusion of consummatory experiences. Just as poetry is a prelude to science, the consummatory experiences of appreciation in literature and aesthetics may be the resources persons seek to draw on for later solutions. Or, they may exist as satisfactions in their own right.

Moreover, I should not want to see social group work as an activity for activity's sake, but, as Coyle implies, see it in relationship to personal development and social effectiveness. Much of the concern we naturally may have about overstepping boundaries can be alleviated when we define our own orientation. Thus, the problem of group observation, which Coyle mentions as one which merits special comment, is one which I see as related primarily to the purposes which such observation is to serve. A group observer can be very effective and not at all threatening if his function is directed to the group task and not the "why" of the members' behavior. In this sense the dichotomy of "deep" vs. "superficial" becomes rather meaningless, for an observation on group process which is clearly task oriented may perform for the group the needed penetration appropriate to the group's conception ot its own socio group process. If it becomes focused on the individual, quite remote from this task, then the observation is not deeper, but only irrelevant, and destructive because of its irrelevance.

IMPLICATIONS OF THEORETICAL FRAMEWORK

The problems of training workers in the different fields and of decisions concerning the appropriate skills naturally cannot be discussed in detail. There are, however, certain implications which can be drawn from the theoretical framework proposed. Certainly all leaders should understand the generic group process. It is hoped that this understanding will clarify their roles in a more comprehensive fashion than prescriptions about "hands off" and "hands on." A knowledge of the structure and purposes of groups can indicate to the worker the varying emphases he will make in relation to both the setting and the primacy of the socio or psyche group aspect.

Because the criteria of help to the patient are always essentially private and the function of the group in group psychotherapy is always directed toward the individual, the group therapist must have an understanding of individual dynamics and perhaps experience as an individual therapist. Likewise, the social group worker brings to his task a familiarity with programming activities which few group therapists need and in which they may have little aptitude. The adult educator is in the process of re-defining his role in relation to a more dynamic and, perhaps, accurate, concept of learning. If the problem-solving milieu is one in which learning takes place more readily, then it is essential that he understand group process and utilize his understanding within his organizational setting.

If we can agree that modern society suffers from fractionalization and formalization, then perhaps we can see that the interweaving of the socio and psyche group processes leads simultaneously to the fuller personal development of the individual as well as to a more creative approach to solving the social problems of our time. Then, too, we can emphasize the generic and overlapping character of these three fields. No one feels that such an emphasis should lead to an obliteration of all lines of differentiation. But such an emphasis should lead to an appreciation of each other's contribution and insight into many emerging interrelationships — all in the pursuit of objectives which have more in common than we have heretofore envisioned.

"The rising ascendancy of the purely functional group in American life," to quote Paul Sheats,[2] "and the declining importance of the primary group face-to-face relationship means that there are fewer and fewer opportunities for widely shared experience and self expression. If we agree with many social scientists that it is in the psyche groups that the individual's value patterns are formed and modified, then the trend which reduces the potency of such group influences means that we are in part at least undermining the fraternal and friendship base of democratic society and substituting a kind of social environment which is favorable to a growth of intergroup tension and conflict, authoritarian practices, and irresponsible citizen behavior. Hence, our efforts to improve the processes of group problem solving in the socio group, but utilizing insofar as we can the value and strengths of the psyche group, take on an even wider social significance."

[2] Western Training Laboratory for Group Development, Idyllwild, California, University of California Extension, UCLA, August 1952, "Materials." (Mimeographed.)

PART TWO · THE GROUP

Section D

GROUP PATTERNS

The three commonly accepted group patterns are authoritarian or aggregate, democratic or organic, and group-centered. Each pattern is based on a different view of the capabilities and motivation of the group members. In the authoritarian group the leaders are considered more capable than the members, whose motivation must be strengthened through extrinsic rewards and punishments. In the democratic group the capabilities of the members and leaders are considered to be similar and motivation intrinsic, arising from common concerns. In the group-centered group the members choose the topic or problem and the method of procedure and carry out the evaluation.

Three readings are provided, one for each group pattern. The authoritarian (aggregate) and democratic (organic) patterns are discussed by L. Thomas Hopkins under the titles, "The Authoritarian Group" and "The Democratic Group," from his book, The Emerging Self in School and Home. The third selection, by Thomas Gordon, "The Group-Centered Group," from Client-Centered Therapy, by Carl Rogers, describes the group-centered pattern.

6

The Authoritarian Group

L. Thomas Hopkins

. . . .

WHAT IS AN AGGREGATE GROUP?

The word group should be applied to people only when they develop the high quality of internal relationship which results from resolving their disturbances through cooperative interaction. Yet it is frequently used to describe interpersonal relations that are on a very low operating level. An adjective must be inserted before "group" to let the listener or reader know its position on a qualitative scale. The term "aggregate" is most frequently used to specify that the group is merely the mathematical sum of its parts — of the individuals who compose it. The word "authoritarian" indicates the dominant internal structure which causes the operating quality to be low. Some writers use the term "categorical" to describe this group. It means that the organization and probable action can be defined and classified in advance of the actual operation of the members. Others have given it the pathological name "heterogenous," meaning that its source of origin lies outside the organism. In sociocultural concepts this group originates from or is formed by some outside person to meet his needs and purposes and is structured by him to that end. Technically, it is not a group, for a group is based upon we-ness or unity or morale, characteristics which such an aggregate does not possess. It is described in practice as a class or an aggregate although the term group is most frequently used. The aggregate group is the psychological field supporting all forms of authoritarian human relations in all life activities in all cultures throughout the world.

The aggregate group has many functional characteristics, a few of which will be stated.

1. The source of origin lies outside the group.

2. The group has a status person designated by the outside source of origin to control it from within. The position is relatively permanent. The particular individual occupies it so long as he has the confidence of his superior,

which means so long as he manages the behavior of the group in the direction of and acceptable to his outside authority. Some writers refer to this individual as a status leader to distinguish him from a real leader who has a relationship of mutual interdependence with all members. Yet any individual with internal status from an outside source of authority has the difficult, if not impossible, task of becoming an emergent leader of the group. His best hope lies in becoming as benevolent in his internal relations as his outside authority will permit.

3. The group is managed around, through, or by the person who is the status leader. What he wants or demands is the focal operating center.

4. The group is organized to a greater or less degree, depending upon the ability and the purpose of the status control. Regardless of the degree or quality from his point of view, the group never has unity, for unity can never be put into a group from the outside. It is *found* by individuals from within. Many people mistake for unity the rigid organization, the good discipline, the regimentation, of an aggregate under external authority. Any interested person can disprove this belief by examining critically how a modern paternalistic family operates or by studying the rise and fall of authoritarian cultures. Learning how to exist in an aggregate organization does not prepare an individual to live in a unified group.

5. The intelligence of the aggregate is the intelligence of the status control. The authorities assume that he knows, and that the members are inadequate in knowledge and in the means of acquiring it. This is why he has to manage them. Yet his control limits their possibilities of ever developing their potential capacity, for their thinking must always be below his and in the direction which he determines.

6. The communication within the group is direct from the status control to each member. Each person reacts to the control but does not interact with it or with others in the group. The communication among the various members has such a low human quality that it can hardly be described as interaction.

7. Preplanning and developmental planning are all managed by external individuals operating through the status control. All major decisions are made for the members. They are allowed to use their judgment only in situations of relatively minor importance.

8. The membership-character of each individual is determined by how well he meets the externally designated or structured ends. This decision is made by the status control. He arrays them in mathematical sequence from highest to lowest, an arrangement in which no individual ever has real security and belongingness with the status control or with his fellows. Members develop various adaptive mechanisms through which one becomes a star while another is called an isolate.

9. The responsibility for the success of the enterprise to which the group is committed rests with the status control. He is held accountable by the external authority which sets the group in motion. He must manipulate it to do what his superiors want. A few failures cost him his position.

10. The internal evaluation of the success of each member is always made by the status control in terms of the qualitative demands placed upon him by the outside authorities for their purposes. The status leader himself is rated

by his superiors on their judgment of the success of his group by their standards. Thus he is not psychologically free to develop and use his intelligence,
a field condition which he willingly accepts and transmits to the members of
his group. Each member finds the kinds and degrees of followership which he
and the leader can tolerate so that neither will be removed from the group by
the superior powers.

. . . .

7

The Democratic Group

L. Thomas Hopkins

. . . .

What Is an Organic Group?

An organic group is the name applied to a number of individuals working
together by a process of meaningful interaction which releases in them a
latent emergent quality of wholeness previously unknown to any individual.
It is found exclusively among human beings, since they alone are capable
of developing the thinking necessary to achieve such a quality. Some persons
use the word "superorganic" to describe this phenomenon, since it clearly
transcends mere organic structure or sensory experience. All of them recognize that this quality emerges when interaction is such as to release the
potential capacities of people. Since this emergent quality is the growth
process which every organism is born with and uses to keep itself intact, I
shall use the term "organic group" to apply to people working under such
conditions.

The concept of the organic group is of relatively recent origin. It was
unknown to peoples in ancient times, when they used the aggregate as the
pattern of organization of their various social institutions. It is a product of
the growing researches in the life sciences, ranging from basic biology to the
more recent studies in group dynamics. It is called organic since individual
members function in a similar dynamic relation to each other and to the
whole as do the various organs of the body to each other and to the whole.
It is called cooperative and interactive since cooperative interaction is the

From *The Emerging Self in School and Home* by L. Thomas Hopkins. Copyright
1954 by Hester R. Hopkins. Reprinted by permission of Harper & Row, Publishers,
Incorporated. Pp. 195–200.

basic process by which the body maintains its unitary wholeness under the various conditions of its environment, internal and external. Granted that there are meanings, values, norms which hold people together and which are above and beyond any wisdom of the body. Yet the operating self, which is the person, is a unity of organic wisdom with superorganic meanings derived through thoughtful criticism and enrichment of sensory experience. The normal way to develop a meaningful self is to extend upward into the psychological area the basic process of learning already established by inheritance in the organic area. In this dynamic interaction within an organism there are some very clear operating principles which offer a clue to cooperative relations within and among groups.

1. The organism as a whole determines the quantity, quality, and direction of its energy output. The quantity is associated with the strength of the need or the depth to which the upset affects the already constituted self. The quality is in the process of meeting the need or the way in which need-fulfillment is obtained. The direction is toward need behaviors which maintain, preserve, and improve the operating wholeness. The direction is paramount since operating wholeness is the very essence of life itself. And it is remarkable how the organism struggles to maintain such wholeness under the most devastating environmental conditions.

2. The organism as a whole regulates the energy output or work of the various parts or organs. All energy is expended through the various parts and all bodily functions are carried on by them. The whole stimulates or retards such action. It concentrates forces at a given point, as in the case of the white corpuscles going into action against a localized infection. It fights against all conditions within or without that tend to destroy its unity. But the organism as a whole is not something added to the parts to give them unity. It is not the sum of its parts plus this regulating entity. The organism as a whole is the cooperative interaction among the various parts whereby each participates in every directional judgment and action. When one part tries to dominate another the process is disoperative and a divided self or a disorganization of inward coherence results. The behavior associated with a disoperative process is described by the observer as neurotic or psychotic. Thus the integrating whole is the normal process of interaction among the various parts, each working in relation to their shared directional decisions.

3. Each organ of the body has a specialized function to perform for the good of the whole. This gives it a permanent but variable membership-character in promoting the organic quality and a continuous status with the whole and the parts. This specialized ability is recognized and respected by all organs. No one tries to usurp the function of any other. And the organism as a whole recognizes that it cannot maintain itself without the specialized services of the parts. It does not place one function on a higher level than another or favor one organ over another. When some part is temporarily unable to perform its services, thereby threatening the integrity of the whole, other organs either stimulate the sluggish one to a normal performance or devise means of taking care of its duties. Such wisdom of the body is now an accepted fact.

4. The unity and direction of the organism are maintained by the highest

form of the cooperative interactive process known to man. The sensitivity of each organ to the performance of all others is maintained at all times through main avenues of communication, which are the blood stream and the nervous system. Some organs have their own private messengers called hormones, which they secrete into the blood if danger is apparent and more energy is necessary. Leadership moves from one to another, depending upon where the need of the whole is centered at the moment. While every organism develops tendencies to action as a means of dealing with internal and external forces, these tendencies do not deny the principle of organic cooperation. At times they make cooperation difficult, as in the case of neurotic persons, but the cooperative process still works to overcome the denial conditions.

5. Each organ self-selects those elements which are best for it as an organ, as in foods to rebuild its tissues and maintain them in healthy working condition. The organism as a whole self-selects those learnings which in its judgment are best for its developing unity. Such selection takes place on the autonomic and conscious level.

6. There is continuous differentiation of new adjustments both in structure and in behavior, except when serious damage prevents such differentiation. The damaged heart develops new blood channels. When varicose veins are blocked, the leg increases the size of other veins to carry the blood supply. The healthy kidney expands to carry on the functions of the diseased one which was removed. The lungs develop seals to enclose and arrest the spread of tuberculosis germs which attempt to destroy them. In the same way individuals develop behaviors to compensate for difficulties of adjustment or select learnings which promote more mature relationships. Variation is in the degree to which they are capable of utilizing it. But these principles of self-selection and differentiation do not deny the process of cooperation. Neither do they reject the regulation and direction of the organism by the whole. For the whole does not set itself up as a dominating entity, forcing the parts to live within its status demands. From the biological evidence available, cooperative action in organic groups is the normal basis of life, while cultural authoritarianism in aggregate groups is cancerous tissue arrested in embryonic differentiation.

The organic group has many functional characteristics. A few of the most important ones will be enumerated.

1. It is autogenous in origin, the members coming together to resolve common needs.

2. Leadership emerges from within and continues so long as it functions to achieve group purposes through cooperative action.

3. Unity and functional organization are developed internally around the group's own purposes in relation to its own need.

4. All of the planning and all of the major and minor decisions are made by the group itself.

5. Large directional policy decisions which regulate the work of individuals or subgroups are made by the group as a whole.

6. Decisions as to policy or action are made by consensus, not by majority rule. Consensus means that every member recognizes and assents to the

mutual fitness of the judgment or action to achieve the purposes which are commonly accepted.

7. The work is carried on by individuals and small groups. The responsibility for such work is delegated by the group as a whole. It should be both genuine and challenging to everyone concerned. The whole group holds subgroups accountable for the adequate performance of their duties. Individual initiative and creativeness in carrying on such activities are encouraged at all times.

8. The group as a whole sets the esprit de corps or climate of opinion or psychological atmosphere in which each individual or subgroup carries on its work. This is a creative emergent from the cooperative interaction among the members.

9. The group as a whole helps each individual member clarify his own concept of need, refine his own meanings, improve the logic of his own experience. It encourages his creative contributions, helps him to evaluate his own self-selections, shows him how to appraise his own value judgments.

10. Responsibility for the success of the total group enterprise is assumed by everyone, each contributing in his own best way through free and open interaction among members which is maintained at all times.

11. Cooperative and continuous evaluation by the group of its own decisions and actions is made in the light of the developing need-experience.

. . . .

8

The Group-Centered Group

Thomas Gordon

. . . .

SOME PROPOSITIONS REGARDING THE ADJUSTIVE CAPACITY OF GROUPS

At this stage of our thinking it would be presumptuous to claim a well-formulated system of theory about groups. Nevertheless, out of our experiences we can begin to construct a tentative outline for a theory that will be

From Thomas Gordon, "Group-Centered Leadership and Administration," in Carl R. Rogers, *Client-Centered Therapy* (Boston: Houghton Mifflin Company, 1951), pp. 323–329. Reprinted with the permission of the publisher.

consistent with these experiences. Admittedly, this will be a sketchy outline. At present it exists as a mere skeleton, devoid of flesh at many points. Its inclusion here is based upon the hope that it will make more clear our subsequent formulation of the group-centered approach to leadership and administration.

This theoretical basis for thinking about groups will be presented as a series of propositions. Many of these are of the nature of assumptions, and are stated in a form that would make it difficult for them to be tested experimentally. It would be correct to say that these propositions simply represent one of several possible frames of reference for thinking about groups.

1. A group is defined as two or more persons who have a psychological relationship to each other. That is, the members exist as a group in the psychological field of each other, and they are in some kind of dynamic relationship to each other.

Here we are attempting to set up certain criteria that can be applied to differentiate a group from other collections of individuals. Borrowing from the definition of Krech and Crutchfield,[1] a group is made up of persons whose behavior has direct influence upon the behavior of the other members.

2. Groups demonstrate during some specific time period some degree of instability or disequilibrium as a result of forces within the group. The group, then, is a dynamic system of forces. Changes in any part of the group produce changes in the group as a whole.

This proposition re-emphasizes the notion that the behavior of members of a group affects the behavior of other members. But it also gives to groups the qualities of a system of inner dynamic forces that are in a state of continuous change and reorganization. Take, for example, an industrial organization whose personnel manager decided to introduce a new system of evaluating employees. According to Proposition 2, such action on the part of the personnel manager will produce changes in other parts of the organization. Supervisors may resent the added paper work made necessary by the new procedures; certain employees may perceive the new procedures as a means of weeding out the less capable workers; the union steward sees this action as a breach of the merit-rating system agreed on by the union and management; a line supervisor resents the authority of the personnel department over the "line." A seemingly isolated act, then, actually upsets the equilibrium of the entire plant structure.

3. Group behavior which serves to reduce the disequilibrium produced by changes in the inner forces of the group may be described as adjustive behavior. The degree to which the group's behavior is adjustive will be a function of the appropriateness of the methods employed by the group as they are related to the nature of the internal imbalance.

This proposition states in a more technical way a fact which we all recognize. That is, how successfully a group adjusts to an internal disruptive force depends upon its employing direct and appropriate methods of attack on the problem. This principle has its counterpart in individual behavior. A person

[1] David Krech and R. S. Crutchfield, *Theory and Problems of Social Psychology* (New York: McGraw-Hill Book Co., Inc., 1948).

finds himself in a conflict-producing situation which upsets his own equilibrium. He becomes tense and uncomfortable. His turning to alcohol may produce a temporary relief from the tension, but it is far from being an adjustment appropriate to the state of conflict which exists in the total organism. Until the person becomes aware of the nature of the conflict, his behavior is not likely to be adjustive. In the same way, groups frequently exhibit nonadjustive or partially adjustive behavior, examples of which are so numerous as to defy classification. Scapegoating, projecting, inhibiting expression of feelings, blaming the leaders, attacking other groups, withdrawing, regressing to a strong dependence relationship to the leader — these are some of the more obvious partial solutions employed by groups.

4. A group's adjustive behavior will be most appropriate when the group utilizes the maximum resources of its total membership. This means maximum participation of all group members, each making his most effective contribution.

This proposition is a way of saying that the best decisions or the most appropriate actions of a group will be those based upon the maximum amount of data or resources of its members. Thus the most effective group will be the one in which there is participation of all group members, each member making his most creative contribution. This idea has been expressed in the report of the President's Committee on Civil Rights:

> Democracy assumes that the majority is more likely as a general rule to make decisions which are wise and desirable from the point of view of the interests of the whole society than is any minority. Every time a qualified person is denied a voice in public affairs, one of the components of a potential majority is lost, and the formation of a social public policy is endangered. . . .
>
> How can the concept of the marketplace of thought, in which truth ultimately prevails, retain its validity if the thought of certain individuals is denied the right of circulation?[2]

Although these statements are taken from the context of "civil rights" for citizens of our nation, they reflect the essence of the proposition above — namely, that what is best for a group is that which has been formulated out of the contributions of all of the group's members.

If this proposition is valid, it helps to clarify the value of "participation." The concept of group-member participation can be found in almost every article dealing with the problems of group leadership and administration. It has been stressed as a principle of industrial supervision, community action, and labor-management relations. In psychology this concept has earned the label "ego-involvement." Too frequently, however, one gets the impression from some of this literature that participation and ego-involvement on the part of group-members are things to be achieved so that the group-members will more readily accept the plans, goals, or decisions *already formulated by the leaders*. Obtaining participation thus becomes a *leader technique* for

---

[2] The President's Committee on Civil Rights, *To Secure These Rights* (New York: Simon and Schuster, 1947), pp. 8–9.

satisfying the members' natural desires for achievement, status, and recognition. True, participant groups do seem to have better morale than leader-centered or authoritarian groups. Nevertheless, not always is participation also seen as contributing to the total efficiency of the group. Not always is there a genuine belief on the part of leaders that participation pays off in terms of better decisions, more production, economic gains, more appropriate group adjustment.

This narrow conception of participation as a method of obtaining willing compliance has been noted in the attitudes of some industrial executives, as pointed out by French, Kornhauser, and Marrow. They define three main patterns of control in management, one of which is characterized by efforts to obtain through "participation" and "cooperation" the workers' compliance, loyalty, good will, and welfare. These writers emphasize that such dealings are a device employed by management.

> Under these circumstances, "democratic cooperation" is at best a euphe-
> mism, and at worst a deceptive make-believe process. Sometimes manage-
> ment is deliberately using the attractive symbols of democracy, participation,
> man-to-man discussion, group decision, etc., to create the desired atmosphere
> within which it can smoothly manipulate the attitudes of its employees,
> retain their loyalty, and still run the business "as it should be run," without
> irritating interferences from below.[3]

I am reminded of the remark of a training-group leader to the effect that his greatest concern was how to reconcile his intellectual convictions that the group must decide its own goals and methods of reaching those goals with his equally strong ideas of what those goals and methods *should* be. This same dilemma is seen in individuals in the initial stages of learning client-centered psychotherapy as they come to examine whether their own basic attitudes about people are consistent with the "technique" they are learning. A minister in one of the courses in psychotherapy once asked, "How can I as a minister use this approach in my counseling and yet get the client to end up with the conviction that it was his faith in the Divine which was responsible for his recovery?"

5. A group has within itself the adjustive capacities necessary to acquire a greater degree of internal harmony and productivity and to achieve a more effective adjustment to its environment. Provided certain conditions are met, the group will move in the direction of greater utilization of these capacities.

This is a re-statement of the basic client-centered hypothesis as applied to a group rather than to an individual. Like that hypothesis about the individual, it stresses the positive growth forces which, if released, result in greater internal harmony and productive efficiency and more effective adjustment to the environment. It is an hypothesis that emphasizes the inner capacity of a group. It states that every group *has* this capacity, but implies that it is a matter of process or development for a group to approach the *realization* of that capacity. In other words, a group may not be able to solve

[3] J. R. P. French, Jr.; A. Kornhauser; and A. Marrow (eds.), "Conflict and Cooperation in Industry," *Journal of Social Issues*, II (1946), pp. 44–45.

immediately an existing problem, yet it can and will develop in a direction which will lead to the best solution of that problem provided certain essential conditions are met.

It will be apparent that, although expressed in the form of a proposition, this idea is more in the nature of an hypothesis which the group-centered leader chooses to hold in his relations with members of a group. He could choose to hold an entirely different belief about groups — one that placed less stress upon the inner capacities of the group and more stress upon its inherent weaknesses and tendencies toward submission to outside forces. Such an hypothesis seems to be preferred by many writers, as is indicated in the following quotation from the writings of Freud:

> A group is extraordinarily credulous and open to influence, it has no critical faculty, and the improbable does not exist for it. . . . Inclined as it itself is to all extremes, a group can only be excited by an excessive stimulus. Anyone who wishes to produce an effect upon it needs no logical adjustment in his arguments; he must paint in the most forcible colors, he must exaggerate, and he must repeat the same thing again and again. . . . It respects force and can only be slightly influenced by kindness, which it regards merely as a form of weakness. . . . It wants to be ruled and oppressed, and to fear its masters. . . . And, finally, groups have never thirsted after truth. They demand illusions, and cannot do without them. They constantly give what is unreal precedence over what is real; they are almost as strongly influenced by what is untrue as by what is true. They have an evident tendency not to distinguish between the two. . . . A group is an obedient herd, which could never live without a master. It has such a thirst for obedience that it submits instinctively to anyone who appoints himself as its master.[4]

It is true, perhaps, that history provides many examples of groups in which such characteristics have predominated, and this fact makes it understandable why some would choose to adopt this kind of hypothesis about groups. It is possible, however, to find in history examples of groups which have demonstrated quite different characteristics — those which require us to have a great deal more respect for the inherent potentialities of the group for self-direction, self-protection, and appropriate adjustments. It is just such a respect that seems a part of the attitudes of those who have chosen to operate with groups in terms of the hypothesis that is contained in Proposition 5. While recognizing that groups have both the tendencies described by Freud and also more positive tendencies, some leaders choose to hypothesize that the latter are the stronger.

This proposition is explicit in its emphasis upon "movement," growth, or development of the group. This is to say that the group's achievement of a state in which it is able to utilize its maximum potential is the result of a certain process of development. Groups usually do not have this characteristic. Quite the contrary, most groups operate far from this ideal. Apparently few groups in our culture are ever provided with the conditions whereby they might move toward maximum utilization of their potential. It is more

[4] Sigmund Freud, *Group Psychology and the Analysis of the Ego* (London: Hogarth Press, and New York: Liveright Publishing Corporation, 1948), pp. 15–21.

common for a group to rely upon the contributions of only a part of its membership while the rest of the group dissipates its energies in *reacting against* the control and authority of the more active members. It is here that group behavior can be deceiving. Often all members of a group are *active*, but upon closer examination it is usually found to be what McGregor[5] has called *reactive* behavior. As Allport has pointed out, "a person ceases to be reactive and contrary in respect to a desirable course of conduct only when he himself has had a hand in declaring that course of conduct to be desirable."[6] Few groups ever reach the state where its members are given this opportunity.

How do groups reach such a state? How do groups approach the maximum utilization of their potential? What kind of process is necessary for groups to move in this direction? These are the crucial questions, yet we have no definitive answers for any of them. Our own experience would lead us to believe that certain conditions facilitate this process. . . .

· · · ·

[5] Douglas McGregor, "Conditions of Effective Leadership in the Industrial Organization," in T. M. Newcomb and E. L. Hartley, *Readings in Social Psychology* (New York: Henry Holt & Co., Inc., 1947), pp. 427–435. [Reprinted from the *Journal of Consulting Psychology*, VIII (1944), 55–63.]

[6] G. W. Allport, "The Psychology of Participation," *Psychological Review*, LIII (1945), 117–132. [Permission to quote given by the *Psychological Review* and the American Psychological Association.]

Section E

VALUES OF THE GROUP

For groups to attain their maximum usefulness, not only in planning and problem-solving but also in making possible the development of increasing inner psychological and spiritual health, there must be a balance between the attention given to needs and aims within the individual and those within the group.

Although certain group patterns may be more conducive than others to the working out of these objectives, much will depend on the quality of the leadership and the creative potentialities of the members.

It is perhaps unnecessary to extend the caution that groups are not a panacea. They can foster regression as well as creative development.

The readings focus on the particular values of the group. Leland P. Bradford, in his article "Developing Potentialities Through Class Groups," discusses learning as a "social affair" and contrasts learning in the class "which has not accepted the common task of group learning" with one which has "come to accept the common task of enhancing individual learning." Bernice Baxter and Rosalind Cassidy in the selection from their book, Group Experience, the Democratic Way, have focused upon the concept that "the felt appreciative attitude of others toward self is essential to personal security and well-being." They diagnose weaknesses and suggest means whereby groups may secure greater values for the individual members, and conclude that "The ways of democracy must be experienced if they are to be lived."

9

Developing Potentialities Through Class Groups

Leland P. Bradford

The class as a group is only beginning to be explored adequately in American education. Group forces, latent or active in every classroom situation and potentially highly supportive of individual learning, have neither been released generally nor, when active, gone the teachers' way. As a result needless struggle takes place between teacher and students as to who shall learn and what; desirable concomitant learning goals are not realized; and students build barriers to present and future learning and frequently end up with lasting anxieties and undesirable attitudes toward education.

The many educational values which may result from developing the class as a group certainly have not been thoroughly understood, nor have teachers been trained to build and maintain effective learning groups. Let us here examine a few of these values, and look at specific group forces affecting learning and their application for the functions of the teacher.

INDIVIDUAL LEARNING THE COMMON GOAL

Class group acceptance of the common task of encouraging learning for all members produces a far different learning situation and widely different learning results from those obtained when individual learning is the responsibility of each student, with appropriate encouragement from the teacher. Obviously the individual must, in any case, decide how far he will enter into any learning situation. However, the class group which accepts the common task of individual learning fosters in the student the wish to learn and aids him in the process, rather than being relatively indifferent to the individual's progress, or tacitly encouraging of mediocre performance.

Let us contrast two situations. In the class which has not accepted the common task of group learning the following factors may be present. Each student tends to be in a competitive situation — winner or loser in the learning game. Some students suffer anxiety in competition and, fearing failure and rejection, become apathetic and are inclined to withdraw.

Some students develop a fairly high commitment to learning, but others

From Leland P. Bradford, "Developing Potentialities Through Class Groups," *Teachers College Record*, LXI (May, 1960), 443–450. Reprinted with the permission of publisher and author.

seek to escape from as much learning as possible. Basically, parts of the class are at war with other parts, and teacher energy and group time are spent in keeping the dissonant parts in some degree of harmony. These group forces present may serve to protect the less committed students and to punish the "eager beavers." Little help in learning is given from student to student. The assumption seems to be that learning is an individual affair somewhat accidentally taking place in a group situation.

Yet people generally do not learn totally alone any more than they live alone. Learning is a social affair, and many learnings can come only from social interaction. Because individuals vary in degree of anxiety about the difficulty and consequences of engaging in learning, these differential anxieties and resistances easily can add up to a group climate of partial resistance to the teacher. The class is pitted against the teacher rather than joining in a common venture. Group forces, inevitably present, do not go the teacher's way.

In the class group which has come to accept the common task of enhancing individual learning, many different forces operate. Difficulties in learning for any individual become the concern of others. Emotional support is supplied by group to student, thereby giving acceptance and membership to the student receiving help. Feedback about performance and corrective information can be given by student to student as well as by teacher to student, when the class group climate is less competitive and individually rejective and punishing and when, consequently, individual defensiveness is reduced. Impacts for learning can also come from the class group itself.

In situations where there is common acceptance of the task of learning, individual students are freer to discover and release feelings of concern about other students. As these feelings are properly channeled into responsible giving of help, students develop ways of healthy living, as well as gain in the subject-matter knowledge of the class.

If properly combined with understanding of individual problems, potentials, and difficulties (to prevent conformity pressures for impossible achievement for some students), forces of group loyalty and pride can give motivational and supportive encouragement to learning.

When a class really accepts the common task of individual learning for all members it is much easier to develop a willingness to work on the joint task of improving the climate and conditions of learning. Teacher and students have now a point of mutual concern: What is there about our class group that is keeping some of us, or many of us, from learning more, and what can we do to improve the situation?

Given the acceptance of this common task, the teacher and other class members can work together in the task of building and maintaining in good working order a group geared to the purposes of learning. Just as research in other fields indicates that well-functioning groups must be carefully developed and maintained if high productivity is to be secured and continued, so also, when the production goal is individual learning, can effective class groups improve learning. Forces resulting from group cohesion, standard setting, appropriate ways of recognizing and dealing with emotional factors, goal setting, and membership acceptance, for example, can be just as influential in increasing individual member learning as in improving industrial production.

GROUP MENTAL HEALTH AND CLIMATE

Much time and attention are devoted to the mental health of individual students. Counselors, clinical psychologists, and psychiatrists are specialized personnel concerned with detecting mental and emotional ill-health and promoting good health. Teachers and administrators have long been alerted to individual emotional problems and some of their causes. Yet class groups vary about as widely as do individuals on the dimension of good and poor mental health. Every student knows that classes differ greatly. Some are supportive and building; some are traumatic and destructive; some induce deadly apathy.

The mental health of a class group is as important to the learning process as the mental health of individual students. Group and individual mental health are interactive. The climate — symptomatic measure of group health — affects the emotional health and development of the individual students as well as his degree of learning.

Students who fear exposure and failure may feel isolated or rejected; may have anxieties about personal ability. If they have been traumatized by previous learning situations with too much competitive stress, they will have difficulty in learning *no matter what the subject may be*. Stress; anxiety; feelings of rejection, failure, and lack of belongingness are strongly contributing factors to the state of mental health of the individual.

Students who are anxious and fearful about self-exposure and who have low personal assessments of their own abilities tend to withdraw from the learning situation. Whether or not these assessments are correct, a class with poor group climate will tend to accept and reinforce them. If the atmosphere of the classroom either does nothing to reduce these anxieties or even acts to increase them, learning of the particular subject matter is very likely to be greatly reduced, whereas anxiety over future learning situations may be increased.

The classroom climate has an impact not only on the overwhelmed student but also on the one who remains unchallenged. Effective learning carries potential stress. Learning typically requires acknowledgment of inadequacy and ignorance by the student to himself alone, or to the teacher, or to other class members. Exposure is fraught with potential threat to one's self-image, the danger of loss of status and importance in others' eyes, and the fear of rejection by others. Learning means venturing into the unknown. Change requires disturbance between the individual's internal world and his relations to his external world. Change means unpredictability for a while, and it increases the potentialities of failure.

The essence of good teaching is not to protect the student from exposure of inadequacies, learning, and change but to create supportive conditions enabling the individual to undergo the process of learning, to handle his anxieties and concerns, to experiment with new ways of thinking and behaving. The important point is that *the teacher alone cannot supply all of the support necessary for all students,* particularly when the classroom climate itself creates more stress for the individual.

Let us take two typical classroom situations. In the first, competition for rewards, for grade promotion, for approval, is fairly heavy. Too little concern for individual feelings is shown by the teacher. Individual anxieties in many students increase. No effort is made to develop a class group.

Curiously, group forces do develop which work against subject-matter learning. Essentially a student mutual protective association builds. It pits the class against the teacher, makes learning a forced and resisted goal, and separates class approval from individual learning. Out of the anxieties and fears of many students a group norm grows which, for all intents and purposes, implies that failure in the teacher's eyes does not bring loss of esteem and status with one's classmates. A second norm tends to put pressure on bright students to work less hard. If the bright student persists he may find rejection. Another norm stresses resistance to the teacher: "Let the teacher teach us if she can."

The second situation might find the teacher giving early and continued emphasis to developing a class group in which norms facilitate learning and in which group climate reduces individual anxiety by building group and peer support for the individual. Such a class group, in addition to facilitating subject-matter learning, can grant the reward of acceptance, belonging, and membership.

Children denied acceptance in home or neighborhood, or forced to secure it at the terrible price of gang conformity, could be helped to gain healthy and supportive membership in a class group. *The important point is that the teacher cannot really confer group membership. She can confer only class membership.* However, she can do much to create an atmosphere and provide leadership and encouragement to build a group in which all students can gain a type of acceptance meeting many personal needs as well as removing blocks to learning. In this way social–emotional and intellectual conditions for learning can be more evenly developed and more adequately integrated and good group mental health may be insured.

Research in group behavior is relatively recent. The upsurge of such research during the past two decades is only beginning to be felt in educational practice and in teacher training. Application of findings about group interaction has unfortunately been more rapid in other social fields.

Why have group forces not been widely known or utilized for educational purposes? The answer is that in many cases they have been. Hundreds of successful teachers in classrooms in various parts of the country have learned through experience to work with group forces and have invented teaching procedures which created good group climates for learning purposes. They have learned the importance of appropriate social–emotional conditions for effective learning, and the importance of group participation and membership in producing such conditions. Teachers recognize, on one level, the existence of a group. They speak of deriving more pleasure from working with one class than with another, of the superiority of "this year's class."

TEACHER–STUDENT RELATIONSHIPS

Again, the great emphasis upon child understanding and teacher–student relationships during the past three or four decades, highly significant and important as this emphasis has been in American education, may have served to distract attention from the classroom as a group. To the extent that this is so there has been a lack of balance in seeing the total child, and an inadequate understanding of the basic functions of the teacher.

The student needs to be understood in the context of the classroom group as well as of family, neighborhood, playground, and other cultural forces. The role and place of the student in the classroom; the extent to which he has secured membership and the type of membership; the degree of acceptance or rejection by peers; the types of peer pressure upon him and their consequences for him — all are important forces affecting his behavior and approach to learning. Learner-centered approaches inevitably must also be group-centered. Only when the teacher's point of view is entirely subject-matter-centered is she able to remain oblivious to the group — to the detriment of student learning.

Concentration only on teacher–student relationships creates almost impossible problems of relationship and manipulation for the teacher. Endeavoring to give support to Johnny may appear to Mary as rejection of her. The problem for the teacher of meeting the frequently conflicting needs of many children, and of establishing varying relational patterns is a difficult one. Relationships are not only between student and teacher but also between student and student. These interrelationships are basic group forces and should be developed and maintained by the group as a whole. The teaching–learning process is basically transactional,[1] involving the interrelations of class members.

Emphasis upon the teacher–student relationship may set the teacher further apart from the class group and so foster the dependency of certain students on the teacher. Building and maintaining a relationship should be the joint responsibility of those in the relationship. When the relationship is between superior and subordinate (teacher–student), it is more difficult for the subordinate to take an active part in developing it. His behavior is generally reactive. More effective learning will take place as the student becomes a more active partner in the establishment and continuance of a learning relationship. The classroom group, where relationships can be developed and maintained among peers, serves to involve students more actively and responsibly in their own learning.

Attention to the teacher–student relationship exclusively may inadvertently cause the teacher to block the emergence of group forces. Taking responsibility for maintenance of a series of relationships, she clutches to herself too many leadership and group maintenance functions. Not knowing how to become an effective group member, she prevents membership for others by exercising too much control over the class.

[1] Leland P. Bradford, "The Teaching–Learning Transaction," *Adult Education*, VIII (Spring, 1958), p. 3.

Fundamentally, the teacher should join with students in developing a group with an effective learning climate, and should share with them the responsibility for maintaining a good group.

Effective teacher–student relations need to be balanced with effective teacher–group relations. Put another way, effective teacher–student relationships should be as much the concern and responsibility of the class group as should be effective student–student relationships.

SOCIAL, EMOTIONAL, AND VALUE LEARNINGS

Desirable social and emotional learnings are obviously important for healthy and effective living. In any classroom situation, no matter what the subject matter, they can be learned but seldom are. Such additional social and emotional learnings need not be separated from the subject-matter learning, but rather can support and increase it.

These social and emotional areas of learning, furthermore, can be learned best in group situations. Teacher emphasis upon building and maintaining a class group will make possible these additional learnings. A brief glance should indicate the importance of such learnings and the extent to which they serve to increase other learning.

Effective Social Membership. In an increasingly socially complex, interdependent world the ability to be an effective member of a variety of social groups is of basic importance. People do not adequately make and implement social decisions alone.

The effective member can be no conforming organization-man, subservient to a higher authority. Today's dynamic and changing society means fewer guideposts from past experience to steer future courses. The ability to live with ambiguity and change, to work interdependently, to be socially inventive, to meet new social requirements are all requirements for effective social membership. Such a member must both give and receive influence.

Today the question of personal identity has taken on terrifying significance for many people. Who am I? cannot be answered alone. As individuals become members of healthy groups, help steer and improve a group, and receive acceptance and influence for personal improvement from a group, they have helped themselves to resolve the question of personal identity, as well as grown in ability to work more effectively with others.

Much has been said and written about group pressures toward conformity, and the dire consequences of reducing individuality and integrity. Unfortunately, not so much has been written about group pressures toward meeting a standard of individual variation and personal integrity.

Research and experience indicate that mature, healthy groups stress the increase of individual differences and encouragement of individual growth. They respect and accept the individual. He counts in effective group operation, because only as the member grows in ability to diagnose and help solve group problems can the group grow and become more productive.

In less healthy groups, little concern is felt for group climate, and standards usually develop which reduce individual freedom and inhibit individual growth.

The choice is clear. If group membership is attained only in the autocratic home, the gang, or the neighborhood, fear, submergence of individuality, aggressiveness, and conforming behavior are likely to develop. If, instead, group membership is enjoyed under carefully guided conditions, opposite behavior characteristics are a natural outgrowth.

Unfortunately, the assumption too frequently has been made that such teachings belong to the youth- and group-work agencies and not to the schools, whose task is teaching necessary information. This assumption implies a dichotomy between school and out-of-school learning. The school has a responsibility for the total growth of the whole child, if only because learnings cannot be completely compartmentalized if healthy growth is to take place. In addition, effective membership ability on the part of students means that the class group can produce more individual learning. There is no better place than the classroom to learn how to become an effective member, and thus secure the emotional gains of acceptance, belongingness, opportunity for creative production. There, growth in membership ability immediately plows back into increased subject-matter learning.

Effective Social Leadership. Significant changes in concepts of leadership have taken place during the past two decades as research has been increasingly directed to the problem. These changes have led away from the concept of the driving, aggressive person — the leader — to one whose efforts were directed toward releasing others to be creative and productive.

Leadership is the other side of the membership coin. Effective leadership encourages members to be increasingly involved and participative in group affairs, and increasingly responsible for group effectiveness, whether in terms of task performance or of ability to develop and maintain productive relationships within the group.

The class, with its continuing problems of group maintenance and group tasks, provides opportunity from time to time for students to experience, with careful guidance, leadership activity which involves, assists, and releases others. This can be contrasted with leadership experience in gang and neighborhood, in which ability to exert power and control over others is the dominant learning and the interests of others are secondary.

Creative Social Organization. In days of rapid social change, when new organizational patterns and new social inventions are emerging, people need to learn not merely about present social organization and their place in it but, more importantly, about the process of social and organizational development, the need for social invention, and the skills of bringing about change.

Each class situation provides an ideal laboratory situation in social creativity. A group is to be formed, built, developed, and maintained. If this process of group formation is a conscious one (as it should be); if the students are involved in the process of formation; and if they are helped from time to time to look at the process of development through which they have passed, they will have gone through a unique experience in social creation during each year of their educational career. Two results should accrue. In each succeeding experience they will be more adept at creating an effective learning group with resultant increased individual learning. They should, at the end of their formal educational career be far more competent members of families, organizations, communities, and the nation.

Ability to Help Others. Caring behavior needs encouragement. The ability to accept others, to care for them, and responsibly and effectively to give help, particularly on a peer level, enriches the caring individual, builds warmer and more effective human relationships, and makes it easier to receive help, in turn, without developing dependency.

Too many teaching situations create indifference to the problems of other students, with consequent feelings of rejection and failure. Competitive forces block off concern for others.

The classroom situation provides a particularly effective opportunity to encourage and develop the desire to help others. All in the class are engaged in the difficult, threatening, and often painful task of learning. Each, in varying degrees and in differing ways, can be helped. The most effective help may be companionship, acceptance, emotional support. This may lead to other kinds of help as the group improves in ability to diagnose and remove barriers to learning in the class climate, procedures, and behavior.

Such help is best given by the group to its members. Help and support given only by the teacher do not provide opportunity for caring behavior to be learned.

Emotional and Intellectual Learning. So that in his study of algebra the student will not acquire a dislike for all mathematics, or in his study of French an aversion to languages, attention should be given to the integration of emotional and intellectual learning. There has been an unfortunate effort to separate thinking and feeling; to dichotomize the intellectual and the emotional. Learning should lead toward change in the being and behaving of the individual, and this obviously includes thinking, feeling, doing.

Emotion may inhibit or encourage learning. Diagnosis of learning difficulties should include examination of emotional as well as intellectual causes. Intellectual and emotional learning need to proceed together. The individual who grows intellectually but remains immature emotionally may be as ill-equipped for the problems of living as the person whose intellectual growth is slowed.

Emotional learning deals with the ways in which the individual treats forces impinging on him and relates to others. If the class becomes a group in which concern is present for the growth of each member, feelings of rejection can be eliminated, feelings of inadequacy tempered, and more effective ways of seeing oneself and of relating to others developed.

Values. Acceptance of others, caring for others, concern for the rights of others, the discussion of common problems, the development of shared goals, and participation in joint problem-solving are only a few of the democratic values needing to be taught and learned.

Values such as these are most easily learned through the shared experiences of the class group, and are best learned not from imposition by the teacher but experimentally from the trials and tribulations of the class group as the values are diagnosed openly by all. Traditionally, schools have taught *about* values, but have not made the learning of values possible.

These are some among the many desirable learnings which can accrue from any class group, regardless of subject matter, if the group is systematically built and if it takes responsibility for uncovering and solving its learning difficulties. These learnings are not in opposition to subject-matter learning or entirely in addition to them. Rather, they are integrated with, and make possible, more effective learning of other subjects, as well as the development of the many-sided potentialities of every member.

10

Group Experience: The Democratic Way

Bernice Baxter and Rosalind Cassidy

. . . .

Democracy's concern is with the individual. Unless through co-operative action the individual has opportunity to serve others, he is deprived of experiences which stimulate him to fuller and more magnanimous living. By working with others the individual satisfies his basic needs for status and approval. He is stimulated by others and becomes enriched in his own living while serving others of his own society. The process of individual growth in co-operative, interdependent living is democracy in action.

Face-to-face groups take on particular significance if democratic behavior is the aim. The felt appreciative attitude of others toward self is essential to personal security and well-being. Co-operative behavior creates the climate of democratic effort and accomplishment. To counteract the influences in modern living which make relationships complex and involved it is particularly necessary to encourage group organization and participation as an assurance of individual emotional and mental health.

All behavior is emergent, resulting from the interplay of persons and their surroundings. Whatever individuals within a group accomplish together will

From *Group Experience* by Bernice Baxter and Rosalind Cassidy. Copyright 1943 by Harper & Brothers. Reprinted by permission of Harper & Row, Publishers, Incorporated. Pp. 18–21.

be determined by the degree to which the environment in which these individuals operate encourages the free and full development of every person therein. The environment, in turn, will be the resultant of the attitude of one person toward another or persons toward persons. Democracy then comes to be a belief in the importance of every individual both to himself and to society.

To become emotionally conditioned for democratic living, individuals must learn to conform and contribute to group needs through a continuing experience which begins in early childhood to modify their individualistic tendencies. For example, as young as nursery school age, the child may and should learn that the sharing of toys and space is part of the conformity demanded by being in a situation with others of his own age. From then on through life his purposing, planning and realization of plans should be governed by his readiness and willingness to merge his own desires with those of his associates. The group makes constant demands upon the individual. There will be times when inflexibility of forces will exert an irresistible pressure upon him. He will need to learn to make such adjustments as are necessary. On the other hand, the individual person should have an active part in the making of group decisions. He should not be satisfied to have others make his decisions for him. Only as he learns to see his own purposes to successful conclusion will he grow in self-confidence and self-dependence.

The interaction of individuals in groups constitutes complex guidance problems. The unique personality of each individual must be maintained while the cohesiveness and solidarity of the group are fostered. Experiencing the oneness of self with others has a positive influence upon the person. Face-to-face group participation should be planned and guided as an essential in developing the social personality.

Groups differ in their cohesiveness. Not all aggregations of individuals have sufficiently common interests to be regarded as true groups. They may be mere assemblages of persons quite unlike in characteristics and not drawn together because of a central compelling purpose. Cohesive groups possess natural internal relationships between individuals within the groups and have certain distinguishing characteristics which to some degree are resident in all members of the group. This very alikeness in individuals is responsible for a prevailing atmosphere within the group organization.

In the integrated group, there is a "belongingness" in which all share. Persons within the group like to be together. Each is impelled to give of his best without restraint, without question as to how it will be received and without undue introspection. There is an outgoingness on the part of each member which is conducive to full and free self-expression.

In a genuinely unified group, there is no reason for one individual to mistrust another. Every individual has a unique worth to himself and to the group. Both he and all other members are aware of this value. Each member has found his relationship to a common purpose. The bond which unifies individuals is, therefore, to be found in the group purpose which is greater than any separate individual and yet is one to which all are willing to subscribe.

With the subscription to a common purpose there is also an acceptance of a social control by the group. There is a willingness without effort, on the part of members, to trust majority decision and majority action. Not always of a unanimous nature, judgments of the group will not alienate completely any individual. Since true group decisions emerge without force and without pressure, every contributing person will have a part in shaping these decisions. Each will abide by the control which all have been instrumental in establishing.

The group which is characterized by unity of purpose, commonly held values and member-accepted control will have afforded to its members opportunities for becoming acquainted with one another, with each person's modes of thinking, individual habits of action and needed satisfactions; otherwise, completely unified outcomes would not be possible. Sensitivity to the needs of others has to be acquired through practice.

All groups in American life do not reach this stage of unity. Time limitations often cause potentially unifiable groups to remain in the mere aggregate state. Individuals may meet together regularly and have a selected purpose without ever enjoying the full synthesis of thought and the complete integration herein suggested. In fact, most groups only approach the ideal. Since American society is pluralistic, that is, every person is a member of several groups, it seems increasingly important that the process through which group unification results should become part of the experience of everyone. The ways of democracy must be experienced if they are to be lived.

● ● ● ●

SUMMARY, QUESTIONS, AND SUGGESTED READINGS

SUMMARY

Much remains to be learned about groups. The complexity of the interaction and the stage of development of the instruments of research have necessitated an interpretation that is much too simple. Nevertheless, progress has been made, and the available knowledge serves a necessary and useful basis for advance.

Groups have been differentiated from a collection of objects. It is agreed that the group is not the sum of its parts but a structure that develops from the interaction of the individual members. There is agreement that the members of the group share norms, have interlocking roles, satisfy one another's needs, and work for the total good of the whole.

The group has its foundations in many disciplines. Anthropology and sociology have made possible the understanding of groups in relation to their community settings; psychology, the understanding of interpersonal, intrapersonal, and leader–member relationships; philosophy, the place and function of imagination and symbolism; religion, the nature and destiny of man. The combined enlightenment of these disciplines provides the framework within which study and research may proceed with increasing intelligence.

The group is better understood in terms of its various dimensions such as types, levels, and patterns. Examination of the types provides information regarding various kinds of groups; study of the levels clarifies the purposes of groups; and exploration of patterns discloses the character of the interaction and functioning of leader and member and of members with one another. Such an examination helps one to comprehend the complex structure of group functioning and to appreciate the possibilities and limitations of groups in relation to leadership and membership.

People will continue to work, play, and pray in groups. Although groups satisfy needs which individuals cannot satisfy alone, they are not necessarily constructive. Their usefulness in solving problems and developing the individual member depends on many factors. In determining the usefulness to the members, the qualities and performance of the leader play a vital part.

Questions

1. In modern society, what influences have a tendency to decrease the opportunities within the group for the growth of the personality of its members?

2. Why is a knowledge of the nature of man basic to the dynamics of group structure?

3. What are the implications of "congruence" for the improved functioning of groups?

4. Explain the important differences between a group-centered and a democratic group.

5. Name the significant differences between an instructional and a counseling group.

6. Why are the possibilities for self-understanding and the understanding of others minimized in an "aggregate" group?

7. What conditions enhance the value of the group for its members?

Suggested Readings

Section A: Definitions of the Group

Asch, Solomon E. *Social Psychology.* New York: Prentice-Hall, Inc., 1952. pp. 259–264.
    A well-reasoned and careful definition of the group.

Krech, David, and Crutchfield, Richard S. *Theory and Problems of Social Psychology.* New York: McGraw-Hill Book Co., Inc., 1948. Chapter 1.
    An excellent definition and discussion of the characteristics of the group.

Section B: Foundations of the Group

Fromm, Erich. *Escape from Freedom.* New York: Rinehart and Company, Inc., 1941. Chapter 1.
    Man's fear of isolation is powerful. This discussion provides a basis for the necessity for group process and also indicates some dangers.

Wrenn, C. Gilbert. "Symposium: The Counselor and His Religion," *Personnel and Guidance Journal,* XXXVI, No. 5 (January, 1958), 331–334.
    Provides insights into the complementary relationship of religious and psychological values and indicates the operational functioning of these values in interpersonal relationships.

Section C: Types and Levels of Groups

Haiman, Franklyn S. *Group Leadership and Democratic Action.* Boston: Houghton Mifflin Company, 1951. Chapter 4.
    A concise and well-formulated statement on the dynamics of a group. Included are definitions, and descriptions of types of groups and communication within the group.

Lloyd-Jones, Esther, and Smith, Margaret Ruth. "Helping the Student to Gain Self-Understanding," Chapter 6 in *Student Personnel Work As Deeper Teaching.* New York: Harper & Brothers, 1954.
The self-understanding of the student may be promoted through group experience. Methods are described in this chapter.

Section D: Group Patterns

Bales, Robert F. *Interaction Process Analysis.* Reading, Mass.: Addison-Wesley Publishing Company, Inc., 1950. Chapter 2.
A clear consideration of the characteristics of the small group.

Cronbach, L. J. *Educational Psychology.* New York: Harcourt, Brace & Co., 1954. Chapter 15.
Discusses the reasons for the superiority of group-controlled activities and presents three areas of group work.

Section E: Values of the Group

Humphreys, J. Anthony, and Traxler, Arthur E. "Why Have Group Guidance?" *Guidance Services.* Chicago: Science Research Associates, 1957.
A consideration of the reasons why group guidance should have a place in our society, with emphasis on how it assists the normal student.

Kirkbride, Virginia. "Group Approaches to Student Personnel in Higher Education," *Journal of the Association of Women Deans and Counselors,* XXIV, No. 3 (April, 1961), 127–131.
A description of the values of group procedures on the college level.

PART THREE

The Group Process

The study of group process is permeated with difficulties. These difficulties include the recognition and definition of the important variables, the ability to exercise the desired control, and the difficulty of securing normal groups under normal conditions for study.

In time, these methodological problems may be overcome. Under the best conditions, however, statistical studies may be unable to provide a complete understanding of the interaction and change which take place within a group. One explanation for this is that "the group is more than the sum of its parts." Another is offered by Tournier, who says that "in order for men to unite together, they need a basis of unity that is beyond them."[1]

The outcomes of group process are determined only partially by the knowledge, experience, and skills of group members and leaders. They are also a result of other factors, such as the values held by each member of the group. Basically, group harmony is dependent upon the degree of responsibility accepted by each member to contribute to a good psychological climate, including the acceptance and respect of each person for each other person. These matters of responsibility and respect evade scientific attempts at analysis.

The assumption that better designed research will enhance group functioning does not necessarily limit the use of intuitive insight of the kind described by Reik in his review of the interrupted treatment of a patient:

After an interval we return to the analytic treatment of the patient. Nothing essential is changed in his symptoms in the meantime; the neurosis or the character-difficulties remain the same. And yet their hidden meaning has suddenly become clear to us; we recognize some relation hitherto unconscious, veiled from our sight; we conjecture the purpose of the repression. Something has happened within ourselves, in the relation between the pre-

---

[1] Paul Tournier, *Escape from Loneliness*, translated by John S. Gilmour (Philadelphia: The Westminster Press, 1961), p. 63.

conscious and the unconscious, that has clarified our dimmed sight. We hear again what we have heard so often, but we hear something different in it. Now, at last, we feel psychologically at home after a long absence.[2]

Insights from research will increase the possibility of reaching better solutions and making more satisfactory plans. Incidentally but importantly, group interaction will lead to a greater understanding of self and others, especially in groups in which members are interested in helping one another.

Group process is not an end in itself. Its goals are general improvement in order to reach the desired level of attainment and the improvement of a specific function such as problem solving or therapy.

Part Three considers five aspects of group process. Section A, "Characteristics," acquaints the reader not only with the characteristics of the process but also with its complexity. Section B, "Special Problems in Interaction," discusses such problems as cliques, silent periods, and group size, which have a significant influence on the quality of group performance. Section C, "Problem Solving," examines the methods and approaches which affect learning and the solving of problems in groups. Section D, "Group Counseling," illustrates the process, clarifies the difficulties, and provides some evaluation of group counseling. Section E, "Evaluation," is self-explanatory.

[2] Theodore Reik, *Listening with the Third Ear* (New York: Farrar, Straus & Cudahy, Inc., 1952), p. 212.

Section A

CHARACTERISTICS OF THE GROUP PROCESS

The words "group process" connote movement and change within the members of the group as well as within the group as a whole. The characteristics of the process are directly related to the members considered individually and together.

The process in each group has characteristics in common with other groups, but its expression is unique to each group. There is a listening process, a thinking and feeling process, and a decision-making process. These interlocking processes are common to all groups, but the particular pattern of interrelationships varies from group to group.

In some groups the members try to understand how they themselves feel and think about an issue, while in others they devote their attention to the desires of the leader. Some groups, through their interaction, reach decisions cooperatively. Others, because of a different process, accept the decisions of the leader.

Solomon E. Asch, in "The Causal Relation of Person and Act," introduces the concept that objects and persons take on meaning which are in part a projection of past experiences. L. Thomas Hopkins, in "What Is Group Process?" explains the dynamics of the process with great discernment.

11

The Causal Relation of Person and Act

Solomon E. Asch

In the actions mentioned above we observe a certain direction of the person to his surroundings. When a person "points" with his arm or eyes, we turn our gaze to the object pointed at, not at the arm or eyes. It is similar when we see a child crying and straining toward a toy; his movements have the quality of straining *toward* the toy. Further, in following an action we see, as Heider[1] has formulated, the person as the cause or author. We perceive action as *issuing from* a person and moving into the surroundings with the force he imparts to it. The person and his actions form a unit, of which one is the source, origin, or cause, and the other is the effect. When a boy throws a stone at a window we note more than a sequence of movements — the extension of the arm, the flight of the stone, and the shattering of the window. Although the stone, when it has left the boy's hand, is handed over to external forces, we see the later events as consequences that belong to the act. Similarly, we do not see simply two men running, one in front and another behind, and a distance between them, now greater and now shorter. What is present to us is an act of pursuit, one man fleeing and another aiming to overtake him; the position of the first, though continually changing, is perceived as the constant goal of the other; the distance between them is the gap that one is trying to enlarge, the other to eliminate. These simple examples provide an illustration of a fundamental mode of organization in our experience. Causal relations are directly experienced data, indispensable for our orientation to the surroundings. Instead of a bewildering sequence of movements and changes, which follow each other arbitrarily, we perceive the movements as properties of figural units. By referring the movements to definite origins and by referring the later developments to their antecedents, we relate the passing and changing to what is stable.

Recently, Michotte[2] has demonstrated in an investigation of fundamental

From Solomon E. Asch, *Social Psychology*. © 1952. Prentice-Hall, Inc., Englewood Cliffs, N.J. Reprinted by permission. Pp. 152–157, 169.

[1] F. Heider, "Social Perception and Phenomenal Causality," *Psychological Review*, LI (1944), 358–374.

[2] A. Michotte, *La Perception de la Causalité* (Louvain: l'Institut Supérieur de Philosophie, 1946). See also A. Michotte, "The Emotions Regarded as Functional Connections," in M. I. Reymert (ed.), *Feelings and Emotions* (New York: McGraw-Hill Book Co., Inc., 1950).

importance that causation is an authentic mode of perceptual organization. By means of a simple technique he showed an observer two or more small colored rectangles whose speed, direction, and distance of movement he could control at will. Michotte demonstrated that certain sequences of movement, defined in terms of velocity and direction, produced specific impressions of "functional connections" or caused action. If A moved until it touched B and stopped and then B began to move, the observers reported that A set B in motion. If the movement of A was rapid and the duration of contact short, observers reported that A threw B forward. If A moved toward B, touched it, and then both A and B began to move together at the same speed and in the same direction, the impression was that of A carrying off B. If A moved near to B, came to a stop, and then B began to move, the reports stated that B moved out of the way of A. The effects obtained were strictly dependent on factors such as change of distance and rate of movement.

These observations add the category of causation to the forms of perceptual organization. They demonstrate that cause-effect relations are properties of the same immediacy as shape or the relation of figure to ground. When objects move in our field in a defined relation to other objects, we perceive specific causal effects. These are not the result of past experience or the attribution of meaning; given the proper conditions of timing and speed, the causal perception is present; if the proper conditions are not present, continuous repetition cannot bring about the perception of causality.

These facts have a direct relation to the perception of social action. Michotte, indeed, noted that in reporting on the movements of these inanimate figures the observers spontaneously used the language of human emotions and attitudes. They spoke in terms of "A joins B, then they fall out, have a quarrel, and B goes off by himself," or "It is as though B was afraid when A approached, and ran off." To be sure, such reports are dependent on past experience, or on the communication of present precepts with traces of previous social-human situations in which similar movement patterns had a certain psychological meaning. The manner in which such movements initially acquired meaning is not settled by the present experiment. But it opens the important possibility that we identify certain human actions in part because they are kinetic structures of a particular kind.

Heider and Simmel[3] have independently of Michotte provided an ingenious demonstration in support of this interpretation. Several groups of adults viewed a moving-picture film, about two and one-half minutes long, in which three geometrical figures — a large triangle, a smaller triangle, and a circle — moved in various directions and at various speeds in a field containing a rectangle, one portion of which could be opened and closed. (See Figure 1.) One group was asked to state what they saw; a second group was asked to state what they saw considering the figures to be human. Though the concrete features of human action were eliminated and only the geometrical-perceptual characters of movement retained, nearly all subjects in the first

[3] F. Heider and E. Simmel, "A Study of Apparent Behavior," *American Journal of Psychology*, LVII (1944), 243–259.

Figure 1

Figures Exposed in Various Positions and Relations
on the Moving Film

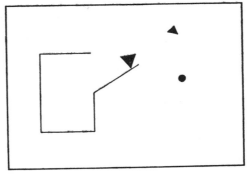

From F. Heider and E. Simmel, "A Study of Apparent Behavior," *American Journal of Psychology*, LVII (1944), 243–259. Reprinted with the permission of the publisher.

group reported what they saw in terms of animated action. The geometrical figures became personalities with definite characters. Also, a majority of the observers reported a connected, meaningful series of events. Only one subject managed to keep "animism" out, but even she finally succumbed when, toward the end of her account, she referred to the large triangle as "he." The results in the second group were even more striking; all subjects made the figures human. The reader will find the following report of one subject instructive:

A man has planned to meet a girl and the girl comes along with another man. The first man tells the second to go; the second tells the first, and he shakes his head. Then the two men have a fight, and the girl starts to go into the room to get out of the way and hesitates and finally goes in. She apparently does not want to be with the first man. The first man follows her into the room after having left the second in a rather weakened condition leaning on the wall outside the room. The girl gets worried and races from one corner to the other in the far part of the room. Man number one, after being rather silent for a while, makes several approaches at her; but she gets to the corner across from the door, just as man number two is trying to open it. He evidently got banged around and is still weak from his efforts to open the door. The girl gets out of the room in a sudden dash just as man number two gets the door open. The two chase around the outside of the room together, followed by man number one. But they finally elude him and get away. The first man goes back and tries to open his door, but he is so blinded by rage and frustration that he cannot open it. So he butts it open and in a really mad dash around the room he breaks in first one wall and then another.[4]

[4] *Ibid.*, pp. 246–247.

The three forms emerged as distinctive characters who were acting upon one another and upon the surroundings in a causal and, indeed, a motivated way. Their movements had the significance of entering and leaving; of fighting, bullying, hiding, and chasing; of hesitating, winning, and raging. Particularly striking was the strong agreement among the observers about the "participants" in the drama. The majority judged the large triangle to be aggressive, mean, bullying. Though less uniform, the view of the small triangle was predominantly that of a heroic, defiant character. Similarly, the circle was predominantly fearful, timid, and female. The actions taking place were soon perceived in terms of the preceding events and of the developing nature of the characters. The observers organized the sequence of events in a consistent way so that a given event fitted with what preceded. A given pattern of movement did not possess a fixed psychological content regardless of what preceded or of the way in which the characters were seen.

The observers uniformly divided the film into units or scenes, each of which comprised a meaningful action. Further, there was striking agreement among their reports about specific incidents in the film. For example, 92 per cent of one group reported that at one point the circle entered the "house" (i.e., the rectangle) in order to escape the fight, and 95 per cent stated that the big triangle in anger pulled down the house; and so on.

Heider analyzed some of the uniformities and pointed to their gestalt character: (1) Instances of successive movement with contact were seen as hitting. The relations of temporal succession, of spatial proximity, and good continuation seemed to be decisive. (2) In instances of simultaneous movement of two parts of the field with prolonged contact, such as opening or closing the door, the figure that had previously acquired the significance of a person became the origin of the movement and the door the recipient. This brought the scene into conformity with the previous experience of the figure as capable of independent movement. (3) When two units of the field moved simultaneously with no contact they gave the appearance of chasing or of one leading the other, depending on the course of the preceding events. With A in front and B in back, A could be seen as the origin, and so leading B, or B as the origin chasing A.[5] Successive movement without contact was almost always seen as chasing or aggressive action.

One cannot doubt that the observers saw what they reported only because they had in the past observed the actions of humans. The fact that the figures turned into human characters is enough to establish this point. But it would not be correct to conclude that the reports (as those of Michotte's observers) were due solely to past experience. For past experience would have been of no value if the observers had failed to note definite qualities in the present visual situation similar to those of which they already had knowledge. Whatever our conclusions about past experience, there is no way to escape the assumption that the movement-forms of the figures were perceptually similar to actual movement-forms of persons. It would seem to follow that we

[5] *Ibid.*

initially perceive movement-forms in persons in a dynamic-causal way *for the same reason* that we perceive them under the experimental conditions.

We conclude that movements which form given kinetic structures possess the properties of happenings or actions. When we perceive a given act issuing from a person it is represented phenomenally as a motive, need, or intention. Just as we perceive certain happenings as swift or turbulent, so we perceive others as aggressive, gentle, reckless, or uneasy. It becomes evident that the doctrines described earlier sought for a solution in the wrong place and failed to find it where it was most obvious. The inference doctrine assumed that actions of persons were psychologically characterless and therefore could acquire a psychological content only indirectly. Stimulus-response doctrine also neglected the perceptual-cognitive processes while introducing them naively.

The realization that we can directly perceive certain qualities of action in the relation of persons to objects and to other persons removes one stumbling block in thinking about social perception: it becomes unnecessary to refer as a matter of principle one's knowledge of others to knowledge about oneself. This removes the force from the assumption that one can observe in another only what one has experienced in oneself. To be sure, our grasp of such events as bullying, chasing, seizing, or receiving would be relatively pale had we not experienced them as agents or recipients; our active participation doubtlessly endows them with further meaning. There is therefore considerable truth to the statement that we can better understand the situation of others when we have faced similar conditions and problems. But the egocentric detour is unnecessary as a general requirement. It should be equally apparent that we gain an increased understanding of ourselves through knowledge of others. Generally we learn about others through ourselves, and conversely. For the present we must leave open the role of each of these sources of knowledge. It seems appropriate to conclude that the *same* capacities for observing and understanding enable us to follow the actions of others and to take part in them ourselves.

· · · ·

12

What Is Group Process?

L. Thomas Hopkins

. . . .

The term "process" has been used in various contexts in previous chapters. Here I shall explain further its meaning to distinguish some behaviors of people which are usually associated with the word group. A process is described by such words as movement, change, action, development, behavior, depending upon the point of view of the individual. It is continuous, dynamic, directional. It begins at conception and lasts until death. It is so completely coexistent with life that when process ceases life also ceases. These descriptive terms may be brought together into one sentence: A *process is a continuous, dynamic, directional life movement of an individual within his phenomenal field.* This movement includes everything that takes place inside the individual, as well as all his relationships with his external environment. It is what he thinks and the unconscious data that he registers in his viscera. It is what outsiders hear him saying or observe him doing, together with all that they construe within such action. It has both covert and overt implications. It is everything that he does, feels, or thinks. It is everything that others see him do, believe he feels, or infer he thinks.

This continuous life process is called experience, which is defined as the continuous interaction of an individual with his environment. Experience or life moves through a series of disturbances called situations, which are not of equal duration, depth, or value. While they are all upsets in the individual, some are problems which can be adjusted by using old behavior patterns with relatively minor modifications; others cut so deeply into his previously constituted self as to be called needs. The latter are of longer duration, greater area and depth, and call for major reorganization of the self by the growth-learning process in order to promote self-enhancement. The series of situations arising out of and integrated through the need–action process is sometimes called *having an experience* instead of just experience, since it has a unit quality which gives it a name or at least a definite and distinctive recognition. Regardless of how the individual or others may view his life, whether he accepts it or rejects it, whether others approve or disapprove it, a process of some type is ever present. So the growing child in his environment and the adults in theirs should have the same common area of need. They should all work together to develop such high quality in the process of living, growing, learning that each self may continue its upward movement in the never-ending quest for self-enhancement.

When I explain to students that all life is process, someone immediately asks, "What is group process?" Whenever two or more people work together on anything for any purpose, by any method of study, inquiry, or human relations, the process used is group process since two or more interacting individuals constitute a group. Reversing this statement, group process means that two or more people are working together on some need or problem toward some recognized end, by some form of interpersonal relations, with some covert or overt effect on each. A few students immediately point out that this definition of group process is too general. Any form of human relations can qualify under it, even the most arbitrary and ruthless persecution of a weak person by a more powerful individual. Of course this is true. Other students reply that every act of any individual is modified by others and in turn affects others, hence life process is really group process. This is true also.

But a distinction must be made between the social behavior of an individual and the behavior of social group. The former refers to the actions of a single person in relation to other people, individually or collectively, within his own phenomenal field. The latter has to do with what constitutes a group, how it operates to develop and maintain its groupness, and what effects it has upon the individuals who compose it. In either case, the same number of people may be involved, but there is a different relationship among them. In social behavior the movement is largely from individual to individual, whereas in group behavior there is a tangible qualitative interdependence of each upon others which operates three ways: individual to individual, individual to whole, and whole to individual. When this three-dimensional relationship breaks, the group ceases to exist. Everyone knows that some associations with people are unsatisfactory since they tend to depress the self, while others are desirable since they tend to elevate the self. There is a quality in human relations which can be distinguished and explained intellectually, even though the more subtle emotional effects are difficult to symbolize.

This quality in the relationship of individuals is the group and the way they work together to produce it is the process. It is not the social behavior of individuals, it is not any old way by which people work together, it is not any effect which one person may have on someone else. Group process is the way people work together to release an emergent quality, called psychological climate, group morale, esprit de corps, or cooperative unity, through which each discovers and develops his inner capacities, realizes better the nature of his self, releases more of his past experience, and learns how to create this emergent quality in all life situations. This does not affirm a group mind existing apart from the individuals who compose it. Neither does it mean that individuals in a group generate a common mind superior to that of any member. For there is no common mind or superior group mind which imposes actions on anyone. By the need-experience process, individuals release into the environment potential creative ability heretofore unknown to them or to others. A higher level of thinking emerges than was possessed by any individual prior to the qualitative interaction. Thus interacting individuals furnish the environment in which to bring forward their creative meanings, thereby giving each the opportunity to become a better self. It is the need–experience process previously discussed which produces the quality called the group. And only as individuals conceptualize it while they use it, can the group continue to function on a high level.

• • • •

Section B

SPECIAL PROBLEMS IN INTERACTION

Interaction is the heart of the group process. The conditions which affect it are so complex and interrelated that present research methods are inadequate for their evaluation. Some of the conditions are more common than others and have therefore received greater attention. Three of these, "group size," "cliques," and "the silent period," have been selected for presentation.

A question of great practical significance is the number of members that can participate in a group before it loses in both its intellectual performance and its possibilities for personality change. For what purposes may the number in a group be significantly increased without destroying the functioning of the group?

Another problem of a different nature is that of the evolvement and functioning of subgroups within the group proper. Such subgroups or cliques materially hamper the functioning of the total group. Why do some groups have cliques, while others do not? What conditions encourage them? What needs of the members are met by them? When cliques are formed, how may the situation be improved?

Another problem in interaction is the period of silence. Some consider it to be of negative or questionable value. They tend to find it a somewhat frustrating, although common, experience in all groups. Is the silent period to be considered the norm? May it be a means of growth? Are all silent periods of equal value? What is the best means of utilizing a silent period? The meaning of the silent period can be determined only in relation to the character of the interpersonal relationships, especially the feeling tone which exists between each member and the leader. The silent period may be used for thoughtful resolution of conflict, for gaining insights, for recognizing ideational relationships. In other situations it is an expression of hostility or of confusion, discouragement, or withdrawal.

The problems in interaction that are associated with group size, cliques, and silent periods originate in various types of groups. All of these problems may be expected to diminish as the group members grow in the ability to accept themselves and one another. This degree of acceptance is directly related to the quality and kind of leadership and to the amount and quality of group interaction. To understand the true significance of any of these problems, a careful study must be made of the dynamic interrelationships within the group.

The problems associated with group size are discussed by James A. Schellenberg in "Group Size as a Factor in Success of Academic Discussion Groups." The nature and treatment of cliques or small subgroups within the large group are treated by Charles A. Tonsor in "The Small Group: An Atom the School Can't Split." The third common problem is analyzed by D. Patrick Hughes in "The Silent Period in Group Process."

13

Group Size as a Factor in Success of Academic Discussion Groups

James A. Schellenberg

This paper reports a study of the effects of group size upon satisfaction and scholastic achievement of academic discussion groups. It is an attempt to apply to an academic setting an area of social research which may have important consequences for educational administration.

Sociologists and social psychologists have developed a growing body of data concerning the effects of size upon small groups.[1] Among some of the more interesting of various findings are that idea productivity appears to vary inversely with size;[2] that groups of four are slower on concrete problems than groups of two, but faster on abstract problems;[3] that consensus, interaction, and satisfaction are all higher in groups of five persons than in those of twelve;[4] that accuracy in decision-making is better in groups of six than in those of two or three persons;[5] and that member satisfaction is greater for groups of five persons than for either larger or smaller groups.[6]

At first glance these studies may seem directly applicable to problems of educational administration — especially those involving discussion-type classes.

From James A. Schellenberg, "Group Size as a Factor in Success of Academic Discussion Groups," *Journal of Educational Sociology*, XXXIII (October 1959), 73–79. Reprinted with the permission of the publisher.

[1] For a recent survey of the literature on this problem see Robert F. Bales, A. Paul Hare, and Edgar F. Borgatta, "Structure and Dynamics of Small Groups: A Review of Four Variables," in Joseph B. Gittler (ed.), *Review of Sociology: Analysis of a Decade* (New York: John Wiley & Sons, 1957), especially pp. 394–402. See also Harold H. Kelley and John W. Thibaut, "Experimental Studies of Group Problem Solving and Process," in Gardner Lindzey (ed.), *Handbook of Social Psychology* (Reading, Mass.: Addison-Wesley Publishing Company, Inc., 1954) Vol. 2, especially 761-762.

[2] J. R. Gibb, "The Effects of Group Size and Threat Reduction upon Creativity in a Problem-Solving Situation," *American Psychologist*, VI (1951), 324 (abstract).

[3] D. W. Taylor and W. L. Faust, "Twenty Questions: Efficiency in Problem Solving as a Function of Size of Group," *Journal of Experimental Psychology*, XLIV (1952), 360–368.

[4] A. P. Hare, "A Study of Interaction and Consensus in Different Sized Groups," *American Sociological Review*, XVII (1952), 261–267.

[5] R. C. Ziller, "Group Size: A Determinant of the Quality and Stability of Group Decisions," *Sociometry*, XX (1957), 165–173.

[6] Philip Slater, "Contrasting Correlates of Group Size," *Sociometry*, XXI (1958), 129–139.

However, there are several considerations which make such direct applications hazardous. First, the studies in the literature on the effects of group size are nearly all those of specially created and temporary groups. This minimizes certain forms of prior expectations on the part of students and teachers which are often of central significance in the culture of the classroom. More specifically, such studies typically refrain from imposing any leadership structure or pattern of interaction upon the group, for the observer is usually interested in the forms which will evolve "naturally." In the classroom, on the contrary, the teacher usually makes a most deliberate and thorough attempt to control the situation of interaction. Finally, the criteria of satisfaction or success may be quite different in the classroom from those of artificially created groups. These considerations all underline the importance of studies which may deal directly with academic settings if the results are to be considered relevant for educational application.

STUDY PROCEDURES

The present study was designed to discover whether there is any relationship between the size of discussion group and measures of student satisfaction, instructor satisfaction, and student achievement. To achieve this, thirty-two discussion groups in Western Civilization at the University of Kansas were set up as experimental groups during the fall semester, 1958–59. The Western Civilization Program at the University of Kansas is a general education requirement for undergraduates in liberal arts, education, and journalism. The reading materials are selected to represent the ideas of leading thinkers concerning the civilization of the past five centuries (Machiavelli, More, Luther, Locke, Voltaire, Mill, Marx, Mussolini, and Dewey are among the perennial authors used) and to challenge the student to think about central issues of modern civilization. Self-responsibility on the part of the student is emphasized, and the only classroom instruction is in the form of small weekly discussion groups.

Each of four participating instructors[7] was given two groups of each of the following original number of students: four, six, eight, and ten. Care was taken to keep the groups at the original sizes throughout the semester, although additions and withdrawals were necessary in some cases. In the results reported below group size is figured as the actual size at mid-semester, which in no case differed by more than one from the originally scheduled size.

Groups were scheduled in such a manner that effects of the day of the week or time of day would be minimized. Students involved were all sophomores in the College of Liberal Arts, enrolled for the first time in "Western Civ" and assigned by random to their particular discussion group.

At the last meeting of the semester each of the experimental groups was given a questionnaire which each member was to fill out anonymously. Completed questionnaires were thus obtained from 95 per cent of the students

---

[7] Instructors of groups used as experimental groups were William Cozort, Jack Gibson, Bruce Hood, and Mark Plummer. The writer is indebted to these instructors for help in both planning and carrying out the study.

enrolled in the experimental groups. The questionnaire included the following questions:

1. In general, how satisfied have you been with this semester's discussion group?
2. How satisfied are you that you have been able to express yourself freely and fully in your group discussions?
3. How satisfied are you that your group has adequately covered the main points in each week's readings?

For convenience in the following discussion the results of these questions will be referred to as reflecting criteria of "general satisfaction," "freedom of expression," and "content coverage" respectively.

To answer each question students checked the appropriate response of a nine-item scale which ranged from "extremely satisfied" to "extremely dissatisfied." In scoring, the scale was treated as an equal-interval scale with weights given to the responses ranging from 1 to 9. For each group the mean score was obtained to represent the degree of satisfaction for the group as a whole.

Instructors were asked corresponding questions concerning their groups (e.g., "How satisfied are you that the students of this group have been able to express themselves freely and fully in the group discussions?"), and instructor questionnaires were scored in the same manner as were those of students.

To allow a rough measure of academic achievement, semester grades were recorded for all students, and grades for an essay hour exam given during the seventh meeting of the semester were also noted. Scores on the *American Council on Education Psychological Test* were also available in all but a few cases, and these were used to check the assumption that the experimental design successfully randomized the factor of initial ability.

RESULTS

Student Satisfaction. Before conducting the study it was considered likely that the optimum group size would be somewhere between four and ten. However, nearly all the results which showed a systematic pattern appeared to vary inversely with group size. Therefore the results may be presented in the form of linear correlations.[8] Product-moment correlations between group size and criteria of student satisfaction (based on the mean satisfaction score for the group) were as follows:

Criterion of Student Satisfaction	Correlation with Group Size
1 (General Satisfaction)	−.37
2 (Freedom of Expression)	−.59
3 (Content Coverage)	−.47

All of these correlations are significant at the .05 level, and both the second and third are significant at the .01 level.

[8] A preliminary report which gives detailed results for each size of group and for each question may be obtained upon request to the Western Civilization Program, University of Kansas, Lawrence.

From this one may simply conclude that student satisfaction decreased as the size of the group increased. This is true no matter what criterion of student satisfaction is used.

Instructor Satisfaction. It will be recalled that instructors also filled out questionnaires to indicate their degree of satisfaction with their groups. Product-moment correlations between group size and criteria of instructor satisfaction were as follows:

Criterion of Instructor Satisfaction	*Correlation with Group Size*
1 (General Satisfaction)	−.21
2 (Freedom of Expression)	−.21
3 (Content Coverage)	+.18

None of these correlations is statistically significant; however, this in itself is important when we remember that *all* the correlations with student satisfaction were significant. Evidently the size of group was much more important to the students (even though they may not have been aware of it as a factor in their satisfaction) than to their instructors. In fact, according to the third criterion of content coverage ("How satisfied are you that this group has adequately dealt with the main points in each week's readings?"), there was actually a slight tendency for *larger* groups to be rated higher by their instructors than were smaller groups.

Academic Achievement. Granted that the size of group may have an effect upon student satisfaction, the question remains concerning the relationship between size of discussion group and academic success. Do students in the smaller groups learn more? Data on this question are not as adequate as might be desired, but that which is available favors a positive answer. The central piece of evidence in this regard is that there was a correlation of −.46 between the semester grade average of a group and its size. This is statistically significant at the .01 level. That this cannot be due to a failure to achieve a random distribution of original ability is indicated by the low positive correlation of .03 between group size and the A.C.E. average of groups.

However, it is unlikely that so large a correlation as −.46 could reflect directly differences in the degree of academic success of persons in groups of different sizes. Even though there was no very marked tendency for instructors to be more satisfied with smaller groups, they still may have unconsciously graded their smaller groups more generously. This could conceivably be the case if an instructor's semester grade (which is based largely on discussion) happened to be based in large part upon the *amount* of discussion which an instructor could observe from a particular student — for larger groups obviously allow less time for participation for each student.

Quite possibly the high correlation between group size and semester grade average is partly to be explained on the basis of such considerations and in part the result of greater real achievement which the smaller groups were better able to stimulate. In this respect it is worth noting that the correlation between essay hour exam grades taken after six weeks and group size was −.23. This is in the direction of showing better results for the smaller groups, although this correlation is not statistically significant at the .05 level. Although one hopes that the final semester grade better reflects real achievement than grades for the essay hour exam, the latter criterion does have the advantage of being free from the influence of the amount of participation which an individual may show in group discussions.

DISCUSSION

It must be made clear that all the above results are based on the group as the unit of analysis. Thus all correlations are between group size and various measures representing the group as a whole. Because of this these results can be important only in showing the presence and direction of a relationship. The results are not in a form allowing direct prediction for individual persons.

The outstanding finding was the consistency with which students in smaller groups showed greater satisfaction. This suggests that the smaller the group, the greater will be the satisfaction — although there is no evidence concerning groups with less than four students. This finding was something of a surprise in that the department had been operating under the untested assumption that groups of five to seven were of optimum size. Even among instructors of the experimental groups there was a tendency to consider such a middle-sized group as preferable to either a group of four or of ten students.

But the finding of greater student satisfaction with smaller groups needs to be qualified in several ways in making generalizations which would be applicable to other educational settings. Of first importance is that "Western Civ" is presented to students at Kansas as a program in which they are placed on their own responsibility. It is emphasized that the student should search for his own answers to the issues presented by the modern world. With this presented as a large part of the purpose of the course, it is perhaps not surprising that the more informal classroom setting (such as the smaller discussion groups) may be evaluated by students as more successful. Also, students have come to associate the course with a rather informal discussion setting. Thus there may be expectations in the student culture as well as educational objectives of the faculty which combine to make this Kansas course in general education considered more successful by students when placed in smaller discussion groups.[9] It is quite possible that most courses in a university setting would not fit into the same pattern — especially courses with a more technical orientation to subject matter.

The results favoring the smaller size of discussion group lead to further implications concerning studies of the success of the discussion method of teaching. Most studies comparing discussion and other methods have reported rather inconclusive results — indeed, in the classic Michigan psychology experiment there was slightly higher achievement with the recitation-drill

[9] It is here of interest to note the following observation: "It is in this area of expectations that differences between colleges are important. For example, students at Brooklyn College rate large classes as favorably as small classes, while students at Grinnell College rate instructors less favorably in classes of over thirty. I would interpret this as being due to differences in student expectations." Wilbert J. McKeachie, "Students, Groups and Teaching Methods," *American Psychologist*, XIII (1958), 583.

method.[10] However, most such comparisons of discussion and other methods have used discussion classes considerably larger than those of the present study — such as classes of twenty-five to thirty-five in the Michigan study. From the present study it appears quite likely that a very small class would be necessary to show the greatest possibilities of the discussion method in such comparisons.

Finally, a few comments are warranted by the rather surprising difference between student measures and instructor measures of satisfaction for groups of different sizes. Perhaps this, and especially the divergence concerning satisfaction with "content coverage," may be explained as follows: The larger groups are more likely to include several good students than are the smaller groups. Thus in the larger groups the instructor, while he may note that some of the students participate very little, is more apt to be satisfied with the level of discussion of those who do participate. Meanwhile, the average student is apt to be much more aware in these groups of instances in which he is not able to get from, or give to, the discussion what he would like. This must be seen as evidence for the idea that an instructor is not always the best judge of the conditions under which students may be best stimulated educationally. At any rate, sometimes the students may have quite another perspective.

SUMMARY AND CONCLUSIONS

Thirty-two academic discussion groups were varied in sizes from four to ten students to measure the effects of group size upon student satisfaction, instructor satisfaction, and student achievement.

The most significant finding was the surprisingly consistent inverse relationship between group size and student satisfaction. Students claim greater satisfaction in the smaller groups.

A second important result was the difference between the perspective of instructors and those of students. Instructors are more inclined than students to show satisfaction with larger groups.

There was limited evidence that smaller groups also showed slightly higher academic achievement than did larger groups.

[10] For a summary of such studies see Philip E. Jacob, *Changing Values in College: An Exploratory Study of the Impact of College Teaching* (New York: Harper & Brothers, 1957), especially pp. 92–95. For the Michigan study see Harold Guetzkow, E. Lowell Kelly, and Wilbert J. McKeachie, "An Experimental Comparison of Recitation, Discussion and Tutorial Methods of College Teaching," *Journal of Educational Psychology*, XLV (1954), 193–207.

14

The "Small Group": An Atom the School Can't Split

Charles A. Tonsor

A large school, like a large factory, may by its very size and methods of operation give rise to personality problems. The stress and strain imposed by assembly-line procedures, the isolation from mates required by close concentration start a chain reaction that leads to all sorts of personality problems — drinking, quarrelling, absenteeism, and the like. Industry accomplished little toward breaking up this condition until relaxation and recreation periods in which small groups could get together were established. This changed conduct completely. Industry found that it paid to take note of the personality building power, the therapeutic power of small groups.

Business also found that workers did not conform to measures taken in their behalf. Those measures were best which they initiated when given the opportunity. No matter how carefully administrators formulated activities, they were suspect as trying to control the crew so as to get more out of them than the workers would ordinarily be willing to grant. . . . Workers have their own value system, one which cannot be changed by fiats. They have their own ideas of a day's work and their own ways of punishing laggards or those who produce beyond the unwritten limit.

That same system rules in any large high school, and administrative fiats will not break it up. The only way that change will come about is through small groups or giving an opportunity for small groups to form which will accomplish the desired results in their own ways. The only control which can be utilized is an indirect control through those who are recognized by the small groups as leaders.

Administrators must study small groups, their formation, and their operation, because these small groups will form willy-nilly among faculty and pupils. These small groups may consist of duads, triads, quartettes, or sextets, rarely more because even within so small a group as twelve or thirteen, smaller groups tend to form; witness Peter, James, and John among the Apostles!

The nexus that holds these groups together is the personal satisfaction the members gain from one another's company. They stand in a group of two or three outside a classroom and just talk, dodging into the room as soon as

From Charles A. Tonsor, "The 'Small Group': An Atom the School Can't Split," *The Clearing House*, XXIX (December, 1954), 195–198. Reprinted with the permission of the publisher.

the commencement bell rings. They wait for one another for the bus, stand in the same spot day after day before or after school. They are seldom anti-social, nor do they cause trouble through acts of violence. They are often late for school merely from failure to duck in on time. They are just satisfied with one another's presence and small talk.

Sometimes there is a leader, and if there is, he is a leader by common consent. The others gravitate to him. No by-laws, no organization. If there are such rules, the group has formalized and soon disintegrates. Reach the leader and you reach the group, but you cannot supply the leader for the group. Usually all actions are informal. "Let's go to Confraternity tonight" or "Let's go to the beach." Like Lucretius' atoms, they bang into one another during the stream of school life and then adhere to form a definite group with definite tastes and opinions — and a definite code, even though it is never formulated. Different groups will have different codes.

Such a group cannot be dissolved by force or fiat. It will re-form as soon as the individuals are free. But strangely enough, it will disintegrate if the leader or one or two members go elsewhere. The group may re-form if those who caused its dissolution return, but it seldom continues its existence by admitting new members. Nor may anyone apply for membership. One may be brought by a friend and gradually be accepted, but as often, one may not.

In these small groups behavior is relaxed, as in a real family. The situation is one in which the young people can let their hair down. There is no need of being on guard against anyone. There may be a Judas among the thirteen but not among Peter, James, and John. In the small group you can say what you please and nobody holds it against you. You can say what you feel, you can be yourself without any fear of being called to order or called down. The proverb runs, "Misery loves company," but these birds are far from miserable. "Birds of a feather flock together" — but often they are very unlike, complementary instead. In fine, the small group provides a situation in which you can be a person and not a lost sheep in the large flock called the school, or a small cog in the vast machine.

These groups are non-secret. Everybody knows the membership. All you have to do is ask, "Whom does John pal around with?" Often you don't have to ask. Watch who sits on the steps, the same spot, day-in-day-out. No one will take that spot from the group without a struggle. Watch for who waits for whom. You will have no trouble getting the information you want, even if the group does get into trouble now and then. As to a gang — that is a different story.

What do they find to talk about? For talk they do. They cut classes to meet one another in the hall, or in the lavatory, or in any out-of-the-way corner just to talk. You may punish them, you may order them to stay away from one another, you may tell them they are not good for one another, parents may try to keep them apart. No use — at the first opportunity they will be together again. All this just for chit chat, incidents in their daily lives, class, events of the preceding day, what's cooking, and so on, plans for this, plans for that, whether to go to the movies, to a particular confraternity, or what have you.

The group members don't hesitate to tell what they have been talking about. There's nothing secret, nothing illegal. They'll talk about a teacher or a dean, and when questioned will make no bones about telling another dean. They are brutally frank. Our experience with many such groups, whose interpersonal attraction leads now and then to infraction of school regulations, is that they admit the need of regulations. But the excuse is, "I wanted to tell Joe something" or "I wanted to ask Bill about John." That's not a lie to conceal the real situation, for time and again when one checks with Joe or Bill before there is any opportunity for cooking up a common story, the statements agree.

Although you cannot force another member upon a group, there are "isolates" to whom these groups go either for small talk, for advice, or for specific guidance. These isolates are not members of any one group, at least in school, but are respected by all, and the groups value their decisions or opinions. Often they are so familiar with the workings of the administration that they advise the group on how to approach the administration. Often these isolates are more mature than their fellows and form a very important means of making the school what it should be. Their status does not grow out of any selection by the administration but from their natural relation with the faculty and the school. They are old enough to see the school point of view, young enough to see the student point of view. They are thus a valuable asset in forming the student climate of opinion. However, they cannot be selected for the part or thrown into it. They may be selected for responsible activities *after* they have become recognized as advisers for a group or groups.

But there are isolates whom groups shun. They may be the "trailers" who tag along hoping to get into a group but who never are admitted. Or they may be self-rejects because they cannot find any group with whom they are at ease. Sometimes they seek the company of older people and assist in projects, service, and activities. We cannot form a group for one no matter how hard we try. Yet groups eventually may form among them, for in working with older people, such an isolate may meet others sufficiently congenial to form a group. However, the isolate who believes the world is against him is likely to become dangerously anti-social.

How long does a group last? Nobody can say. Some have great persistence. Often, where one member goes another follows. Sometimes they disintegrate for a time when members go elsewhere, but regroup if members return. Often they persist through the years when these students have become alumni. . . .

What significance have these small groups for a school? Small groups set the pattern for achievement, just as people in industry do. No matter how high his IQ, an individual will not function accordingly if the group limit is set below it, not by vote but by "common consent." We may cajole and urge, to no avail. An individual within a group who exceeds the pattern of the group will find himself talked down. Other members will not let an individual rise above the level set by the group. You may try to break the hold by cutting a bright individual out of the group, perhaps through shifting his recitation class, but even that is a gamble. The standard which the leader sets, the rest follow. If his is a C average, the rest will be content with a C average. The same situation holds in extracurricular activities. That explains in part why athletes of ability don't live up to their capacities.

We would like to know how pupils are brought into small groups or talked out; but we don't know. And we would like to know the best way to operate on those group members who act against school policies. One thing we know. Change the environment and you split the group. If a class is changed so that an individual can seldom meet with his group, that individual soon is out of that group. But we still cannot determine who will take his place.

Remember, too, that small groups operate on all levels — among teachers, parents, and board members, as well as pupils. These small groups may be a help or a hindrance, according to the skill with which we manipulate the environment or handle situations that promote or discourage their formation or persistence.

Nearly a quarter of a century ago when we organized Grover Cleveland High School, we provided as many opportunities as possible for pupils. We had a very large number of activities. This made groups small. Our orchestra was a body of smaller units. Fifers, trumpeters, drummers were entities. They performed as entities within the larger group. They recruited their own replacements, often giving instruction themselves to "friends" so that they could be members of the group. Dance band, accordion band, trios with guitar, bass fiddle, and piano were organized and proved of inestimable value in establishing school spirit and a proper social atmosphere.

The same condition was true in dramatics, in the student cabinet, and student court. One had to be the natural leader of a small group to be eligible for selection to school positions. Pupils as well as teachers could make recommendations of qualified persons. Even in athletics, the intra-mural program was arranged to provide for self-organized small units — handball, tennis, badminton, basketball, softball, six-man football, and the like. The resulting ability of the student body was noteworthy.

Now, in spite of the decline in voluntary activities caused by unsatisfactory experiences of the teachers in salary matters, the spirit still continues and teachers find it hard to resist the appeal of small groups who come pleading for a sponsor. Pupils, not sponsors, form the groups. Therefore pupils, not teachers, are the active force, the teachers being guides and advisers, as they should be.

The small groups keep up their contact with the school long into the days of alumni status. Julius La Rosa, for example, still comes around on occasion and still maintains contact with the small group of which he was a part at school. When we adopted the small-group plan, we did so not because we were experts in anthropology but because we were solicited by small groups [and] saw the advantages, and experience has justified the wisdom of our action.

15

The Silent Period in Group Process

D. Patrick Hughes

One of the criticisms of group processes is that there are long, inefficient periods of silence. Critical comment characterizes these periods as wasteful, laments that nothing is being accomplished, would have group members drive through to immediate problem solutions and obtain quick, clear-cut results.

These criticisms contain two assumptions, self-made: (1) that the *total* value of group processes should lie in the result, and (2) that absolutely *nothing* is being done during the period when the apparently awkward silence obtains.

Criticism focused on results ignores the value of the process. Actually, the silent period may be the most fruitful portion of the meeting, for here the participant is balancing the turn of the group discussion with his own experience, background, and observations in the practical situation in his own community. When there is a period of silence, *everyone* is thinking, weighing possible solutions to the problem under consideration, perhaps making and rejecting possible decisions.

It must be remembered that in any discussion, when one person is talking, the group membership with but *one* exception is silent. During any speech or lecture, only *one* individual is talking and the many are silent. So, actually, in group dynamics when all are silent, it does not necessarily mean that an impasse has been reached; the period of silence is but a very small departure, for *only one more* person than usual is silent.

During this "awkward" period, experience hints it is not unsafe to guess that more creative thinking takes place than during any other part of the discussion. Group members can deliberate without being whisked from one point to another by the speaker. It is awkward only to those who are in a hurry to get things done, who ignore the danger that snap judgments and *ad hoc* solutions may be concomitants of this haste.

The floor is open during the silent period. Anyone can talk; a "free" atmosphere prevails. Because the group is waiting for the first one to speak and because it could be any individual in the group, each is preparing a

From D. Patrick Hughes, "The Silent Period in Group Process," *The Clearing House*, XXXII (December, 1957), 230–231. Reprinted with the permission of the publisher.

carefully thought-out statement. This very freedom to speak, to be the one to resume the discussion, is self-enhancing to each group member; possible statements are fashioned and refashioned, clarified and reclarified, though they go unspoken. And though they go unvoiced, their very completeness increases the eventual chance for a core of agreement throughout the thinking of the group members; this core becomes the basis for mutual understandings that lead to effective results.

Very little of what is thought ever reaches the group orally. How then is this silent period of thinking of value beyond the aforementioned understanding?

When one seeks answers and solutions, one constantly re-examines the question or problem. Careful, unhurried, reflective thinking increases opportunity for both sides of a question, or all pertinent aspects of a problem, to come into focus and consideration. This not only leads to a greater understanding in the group but makes possible a more complete rapport and, in turn, a more solid, effective, two-way co-operation.

In educational groups, much of what never comes to be said, much of what was thought, goes back to the individual districts, systems, schools, and even classrooms, and ultimately works for improvement. This thinking has been modified by the group, this modification has had time to crystallize, consciously, maybe even unconsciously, during periods when no one seems to have anything to say.

For during this silent period, ideas swarm, each a direct result of group thinking and group stimulation. Since there *is* time, all possibilities of each idea are examined carefully, because the mind is preparing it for submission to the group. This process is repeated numerous times.

Though an idea may never be submitted to the group, this opportunity for the individual to examine it and the ideas of others critically, in reference to his own situation, gives perspective, and one day appears in action.

Section C

GROUP DECISION AND
SOCIAL CHANGE

Conditions that are conducive to group change and the method used for its accomplishment are basic problems in any consideration of groups. It is generally accepted that the group changes as a unit rather than member by member.[1] The more cohesive the group, the more it can be expected to move to a new attitudinal position as an integrated whole.

But cohesiveness itself is a condition which is complex and not easily understood. Cohesiveness exists when each member believes that every other member is appreciated by and necessary to all others in the group. This sense of being bound together may result through pressures from without the group or from the growth of respect, acceptance, and affection developing from within. The results of outside pressure may appear to the observer to be genuine unity. This type of cohesiveness is not stable, however, and it dissolves when the threatening condition or fear of a punitive status authority is no longer present.

Any method used to induce social change must take into account the quality of cohesiveness of the group. The leader upon whom the responsibility generally rests for initiating the conditions leading to social change must appraise the degree to which he can expect a total group response.

One method of accomplishing group change is based on the assumption that the members change either to improve their present condition or to avoid a worse condition. This method of changing groups has three stages: (1) the creation of a state of disequilibrium among the members (a dissatisfaction with the present and a readiness to change); (2) an inducement or reward if and as the new level of behavior is attained; and (3) the "freezing" or establishment of an equilibrium "set" after the new level of behavior has been reached.

---

[1] Kurt Lewin and Paul Grabbe, "Conduct, Knowledge, and Acceptance of New Values," *Journal of Social Issues*, I (1945), 64.

The "self theory" of Carl Rogers takes a very different approach. Basic to this theory is the assumption that if the leader is able to provide a non-evaluative "climate" of acceptance in which the members make and put into effect their decisions, then constructive change will take place. This change occurs in an atmosphere in which individuals are free either to change or not to change. The process includes the recognition and expression of negative feelings and motives which are accepted by the leader and which yield almost imperceptibly to increasingly positive feelings and motives.

Difficulties of the group in making decisions is discussed by Kenneth Herrold, Joel Davitz, David Fox, and Irving Lorge in "Difficulties Encountered in Group Decision-Making," and one method of working toward social change is described by David Jenkins in "Social Engineering in Educational Change: An Outline of Method."

16

Difficulties Encountered in Group Decision-Making

Kenneth F. Herrold, Joel Davitz,
David Fox, and Irving Lorge

The purpose of this study was to evaluate and describe some of the difficulties encountered by individuals in group decision-making.[1] Attention was directed to the procedural difficulties experienced by groups in decision-making wherein the problem, related information, and the time and other conditions were rigorously controlled. The nature and degree of difficulty experienced with respect to the group procedures was related to the quality of the group decisions determined in other research related to this study.[2] A knowledge of these difficulties has important implications for the training of professional personnel for effective staff and other decision-making.

The subjects in this pilot study were one hundred graduate students at Teachers College, Columbia University. These subjects were enrolled in an introductory course in group development and group process. They represented a wide range of professional occupations related to education. The subjects were tested before they had received instruction or skill training and at the close of the instruction period. Therefore, it is possible to speculate as to the effects of the specific training experience on this particular group skill and to derive some indications as to where the training led to improvement in the skills of the participants and what areas of difficulty persisted even after training.

The subjects were organized into groups of five. Each of the five members of each of the decision-making groups was given a different tab or protocol of information regarding the common problem they were all requested to solve.

Although the group problem, in the first and final decision-making tests, concerned personnel relations at an Air Force Base in either the United States or Korea, the basic nature of the problems involved common character-

From Kenneth F. Herrold, et al., "Difficulties Encountered in Group Decision-Making," *Personnel and Guidance Journal*, XXXI (May, 1953), 516–523. Reprinted with the permission of publisher and authors.

[1] Studies on Decisions: No. 3, conducted under Contract AF 33 (038) 28792 with the Human Resources Research Institute, Maxwell Air Force Base, by the Institute of Psychological Research, Teachers College, Columbia University, Irving Lorge, Principal Investigator.

[2] See report by Joel Davitz et al., "Individual versus Group Decisions."

istic conditions, factors, and responsibilities which were also similar to those one might encounter in school, college, or civilian community life. One problem, the first, involved the deteriorated morale of airmen stationed at an Air Force Base in the United States. The second, and final test problem, presented essentially the same type of problem but at an Air Force Base in Korea. In both situations the conditions at the Base were unsatisfactory; relations with the local civilians were strained; the superior-subordinate Base relations were encumbered with misunderstandings and poor communications; and there were poor recreational and educational facilities and programs. Important in both situations were the poor housing and living conditions.

PROCEDURE

A statement of the problems was presented to the subjects along with the unique individual information tab or protocol. The individual participant first listed what he considered the most important causal factors on the back of the tab and returned it to the observer assigned to each group. In groups of five the participants then attempted to follow these instructions:

> Briefly state, in order of their importance, the important factors related to the solution of the problems; state a plan of action to solve this problem. Your plan should be complete, that is, it should cover all aspects of the problem. Your plan should be specific, that is, each step or action should be specified concretely; and finally, what is the first step you would take?

Following the group decision-making test each of the participants was asked to evaluate the participation of his group, the quality of his group's decision or problem solution, and to state the degree of confidence in his group's decision or plan. During the group decision-making phase of the test an observer, assigned to each group, made periodic observations of the group's procedures, member participation, and other group process related factors.

The procedural design in the initial and post-tests were identical. First, the individual subject appraised the unique information given to him. Second, with the other members of the decision-making group of five, an attempt was made to arrive at a plan or decision as a group. During this second phase, the behavior of the participants was observed by the non-participating observers assigned to each group. The observations were made according to pre-defined categories to which scores or values had been assigned. Finally, the subject, as an individual, made a personal evaluation of his experience with his group.

The observer records and the participant reactions were analyzed[3] and their implications form the basis of this report. The scores accumulated for each category and for all categories were totaled and analyzed. These data were then compared with the rankings of the groups in terms of the quality of their decisions.

[3] The writers were assisted in the organization and analysis of the data for this report by Jayne Culver, Lydia Hall, Burns Crookston, Betty Worley, Joe Adegbite, William Haug, Isabel Berry, and Jack Metler, graduate students in Group Development at Teachers College.

RESULTS: AS RATED BY OBSERVERS

If it is assumed that the total possible score indicates maximum operational efficiency then the mean scores indicate that in all categories of process observations the mean efficiency score in the first test was approximately 40 per cent of that considered maximal. In the second or final test, after training, they had improved their efficiency by 18 per cent and were thus operating at approximately 60 per cent of that considered maximal. Therefore, all of the group experienced difficulty with the procedural behavior observed. In general, the greatest difficulty was experienced in the first test with the development of a constructive atmosphere which reflected positive attitudes toward one another as members of a group. These were nontraditioned groups and they had not yet developed a sense of belonging to either the class or group. Difficulty was also experienced with the problems (1) of keeping the discussion centered on the problem and the pertinent information, (2) where the group elected a discussion leader there was over-dependence on the leader, and (3) the participants tended to compete with one another rather than to cooperate in making the decision. Of all areas of difficulty the groups seemed to have less difficulty with involvement, interest, verbal participation, the influence of the observer. The observers also seemed to feel that in general the group members progressed toward their own expectations or goals.

After the instruction period and in the final group decision-making test certain changes appeared to be in evidence. First, all of the groups demonstrated a marked increase in the quality of their participation as individuals, they appeared to be less influenced by the observer (who might be considered a critic figure), and, as indicated above, the members were much more cooperative. Apparently the observers felt that the groups were less able to demonstrate marked gain in the skill of moving as a group toward their own perceived goals, they showed only a slight gain in interest and involvement in the task, and again, though somewhat improved, the individuals in the groups were still handicapped by their attitudes toward one another. The groups, in general, seemed to look more to the discussion leader, whom the subjects selected or elected, to keep the discussion goal-centered. Possibly this increased use of the leader or coordinator role was the result of emphasis on the use of the coordinator role in the late phases of the instruction and training. It may also have been due to the fact that the influence of cultural factors and the restriction of the problem and the process in the decision-making test encouraged a form of authoritarianism in which responsibility rested with a leader. It is suggested therefore that training for group decision-making must do more than improve verbal participation. In this test every group presumably had available all of the informational resources necessary to solve the problem. Obviously individual differences in the people who composed the groups did make a difference in the group productivity. Nevertheless, until those involved in decision-making are able to understand and create attitudinal atmospheres that provide for mutual respect, the resources each member possesses will not be brought to bear on the problem. Furthermore. as long as there is any competition between the participants in a decision-making group the resources of the group will not be properly and effectively utilized. These two areas of difficulty require a great deal of internal development which cannot easily be developed by prescribed circumstances and conditions.

RESULTS: AS REPORTED BY SUBJECTS

Again if it is assumed that the total possible score indicates maximum participant satisfaction with the operational efficiency, then the mean scores would indicate a measure of the general satisfaction of the participants with the operation of the members of the group and of themselves. Therefore, examination of the satisfactions of the members of all of the groups as a total population indicates that members were best satisfied with their group's problem-solving skill, ability to communicate, and their group's achievement. They were somewhat less satisfied with their group's capacity to get organized actually to make the group decision, to plan as a group, and to cooperate. They did not feel they were very objective about the task. In other words, they seemed to express the feeling that they could not help but get involved in other aspects of the process and relationships which took priority over solving the problem. It may be pertinent to note here that it was discovered that the best relationship between the quality of the decisions and another factor was established with the scores of participant confidence in the outcome of the group's decision-making.

Examination of the observer data and the subject or participant reaction data shows that certain similarities and differences do exist. The subjects had the most satisfaction with their problem-solving skill, ability to communicate and to achieve, while the observers perceived the most effective skill in participation (verbal ability primarily), progress, and interest or involvement. Next in order the members were somewhat less satisfied with their organizational ability, group planning, cooperation, and confidence in the group product. The observers were also less impressed with the cooperative ability, the leader dependence, and the goal-centered quality of the participation. The members were least satisfied with their capacity to be objective, and the observers felt that the participants were much too influenced by external factors typified specifically by the observer's presence and what he represented.

In the final decision-making test the observer and member reaction data compared as follows: The members were most satisfied, as in the pre-test, with their problem-solving and communication ability. In this second test they were much better satisfied with their ability to cooperate. The observers, on the other hand, were also impressed with the participation ability of the group members, as well as with the goal-centered nature of their work, and with the reduction in the degree of influence of outside factors such as the presence of the observer. Next in order of satisfaction for the members were their organizational ability, planning, objectivity, achievement, and confidence in the group product or decision. The observers seemed to agree with the members' reaction to the improvement in progress [and] interest in the problem, but did not seem to be impressed to the same degree with the groups' ability to cooperate. The observers were even less impressed with the leader-dependence of the groups and with their interpersonal attitudes.

. . . .

It is undoubtedly premature to conclude, but certainly indicated, that the feelings of the members of decision-making groups are apparently as reliable, if not more so, as the perceptions of observers who may not be sufficiently sensitive to the real quality of the group relationship and behavior.

17

Social Engineering in Educational Change: An Outline of Method

David H. Jenkins

. . . In this article we would like to explore one approach toward problems of social engineering and to see how it might apply to the kinds of problems we find in the school setting. Suppose, for example, we feel that there is not enough teacher-pupil planning in the classrooms in our high school, and we want to see a change from the more teacher-centered methods of working with a class to methods using more pupil participation in planning. As a group of interested teachers, how can we begin to tackle a problem such as this?

STEPS IN SOCIAL ENGINEERING

There seem to be four general steps which must be taken if the changes which are desired are to be effected: (1) analyzing the present situation; (2) determining the changes which are required; (3) making the changes indicated by the analysis of the situation; and (4) stabilizing the new situation so that it will be maintained. Let us look at these steps in detail to see what they may imply.

ANALYZING THE PRESENT SITUATION

Before effective plans for change can be made the present state of affairs must be defined as accurately as possible. This is the step familiar to most of us under various names such as "diagnosis" or "definition of the problem."

From David H. Jenkins, "Social Engineering in Educational Change: An Outline of Method," *Progressive Education*, XXVI (May, 1949), 193–197.

The specific question that we might ask about our problem is, "Why don't we change our teaching methods, or *what are the forces which are keeping our methods in their present 'groove'?*" At first glance we often feel that the present condition exists because no one has the energy to make it any different — there is just too much "inertia." Yet, as we explore further it becomes clearer that there may be some very strong forces preventing substantial changes of any kind from occurring, [as well as equal forces pressing toward change].

In our example, there might be several forces which point toward more teacher-pupil planning in the classroom: (a) a generally progressive philosophy of education may be accepted by a large number of teachers; (b) the teachers want to train students in the ways of living as citizens in a democracy; (c) the pupils desire some freedom in making decisions.

But there are also some forces which seem to be opposed to changes in that direction, such as: (a) many teachers lack training and skill in methods of planning cooperatively with pupils; (b) leaving the present methods and experimenting with the "unknown" makes us, like anyone else, feel insecure; (c) criticism may be directed against the school by the more conservative parents; (d) pupils have little skill in planning together. Forces like these which oppose each other determine the present level of methods which are used in the classroom.

DRIVING FORCES AND RESTRAINING FORCES

Forces such as those above seem to be of two kinds. *Driving forces* are those forces or factors affecting a situation which are "pushing" in a particular direction; they tend to initiate a change and keep it going. One's desire to be a more effective teacher is an example of a driving force; one is continually trying to improve regardless of his present skill.

Restraining forces may be likened to walls or barriers. They only prevent or retard movement toward them. . . . Any lack of skill we may have in using teacher-pupil planning methods in the classroom may be termed a restraining force against practicing this method.

As we see later, these two types of forces become particularly important when we attempt to stabilize a new condition to be sure it is continued.

THE FORCE FIELD

A group of forces such as are shown in Figure 1 may be called a "force field." The top of the figure may be designated as teacher-pupil planning method and the bottom of the figure as teacher-centered method. The arrows pointing downward represent the restraining forces which are keeping the methods from including more pupil participation and the driving forces toward more teacher-centered methods. The arrows pointing upward represent the restraining forces which are keeping the methods from becoming more teacher-centered and the driving forces toward more pupil participation. The length of each arrow represents the relative strength of the force at that particular point — the longer the arrow the stronger the force.

Figure 1

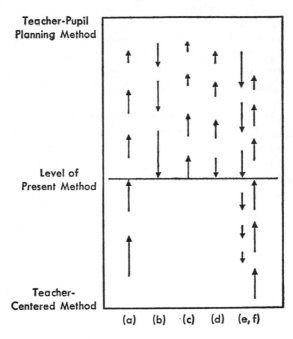

As we see, the force field is made up of several forces of varying strengths which oppose each other. The strength of a particular force may itself vary at different levels (force (a) in Figure 1 is weak at levels near teacher-pupil planning but strong at levels near teacher-centered method). *The present condition (the present level of the method) is at that level where the sum of all the downward forces and the sum of all the upward forces are equal.*[1] It is represented for our example by the line near the center marked "level of present methods." This means that all the forces which are affecting the methods being used in our school are such that our methods are being maintained at a level about half way between teacher-pupil planning and teacher-centered methods — we are probably doing some of each. If we analyze our situation and find that the opposing forces do not seem to be equal we may have overlooked some important factors.

SOME EXAMPLES OF FORCES

Let us look briefly at some examples of the different kinds of forces we might find in our situation:

If the teachers in our group have a generally progressive philosophy of education it might be described by force (a) in Figure 1. This is a driving

[1] This type of analysis of the "equilibrium of change" was developed by the late Kurt Lewin in a pioneering article, "Frontiers in Group Dynamics: Concept, Method, and Reality in Social Science; Social Equilibria and Social Change," *Human Relations*, I (June, 1947), 5–41.

force having some effect throughout all levels of teaching method, but the more teacher-centered the current method (i.e., the lower the level of equilibrium) the greater pressure this force would exert toward increasing the amount of teacher-pupil planning.

If we lack skill in using pupil participation in planning, it might look like force (b). Here is a strong restraining force effective only at levels above our present level.

Force (c) represents our belief that as teachers increase the pupil participation in planning they will gain greater personal satisfactions from their teaching. These satisfactions will stimulate them to increase their use of this method. This force, one which acts as a driving force after some change has occurred, is described by the statement, "If I can only get them started, I know they will like it."

Sometimes we might find that the administration in a school is hesitant to make changes because of the administrative procedures involved. However, once changes are decided upon, they may take a very active part in seeing that they are carried through. The hesitancy to make changes might be represented as a restraining force which reverses its direction when the change is decided upon and becomes a driving force when a change has been initiated. It would look something like force (d).

In our community there would be wide differences of opinion among the parents toward teacher-pupil planning. Some might feel that it was a valuable experience, others might feel that it was time wasted. Forces (e) and (f) together could represent these influences. As more parents come to feel that teacher-pupil planning is valuable, force (e) would be reduced, and force (f) would be increased.

These are some examples of a few of the different kinds of forces we might discover in any particular situation. They may be either driving or restraining forces in either direction, of varying strengths, and effective throughout the entire field or only a portion of the field. All of these characteristics help us do a thorough analysis of the present condition.

PLANNING FOR CHANGE

Carrying through such an analysis as we have started, in terms of a specific situation, supplies the basis for planning change. When we have determined the nature of the forces which are affecting the present state of affairs we can think more clearly in selecting the forces or factors which should be modified if the conditions are to change in the direction we desire. *Changes will occur only as the forces are modified so that the level where the forces are equal is changed.*

As we wish to change our teaching methods in the direction of increased use of teacher-pupil planning, our task then becomes either to increase the total strength of the driving forces in that direction (upward in Figure 1), or to decrease the total strength of forces opposing that direction (downward in Figure 1) or both.

WAYS FORCES CAN BE CHANGED

The component forces can be modified in the following ways: (1) reducing or removing forces; (2) strengthening or adding forces; (3) changing the direction of the forces.

In our example, one important force which almost necessarily requires reduction or removal is lack of skills in ways of using the methods of teacher-pupil planning. As we increase our skill in these methods we will, in effect, be reducing or removing a restraining force like (b) from being effective at the present level.

If we come to feel that these methods are essential if we are to put into effect our philosophy of education, we have probably added a new driving force or strengthened one which was already present.

When it is possible, one of the most efficient ways to get change to occur is to change the direction of some of the forces. For instance, all teachers probably hold a common goal of training students to be good citizens in a democracy. However, there may be differences of opinions about the best way to do it. Many teachers may feel that an "efficient" classroom, directed by the teacher, will make the greatest contribution to good citizenship. For these teachers, the force representing their goal of good citizens would be in the downward direction in Figure 1. If these teachers come to believe, instead, that better citizens are trained through cooperative planning between teachers and pupils, this force toward citizenship training would be reversed in direction, now pointing upward toward teacher-pupil planning. A change in the direction of a driving force has something like a double effect — it acts as a removal of the force in one direction, and an addition of a force in the opposite direction.

SELECTION OF THE FORCES TO BE MODIFIED

After we have analyzed a situation we are still faced with the problems of selecting which forces it will be possible and strategic to modify.

From the analysis, *the first step may be to determine what forces, if any, must be dealt with before a change can occur.* In our example it seems very likely that the restraining force representing lack of skill in actually using pupil participation in planning is one which must be removed before change can occur in that direction. We probably would find this force is of "infinite" strength and could not be overcome by adding strong driving forces. It must be reduced or removed.

When we have become aware of the forces which *must* be modified, we can then determine which of the remaining forces can most efficiently be modified to encourage a change in the level of present procedures.

Are there some forces whose direction can be reversed? How do we look at teacher-pupil planning? Do we see it as a means for training pupils for good citizenship in a democracy? Do we see it as a way to encourage more creative development and ideas? How do the parents look at pupil participation in planning? If they question it as a worthwhile method can their questions be satisfied?

Which opposing forces can be reduced with the least effort? Does the administration encourage alterations in classroom procedures such as might be suggested by this method? Are there opportunities for getting increased experience and skill in using such methods in the classroom? How much of a job would it be to retrain the students to accept planning as a part of their responsibility in the classroom? How can we reduce our own insecurities which seem bound to arise whenever we try to do something in a different way?

Which augmenting or upward forces can be increased? Do all of us feel that one of the legitimate tasks of the classroom is to help the class gain maturity in making decisions for itself? Do we feel, as teachers, that we have freedom to experiment with new methods in the classroom and to participate in decisions with the administration in establishing new procedures?

Questions like these represent the kinds of forces which will need to be considered when we make plans to initiate change in our classroom methods. They are the ones from which the forces to be modified in securing changes will be selected.

We might select, as a first step, for instance, getting parents interested in having more pupil participation in planning in the classroom. As a result there may be no immediate change in classroom methods but, as the parents become interested, we, as teachers, may feel encouraged toward increasing our skill in these methods. With increased skill and increased parent interest two important forces in the situation have been modified and the level of equilibrium of forces (the level of present method) should move upward toward more teacher-pupil planning.

The criteria in selecting forces to be modified, then, are: (1) what forces, if modified, will be most likely to result in changing the level of the present condition in the desired direction, and (2) what forces can be modified most easily or quickly? When we take action on a sound analysis of the forces in the situation we are most likely to move effectively toward the desired results. The ineffectiveness of many of our attempts at change which may be due to the "shotgun" approach is removed.

Modifying the Forces

When we are ready to modify a particular force we may find it necessary, of course, to analyze that particular force in the same manner as has been done for the more general problem. If we wish to train ourselves in the skills of securing pupil participation in planning we may find some specific forces which are directly related to the training program. Some of these might be a general resistance to being in a "training" situation, confusions of philosophy, and time limitations. Analysis of these problems, in turn, becomes the step required.

Clearly this process of analysis in planning change is a continuous one. We are able to make from our first analysis intelligent judgments for taking action. This action leads to the change in the situation, and a change to the new level of equilibrium calls for renewed analysis.

STABILIZING THE NEW CONDITION

Often, when changes in a situation have been achieved we "rest on our oars" and feel that the job has been completed. Later, upon examination, we may be surprised to find that the old situation has gradually returned and the changes need to be made all over again. *Whenever change is planned one must make sure that the new condition will be stable.* We need to develop in our analysis as clear a picture as possible of the forces which will exist when the new condition is achieved.

If we have secured a change by overcoming restraining forces, we can be assured that the new condition will continue. The restraining forces which have been overcome will not "push it back" to the old level. Such is not usually the case, however. More often the change has been made by overcoming some driving forces. In this instance there must be careful planning to make sure that the forces which support the new condition are stable, otherwise there will be a return to the old condition because of the opposing driving forces.

For example, we may become stimulated by a visiting teacher to try out some new methods. After she has left, however, we may run into difficulties, become discouraged, and return to our usual ways. If the change which has been initiated by this visiting teacher is to continue there will need to be some other force ready, when she leaves, to take the place of her stimulation. . . .

The method which we have discussed here is a general method which can be applied to any problem of changing human behavior. It supplies a framework for problem solving. We have used a problem of classroom technique to illustrate our discussion, but the method can be equally well applied to problems of changing the curriculum, changing pupil behavior in the classroom, school-community relations, administrative problems, etc. Clear analysis of any problem is the first step in problem solving.

Section D

PROBLEM SOLVING

Group problem solving has been studied through the use of various methods. Some of these methods have been designed to examine the effects of different kinds of leadership; others, to scrutinize the effects of internal conditions within the group or to determine the optimum size of the group for this purpose; and still others, to compare individual and group results.

One of the chief difficulties in studying groups is that of obtaining "true" groups. Most groups that might be studied have been established for the purpose of the study, and the members lack, among other things, the involvement which is present in spontaneous, developing groups. The results tend to be artificial, perhaps increasingly so in those situations in which "stooges" are used to obtain certain effects. Frequently the tools used for the comparison of groups under various controlled conditions are inadequate for the assessment of incidental learnings and personality changes. The inconsistent results obtained in comparisons of individual and group problem solving may in part be due to the difficulty of accounting for the error variance of intangible and yet significant variations in interest, motivation, and interpersonal relationships.

The methods used in problem solving and the difficulties encountered are discussed in the readings in this section. Harold H. Kelley and John W. Thibout, in "Theoretical Analysis of the Factors Uniquely Affecting Group Solutions," introduces us to the complexity of the process and the factors which influence the outcomes of group problem solving. A description of the factors within the group which improve the quality of learning is discussed by Leland P. Bradford in "Group Forces Affecting Learning."

18

Theoretical Analysis of the Factors Uniquely Affecting Group Solutions

Harold H. Kelley and John W. Thibout

. . . .

The foregoing studies have compared pooled individual solutions (judgments, opinions) with group solutions arrived at by some process of discussion and group decision or vote. It is apparent that the group solutions differ from the pooled individual solutions. In most of the instances reviewed above, this divergence is in the direction of superiority of the group products. It is clear, however, that group solutions are not always superior. Furthermore, as careful analyses of products are made, it seems likely that qualitative discrepancies will appear which are not capable of being described on a simple dimension of "goodness" of solution.

The question now arises as to what accounts for the unique properties of group solutions as compared with pooled individual solutions. There are two logical possibilities, not mutually exclusive, either or both of which can account for this uniqueness. As a result of the group problem-solving situation and the interaction process involved, (1) *the individual solutions available for pooling or combination differ from the individual solutions derived under conditions of independent problem solving,* and/or (2) *the individual solutions are combined or assembled in a manner not reproducible by simple averaging, use of majority vote, or similar methods.*

In the present section we shall speculate a bit about the social processes and psychological phenomena which these two logical possibilities suggest. The subsequent parts of the chapter will be devoted largely to the concrete research evidence bearing upon the factors and relationships which we shall postulate here.

From Harold H. Kelley and John W. Thibout, "Experimental Studies of Group Problem Solving and Process," Chapter 21 in Gardner Lindzey, *Handbook of Social Psychology*, Vol. 2, 1954. Addison-Wesley, Reading, Massachusetts. Pp. 741–747, 782–785. Reprinted with the permission of the publisher.

The Social Modification of Individual Solutions

Here we wish to explore the possibility that the individual products available for incorporation into the group product are modified by the problem-solving situation and process.

Modifications produced by direct social influence. Perhaps the most obvious as well as the most important way in which individual solutions are modified is through the direct social influence exerted in the course of the group discussion. An example of change in individual opinions as a result of discussion is provided by Timmons'[1] investigation, described earlier. As a result of the group discussion of the parole problem, the subjects in the experimental groups were significantly more accurate in their subsequent individual rankings than were the control subjects, who had merely restudied the parole problem. It was also found that the subsequent rankings made by individuals who had participated in the discussion groups correlated fairly highly with the rankings agreed upon by their respective groups (i.e., the rankings constituting the group solutions to the problem). Thus it is clear that not only did individual judgments change, but they changed in the direction of the group consensus. The importance of this phenomenon for understanding group solutions is obvious: If persons change their opinions as a result of interaction, then the individual solutions available for combination into the group solution will differ from what they would have been if there had been no interaction.

As to the process by which such opinion changes are mediated, several generalizations can be made. To begin with, the views held by a given person will be influential only if they are communicated, either by him or by someone else, to others within the group. In other words, shifts of opinion need be analyzed only with respect to those ideas and views which are expressed in some manner. This immediately suggests that an analysis of the influence process must start with an investigation of the factors which act to facilitate or inhibit communication. In the terms used by Festinger,[2] what are the forces to communicate and what are the restraining forces against communication?

Once a person communicates his point of view, his effectiveness in producing covert changes in other persons' opinions depends upon a variety of factors. In the analysis of influence transmitted through mass media, it has been emphasized that for a communication to be successful the recipient must attend to it, comprehend and learn its contents, and accept them. . . . Although the attainment of these stages of influence may present somewhat different practical problems in direct interpersonal influence, they seem to be as essential here as in mass communications.

---

[1] W. M. Timmons, "Decisions and Attitudes as Outcomes of the Discussion of a Social Problem," in *Contrib. Educ.*, No. 777 (New York: Bureau of Publications, Teachers College, Columbia University, 1939).

[2] L. Festinger, "Informal Social Communication," *Psychological Review*, LVII (1950), 271–282.

To simplify the discussion, consider member A communicating his solution or judgment to member B. Since it is essential that B attend to A, influence will be facilitated if B has some tendency to orient himself toward A or if A has abilities, mannerisms, or striking characteristics which elicit attention. Likewise, at the comprehension stage, influence will be facilitated by A's skill at expressing clearly his ideas, and/or by B's verbal and intellectual ability.

Assuming the attention and comprehension requirements are fulfilled, the extremely complex problem of acceptance is encountered. In some instances, acceptance will depend largely upon the intrinsic properties of A's solution and the arguments with which he supports it. For example, the solution may interact with and fit into B's prior cognitive structure so as to produce a new structure more tenable and satisfactory than the old one. The new cognitive structure may take account of more factors, be simpler, or more aesthetic, etc. In other instances, B may be able to test or prove the suggested solution by logical processes. These possibilities suggest that the individual may sometimes change his opinion after simply hearing other opinions, regardless of their source. It has been held that if the person is aware of the great variety of solutions or judgments possible in any given situation, he will be better able to reach a correct judgment.[3] If this is true, the simple fact of making public the opinions held by various members would provide the basis for an improvement in the average quality of their contributions. Relevant to this process would be any factor such as group size or permissiveness which affected the number and range of ideas made public within the group.

When the problem at issue requires opinions and judgments which cannot be validated by logic or by empirical tests, people tend to seek support for their opinions through agreement with their associates. There appear to be at least two general types of relationship between the initiator and the recipient of a suggestion that can function to determine the degree to which the recipient agrees with and accepts the suggestion. In certain instances, the initiator may be viewed instrumentally as a "mediator of fact" by virtue of his perceived expertness, credibility, and trustworthiness. In other instances, the recipient may be motivated to agree with the initiator without regard for his "correctness"; agreement may become an independent motive. The strength of this motive seems to depend partly on the strength of positive attachment to and affection for the initiator. Thus, A can produce a change in B's opinion if he is liked by B or provides the means whereby B satisfies important drives. When the group member has a strong positive attachment to his group and its members, he will tend to conform to the modal opinion expressed in the group. In such instances, the opinion change resulting from discussion may produce a convergence upon the opinion initially held by the majority, as noted by Thorndike.[4] (Majority opinion may also be effective in the absence

[3] J. F. Dashiell, "Experimental Studies of the Influence of Social Situations on the Behavior of Individual Human Adults," in C. Murchison (ed.), *Handbook of Social Psychology* (Worcester, Mass.: Clark University Press, 1935), pp. 1097–1158.

[4] R. L. Thorndike, "The Effect of Discussion Upon the Correctness of Group Decisions, When the Factor of Majority Influence Is Allowed For," *Journal of Social Psychology* IX (1938), 343–362.

of positive feelings for the group. Where no expert opinion is available, the opinion held by most persons may be perceived as the "safest bet.")

Another relationship which may be relevant to the acceptance of the initiator's opinion is that in which the recipient's real or apparent acceptance is motivated by a desire to avoid punishment or unpleasantness in general. A is able to deliver punishment to B even though B has no positive feelings toward him. Thus, a powerless B may be physically or socially constrained to the relationship with a punitive A. In the case of group membership, B may be physically unable to leave the group or may maintain membership merely to avoid dangers that exist outside the group. Festinger[5] proposes the hypothesis that such relationships can produce overt compliance to social influence but do not lead to covert acceptance of it. Other theories and evidence suggest that certain of these situations, where pressure can be exerted on a person to express an opinion different from the one he privately affirms, do tend to produce covert opinion change.[6] However, in the following discussion, we shall consider these conformity-producing pressures primarily from the point of view of the *behavioral* changes they produce.

Finally, no discussion of the factors affecting opinion change would be complete without mention of those determining the degree to which change is resisted. Broadly speaking, resistance stems from the strength of initial opinions; the basis they have in fact, experience, or logic, the person's "anchorage" through loyalty to other groups; and possibly the fact of overt commitment to a given point of view. The amount of change produced in any case may be considered to be a resultant of the strength of influence exerted minus the strength of the resistance to change.

Modifications Produced by the Social Context of Individual Problem Solving. Even in the absence of direct social influence, the group member's problem-solving activity may differ from what it would be if he were working as an independent individual, by himself and for himself. Thus, his motivation and thought processes may be modified by the social context in which he works — by his group membership, the social situation in which the task is presented or decided upon, the presence of others who may be working on the same problem, the eventuality of communicating his product to others, their anticipated social reactions, etc.

Of great importance in determining an individual's effort and concentration on a task is the strength of his motivation to complete it. This can be quite different when working for oneself than when working for a group, depending upon such factors as the degree of identification with the group, the amount

[5] L. Festinger, "An Analysis of Compliant Behavior," in M. Sherif and M. O. Wilson (eds.), *Group Relations at the Crossroads* (New York: Harper & Brothers, 1953), pp. 232–255.

[6] Cf. H. C. Kelman, "Attitude Change as a Function of Response Restriction," *Human Relations*, VI (1953), 185–214; I. L. Janis and B. T. King, "The Influence of Role Playing on Opinion Change," *Journal of Abnormal and Social Psychology*, XLIX (1954), 211–218; and C. I. Hovland, I. L. Janis, and H. H. Kelley, *Communication and Persuasion: Psychological Studies of Opinion Change* (New Haven: Yale University Press, 1953), Chapter 7.

of responsibility felt for the outcome of the problem-solving process, and the kinds of rewards given for successful task completion.

Also of relevance here are the investigations of social facilitation, which we shall discuss more fully in the next section. These indicate that working in the presence of others who have the same task (or even working with the belief that other persons have the same task) produces variations in accuracy, speed, and quality of output.

A related notion is contained in the suggestion by Bos[7] that the very act of formulating an opinion or idea for communication to the group leads to a sharpening and refining of the idea. Thorndike[8] also comments that in a problem-solving group, individuals appear to think about an issue more carefully and more cautiously before announcing an opinion to the group. Of course, the latter suggests the existence of restraints in the communication process, which might seriously modify the assembly of individual solutions. However, Bos and Thorndike appear to agree that even prior to communication the group member's covert opinion undergoes some change toward greater sharpening and clarity.

A series of experiments by Bos[9] may be taken as illustrating the effects of a hypothesized process of sharpening and clarifying, not because her research provides a test of the hypothesis but because she interprets much of her results in these terms. In her first experiment Bos studied sixty-eight children eleven to thirteen years old. One group of subjects worked first individually and then after "some weeks" repeated the same tasks in pairs. A second group began as individuals and was retested individually. The third group began work in pairs and later worked as individuals. The tasks set for the children involved the identification, from sets of reproductions, of paintings done by the same painter. Children working in pairs were encouraged to talk freely. The experimenter observed informally.

In her second experiment, Bos studied forty-three younger children (ages six to nine), this time eliminating from her design the treatment in which pairs preceded individuals. The tasks were to arrange five sets of pictures in such a way that each series conveyed a sensible story. Again paired children were encouraged to interact and the process was observed. In both experiments children in pairs were substantially more accurate than as individuals. Part of this superiority Bos credits to the resistance offered to vague ideas by the demands of communication. She also observes, however, that this process occasionally has a negative effect, as when a person attains a correct insight based on a general intuition which he finds difficult to communicate in a rational, persuasive way.

THE COMBINATION OR WEIGHTING OF INDIVIDUAL SOLUTIONS

The second possible way of accounting for the unique properties of group solutions as compared with individual solutions is that the latter are com-

[7] Maria C. Bos, "Experimental Study of Productive Collaboration," *Acta Psychologica*, III (1937), 315–426.

[8] *Op. cit.*

[9] *Op. cit.*

bined and weighted in a complicated way in arriving at the group product. The focus here is upon the processes of proposal, compliance, concession, compromise, and rejection whereby some sort of group decision is reached. These processes affect the outcome only if the discussion preceding the decision fails to produce covert agreement among the various members as to the most appropriate solution. If the discussion produces complete consensus at the covert level, the decision process usually can have only one outcome, however it proceeds. (An exception to this generalization is the state of "pluralistic ignorance," where the covert consensus so sharply violates some cultural norm that group members will neither express their covert opinions nor even expect one another to hold them.) We shall consider, then, instances where at the time of deciding upon a group solution there are differences among the members with respect to what they privately believe to be the best solution.

To arrive at a group solution, there must be a presentation of alternatives and a process of decision in which one alternative is selected as the group's response to the problem under consideration. Under the conditions specified in most experimental studies, this decision involves the achievement of some sort of agreement which is mediated by the proposal of solutions and formal or informal voting upon them. In this decision, the *overt* proposal and the *overt* vote are crucial. The unexpressed and unsupported covert opinion, no matter how strongly held, is not recorded in the outcome. Furthermore, only if there are discrepancies between overt votes and covert opinions does this aspect of the total problem-solving process contribute to the unique properties of group solutions. If all members vote and if they vote in accordance with their private opinions, the group vote can be determined simply by summarizing their individual private solutions. However, if persons with one opinion support a different one or fail to vote *or* if persons without an opinion take a definite stand, then the group product is not related in any simple way to individual covert opinions. In other words, during the decision process persons who fail to act in accordance with their private opinions (by withholding their vote when they have some opinion, voting when they have none, or voting for an alternative other than the one they privately think best) give extra weight to others' opinions at the expense of their own.

To understand this process of weighting it is necessary to examine factors which make for discrepancies between covert and expressed opinion. Sometimes these discrepancies are to be traced to external social pressures; on other occasions, they are due to self-imposed restraints which we shall refer to as "self-weightings." In particular instances, it may be difficult to locate the cause of a given discrepancy, but in principle it seems desirable to distinguish between externally initiated weighting (direct social pressure) and internally initiated (self) weighting.

Weighting Produced by Direct Social Pressure. One of the obvious situations in which expressed opinions diverge from covert ones is when external social pressures are brought to bear upon behavior. Festinger[10] has

[10] *Op. cit.* (1953).

analyzed the relations between a group and its members which lead on the one hand to covert acceptance of the group's norms and, on the other, to mere overt compliance with them. He suggests that overt compliance without covert acceptance occurs when (a) the member is constrained to membership in a group by physical or social restrictions or by external dangers, but (b) the group does *not* provide positive satisfactions or mediate positive goals for him. Thus, the group or its representative is able to produce behavioral conformity through punishment or threats of punishment, but the recipient has no basis for positive feelings toward the group and no desire to be like its model members.

Members who stand in this relation to a group can be expected on occasion to support solutions or judgments which they do not privately accept. They will support what they believe to be the opinions held by the majority of the members or by the most powerful members, i.e., those who are most influential in setting the group standards and in applying group sanctions. In general, the discrepancies between private opinion and public vote will be maximal in groups where membership results from restraints and external threats and minimal in groups where membership is characterized by positive satisfactions. In the latter groups, a high degree of covert consensus will develop in the course of the discussion and, as noted before, the group decision will be a relatively simple reflection of this consensus. In the former groups, the greater the power differential among members, the greater will be the tendency toward differential weighting of their private opinions in arriving at the group solution.

The process by which compliance occurs need not involve explicit threat or pressure. On the basis of prior experiences of pressure, a person may express opinions he expects more powerful members to hold. But frequently the less powerful member waits for others to express their opinions or follows closely the social reactions to others' contributions and to his own trial balloons.

Social reactions to various proposals — reactions of rejection, approval, or toleration — can play an important role in the success of a problem-solving group. The high quality of group products has been attributed to the "corrective" responses made by the group to various contributions and proposals.[11] In this process the group is reported to reject, modify, and correct at least some of the ill-conceived and erroneous conceptions of its members. Obviously, this process, in part, results in changing the initiator's or other persons' opinions or solutions. At the same time, however, such social reactions may cause a person either to withhold his opinion (without necessarily changing his mind about it) or to publicize it even more strenuously. In either case, the social reactions may modify markedly the weight his individual opinion carries in the final group decision. Whatever the nature of this process, as long as the social response is cued to the contribution and not to the contributor (his status, friendliness, etc.), its result seems to be a reduction of errors in the final group product.

[11] M. E. Shaw, "A Comparison of Individuals and Small Groups in the Rational Solution of Complex Problems," *American Journal of Psychology*, XLIV (1932), 491–504.

Self-Weighting. On certain occasions, a member may voluntarily with-hold his vote or support a position not his own. Gurnee's investigations suggest that this may be due to the degree of confidence a person feels in his private opinion. Consider first his study of maze learning by individuals as compared with groups. At the end of the learning series, the groups per-formed much better than their individual members. Therefore, the superi-ority of the groups cannot be accounted for by improvement in individual solutions as a result of the group problem-solving situation or discussion. Rather, the superiority of the groups seems attributable either to a cancelling out of individual errors or to the voting process. The acclamation method of voting constituted the means by which individuals' ideas were combined into the group decision at each choice point in the maze. This method provides the opportunity for people who are most confident to carry greater weight in the group vote than those who are less confident. In his second study, Gurnee explicitly attributed the superiority of his groups to the process of voting. He observed that correct subjects were apt to respond more quickly and hence carry more weight than the more doubtful subjects. Thorn-dike also found that higher confidence on the part of those subjects initially holding the correct views accounted for part of the discussion-mediated shift toward more correct answers.

These results suggest a *self-weighting* process whereby individuals con-tribute or withhold their suggestions according to the degree of certainty they feel about them. (We may not, of course, always find a positive relationship between confidence and correctness, such as apparently existed in the fore-going studies.) It may be hypothesized that this tendency toward differential self-weighting would be most marked in groups where there is great hetero-geneity among the members in their ability or expertness on the problem at hand.

A variety of other factors may also affect the weight a person gives his private opinion in voting for the group decision. There may be personality predispositions related to self-confidence which lead certain individuals con-sistently to place great or little weight upon their own opinions. The percep-tion that others will be more affected by the decision than himself might be expected to heighten an individual's tendency to permit their opinions to carry the decision. For example, if a particular member has a very great stake in the quality of the decision (e.g., he must act upon it; it determines his future success), other members may defer in their voting to his opinions. Other self-imposed restraints against expressing one's private opinion may arise out of desire to avoid hurting the feelings of a friend who holds an opposite opinion. Similarly, if a high premium is placed on group unity or if schism within the group would place its existence in peril, members may suppress their private feelings and at the behavioral level present a united front.

Finally, it should be noted that the process of voting can be formalized to minimize differential weighting tendencies, whether self-imposed or due to external pressures. Everyone in the group may be required to vote simul-taneously, privately, and anonymously, with all votes being given equal weight in the decision. Even this type of procedure, however, may fail to eliminate all sources of differential self-weighting. "Game" considerations, as described by von Neumann and Morgenstern[12] may frequently lead to distortion of covert preferences, as for example in the common practice of supporters of a minor party who actually vote for a major party candidate rather than "throw away their votes."

SUMMARY

In brief, it appears that a variety of factors may affect the group product and account for its unique character as compared with a simple pooling of individual products. These factors can be analyzed in terms of whether they affect (1) the individual solutions, judgments, opinions, etc., which are available to be combined into the group product, and/or (2) the actual combination or voting process in which individual contributions are "weighted" in some way to determine the final group outcome. With regard to the first, modifications in individual solutions can be traced to (a) the operation of direct social influence or (b) the social context in which the individual works on the problem. With regard to the second, the differential weights given individual solutions are reflected in discrepancies between private opinions and public votes and these discrepancies are attributable to (a) the operation of external social pressures or (b) self-imposed restraints in voting behavior.

Observation of the problem-solving process in natural informal groups reveals that all of the above aspects of the process frequently proceed simultaneously. Often, members are considering the problem for the first time even as the discussion goes forward. The "voting" process usually goes on implicitly during the discussion — persons indicate their position and make it clear how they will vote. After a thorough airing of opinions, a formal vote is often unnecessary. However, this typical collapsing and overlapping of the various aspects of the process does not mean that factors shown to affect the total outcome need remain unanalyzed as to their more specific effects.

To determine which aspects of the total process are affected by any given variable (in this instance, *group size*), we propose the scheme of procedure and data analysis outlined in Figure 1. To study only the relative effects of large and small groups, the first two columns of the scheme would suffice. The investigation begins by obtaining independent judgments or opinions after a period of individual consideration. Assuming that no person has prior familiarity with the problem, the data obtained at 1 and 1' represent the solution attained by individuals while operating as group members and in a specific social context. Differences between 1 and 1' indicate the effect of size upon the social context relevant to individual problem solving. (If he desires, the investigator can estimate the effects of the social context in either a large

[12] J. von Neumann and O. Morgenstern, *Theory of Games and Economic Behavior*, Second Edition (Princeton, N. J.: Princeton University Press, 1947).

Figure 1

PROCEDURE FOR ANALYZING SPECIFIC EFFECTS OF GROUP SIZE
ON GROUP PROBLEM-SOLVING PROCESS

PERSON WORKING AS A GROUP MEMBER		PERSON WORKING AS AN INDIVIDUAL
SMALL GROUPS	LARGE GROUPS	
Independent thought	*Independent thought*	*Independent thought*
1. Initial private opinion	1'. Initial private opinion	I. Initial private opinion
Group discussion	*Group discussion*	*Further independent thought or other interspersed activity*
2. Final private opinion	2'. Final private opinion	
3. Overt vote for group solution	3'. Overt vote for group solution	II. Final private opinion.
Other members' votes } → Group solution	Other members' votes } → Group solution	

or small group as compared with none. For this purpose, he would have some subjects work on the problem alone, as individuals, and compare the data at point I with that at 1 or 1'.)

Following the recording of initial private opinions, the groups are permitted to discuss the problem. At the conclusion of the interaction, the investigator can determine, by appropriate interview techniques, covert individual opinions (2 or 2'). He can also note the manner in which each person votes or openly contributes to the group decision (3 or 3'). A comparison of the opinions at 1 with those at 2 (or 1' vs. 2') indicates the contribution to the group decision of changes in individual opinions resulting from the group discussion. (To isolate the effects definitely attributable to social interaction, it may be necessary to take account of I vs. II, which indicates the changes produced by further individual thought or by some other form of interpolated individual activity.) Finally 2 vs. 3 (or 2' vs. 3') indicates the contribution to the group decision of the voting process with its social pressures and self-imposed restraints on overt behavior. The effects of size on the *discussion* process can be estimated by comparing the changes from 1 to 2 with those occurring from 1' to 2'. Similarly, the effects of size on the *voting* process can be estimated by comparing the difference between 2 and 3 with the difference between 2' and 3'.

In brief, by obtaining covert individual opinions before and after group discussion and by observing the opinion overtly supported in the decision process, it is possible to estimate the contributions to the group solution of the various phases of the process and to investigate how other variables affect these phases.

. . . .

The research summarized above suggests some of the consequences of high member motivation toward achievement of the group's goal. Although not all behavioral aspects of this situation have been described, we obtain a picture of a person who puts considerable effort into the group task, thinks about it until he or a co-worker complete it, works and communicates effectively with his colleagues, and achieves a sense of satisfaction from the group process and progress. From the viewpoint of the group product, these sentiments and behaviors of the member augur well for group output; other things being equal, quantity and quality of output seem to depend on the degree to which members are concerned about the shared goal rather than their more private goals.

Given these outcomes of individual motivation to achieve the group goal (sometimes referred to as "acceptance" of the group goal or "identification" with the group), in what circumstances does this sort of motivation develop? In short, under what conditions does the individual member accept the group goal?

Some of the studies of group decision performed by Lewin's students suggest a general answer to this question, and at the same time they provide additional evidence as to the effects of member acceptance of group goals. Let us now briefly consider the most relevant studies. [Cf. Lewin[13] for a more complete discussion of the group decision investigations. Those studies not summarized here deal mainly with changes in individual opinions and behavior, mediated by specific social situations. They have little or no bearing on the goals of small groups. To enter this general area of individual changes which are produced by various social situations, which includes not only what is conventionally understood as group-decision research but also the literature on individual and group psychotherapy and the research on discussion versus lecture methods in teaching, would take us further from our central focus of group problem solving than space permits.]

Bavelas (reported in Maier,[14] used a group decision method to increase the output of a group of sewing-machine operators. These workers were paid on an individual piecework basis with a standard of sixty units per hour set by a time and motion analysis. A group of the operators held three weekly meetings with the plant psychologist to decide on definite production goals to be attained within a certain time. Presumably as a result of the series of decisions, productivity increased to almost ninety units per hour and stabilized at that level. Meanwhile the total plant production was around fifty-eight units. Two other work groups also had three weekly meetings with the

[13] K. Lewin, "Group Decision and Social Change," in G. E. Swanson, T. M. Newcomb, and E. L. Hartley (eds.), *Readings in Social Psychology*, Second Edition (New York: Henry Holt & Co., 1952), pp. 330–344.

[14] N. R. F. Maier, *Psychology in Industry* (Boston: Houghton Mifflin Company, 1946).

psychologist at about the same time and received attention and friendly encouragement from him but did not make group decisions in regard to a production goal. These groups showed no tendency to increase their production and continued at around fifty-eight units per hour. Furthermore, the groups did not increase their output when simply reassured that such an increase would not lead to a change in piece rates or standards.

Coch and French,[15] also working in a factory setting, studied the effectiveness of different methods of introducing job changes. It was plain before beginning the study that the workers strongly resisted changing jobs and working under new piece rates. However, such changes were frequently necessary because of the demands of the business. This resistance to change seemed to manifest itself in informal group standards to restrict production whenever a new piece rate was introduced with a transfer of jobs. Using groups of workers doing roughly comparable work, the following methods of introducing job changes were used:

(a) Total group participation in planning change: all the workers involved in the change learned the new operation, gave suggestions for eliminating unnecessary work, and served as subjects in the time and motion study.

(b) Representative participation in planning change: several workers, chosen by the group, went through the above steps and then trained their associates in the new method.

(c) Control method: as was customary before the experiment, the change was planned for the workers and they were told about it at a meeting.

The production curves following these procedures were strikingly different. At the time of changeover, the control group exhibited the considerable drop and very slow recovery in output which had been characteristic of prior transfers. Both participation groups showed an initial drop in production but their recovery rates were far faster than that of the control group. In this respect, the total participation method was somewhat superior to the representative method. In addition, in the participation groups fewer workers quit after the transfer and less aggression was expressed towards supervisory personnel and time-study engineers. Very similar results were obtained in a second experiment two and one-half months later when a second transfer was necessary for the original control group and when the total participation procedure was used; the superiority of this method of change was again apparent.

The results both of Bavelas and of Coch and French require at least some mention of group norms, a topic that we shall discuss more fully in a later section. The problem in both cases was essentially one of gaining member acceptance of and adherence to standards of behavior that were beneficial to the total business but were initially resisted by common agreement among the members of work groups. The implication of these studies is that under certain conditions, the new standards are more readily accepted when the individual participates in setting them than when they are introduced by fiat or with exhortations and assurances.

[15] L. Coch and J. R. P. French, Jr., "Overcoming Resistance to Change," *Human Relations*, I (1948), 512–532.

That the same general principle probably applies to producing member acceptance of group goals is indicated by Willerman's early investigation of the group-decision method.[16] In eight college dormitories at meal time, a student proctor read a letter from a university official, the general purpose of which was to increase the consumption of whole-wheat bread in the dormitories. In four of the groups, the letter suggested a group decision and the proctor asked for a discussion of the proposal. If the group agreed to cooperate, he then asked the members to decide how much they would increase their whole-wheat consumption for the following week. In the other four groups, the letter merely requested that the group raise its consumption of whole-wheat bread and suggested a specific goal. The goal specified for a particular "request" group was set at the same level as the amount which had been chosen voluntarily by the particular decision group with which it was paired. Subsequent analysis revealed greater whole-wheat consumption by the decision groups and, in general, the members of the decision groups reacted more favorably to the proposal and rated themselves and their group as more eager to reach the goal. There was, however, one decision group in which a high goal was set by a bare majority of the membership and rejected by the minority, with the result that of all the groups the members of this one were the most discontented with the goal and the least eager to reach it. An important finding was that in the decision groups, eagerness to reach the goal had no relation to the individual's own preference for white as compared with whole-wheat bread. In the request groups, on the other hand, a relation existed between these two variables. This result parallels that of Horwitz, that the group goal can override a person's personal preference on an issue if he subsequently accepts the goal. In general, Willerman shows that members are less motivated to reach group goals set by external figures than goals set through discussion and decision within the group.

In summary, the group-decision studies suggest that member acceptance of group goals is heightened by a goal-setting procedure involving discussion and participation in selecting the goal. Incidentally, Marquis, Guetzkow, and Heyns[17] provide data which suggest that the *possibility* of participation is more important than whether or not the person actually participates. In a series of studies of decision-making conferences, they found that member satisfaction with the meeting and the decisions reached does not correlate with amount of overt participation but is related to whether or not the member feels he has had an opportunity to say what he wanted to during the meeting.

A beginning has hardly been made at exploring the basic factors underlying this relation between participation procedure and goal acceptance, or the exact conditions under which this relation holds. One possibility is that a participation procedure increases the likelihood that a goal will be set which

[16] B. Willerman, "Group Decision and Request as Means of Changing Food Habits" (Washington, D.C.: Committee on Food Habits, National Research Council, April, 1943). (Mimeographed.)

[17] D. G. Marquis, H. Guetzkow, and R. W. Heyns, "A Social Psychological Study of the Decision-Making Conference," in H. Guetzkow (ed.), *Groups, Leadership, and Men* (Pittsburgh: Carnegie Press, 1951), pp. 55–67.

is congruent with individual goals. That this is not the whole story, however, is indicated by the fact that initial preferences are sometimes set aside in favor of the group goal. Another possibility is that because of the discussion involved in setting the goal, members are more likely to have adequate knowledge of the goal and of its value to themselves and to the group, as well as a realistic view of its attainability. A somewhat different explanation would be that a positive evaluation of the goal is derived from hearing that other group members value it. Thus, if the goal is definitely desired by some members and this becomes apparent through the discussion, their associates may either change their judgments of the goal or work toward it simply as a means of helping their friends. On the other hand, when the goal is imposed from without or by group leaders, hesitance or apathy may be attributable to the fact that no member gets a chance to communicate his preference for it. Over and above any tendency to resist being told what to do, which is probably quite general, there may well be a hesitancy to change in any way that might be felt to violate the expectations of one's associates. These suggested explanations for the effectiveness of group decision do not begin to exhaust the possibilities. Determining the specific mechanisms underlying this phenomenon is an important research problem for the future.

. . . .

19

Group Forces Affecting Learning

Leland P. Bradford

Forces affecting group behavior are many and dynamic. Group morale and efficiency are easily disturbed. Relationships shift in the group. Understanding of the major forces present in most groups and diagnostic sensitivity to their interplay is necessary if group forces are to increase individual learning. Of the many group forces which may affect learning, a few are singled out for elaboration.

1. *Group Cohesiveness.* The desirability of the group largely determines the degree of influence it has upon the individual member. If the group is

From Leland P. Bradford, "Group Forces Affecting Learning," *Journal of the National Association of Women Deans and Counselors,* XXXIII (April, 1960), 116–120. Reprinted with the permission of the publisher.

prevented from consciously forming as a group; if individual relations are set between teacher and pupil and not among pupils; and if no group goal or product is possible, forces of group belongingness and pride leading toward cohesiveness are inhibited. If present, they have arisen because the group coalesced in a resistance to teacher and learning activities, and in this case group cohesive forces serve to inhibit learning.

Sometimes teachers, seeking to develop group cohesive forces, inject group tasks periodically and sporadically, frequently of an extracurricular nature. This may develop a temporary group cohesiveness, depending upon whether the task is competitive or cooperative, upon the group climate, and upon the interrelationships among members and with the teacher. It will not, however, bring the steady group strength which will ultimately result if the group is encouraged to deal with its own basic group problems. Working with others on the serious and personal task of improving one's own learning will make for greater group cohesiveness and will increase the influence potential of group on member.

2. *Standard Setting.* All groups set standards affecting the behavior of their members. Too frequently, standards about learning are set from community, gang, or playground forces, or from the anxiety and withdrawal of certain students. A few students having power and prestige with other students can very rapidly develop class standards of mediocre production. Efforts of the teacher to set standards for the group and support them with extrinsic reward and punishment systems are only partially successful and at best result in the continued clash between teacher standards and class standards.

Group standards can and should cover a variety of class situations. For example, standards may be set regarding expected levels of production, differentiation in contributions and learning production, mutual concern for the difficulties of all, role differentiations among teacher and students (what should the teacher do to give most help to the class and where are the boundaries of her power), degree of concern for class procedures, appropriate time to inject personal problems into sessions dealing with group problems, ways of showing caring and helping behavior to others, freedom to disagree with the teacher, extent to which information and experimental evidence is sought in problem-solving.

3. *Group Climate.* A group climate which reduces individual defensiveness and anxiety about exposure of one's inadequacy and gives acceptance and emotional support to all students will do a great deal to prevent or repair feelings of rejection, of inadequate self-image, of failure. Such a climate is paramount in creating readiness for learning, and in being able to face and solve difficulties inhibiting individual and group growth and development.

4. *Involvement and Participation.* Research and experience indicate the much larger degree of learning, and of retention and utilization of learning, that occur when the individual is involved and participates in the activity in which learning takes place. This is obvious and well-known. What is not so

well-known, at least in regard to general classroom practice, is that such involvement and participation are necessary in all parts of the learning process.

Generally teachers attempt to involve students in participation in classroom activities set by the teacher. This, at best, is still only *partial* involvement. The student is being prevented from fuller involvement in and responsibility for his learning. If he, with his peers, could be invited to supply data from their own feelings and learning experiences concerning the effectiveness of the procedures and activities, could jointly test the accuracy of their perceptions, could diagnostically explore individual emotional problems affecting learning, and could join in experimenting with different procedures for learning, involvement would be much deeper.

Such involvement of the class group would, in addition, serve the teacher as a good diagnostic instrument to determine motivational, perceptual, and actual difficulties in learning and would thus enable him to encourage group help to student members.

5. *Effective Group and Interpersonal Relationships.* The teaching–learning process is generally a transaction among people. The transactional relationships lie between teacher and individual learner and among learners. These relationships are delicate and subject to drastic change. The process of learning, if it is at all central to the individual, can rapidly mobilize defensive reactions.

Increasingly the importance of the meaning, value, and strength of relations between and among individuals is seen as crucial in fields of therapy, industrial production, even brain washing, as it is erroneously named. Equally the quality of the intra-group relations have meaning for all in the group. If there are strong sub-groups that continue to operate within the class or if there is such partiality in relationships that uncertainty of position and acceptance is created for others, learning will be inhibited for some.

6. *Increased Member Participation.* Two of the difficulties facing any group are freeing members to participate, and integrating and regulating their participation. One initial block to participation in most groups is the concept that all participation should be similar in function. Only as groups explore the many different member functions which need to be performed for effective group operation is the myth of similar and equal participation buried. As a wider range of necessary participation is recognized (group maintenance functions of encouraging, harmonizing, bridging, gate-keeping for others, etc., as compared with the customary task functions of supplying ideas, opinions, and facts), wider student participation in class activities can be secured.[1] Successful participation, in time, may free some anxious students from inhibiting learning.

7. *Solving Emotional Problems.* Individual problems of anxiety and uncertainty loom larger when hidden. As the class group works on its problems of individual learning and brings to the surface individual fears and uncer-

---

[1] K. Benne and P. Sheats, "Functional Roles of Group Members," *The Journal of Social Issues,* IV, No. 2 (Spring 1948).

tainties, then support, reassurance, and assistance can aid each student in increasing his learning. As such emotional problems blocking learning are brought out in the group, other students feel freer to talk about their problems. Many students in such an atmosphere find their anxieties reduced and come to solve many of their own problems without recourse to group concern.

8. *Motivation for Learning.* Teachers frequently have failed to utilize some of the most important motivations for learning possible to them. Motivation for learning doesn't lie only in the subject-matter value, classroom procedures, extrinsic reward and punishment systems within the classroom system, or external pressures from family and community.

Opportunities for acceptance rather than rejection by peers, for belonging to a desirable group, for participation in joint membership ventures, for occasional leadership, provide powerful motivation for learning the subject-matter of the class.

In a fourth-grade class the children faced a class problem. They asked the teacher's help. She said she was occupied during the lunch period and suggested that after lunch they return and work out the problem themselves.

During the luncheon period she returned and looked through the window in the door. The children had formed two groups to work on the problem more effectively. Most of the stronger leaders in the class were clustered in one group. Typically, rather than face the struggle as to which of them would emerge as leader, they chose one of the more timid members of their group as leader and supported him in his leadership efforts. Their group was the most successful of the two in working on the problem. The timid member emerged with a flushed and happy face.

The next day he confided to the teacher that he couldn't get to school early enough that day and that he had never known a time when he liked school so much.

These group forces enhancing learning will be realized only as attention is given to group building and maintenance as well as to subject-matter teaching. Fundamentally, the first serves the second as well as widens the areas of learning.

Given the educational purpose of helping children and youth learn and grow, a basic mechanism for learning needs to be developed which most effectively releases the student from his anxieties and inhibition concerning learning, encourages him to enter fully into the learning situation, supports him during the process of learning, and facilitates the utilization of systematic subject knowledge and experimental evidence.

Such a mechanism is the learning group, in which the efforts of all involved, both teacher and students, are directed toward eliminating blocks to learning. Just as other fields have found that attention to the development of effective groups increases productivity in that field, so can this be true of learning.

If the teacher succeeds in developing a class group, he has gained twenty to thirty partners, rather than an equal number of potential antagonists.

Group Building and Maintenance

If group forces are to be generated or released to serve educational purposes, then an effectively functioning group must be developed and maintained. Group development is not easy. Effective groups do not grow without guidance. Natural groups all too frequently serve the ends of a few, are destructive of others, and spend a large proportion of energy in malfunctioning behavior.

Group members need to be involved in group building and maintenance activities. With this point in mind, some of the major requirements for cooperative group building and maintenance can be listed:

1. Shared decision-making about group goals and behavior whenever possible.
2. Shared diagnosis of group difficulties and shared analysis of group successes.
3. Shared analysis of required teacher and student roles and functions.
4. Acceptance of all individuals as members of the group.
5. An accepted standard of working on individual and group problems holding up the group task of developing a learning group.
6. An accepted standard of willingness to be experimental in procedures clarifying or changing goals and modifying group behavior.
7. Efforts to utilize member resources.

Requirements for the Teacher

Learner-centered and group-centered educational leadership calls for additional and different requirements than traditionally expected. However, when successful in developing a learning group, the roles required for teaching–leading–involving are more satisfying and successful than is normally true.

What, then, are the requirements for the teacher?

He must be sincerely committed to the concept of a class group and convinced that group forces can increase individual learning. He must have diagnostic sensitivity to the emotional factors present in the group, as well as to the consequences of behavior on both task and building levels. He must be able to hear the music as well as the words in group behavior.

He must be able to help develop a structure within the class group by which learning goals can be established and accepted, learning tasks can be accomplished, learning difficulties in individual or group analyzed.

He can then be able to relinquish carefully and deliberately to the group much of his traditional control. This, perhaps, is one of the most difficult barriers to overcome. If he has sought gratification through maintaining a central, controlling, dominating, distant teacher role, he may too easily seek evidence that the class cannot take responsibility for improving learning climate and approaches, and quickly take back the control he has relinquished.

He needs to be able to recognize the even greater gratification of class success even though the credit is spread throughout the class.

It needs to be clearly seen that there is nothing soft in working with a group. The path to group development and continued group maintenance can be studded with difficulties. The generation and release of human forces through involvement and participation do not result in easy agreements or an even flow of action. Yet the results in increased learning and growth usually far exceed any difficulties encountered.

At the same time that he must relinquish some controls, he needs to be clear as to which controls to maintain for a while and what his various functions should be.

He needs to be able to mix the roles of class builder with subject-matter teacher. To do this, he needs to be comfortable as a group member. For the process of group formation to be successful, he must assume a member role, although a special one.

Perhaps the most difficult problem for the teacher is to be willing to accept spoken, and not covert, criticism for past behavior and suggestions for future action. If the teacher has strong personal needs to control other people and to maintain distance from them, he will have difficulty in group formation. On the other hand, if interest in professional development and improving himself as a person is paramount to him, he will find the experience of special membership in the class group a rewarding one.

Finally, he needs to be in sufficient control of his own need systems that his needs to punish, to control, or to secure love do not obtrude on the class.

· · · ·

Section E

GROUP COUNSELING

Group counseling is only slowly gaining recognition as a method having therapeutic usefulness. Some have limited its usefulness by treating it only as a method for giving information and for planning. Others have hopefully and erroneously considered it as a means of replacing or substantially decreasing the need for individual counseling or have been unable or unwilling to differentiate its purpose and method from group psychotherapy conducted by psychiatrists or psychoanalysts. Some have rejected it as a possibility for use in schools. Others have openly accepted it but have equated it with group guidance.

Preoccupation with the problem of whether or not group counseling should be considered counseling appears to have interfered with the evaluation of its usefulness. Coffey's consideration of group counseling as psyche-process concerned with planning, giving information, and problem solving might redirect our thinking in more useful directions.

The readings in this section discuss the meaning, describe the process, and evaluate the outcomes of group counseling. "Multiple Counseling: Why? When? How?," by E. Wayne Wright, compares group counseling with individual counseling and describes the function of the leader and the outcomes which can be expected. "Counseling Within a Group Setting," by Merle M. Ohlsen, defines the process and then reports a study based upon the definition provided, concluding with a clear statement of the changes which took place in individuals. "Group-Centered Counseling," by Nicholas Hobbs, illustrates the functioning of the counselor.

20

Multiple Counseling: Why? When? How?

E. Wayne Wright

. . . .

One issue that has persisted throughout the transition in counseling theory is inherent in the concept still held by many that counseling, by definition, is, and must be, a one-to-one relationship. It is with this concept of counseling that the present paper takes issue as the writer discusses a process of "multiple counseling" and attempts to show some of the benefits to be derived from counseling with groups.

It goes almost without saying at this point that those who ascribe to the one-to-one concept of counseling have difficulty accepting the idea of group counseling because of the obvious inconsistency in using the term *group* with the *individual* connotation of counseling as defined. These unbelievers in group counseling circumvent the problem of semantics by referring to counselor–individual relationships as "counseling" and to counselor–group relationships as "group guidance," "study groups," "group procedure in counseling," or the like. A problem with defining counseling this way is that such a definition becomes meaningless when one considers the variety of situations in which a counselor may have "individual" contacts that are not counseling and "group" contacts that are not group guidance. On the other hand, if a counselor is able to establish an effective counseling relationship and achieve some of the goals of counseling even when working with several counselees simultaneously, is he not actually counseling? Many would concede that he is doing more than just group guidance, broadly conceived. It would seem that modifiers such as "individual" and "group" could be reserved to designate conditions under which counseling takes place and not be used to define the term itself.

MULTIPLE COUNSELING — WHAT IS IT?

In recent years, the concept that counseling must be a one-to-one relationship has been challenged. One who has led in this respect is Froehlich,[1] who

From E. Wayne Wright, "Multiple Counseling: Why? When? How?," *Personnel and Guidance Journal*, XXXVII (April, 1959), 551–557. Reprinted with the permission of publisher and author.

[1] Clifford P. Froehlich, "Multiple Counseling: A Research Proposal" (Unpublished manuscript, University of California, Berkeley).

asserts that as long as the process has the same objectives of individual counseling and attempts to achieve these objectives it can be called counseling.

The objectives of counseling, whether individual or group, Froehlich sees as being essentially to assist the individual in the following: (1) evaluation of himself, or gaining knowledge necessary for wise choices — *i.e., learning;* (2) decision-making and self-direction — or *growth* in the ability to make decisions and be responsible; and (3) carrying through of learning to action — *i.e., changed behavior.* With these objectives for counseling in mind, Froehlich originated the term "multiple counseling"[2] to describe a situation in which the counselor counsels with more than one individual at a time, but each on a coordinate basis. In other words, multiple counseling, thus conceived, is concerned with helping each counselee make individual decisions within a group situation.

The term "multiple counseling" fulfills several needs for counselors who believe that effective counseling can and does take place in group settings. (1) It provides for a broader concept of the conditions under which counseling principles are operative. (2) It avoids, to some degree, the semantics problem felt by those who cannot accept the term "group counseling." (3) It makes for a clearer distinction of the multiple counseling process from the already-confusing terms "group guidance," "group procedures in counseling," "group therapy," etc.

While the process of multiple counseling as described by Caplan[3] "differs somewhat from teaching and group guidance (with their emphasis on the imparting of facts) and from group psychotherapy (with its emphasis on treatment), the multiple counselor may at times 'teach' (impart facts), and he may at times aid the individual to understand and objectify his emotions (do therapy)."

The unique characteristics of multiple counseling as expressed by Froehlich[4] and reported by Bennett[5] are summarized as follows:

1. *All members of the group have a common problem.* The common element may be the need for making an occupational choice; it may be that all are low scholarship students; all may have an interest in the results of tests they have taken; they may all be having difficulty resolving the same personal problem; or some other common element may exist which helps them identify with the group. This common element for the group does not mean homogeneity in the strictest sense. Instead the common element may exist more in terms of a situational problem than as a psychological dynamic. For example, the common problem may be that all members of the group are on academic probation. However, one student may be failing because of low ability, another may lack interest or motivation for school, while a third may be failing deliberately as a means of expressing hostility toward his parents.

---

[2] *Ibid.*

[3] Stanley William Caplan, "The Effect of Group Counseling on Junior High School Boys' Concepts of Themselves in School," *Journal of Counseling Psychology,* IV (1957), 5.

[4] *Op. cit.*

[5] Margaret E. Bennett, *Guidance in Groups* (New York: McGraw-Hill Book Co., Inc., 1955).

2. *All of the members identify with this common element which has real meaning for them.* The effectiveness of the counseling function is dependent upon the ability of each individual to identify with and participate in the thinking of the group. His ability to do so depends upon the importance of the common element to him.

3. *The counselor functions as the leader of the group but does so from within the group.* In this role, the counselor at times serves "as a resource person, providing needed information," at other times as a "stimulator of discussion," and sometimes as merely a "listener."[6] The skillful counselor will attempt as much as possible to keep the locus of responsibility for the discussion centered within the group members. At the same time, however, he must be alert to the dynamics of the group and be ready to counteract or redirect undesirable elements without destroying the permissiveness of the situation. He is also trying to identify those who might profit from additional help through individual counseling.

4. *A permissive atmosphere favors free expression.* This characteristic is an axiom for any kind of counseling. For effective interaction, the relationship among all of the group members must be permissive, free, and safe.

5. *Interactions and mutual help among members is essential, and members have the opportunity to evaluate pressures created by the group situation.* After the counselor has been able to establish rapport and structure the permissiveness of the situation, he can point out the common element that he feels exists in the group and give each individual an opportunity to identify with the common element. This can be done by letting each individual express his own reactions about the problem or his suggestions for handling it. By this sort of interaction, group members help each other to express feelings and to gain insights concerning the problem as it affects each individual. In a sense, the group members serve as "multiple counselors" for each other in that they assist each other in expression of emotions, they interpret meanings, they exert some influence on behavior, etc.

6. Finally, if the multiple counseling is effective, *the participants are stimulated by group standards to accomplish the goals of counseling suggested earlier, i.e., evaluation of self and opportunities, making wise choices, accepting responsibility, and initiating courses of action.*

Why Use Multiple Counseling?

Some of the benefits of multiple counseling which are not obtained by the exclusive use of the traditionally accepted individual approach to counseling have their basis in principles of group dynamics. Therefore, the use of multiple counseling can be supported in terms of previous research with similar group processes. A review of the literature dealing with theories of group dynamics and with the recent widespread growth of group work follows.

In discussing the influence of interpersonal relations on everyday psychological processes, Katz and Lazarsfeld[7] give persuasive evidence to support

---

[6] Froehlich, *op. cit.*

[7] Elihu Katz and Paul F. Lazarsfeld, *Personal Influence* (Glencoe, Ill.: The Free Press, 1955).

the thesis that groups influence individual opinions, attitudes, and actions. Theory and research reported by these writers indicate the following as social factors which influence individuals' opinions and actions: (1) benefits which befall the individual who conforms to group norms. These benefits are experienced in terms of satisfaction which comes with acceptance by the group and achievement of desired status; (2) the individual's dependence on others about him for the definition of "social reality." "What exists as 'reality' for the individual is to a high degree determined by what is socially accepted as reality"; (3) interaction among individuals operates to produce shared standards of judgment, opinions, and ways of behaving. Friendship groups adopt shared ways of thinking, and private opinions and attitudes are developed through association with others of similar opinions and attitudes; and (4) groups of people demand conformity of individual members to maintain the status of the group. Katz and Lazarsfeld conclude that (1) individuals in primary group interaction develop norms governing their interactions, (2) even an individual's personal opinions and attitudes may be by-products of interpersonal relations, and (3) any attempts to change an individual's opinion or attitude will fail if his opinion is one which he shares with others to whom he is attached and if the others do not concur in the change. Katz and Lazarsfeld, therefore, suggest *group change* as the "target" for initiating individual attitude and behavior changes.

Growth of Group Work.   Recent years have seen a considerable increase of research in the field of group dynamics. Crutchfield[8] feels that this evidenced growth in group research demonstrates quite convincingly "how crucial psychological variables can be dealt with experimentally in genuine group settings." According to Crutchfield, the size of the group can be reduced to as few as three members without loss of effective group pressure.

With the growth of group dynamics research has come an increased acceptance and use of group approaches in many psychological and guidance processes. This diversified application of group procedures is evidenced by studies reporting the use of groups in the treatment of psychotics,[9] as a training device for doctors, nurses, and patients in a private clinic,[10] as seminars with executives in business,[11] in industry,[12] in counseling with families in a casework agency,[13] in penal institutions,[14] with alcoholics,[15] for marriage

[8] Richard S. Crutchfield, "Social Psychology and Group Processes," *Annual Review of Psychology*, V (1954), 171, 182.

[9] Burman H. Preston, "The Class Method in the Treatment of Psychotic Patients," *International Journal of Group Psychotherapy*, IV (1954), 321–330.

[10] John D. Patton, "The Group as a Training Device and Treatment Method in a Private Psychiatric Hospital," *International Journal of Group Psychotherapy*, IV (1954), 419–428.

[11] Henry P. Laughlin, "A Group Approach to Management Improvement," *International Journal of Group Psychotherapy*, IV (1954), 165–171.

[12] Milton L. Blum, "Group Dynamics in Industry," *International Journal of Group Psychotherapy*, IV (1954), 172–176.

[13] Hanna Grunwald, "Group Counseling in a Case Work Agency," *International Journal of Group Psychotherapy*, IV (1954), 183–192.

[14] Lloyd W. McCorkle, "Guided Group Interaction in a Correctional Setting," *International Journal of Group Psychotherapy*, IV (1954), 199–203.

[15] Arthur Lerner, "Self Evaluation in Group Counseling with Male Alcoholic Inmates," *International Journal of Group Psychotherapy*, V (1955), 286–298.

counseling,[16] as a preventive approach in promoting mental hygiene,[17] as orientation for counseling,[18] in education,[19] and for multiple counseling.[20] In addition, a review of group psychotherapy bibliographies by Locke[21] shows the use of therapy in many new areas.

A number of writers[22] have concluded that counseling and psychotherapy have much in common relative to their process and goals. As stated by Wrenn,[23] "the differences between counseling and psychotherapy appear to be differences in *degree*, not in kind, as existing on a continuum rather than being of a dichotomous nature." Therefore, in light of the growth of group therapy and the status *that* process has achieved, it follows that if one accepts a similarity of process and goals between counseling and therapy, he lends support to the process of multiple counseling.

It is recognized that the group approach to counseling is not without limitations. However, in the opinion of this writer, the limitations of the multiple process do not obviate the values that can obtain from *judicious* use of this process. Some of the limitations in multiple counseling consist of: (1) the inability of some students to relate to the common element or problem, thus never really feeling a part of the group; (2) the need that some individuals have to identify more directly and more closely with one person (presumably the counselor) before being able to relate to or interact comfortably with a *group* of persons; (3) the probability that there is less warmth or closeness of relationship between the counselor and individual group members; and (4) a danger that the relative safety or anonymity of the group, and the expressions of other group members, may lead some individuals to experience catharsis or disturbing insights too much or too rapidly to be adequately dealt with during that particular session. In the latter instance, it is possible that the counselor may not even recognize the individuals in the group who may be experiencing this kind of upset.

On the other hand, the *values* of multiple counseling that do not seem to be experienced in individual counseling can be restated in terms of (1) the life-like setting for making decisions and choices, thus helping individuals

[16] Evelyn R. Gaskill and Emily Hartshorne Mudd, "A Decade of Group Counseling," *Social Casework*, XXXI (1950), 194–201.

[17] Marvin A. Klems and Vern J. Kallejian, "The Group Psychotherapist in Industry: A Preventive Approach," *International Journal of Group Psychotherapy*, V (1955), 91–98.

[18] Everett L. Shostrom and Lawrence M. Brammer, *The Dynamics of the Counseling Process* (New York: McGraw-Hill Book Co., Inc., 1952).

[19] Kenneth F. Herrold, "Applications of Group Principles to Education," *International Journal of Group Psychotherapy*, IV (1954), 177–182.

[20] Froehlich, *op. cit.*

[21] Norman Locke, "Trends in the Literature on Group Psychotherapy," *International Journal of Group Psychotherapy*, V (1955), 181–184.

[22] Edward S. Bordin, *Psychological Counseling* (New York: Appleton-Century-Crofts, Inc., 1955); John W. Gustad, "The Definition of Counseling," in R. F. Berdie, *Roles and Relationships in Counseling*, Minnesota Studies in Student Personnel Work No. 3 (Minneapolis: University of Minnesota Press, 1953); Carl R. Rogers, *Client-Centered Therapy* (Boston: Houghton Mifflin Company, 1951); and Donald E. Super, "Transition: From Vocational Guidance to Counseling Psychology," *Journal of Counseling Psychology*, II (1955), 3–9.

[23] C. Gilbert Wrenn, "Counseling Theory," in Chester Harris (ed.), *Encyclopedia of Educational Research*, Third Edition (New York: The Macmillan Company, 1960).

to discover new ways of relating to others, (2) the influences of peers through group interaction and group norms, (3) the opportunity for free expression of opinions and emotions with less personal reference, and (4) the opportunity to give and receive support as a group member. Other advantages of the multiple process from the viewpoint of the counselor's needs include the following: (1) it permits the counselor to meet more students with common problems and to disseminate information of general interest or value in solving these problems; (2) it provides opportunity to identify students who need individual help while also making more time available to see individuals with specific problems; and (3) it advertises the availability of the counseling services, stimulates demand for individual counseling, and prepares students for individual counseling.

Research with Multiple Counseling. Since the tenability of any premise must be determined by empirical evidence, it is appropriate at this point to review the research studies which have investigated the effectiveness of multiple counseling.

Driver[24] used small discussion groups to test the usefulness of such groups in aiding so-called students to gain self-understanding, understanding of others, and interpersonal skills. The study involved eight separate experimental groups, each consisting of eight to ten persons, with each group holding six sessions over a period of three weeks. Several months after the conclusion of the study, retention and carryover of learning were measured by follow-up questionnaires. The returns indicated that the students learned new facts, appreciations, and/or skill in interpersonal relations. Driver concluded that "small group discussions carried on in a permissive atmosphere are an excellent learning medium for personality growth of high school, college, and adult students."

Froehlich[25] and Bailey[26] working independently with different high school populations, but both using the same criterion of improvement in accuracy of self-knowledge, found no difference in the effectiveness of individual and multiple counseling. In both of these studies, self-knowledge was measured by agreement between self-ratings and test scores before and after counseling.

Caplan[27] tested multiple counseling in terms of its effectiveness in changing the self-concepts and improving the school achievement of a group of high school "problem" boys. Significant differences between the experimental and control groups at the conclusion of the study were in favor of the multiple-counseled. Caplan concluded that multiple counseling is a useful technique for school counselors.

[24] Helen I. Driver, *Multiple Counseling: A Small Group Discussion Method for Personal Growth* (Madison, Wisconsin: Monona Publications, 1954); and "Small Group Discussion," *Personnel and Guidance Journal*, XXX (1952), 173–175.

[25] Clifford P. Froehlich, "Must Counseling Be Individual?" (Unpublished monograph, University of California, Berkeley. In press for *Educational and Psychological Measurement*.)

[26] Bruce Bailey, "A Comparison of Multiple and Individual Counseling in Terms of Self-knowledge" (Unpublished manuscript, University of California, 1955).

[27] *Op. cit.*

In the writer's doctoral dissertation,[28] the relative effectiveness of individual and multiple counseling for disseminating and interpreting test data to students was compared. Both counseled groups were also compared with a non-counseled control group. Comparisons were made in terms of pre- and post-counseling measures on four criteria: accuracy of self-concept, acquisition of information about tests, feasibility of vocational choice, and counselee satisfaction. The results showed that both counseled groups made significant gains on post-counseling criteria measures over pre-counseling measures, and that these gains, through counseling, represented a significant improvement over the non-counseled group. However, no differences of any significance were found between the individual-counseled and the multiple-counseled groups.

Although relatively few in number, the findings of the foregoing studies give credence to the belief that multiple counseling holds promise as an efficient and effective counseling technique.

WHEN TO USE MULTIPLE COUNSELING?

When should multiple counseling be used? Generally speaking, multiple counseling seems indicated whenever one wants to achieve the unique advantages of the group setting suggested earlier, or when the objectives of individual counseling can be achieved more efficiently and/or more effectively by the group process than by individual counseling alone. Greater efficiency in counseling might connote either a conservation of time and effort in seeing the same number of students or in being able to provide counseling for more students in the same period. Efficiency in this sense, of course, assumes that the quality of the counseling does not diminish. The effectiveness of the counseling will be measured largely in terms of the degree to which one is able to achieve the counseling goals he has considered important.

The few research data already mentioned support the value of multiple counseling for achieving most or all of the generally accepted goals of individual counseling. Indications have also been presented that multiple counseling can often be more efficient than individual counseling and at least comparable in effectiveness. It is suggested, therefore, that the use of multiple counseling be considered whenever staff skills and physical facilities permit and when a common problem among groups of students is identifiable. In each case, however, the particular purposes for counseling and the amount of opportunity to evaluate the process employed and the outcomes achieved should ultimately determine the advisability of the procedure selected.

HOW TO DO MULTIPLE COUNSELING?

This is probably the most difficult aspect of the present paper to treat briefly. The problem in trying to present specifics about methods in counsel-

---

[28] E. Wayne Wright, "A Comparison of Individual and Multiple Counseling in the Dissemination and Interpretation of Test Data" (Unpublished doctoral dissertation, Universiity of California, 1957).

ing is that those techniques which are successful for one way may not be successful at all for another. It is therefore unwise for any counselor merely to accept at face value techniques suggested by someone else and to attempt to counsel by employing such techniques if the procedures suggested are not really genuine or comfortable for him. The experience that each counselor has with different techniques will indicate the procedures that are best for him. However, this need not prevent a brief consideration at this point of the skills necessary for effective multiple counseling.

Many may concur with the point of view that multiple counseling utilizes to some extent the same principles applicable in individual counseling. Similarities between individual counseling and counseling with groups have been shown to exist not only in similar objectives, but also in skills and techniques.[29] Therefore, the counselor contemplating the use of multiple counseling should first identify those procedures which he has found successful in dealing with individuals and then utilize these procedures in a manner appropriate to the demands of each particular group setting.

But the mere application of individual procedures is not enough if multiple counseling is to be most effective. The counselor who would work with groups must not only be cognizant of the uniqueness of the multiple counseling situation, but he must also be skilled in principles of good leadership and be able to guide interactions on the basis of a solid understanding of group dynamics. In brief, acting as a leader from within the group, the counselor must provide a warm, permissive atmosphere in which interpersonal relationships and group interaction may develop by each individual identifying with, and contributing to, a discussion of a problem which has relevance for him and some measure of commonality to the group as a whole.

A Need for Multiple Counseling

A last word in favor of continued research with multiple counseling can be stated in terms of a growing concern among school personnel. Since currently increasing enrollments at most educational institutions are already placing considerable stress on counselors' time, and since predicted expansions see the situation as becoming even more critical, it seems desirable to look ahead to the ultimate value of group procedures in counseling. Research to date supports a belief in the potential of multiple counseling. Continued evaluation of this process in various settings may well indicate a need to reorient thinking relative to the practice of complete reliance on individual counseling.

[29] Bennett, *op. cit.*; Gaskill and Mudd, *op. cit.*; S. R. Slavson, "A Contribution to a Systematic Theory of Group Psychotherapy," *International Journal of Group Psychotherapy*, IV (1954), 3–30; and Donald E. Super, "Group Techniques in the Guidance Program," *Educational and Psychological Measurement*, IX (1949), 495–510.

21

Counseling Within a Group Setting

Merle M. Ohlsen

Since group counseling is a controversial term, and in my estimation often misused, I should like to begin this paper with my definition, first of counseling, then of group counseling. When one first observes counseling, he may conclude that it involves nothing more than a friendly conversation between a counselor and his client or clients; even a naïve observer soon realizes that it is an intimate, trusting relationship. The counselor struggles to understand exactly what each client is feeling and thinking. The client, on the other hand, gains increased self acceptance and acceptance of others, with new understandings of himself. He learns to assume increasing responsibility for his actions and to solve future problems more effectively. In other words, counseling focuses attention on the individual, even when provided in groups, and helps the individual learn to do things for himself rather than to rely on others.

The Process Defined

In many ways group counseling is similar to individual counseling. In both, the counselor tries to help the pupil to identify and clarify the problems which disturb him, to improve his understanding of himself and of his situation, to define, examine, and test alternative solutions for his problems, and to select an alternative on which he acts. The relationship which the counselor develops with each pupil enables them to discuss problems which heretofore the pupil was unable to discuss adequately. He learns to examine reasons for his difficulty in talking about certain topics, to challenge and consider the limits within which he is expected to work, and to request information whenever he feels the need for it.

On the other hand, there are some real differences between individual and group counseling. Though the counselor must concentrate his attention on trying to capture the speaker's feelings and to help him tell his story, he also must observe how each speaker's comments affect other members and help each to participate in the discussion. The counselor's behavior gradually conveys to each and every one in the group his warmth, understanding, and

From Merle M. Ohlsen, "Counseling Within a Group Setting," *Journal of the National Association of Women Deans and Counselors*, XXIII (April, 1960), 104–109. Reprinted with the permission of the publisher.

acceptance of them. From the counselor, the members learn to accept one another and to help each talk about his problems.

Group counseling differs from individual counseling in another respect. Each member is given an opportunity to test his tentative solutions in an accepting group of peers and to obtain from them multiple reactions simultaneously, prior to translating his verbalizations into overt behavior. Thus, members learn to help others while they are obtaining assistance from others.

Many have used the term group psychotherapy to label what I have defined as group counseling. I have chosen the term group counseling to indicate that my clients fall within the normal range of adjustment and that I treat them in a non-medical setting. Group counseling is to group psychotherapy what individual counseling is to individual psychotherapy. In both counseling and psychotherapy, the counselor must try to understand each client, and to help each client to understand and to accept himself, and to help each to face and to increasingly improve his ability to solve his problems. Both require special professional preparation, including supervised practice in counseling.

THE CLIENTS

Group counseling, useful with adults, upper-grade elementary school pupils, and to some extent with primary school children, is particularly appropriate for the adolescent because of his very strong desire to be like his peers. Moreover, he is usually struggling for independence from the important adults in his life; therefore, it is easier for him to accept help from other adolescents than from an adult. In obtaining help from his peers, he solves his problems with the assistance of those individuals who he thinks understand him best. Then, too, the fact that others in his peer group have problems similar to his own reassures him, makes him feel that, after all, he is like the other teenagers whose company he enjoys. The adolescent also wants to be reassured that his peers understand and accept him. In a counseling group he discovers that they not only come to understand and accept him, but that he also learns to understand them better — that he can empathize with them and help them solve their problems.

In our own research program at Illinois, on group counseling, we have decided to give special attention to gifted underachievers. We believe that this technique is particularly appropriate for them.

Gowan[1] found that gifted underachievers were self-sufficient, unsociable, hard to reach, hard to interest in social activities, indifferent to their responsibilities, and less identified with their parents than are other gifted youths. Shaw and Grubb[2] and Kirk[3] found underachievers to be hostile. Kirk[4] and

---

[1] John C. Gowan, "The Underachieving Gifted Child — A Problem for Everyone," *Journal of Exceptional Children*, XXI (1955), 247–249.

[2] M. C. Shaw and J. Grubb, "Hostility and Able High School Underachievers," *Journal of Counseling Psychology*, V (1958), 263–266.

[3] Barbara Kirk, "Test Versus Academic Performance in Malfunctioning Students," *Journal of Consulting Psychology*, XVI (1952), 213–216.

[4] *Ibid.*

Drasgow[5] also found that underachievers' failure was associated with goals which were not their own. Generally these perceptions agreed with our observers' descriptions of our clients. Further, our observers' judgments agreed with Shaw's and Grubb's[6] hypothesis that underachievement is not a surface phenomenon which is easily modified, and with their conclusion that others' demands for more and better quality of work tend to have detrimental results. Our observers also concluded that most of the underachievers included in our sample questioned our judgment that they were gifted. From this picture of underachievers, we concluded that if group counseling could improve relations with others and increase acceptance of self, it should play an important part in motivating these youth to accept and to use their untapped resources.

The youth described in the previous paragraph appear to be similar to Caplan's[7] unruly, antisocial, and incorrigible boys and Gersten's[8] juvenile delinquents. Group counseling did improve the attitudes and classroom behavior of Caplan's clients. The members of Gersten's experimental group became less inhibited and evasive, more productive, more responsive to mature promptings from within, and better able to establish wholesome relationships with others. In an even more unfavorable setting, Paster[9] found that suspicious, hostile, psychoneurotic casualties treated in groups in an Army hospital learned to discuss their problems in groups, to socialize with others, and to cope better with their guilt feelings and feelings of inferiority.

METHOD

Our study was conducted in an outstanding four-year high school which provided considerably better than average counseling services. The group counseling described in this paper was provided in an ordinary classroom which was furnished with movable armchairs, arranged in a circle.

The sample was composed of ninth-grade students who as eighth-graders ranked in the top 10 per cent of their class on the *California Test of Mental Maturity* and at the ninth decile or below, in grade-point average earned in the eighth grade. Of the thirty-four pupils identified by this method, twenty-nine actually participated in group counseling. The parents of one child refused to grant permission for their child to participate. Another, at his mother's request, was dropped from the project because his work had improved significantly during the first six-weeks grading period. Scheduling problems prevented the other three from participating in counseling.

The twenty-nine who actually participated in the project were divided into

---

[5] James Drasgow, "Underachievers," *Journal of Counseling Psychology*, IV (1957), 210–211.

[6] *Op. cit.*

[7] S. W. Caplan, "The Effect of Group Counseling on Junior High School Boys' Concept of Themselves in School," *Journal of Counseling Psychology*, IV (1957), 124–128.

[8] Charles Gersten, "An Experimental Evaluation of Group Therapy with Juvenile Delinquents," *International Journal of Group Psychotherapy*, I (1951), 311–318.

[9] S. Paster, "Group Psychotherapy in an Army General Hospital," *Mental Hygiene*, XXVII (1944), 529–536.

four small groups; two experimental and two control groups as follows: E_1 — two girls and four boys; E_2 — three girls and five boys; C_1 — two girls and six boys; and C_2 — two girls and five boys.

After the sample had been selected, every prospective client was interviewed for three purposes: (1) to acquaint him with what he might expect from group counseling and to inform him of what would be expected from him; (2) to answer his questions about the experience; and (3) to appraise the seriousness of each client's problems. The interviews were followed by a meeting of the parents at which the project was described in detail; their questions were answered; and written permissions for pupil participation were obtained. Though the investigators stressed the point that they wanted only those pupils who themselves recognized the value of group counseling and elected to participate, they learned from the pupils' comments during counseling that every counseling group except one contained some pupils who participated as a consequence of parental pressure.

An effort also was made to control the educational and guidance experiences during the experimental period. During the course of the experiment, none of these pupils was referred either for assistance with study skills or for counseling.

Each counseling group met for one class period twice a week for eight weeks. They were excused from a study hall for these sessions. The director of the project was the counselor for all four groups.

Growth of clients was evaluated with reference to three variables: (1) academic performance as measured by the *California Achievement Test Battery* and grade-point averages earned in high school; (2) acceptance of self and of others as revealed in responses to a picture story test; and (3) behavior in interpersonal relationships reported on the Behavior Inventory by the pupils themselves and, also, the five members of each observer team,[10] the clients' parents and the counselor.

Before presenting our major findings, I should like to digress a bit to comment on the selection of clients for group counseling. Those who are interested in introducing group counseling should select group members in accord with their own professional competence and the ability of their prospective clients to profit from the experience. Members selected must not only be able to profit from this type of counseling but also to have a therapeutic influence on each other.

Are there among the prospective members some who are not likely to respond to counseling in a group? Once the pupil knows what the group will expect from him, and what he can expect from others, if allowed to decide without pressure, he will usually be able to determine whether he should join a counseling group.

How will the group affect each individual? How will each individual affect other individuals in the group and the group process itself? Once the pupil

[10] Both observer teams included four of the schools' counselors who observed every counseling session from another classroom by closed-circuit television. The fifth person was the clinical observer who operated the closed-circuit TV.

decides that he would like to join a counseling group, the counselor assigns him to a group in which he can help others as well as receive help for himself. This means, of course, that the pupil will not be assigned to a group until he can be placed in an appropriate group.

Very aggressive, extremely shy, and seriously disturbed persons tend to be poor risks for group counseling. But before the counselor classifies anyone in any of these three categories, he should study all the information available. It is entirely possible that an individual who is a poor risk for one counseling group may fit into another one where personalities are more nearly compatible with his. It is interesting to note, for example, that the child who is socially ahead of his age group and the aggressive child often fit well into a counseling group with children somewhat older than themselves. Their opposites, the shy child and the child who is socially immature, tend to adjust better to groups with children younger than themselves.

Having other members of the family in the group may inhibit the pupil's participation and create unnecessary conflicts outside the counseling sessions. The presence of close personal friends has a similar effect. If they are involved in the personal conflicts which the pupil is trying to work out in the group, their presence may block his free examination of the issues.

Should the counselor try to select a relatively homogeneous group? Even though he may prefer a homogeneous group, the best he can hope to do is to select pupils whose scores on some measurable traits fall within a certain zone. First, however, he should ask whether he wants homogeneity. Different kinds of people, and people with different types of problems, often enrich the counseling experiences for the group. But on the other side, the more heterogeneous group also faces communication problems. Successful untangling of communication problems can in itself contribute to growth, but while adults may be able to overcome such problems, it is usually very difficult for young pupils, even senior high school students, to overcome such problems.[11]

RESULTS OF THE STUDIES

In three of our four groups, clients made significant growth on at least two of the measures, and some of the individuals in even the unproductive group made significant growth.[12]

The significant changes in those groups having the special counseling included increased acceptance of themselves and of others and improved behavior at home and at school. Parents' and counselors' descriptions of clients, pre- and post-counseling on the behavior inventory, indicated that these underachievers' behavior became more congruent with ideal adjustment. Those changes were, for the most, maintained over the eighteen-month period following counseling. But they did not improve their grades significantly.[13]

[11] M. M. Ohlsen, "Counseling Individuals Within the Group Setting," Chapter 14 in *Guidance: An Introduction* (New York: Harcourt, Brace & Co., 1955).

[12] J. W. Broedel, M. Ohlsen, and F. Proff, "The Effect of Group Counseling on Gifted Adolescent Underachievers" (Mimeographed paper, College of Education, University of Illinois, 1959); M. M. Ohlsen, F. Proff, and C. Southard, "The Effects of Group Counseling on Two Groups of Gifted Adolescent Underachievers" (Mimeographed paper, College of Education, University of Illinois, 1959).

[13] Broedel, Ohlsen, and Proff, *ibid.*

An Explanation

In conclusion, I should like to explain what I believe happened to the clients in the productive groups. These are clinical impressions only, but the eight school counselors who observed the groups by closed-circuit television and the four research associates who observed at least the first and last fourths of the sessions, on kinescopes, agreed with these impressions. With varying degrees of depth, each client discovered: (1) that expressing his own real feelings about people, things, and ideas helped him to understand himself and the forces that worried and disturbed him; (2) that at least one adult could accept him and that this adult, the counselor, wanted to understand him; (3) that his peers had problems too; (4) that, in spite of his faults, which they wanted to help him correct, his peers could accept him; (5) that he was capable of understanding, accepting, and helping others; and (6) that he could trust others. When a client discovered that others accepted him he found that he could accept others better, and eventually, that he could accept himself better. After he began to accept himself better, then, and only then, could he accept the fact that he was gifted and make plans which required him to use his potentialities. All of this takes time — these changes come ever so gradually — yet they must precede substantial improvement in grades. What is more, each client must learn to live with his new self, communicate this new self to others important in his life, and teach them to understand, to accept, and to live with the new self. For example, it is difficult for the average teacher to believe that these hostile and uncooperative students have really changed and for the distressed parent to believe that these youngsters are willing to take responsibility for their work without nagging. The setting in which group counseling takes place offers these unique advantages. It provides an accepting climate in which a client can test new and improved ways of behaving. It assists the client in discovering his new self and in revealing it to others, and at the same time, in learning to help others accept and adapt to this new self.

. . . .

22

Group-Centered Counseling

Nicholas Hobbs

. . . .

The experiences in group work which I report here reflect the strong influence of a philosophy of therapy which has been called nondirective therapy, or client-centered therapy, or client-directed therapy. Many of you are doubtless familiar with the more important concepts of this approach to psychotherapy, but perhaps it will be helpful to review them briefly, with particular reference to the group situation.

The basic principles of nondirective therapy apply in the group situation as well as in work with the individual. Of primary importance is one's own personal philosophy, one's attitudes toward people. More and more, techniques seem less and less important. Techniques come later; they grow out of and are demanded by one's orientation to human relationships in therapy. To be effective in therapy, it is believed, requires a deep and abiding confidence in the ability of most people to be responsible for their own lives. It requires some humility about how much a person can do for others, aside from making it possible for them to realize themselves. It requires putting aside tendencies to evaluate what is good and right for other people. It requires a respect for their integrity as individuals, for their right to the strength-giving act of making and living by their own choices. And it requires, perhaps above all, a confidence in the tremendous capacities of individuals to make choices that are both maturely satisfying to them and ultimately satisfactory to society.

When these principles are applied to the group situation, with adults, they require a departure from some of the procedures that have traditionally been used in group therapy. There is no need for lectures, films, pictorial materials, outlines of topics to be covered, or activity programs. Neither is there need for the kinds of things that we have come to expect a group leader to do. There is no need for a predetermined plan, for questions, for encouragement to the person who is slow to participate, for any evaluation of what is said, or for interpretations of what is said. As in work with individuals, the therapist must turn to the group for direction. If he has been

From Nicholas Hobbs, "Group Psychotherapy in Preventive Mental Hygiene," *Teachers College Record*, L (December, 1948), 171–177. Reprinted with the permission of publisher and author.

able to communicate his attitude of acceptance of all of the group, and his confidence that the members of the group can be responsible not only for their lives but, indeed, for the therapeutic experience itself, he will find the group working out its own best patterns. In such an atmosphere, the group will sensitively alter its topic, its pace, its humor, to meet the felt requirements of the moment, and it will give efficient direction and tempo to the series of meetings. In time, the therapist comes to feel that the group is a far more knowing guide in its quest for health than he could ever be.

With this theoretical orientation, let us look at some of the problems that arise in attempting to translate theory into practice.

Experiences in Group Therapy

During the past two years, research has been under way at Teachers College to define theory more clearly and to determine what procedures are most effective in group therapy. Appropriately, this work itself has been a group enterprise. At this stage, the work of the group has yielded some suggestions and some illustrations that may clarify the nature of this approach to helping people with their problems.

An initial problem is to decide who will be included in a therapy group. Current opinion is that about six people constitute an optimum number, and it has been our practice to seek some homogeneity in groups, though there is no empirical evidence that homogeneity is necessary. We have had a group of mothers of problem children, groups interested in reducing religious and racial prejudice, groups of university students of approximately the same age but with a diversity of stated problems, a group of boys from Harlem gangs, and groups of children retarded in reading. It has also been our practice to have an interview with each candidate before he joins a group. This provides an opportunity to identify individuals who might, in our present knowledge, profit more from individual therapy, and it serves to get each group member and the group leader acquainted. Groups normally meet twice a week for a period of one hour.

When the meetings get under way, much depends on the skill and sensitivity of the group leader. It is his responsibility to provide orientations that lift the sessions from the level of catharsis to that of constructive therapy. The first of these orientation points lies in the individual selves of the members of the group. The leader's constant aim is to understand the individual and to communicate this understanding to the person and to the group. He strives to understand how the individual perceives himself, his world, and his relationship to the group.

The second of the group leader's orientation points may be found in his concern with feelings. Recognizing that self-perceptions are charged with feelings (and are indeed shaped by feelings), the leader strives to catch and respond to the emotional quality of what is said in the group. Normative values and psychological judgments are excluded. The therapist proceeds at a pace set by the individual he is trying to understand, confident that this is the quickest method of achieving the goals of the group.

Perhaps one of the best ways of gauging the effect of the group leader's activity is to examine the reactions of group members to their leader. Here are a few statements, from members of a group of students:

> My reaction to the group leader is as if he were a member of the group, a silent partner. His remarks, I feel, are sort of stabilizing.

> For the first time, I noticed how the group leader has tried to keep the discussion on emotional rather than intellectual points, in referring back to previous statements which had not been picked up by the group.

And then, an excerpt from one meeting, in which the members were discussing the nondirective technique:

> MARY: I think that when you are very much distracted emotionally by your own problems, I don't think you are aware of the technique at all.
> NANCY: You can see the technique used on the other person but you can't see it used on yourself.
> MARY: Because I realized that I wasn't aware of it after the first day.
> MARJORIE: I often have trouble afterwards thinking of what you have said. . . . I think I just take it in.

As in individual nondirective therapy, the group leader seems to act as a catalyst. He appears to intrude little, yet his efforts are essential to the progress of therapy. His task is a hard one, for now he must respond sensitively to six people instead of one. But his task is lightened by the presence of strong allies who give help as they are receiving it. The leader sets the climate for the group, and his attitudes seem quickly to permeate it. Possibly this happens because, with the reduction of perceived threat, group members feel less need to be threatening; possibly because, with an increase in feeling of being understood, group members feel freer to understand each other. It is an exciting thing to witness a member of a group making an effort to understand the feelings of another member of the group, and to help him clarify his feelings. The happy and stimulating fact is that the group itself becomes a therapeutic agent.

Below are some excerpts from a recorded group meeting that convey some of the feelings that are built up within a group and suggest how group members help each other gain in self-understanding. Not everyone is able to identify himself so intimately with his group as do these people. Occasionally an individual will become somewhat isolated. But these quotations reflect the main trend in skillfully led groups.

> NANCY: I think this is tied up with the way we try to help somebody else. When I am disturbed, I feel that everybody is with me, somehow.
> LEADER: The whole group is with you.
> NANCY: That's right.
> MARY: Yes, you are not conscious of the individual in the group. It's . . . uh . . . a group rather than a person. . . . I have not been particularly worried about what people feel. . . . I am not worried about personal feelings or criticisms.
> LEADER: You mean within the group?

MARY: Within the group. I feel free to say anything I want to.

NANCY: That oneness of it is the thing I think is so remarkable.

ALICE: Yeah. I have the same feeling that you have, Mary. There is nothing that I would not say in the group. . . . But there is a funny thing. I have the feeling that if I met you in twenty years, I'd still feel as warm with you as I feel now. There is a certain affectional tie that you establish that I have never been able to establish with girls before. I have always either been competitive or felt subordinate, and I've never been able to establish a situation where I felt completely accepted, and I accept everybody.

In a situation of growing warmth and acceptance, the members of the group become increasingly able to examine feelings hitherto denied. With a reduction in perceived threat to self, the individual explores areas previously sealed off by expectation of catastrophe should such exploration be attempted in the absence of therapeutic support. The individual begins to perceive himself as a worthy person, capable of managing his own life. To help us understand such developments, we have asked group members to keep diaries in which they write their reactions to the meetings and to anything that seems important to them. The diary entries often highlight important aspects of the group process, as well as of individual gains. After the thirteenth meeting in a series, one girl wrote:

I felt as if something really cleared up in my mind today. I realized suddenly that I had been saying things that implied this feeling all along but that the concept of what it was was still not clear to me. It was the concept of self worth. I realize that I have been walking around feeling like a sad sack pretty much all of my life, and it has kept me from fighting for my goals. A sad sack never wins, and I took that conviction without ever proving to myself that I was capable. This sort of gave me an added impetus to work for my examinations, I think. I had the feeling this session that we were all coming down to pretty much the same basic problem only that we all have different ways of showing it. It made me feel closer to the group.

The group provides also a matrix of personal and cultural values that appears to be useful to the individual as he explores his attitudes and feelings about himself and others. Thus an element is provided that cannot be introduced in individual therapy, where the counselor, to avoid confusion of roles, must minimize cultural expectations. The counselor requires nothing of the individual other than that he work out his own solutions to his problems. This attitude on the part of the counselor seems necessary in order to avoid threat and to provide a predictable environment essential to therapy. The personal counselor cannot be both mentor and therapist. But in a sense, both of these functions are served in the group situation. The leader seldom varies from the predictable pattern suggested above; yet group members often express opinions and value judgments that are representative of the values of our culture — the culture in which each member of the group is attempting to find a satisfying life. In this situation, the individual finds freedom for self-exploration; and at the same time he is provided with an opportunity to see himself and his values in a larger social setting. Let me illustrate this by quoting again from one of the diaries.

The discussion today of a person's role in life seemed particularly helpful as I have not given this much thought before, except for the fact that I often seem to accept the role which others prepare for me. The group, however, made me realize that I can take a much more active part in choosing my roles than I have heretofore. Now I am uncertain about what kind of a person I really want to be. This calls for a critical analysis of values, something else I have never thought much about before. I am surprised to realize that, although I have made academic and vocational plans for the future, I have made very few, if any, personal or social plans.

Still another diary entry indicates how the feelings expressed by group members opened new prospects to one of the participants.

It seemed to me that the majority of the group members had been guided in their lives by emotional considerations, whereas I have been operating on an intellectual basis. A problem now arises over whether I wish to continue in the same manner or will be willing to break down the wall around my emotions and let them be expressed. Whether this bit of insight is really fundamental I am not sure, but I can see that it might explain much of my behavior.

The group situation seems often to evoke an awareness of a common bond with other people, while sharpening, in a healthy fashion, the individual's conception of his own unique personality. There is a comforting togetherness and a dignifying apartness.

Perhaps one of the most important features of all kinds of group therapy (and certainly it has been evident in the experiences in nondirective group therapy upon which these comments are founded) is the fact that the group itself provides an immediate, firsthand opportunity to gain different, healthier perceptions in interpersonal relationships. Maladjustment most often centers around difficulties in significant human relationships. The realization of satisfying relationships with others may thus be one of the major goals of all therapy. The group situation provides rich opportunity to gain new understanding of others and of oneself in relation to others. It provides opportunity for immediate practice in more mature living. One often observes a member of a group who has successfully worked through his own problems, continuing his active participation in the group because of his concern for other members. His identification with the group, once mainly a source of support, becomes a matter of readily accepted responsibility for others. It is believed that this sharing of responsibility for helping others is itself a primary source of therapeutic gain. Not the least important change in the self-perception of the individual in group therapy is the gained concept of himself as a person capable of mature social living.

PROBLEMS OF EVALUATION

The problem of evaluating the effectiveness of group therapy is a difficult one. The evident growth of some individuals who have participated in groups is heartening, and their spontaneous statements revealing their awareness of being more adequate people stimulate one to desire much further study of this approach to therapy. Such statements as these are common: "I think it has helped me immeasurably." "In social situations, I have so much more confidence in myself." "Deep down, I think how much it has helped me. My situation hasn't changed one iota. It's just the way I look at it. And the way I feel about it. Each day . . . I can see one other thing that has happened to me." "A very concrete evidence of my improvement is that I have found myself humming and whistling. That, I hadn't done in two years." Of course, not all people respond so favorably, and those who do not gain much are less likely to voice their appraisal of the experience. What we need are more objective indices of change. We have been exploring various techniques for measuring the outcomes of group therapy, and I can report some tentative but interesting results.

One of the best techniques appears to be the analysis of verbatim protocols. Here we find a gradual decrease in negative statements toward the self and toward others and a corresponding increase in positive statements. One of the most conspicuous changes is evident in expressions indicative of greater self-acceptance. Participants apparently become more able to differentiate their own values from the values that others would impose upon them, and to live more comfortably in roles they themselves find acceptable. Indirect measurements of gain have been obtained in work with children in remedial reading classes, some of whom were given a combination of individual and group nondirective therapy. Children participating in therapy made significant gains in scores on standardized reading tests, as compared with a control group composed of children who pursued only the regular program of instruction. One cannot partial out the influence of group and of individual therapy, of course, but the technique of measurement seems promising. We are also using observer evaluations, sociometric techniques, initial and terminal interviews, initial and terminal self-appraisal essays, pre-testing, and post-testing. We have encountered some fascinating and perplexing problems in attempting to evaluate group therapy objectively. For example, scores on self-rating scales behave in a curious fashion. When one compares initial self-ratings with terminal self-ratings, there is evidence of only slight gains from therapy. But if, at the end of therapy, group members are also asked to rate themselves as they *thought they were at the beginning of therapy*, striking differences emerge. Thus a person may indicate prior to therapy that he feels "swell"; at the end of the therapy that he feels "cheerful most of the time"; and in remembering how he felt prior to therapy, that he felt "down and out." Or again, pre-therapy: "I like most everyone I meet"; post-therapy: "I get along fine with everybody"; and remembrance of pre-therapy: "Most people irritate me." We are not at all sure of what this means. Perhaps we are sure of only one thing — that the job of objectively evaluating what goes on in group therapy is complex, but that an experimental approach is essential if further progress is to be made in shaping group methods to meet the current great demand for therapy.

. . . .

Section F

EVALUATION

The necessity for evaluation has not been widely recognized, nor has it received adequate attention. This apparent lack of interest may be due in part to the complexity and difficulty of the task. This is especially evident in the great number and the intricacy of emotional and intellectual interactions.

Two kinds of evaluation are necessary: one which takes place during the group process and one which follows it. During the discussion, the leader and members endeavor to understand the individual behavior within the group in order to predict the course of the group and how it will change if certain behavior is introduced. Each member tries to understand what is happening early enough to intervene and to change the course of events if he deems it desirable. The results of this difficult undertaking yield poor or, at best, fair predictions. To improve prediction and evaluation, means must be found to calculate the weights of the various relevant factors under given conditions.

The evaluation which takes place following the group discussion is also exceedingly difficult, even with the help of modern recording and photographic equipment. The careful use of tried techniques makes it possible, however, to gain enough understanding to improve the general performance of leaders and members over a period of time. But these techniques are so inefficient that only general improvement of methodology and psychological climate can be expected.

The selected readings describe methods which, although very inadequate, may add significantly to knowledge of certain conditions. "Group Self-Evaluation," by David Jenkins, describes the function of the observer and the usefulness of this method in the improvement of member interaction. "A Closer Look at the Role of Group Observer," from a report of the National Training Laboratory in Group Development, explains the problems and difficulties faced by the observer and how he may improve his performance and increase his usefulness to the group.

23

Group Self-Evaluation

David H. Jenkins

A group discussion is an ongoing process. It is the group mechanism by which the raw materials of subject matter, stated problem, information, and suggestion are integrated, sorted, and refined so as to produce an end product of solution, decision, or learning. As was brought out in the Basic Skill Training Groups, the efficiency of the mechanism has a direct effect on the time that is required to produce the result and also upon the quality of the result. We wish to interest ourselves here in the mechanism, or process of discussion which for purposes of clear analysis needs to be kept separate from the content, or subject matter of the discussion; *what* is being discussed is different from the *how* it is discussed. An efficient mechanism is usable for a wide range of subject matters.

As an ongoing process the group discussion has three qualities: it has a direction toward a goal, rate of progress, and at a given moment, a position or location on the path toward its goal. It is obvious, of course, in our common experiences with groups, that one or more of these qualities may be neither clearly stated, nor even implicit in the group behavior. Each of us has undoubtedly participated in groups where either the direction of the group was undefined or where, during a discussion, the group attempted to go in several directions simultaneously. But in a productive discussion group there is a clear direction and a goal, and knowledge of both the rate of progress and of the present position of the group.

Frequently members of a group are not aware of the nature of the difficulties in the mechanism of discussion. They may become aggressive toward each other or escape from the topic through apathy and boredom. They may have a vague feeling that "we aren't getting anywhere," or a concern over "what *are* we talking about, anyway?" but they are unable to put their finger on the difficulties at hand. There is the feeling of inefficiency and frustration, but the group lacks the proper information, perspective, and diagnostic skill which is necessary in order to identify the reasons for the inefficiency and to determine some methods for reducing it.

From David H. Jenkins, "Feedback and Group Self-Evaluation," *Journal of Social Issues*, IV (Spring, 1948), 50–60. Reprinted with the permission of the publisher.

Several different kinds of information about itself are required by a group before changes in its own behavior are possible.

1. Do we have a direction toward a goal? How successful have we been in keeping oriented in that direction, staying on the subject, not "wandering off course"?

2. Where are we now located in our discussion? Are we in the stage of diagnosing the problem, in the stage of suggesting solutions, or are we ready for final decisions?

3. What has been our rate of progress? Are we actually moving ahead in our discussion at a reasonable or efficient rate, or have we "bogged down"?

4. Are we applying our total group potential, the creative and analytic abilities of *all* our members, to our problem or are we operating with "half of our furnaces banked"?

5. Are we making any improvements in our ability to work together more efficiently?

Only when the group secures information about itself in answer to these questions does it have a basis on which to make the necessary adjustments to improve its efficiency. Until then it cannot recognize clearly the need to act, nor the nature of the change which is demanded.

Most groups, however, have not set up for themselves any mechanism for the "feedback" of this kind of information into the discussion process — no procedure by which the group can become aware of its own difficulties, the reasons for those difficulties, and the corrections which are necessary. In these groups we have an ongoing process which, by its lack of self-correcting (or self-improving) devices, continues at an unnecessarily low level of productivity. Much of the criticism directed at the "committee method" seems based on the assumption that low productivity is inherent in the group method.

The groups at Bethel, feeling that they had not yet tapped the creative resources in the group approach to problems, were concerned with the improvement of their own efficiency. They had in their groups a mechanism for the "feedback" of information to the members about their own method of operation. This mechanism was the group training observer, or group productivity observer. He served as the feedback and self-correcting device for the group along with the group self-evaluation, the general discussion about the meaning of the observer's comments.

By using the productivity observer, the group increases rather than reduces its own responsibility for analyzing itself and planning for changes and improvements. From the information and stimulation supplied by the comments of the observer, the group spends time examining *how* it has performed as a group. Let us look briefly at a portion of a feedback and evaluation session before we describe the nature of the observer's job and the group self-evaluation process.

(The meeting, which is the third one for this group, has been in session for about two hours. It is now about fifteen minutes before the adjournment.)

LEADER: Well, let's stop and take a few minutes to look at our meeting today. Let's hear from our observer first and then we will all share our ideas. Remember that we will want to see whether we felt as our observer did about what happened here, but we will also want to analyze for ourselves why we did what we did and perhaps spend time on suggesting changes which we may want to make in our procedure. Go ahead, Joe.

OBSERVER: I felt our meeting was pretty fair today. According to my tabulations I find that all of us took some part in the discussion for the first time since we started these meetings. One of the things which seemed important today happened when the leader tried to get the group to pull out some conclusions from the discussion we had been having. He suggested, about three times I think, that perhaps we should summarize our ideas. Each time, however, the group continued talking about the specific problems. I felt that we needed to move ahead at that point, but for some reason we didn't seem ready. How did the rest of you feel about it? (*Note the use of objective data at the beginning and with approving comments. Then come the more critical comments, given as a leader problem, augmented by the observer's own feelings, and then referred to the group.*)

MEMBER A: It seemed to me that we were not quite ready to draw conclusions; there were so many details to clear up. (*Compulsion for details of content causes rejection of the point about process.*)

MEMBER B: There were a lot of details, but perhaps we needed to stop and look where we were going once in a while, and see where we'd been. We were so busy looking at the trees today, I'm wondering if we didn't forget which part of the forest we were supposed to be in. (*Goal-oriented member supports and amplifies observer's suggestion.*)

MEMBER C: Frankly, I think now that I was so interested in the things we were talking about I just forgot that we needed to reach some conclusions. I just didn't realize what the leader was trying to do. (*Member shares his own feelings with the group and accepts personal responsibility.*)

LEADER: At the time, I know, I felt a little lost, I was wondering to myself, "What can I do to get us to move ahead? We are not making the progress we should because we have bogged down in details." Is there something we could have done differently to avoid this? (*Leader shares his feelings of difficulty with group — doesn't assume omnipotence.*)

MEMBER B: Perhaps it would have been better if we had decided before we started our discussion what we were going to do. Then, if one of our aims was to come out with some conclusions by the end of the meeting, we would have wanted the leader, or anyone for that matter, to point it out to us when we were bogging down. We could do something about it that way. (*Members can be creative, make positive suggestions.*)

(Other suggestions were made with the group deciding that they needed to plan an agenda for each meeting so they would know what they were to accomplish during that session. The evaluation continues:)

OBSERVER: One other point which might be worth mentioning: It seemed that during the time we were trying to suggest some solutions to the problems two or three of us seemed to want to criticize the idea immediately. We seemed impatient to tear a new idea apart. I made a little record of how many times new ideas were followed by critical comments. Out of seven suggestions that were made, six of them were criticized immediately. B.J. criticized four of them and J.R. criticized the remaining two. Right after that the group seemed to run out of suggestions for solutions. I was wondering at the time if we might not have gotten more ideas, or perhaps better ones, if we had held our critical comments until after most of our ideas about solutions were on the blackboard. (*Criticism of individuals by using objective data with suggestions for alternative methods.*)

J.R.: I guess you're right. I have been so in the habit of reacting to a new idea critically I fail to recognize that it may not be the most helpful procedure. I never was really conscious, until now you mention it, of what effect the criticism could have on the discussion. (*Member insight through being made aware of his own behavior.*)

B.J.: It sounds to me, though, that your idea would waste lots of time. Why not dispose of the ideas as they come? (*Member needs further analysis of problems.*)

(The entire group then spends several minutes analyzing the effects of improperly timed criticism on their own contribution to the group, with the other members helping the resistant member to see the implications of the problem.)

THE PRODUCTIVITY OBSERVER

With this description as a background, let us turn to the analysis of the role of the productivity observer.

The productivity observer is a member of the group who is assigned a special responsibility in the same manner as the recording secretary or the leader is given a special task. His function is to watch the group during their discussion and then feed back to the group his ideas about what happened during their discussion. In order to give his full attention to the behavior of the group the observer does not participate in the general discussion. The assumption is, of course, that even though the group is deprived of the contributions of one of its members during the problem-centered discussion, the total productivity of the group can be profitably increased through utilizing this member as an observer. Sometimes groups bring in a specially trained person to serve as their observer, especially to get the observer role started and adequately identified. This permits the total group to participate in the problem discussion. Frequently the observer job is rotated among the members of the group to give each a chance for the experience and to keep no one from contributing to the general subject matter which is discussed from meeting to meeting.

Non-participation of the observer is necessary to keep him from thinking about the subject matter rather than about the behavior of the group. To become involved in *what* is being said prevents focusing on the questions of *how* it is being said, its relation to the direction of the discussion, etc. The observer needs to maintain his vantage point of objectivity at almost any cost, yet without losing his feeling of membership in the group.

The attention of the observer may be directed at a variety of behavior in the group. He notes the general level of motivation, the general work atmosphere of the group, the orientation of the group, leadership techniques, and other factors which affect productivity. Here is an example of the kind of observation sheet used in several recent discussion groups with some sample notes of the kind an observer makes.

GROUP DISCUSSION OBSERVATION

A. Direction and Orientation
   1. How far did we get? *Covered only half of agenda. Spent too much time on details.*
   2. To what extent did we understand what we are trying to do? *Several members not clear on goals. Some continual disagreements on purposes.*
   3. To what extent did we understand how we are trying to do it? *Almost no discussion about procedure, resulting in confusion at times.*
   4. To what extent were we stymied by lack of information? *None. Relevant information at hand in group.*

B. Motivation and Unity
   1. Were all of us equally interested in what we are trying to do? *No. Two or three not sure problem is worth the time.*
   2. Was interest maintained or did it lag? *Slowed down during time leader made lengthy contribution.*
   3. To what extent did the group feel united by a common purpose? *Rather low feelings of any unity. Two or three not feeling united with group at all.*
   4. To what extent were we able to subordinate individual interests to the common goal? *Antagonisms between R.K. and L.M. outside of group tended to show up here.*

C. Atmosphere
   1. What was the general atmosphere of the group?
      (a) Formal or informal? *Fairly formal, although some first names used.*
      (b) Permissive or inhibited? *Fairly permissive except for period after leader lectured.*
      (c) Cooperative or competitive? *Little competition, some positive evidence of cooperative feelings.*
      (d) Friendly or hostile? *Lukewarm friendly.*

Observations on the contributions of individual members of the group:

A. Contributions of members
   1. Was participation general or lopsided? *All participated at least to some extent. Some monopolization by B.C. and W.U.*
   2. Were contributions on the beam or off at a tangent? *Hard to determine as goals not clear.*
   3. Did contributions indicate that those who made them were listening carefully to what others in the group had to say? *At points of higher interest in the discussion some were not listening to others.*
   4. Were contributions factual and problem-centered or were the contributors unable to rise above their preconceived notions and emotionally held points of view? *Some tendency toward bias, especially during first hour.*

B. Contributions of Special Members of the Group
  1. How well did special members serve the group?
      (a) Leader: *A little tendency to dominate, but catches himself before group reacts negatively. Tried unsuccessfully to get group to draw conclusions.*
      (b) Recorder: *Asked for clarification occasionally. This seemed to help group to clarify for itself.*
      (c) Resource person: *None in group today.*

Other observations:

J.R. and B.J. criticized solutions while they were being suggested. Is that why so few suggestions came out?

Although an alert, untrained observer can sometimes be sensitive to many of the obvious difficulties in the group, training can greatly increase the value of the observer. Especially is this true in the ability of the observer to detect the causes or relationships which produce the symptoms which he notices. For example, there may be no apparent reason for the sharp remark one member passed to another unless one recalls that earlier in the meeting the second member had criticized unnecessarily one of the contributions of the first member. There may have been some antipathy that developed which had not yet been resolved. With improved sensitivity the observer becomes increasingly valuable to the group [members] in helping them go behind the symptoms and recognize the causes of the difficulty.

A group need not assume that lack of a trained observer prohibits use of this technique for improvement, for the tactful, objective member who is alert to problems of interpersonal relations can function satisfactorily in this role. Increased sensitivity will undoubtedly come with continued experience. The responsibility for self-analysis to which the group commits itself by establishing the role of group productivity observer extends to include assistance to the untrained observer to help him do the best job possible for the group. . . .

The observer is a resource which is available to the group at any time. Sometimes groups set aside ten to fifteen minutes at the end of each meeting to discuss their progress and skill with the observer. Sometimes effective use is made of the observer by calling for his help at a crucial or difficult point in the discussion, using his analysis to assist in untangling the difficulty in which the group finds itself. Only infrequently does the group spend any large amount of time on this kind of discussion, and then only as it is felt to be profitable.

Not only does the observer serve a useful role for the group as a whole, he also becomes a "teammate" working closely with the leader of the group. The leader–observer team often spends considerable time together outside of the group session sharing reactions about the meetings and planning together the procedures and techniques for the future. A special value of this relationship is that the observer can serve as the "eyes" for the leader who, because of his own responsibility for the discussion, is unable to attend as closely to the difficulties in the group process and to be as objective in his own feelings.

FEEDBACK

The first experience of the group with "feedback" of information from the observer is relatively crucial and requires skill by the observer in presenting his comments. As they are not generally accustomed to put themselves voluntarily into a situation where they might be criticized, the members tend to be a little defensive in their feelings even though no points are actually made about them as persons. With experience they find that the observer's comments are valuable information and need not cause self-consciousness.

To reduce the resistance of the group, the observer can use several techniques. If he and the leader have developed the desired "team" relationship the observer's first comments, and perhaps the majority of his comments in the first session or so, will be about the techniques of the leader. Because of his experience and understanding the leader will be able to accept these comments objectively and easily and to serve as an example for the group to copy in their own reactions to the observer. ("If these comments don't upset the leader, who is in a more crucial position than I, I guess my feelings of insecurity are unnecessary.") Later comments about the behavior of the members may be more comfortably received.

The observer frequently phrases his comments about data which he has tabulated or observations he has made in the form of tentative hypotheses or expressions of his feelings and then asks the group if they were feeling the same way. In our description we saw how the observer used this technique. Presenting his observations and especially his interpretations in this tentative manner permits the group to reject them without difficulty if the members are not yet emotionally ready to accept them. The observer can just be "in error" and he can "admit it" at this point with a minimum of damage being done to the relationship.

The skilled observer is alert to the maturity of the group. He is aware of the symptoms of change and the increased capacity to handle conflicts. It may be necessary for the observer to "forget" to mention a serious conflict in the group for several meetings because the group will not have had, in the early meetings, opportunity to develop sufficient cohesiveness to absorb the shock of a discussion likely to arouse strong emotions. By the later meetings they will have gained sufficient experience in group self-evaluation so that they can approach such a problem more objectively.

An untrained observer sometimes feels that he must spend a major part of his time commenting on the "nice" things he observed in the group, and give only casual notice to difficulties and conflicts. Although comments about the effective things that occurred in the group should not be overlooked, the members usually feel that the observer "lets them down" if he doesn't talk about the difficulties. Sometimes the group members wonder if he has enough courage to tell them about something of which they are all quite conscious in the group, but which they, as participating members, feel unable to verbalize. Once the observer suggests such an item, he is usually greeted with nods of agreement and perhaps little sighs of relief — "the problem material is now something we can talk about."

The principal advantage of the use of an observer rests in the comparative case with which comments about behavior which is not usually talked about can be brought into the group discussion. A participating member would find it extremely difficult to offer such comments because of his own involvement and his role in the group. But the observer, although he, too, is an accepted member of the group, can make the comments "as a part of his job." The group is then able to orient their remarks toward "what the observer said" rather than toward "what is wrong with our group." This slightly different direction in the orientation presents major differences in the amount of emotional blocking in the discussion of the same problem, even though the same contributions are made.

GROUP SELF-EVALUATION

We have talked at length about the role of the observer and the feedback process. Let us now look at the direction the group discussion takes during the evaluation session. The leader in our example suggested three things the group needed to do: (1) get a common agreement on what actually happened, (2) analyze the reasons behind the event, and (3) suggest some ways of improving the procedure in the future.

The leader of the evaluation in the basic skill training groups encouraged expressions of recognition about the description that was reported by the observer by asking, "Is that the way the rest of you felt it happened?" There may be disagreement among the group members about the actual event, but a common understanding needs to be sought before the discussion continues to the other phases. Sometimes the individual who is most concerned in the situation may be the only one unaware of the event. Often "problem behavior" of group members is something they do of which they are totally unaware until the observer and the group mention it.

Once the event itself is agreed on, the group turns to the discussion of "why did it happen?" Everyone can express his feelings here as feelings are the facts which are often most relevant in group interaction. In our illustration we found members indicating quite different reactions to the same situation. Recognition of these differences may lead to a relatively quick understanding of the causes of the difficulty.

The leader needs to help the group in its self-evaluation to move from analyzing their difficulties to the discussion of desirable changes in group procedure. To become acutely aware of a problem, and no more, may sow the seeds for group disruption. A consideration of the possible solutions to the problem and a decision to try out a tentative solution allows the discussion to terminate on a positive note. In future meetings attention may be given to evaluating the success of the solution as it has worked out in practice. Satisfactory experiences in changing its procedures encourages the group to become more experimental in instituting new techniques.

Not only, however, does the self-evaluation result in specific changes in techniques or behaviors by the group but it frequently builds improved feelings of group cohesiveness. When one of us, as a group member, becomes able to share his feelings of happiness or frustration with members in our group, others are stimulated to participate in a similar vein. Shared feelings become common property. It is this common property which heightens the identity with the group and feelings of belongingness to the group. Increased cohesiveness makes the group more able to handle constructively larger amounts of overt conflict.

Self-evaluation by the group trains the members to become more sensitive to the difficulties in interaction and discussion which exist in the group, their causes, and some techniques for avoiding them. In truth, this increased awareness is a learning which can be generalized, a new or improved skill which the individual person can utilize when he enters new group situations. As he gains this skill he begins to mature as a productive group member.

Summary

If it is to be an effective producing unit a discussion group must give attention to its mechanics of operation. Awareness of its direction and goal, its rate of progress, present location on its path to the goal, use of the member's potential ability and its ability to improve itself, are important factors which lead to increased efficiency. The use of the group productivity observer as a feedback mechanism and the self-evaluation of its process by the group are techniques which have been worthwhile in improving the functioning of groups.

24

A Closer Look at the Role of Group Observer

National Training Laboratory in Group Development

. . . .

. . . What Is a Group Observer?

The observer is a group member who has been assigned the specific job of observing the group's functioning as a totality and of helping the group

From Watson Dickerman (ed.), *Report of the Second Summer Session of the National Training Laboratory in Group Development* (Washington, D.C.: the Laboratory, 1948), pp. 116–121. Reprinted with the permission of the National Training Laboratories, National Education Association.

evaluate its ways of working in order to help it increase its efficiency. In practice, this has meant that the group observer (who may be a rotating or a fixed member) does not participate in the group's discussion of its various subject matter topics. Instead he makes observations about group process at times set aside by the group for this purpose.

His observational material consists of the notes, mental or written, preferably the latter, which he makes of the way the group operates and which he "feeds back" to the group upon its request, with varying degrees of interpretation. Three "levels" of observer feedback may be shown by the following examples. *Descriptive:* "We were not able to reach any decisions today although we discussed two problems which required decision-making." *Low-level interpretation:* "There were no decisions reached today. Was it because none of us played the role of decision-initiator?" *High-level interpretation:* "We seemed to feel that the issues we discussed today were just too hot to handle. Were we afraid to commit ourselves on them because it would mean taking sides with one or the other of the two members of our group who have strongly opposing opinions?"

The belief is — and practice has justified this belief to a great extent — that the use of an observer will lead to the group's increasing awareness of the problems of group efficiency and to continuously improving its functioning.

. . . WHAT KINDS OF PROBLEMS DOES THE OBSERVER FACE?

It would seem logical for the next step in this "pocket-guide" to be a discussion of those practical problems involved in the actual task of observation: problems of what to observe when, what sorts of notes and records to keep, what to feed back, how and when. Members of the BST group with which the writers were associated during the Second Laboratory did not, however, feel this to be the most helpful next step. A single try-out at the observer role convinced many of them that practice of the skills of observation should succeed an exploration of some of the theoretical and ethical problems inhering in the practice of the role.

For example, according to what standards or criteria should one evaluate a group? That is, what constitutes a "good" group, what *is* "good" group fuctioning? It would seem that the purposes and functions of the observer can more readily acquire form and meaning through the formulation of such a "yardstick." What, then, are the functions of the group observer in the light of this to-be-formulated yardstick? What are the levels of observer-functioning appropriate for the various kinds of group settings? In the exercise of his group function, does the observer have some special kind of ethical and psychological "philosophy," some particular kind of personal "value system," as a foundation for the practice of his specific skills? If so, what kinds of philosophy or value system? What sorts of skills should the observer have? Some understanding of problems such as these seemed to many of the delegates to be essential background to the effective practice of group observation.

1. Problem of an Evaluation "Yardstick." What, then, are the factors to be considered in attempting to formulate even a non-definitive answer to the question: what is a "good" group? Is it possible to formulate a consistent answer to this question in light of the fact that there seem to be as many different kinds of groups as there are group goals or purposes? One writer has made a classification of groups according to the kinds of "production" or "action" goals they have set for themselves and has come out with seven types of groups as a result. The standards of evaluation of a foreman as to how well a group of workers are producing would seem to be very different from the criteria involved in the classroom in the judging of how well a group of children are learning.

But if we suggest that one criterion of a good group is that it reaches its production or accomplishment goals, whatever those goals may be, we may resolve our first objection. The problem then becomes one of examining the steps the group should take in efficiently reaching its production goal and of determining the stages of group growth leading toward efficient group production.

But is a consideration of only the goals immediate to a particular group adequate to the formulation of a "good" group, in a democratic society? Should the group not inquire of itself what its inter-group goals are — that is, how its goals relate to the broader social framework of goals within which it operates? For example, a profession, say the medical profession, may not only be assessing how effectively it is moving towards the standards or goals it has set for itself as a profession; it may also be continually assessing its objectives in terms of what should be the goals of the medical profession in a democratic society. Similarly, a classroom in a school may not only be assessing its immediate objectives and responsibilities, but also the broader responsibilities of the public school within the framework of a democratic society. So it appears that some consideration of how a group's immediate goals relate themselves to the broader social goals of the society in which we live should also be included in formulating the description of the "good group."

A new element has come into our discussion: we are beginning to assume that a good group is one which is conscious of its democratic responsibility. But is it enough for a good group to be aware of its democratic ends on an external basis only, that is, in terms of its work goals? What of its internal functioning? Does it not have a democratic responsibility on the member-functioning level also? In other words, to what extent is it utilizing its member-potential towards the achievement of its work goal? Further, are there not responsibilities which group members have to one another? Are they not responsible for the promotion of each other's growth towards increasingly efficient group functioning?

We have come to the definition of the good group as a democratically functioning group on both the external goal level and the internal member-functioning level. Can we, then, evaluate any group in the light of these four relative, rather than absolute, criteria? (1) How well is this group as a group progressing towards some production or action goal it has set for itself?

(2) How well is this group fitting its immediate goals into the broader framework of our democratic society? (3) How well is this group utilizing the potentialities of its members to contribute towards its work goals? (4) How well is this group "growing" its members, how well is it helping them become even better contributors, to assume a wider variety of essential group roles, than their present potentialities allow them? The assumption being made is that the further the group "grows" along these four dimensions, the more "mature" a group it is.

The fourth criterion contains implications which should not be overlooked. It leads us into the broad area of personality development — how the personalities of individual members can affect the functioning of the group and how the functioning of the group can affect individual personalities. And here, perhaps, is the one criterion which may distinguish the democratically oriented group from one operating within an authoritarian social framework. A wise dictator would probably want groups to achieve their "work" goals as efficiently and rapidly as possible. He may see that full utilization of member-potential results in more effective group production and so advocate it. But it would defeat his own purposes to promote the kind of group interaction that helps persons become secure, independently functioning personalities, persons whose willingness to cooperate with others, to be socially *inter* dependent, arises from their recognition and acceptance of themselves as adequate, *inter* dependent, mature personalities. On the contrary, it would seem to be essential for the continuance of an authoritarian group or society to foster the kind of group process that promotes the individual's continuing emotional and intellectual dependence on the leader.

This point leads us directly into the concept of member-roles, or rather, the concept of the distribution of good group roles throughout the membership. That is, the authoritarian functioning group will tend to keep the group functions or roles necessary for group production concentrated in one person, the leader: the chairman or social-control role, the action-suggester role, the clarifier role, the content coordinator role, the peace-maker role, the tension-reducer role, the information-giving role, the decision-making role, the evaluator role, and so on. The democratically functioning group not only works towards an increasingly wide distribution of these roles among the members of the group but also towards increasing the individual member's repertoire of such group roles.

2. Problem of Observer Purposes and Functions. With these four criteria of the "good group" as our yardstick, what would seem to be the group observer's purposes and functions? Ideally, his role is to stimulate the group to assess its degree and rate of progress in the four areas of: efficient group functioning, awareness of broader social goals, full member-utilization, promotion of member-growth. Accordingly, it would be his duty to make observations pertinent to these four areas and to call the members' attention to their functioning in these areas. It would be his further duty to perform these functions in such a way as to assist the group to utilize these observations to improve its functioning, to make decisions, to do something about the way it has been functioning.

3. Problem of Appropriate Levels of Functioning. The word "ideally" was purposely used in the preceding section. The problem of levels of observer-functioning is the question of to what degree and in what ways the observer should attempt to exercise these functions in various types of groups.

Two general levels of functioning can be differentiated: the calling-to-attention or descriptive level and the why-did-it-happen or interpretation level. The descriptive level in a sense serves the same sort of purpose as would the playing-back to the group of a record of the meeting. However, because such reporting back should be selective, it focuses the attention of the group on specific points or happenings far more than would an all-inclusive play-back of a record. Thus, even on the descriptive level, the observer functions to stimulate group evaluation and decision on specific group problems. This might be termed the most "superficial" but nevertheless the most suitable level for such groups as a single committee meeting, a one-day institute, a week-end conference. Feedback such as, "We were able to arrive at three decisions today," or, "The meeting seemed to drag at the beginning — we didn't seem to warm up and get going until about the second half, when member participation became more active and general" are typical of the descriptive level of observer-functioning.

Such "evaluation" can be made available to the group by the observer at the end of the meeting. Again the observer may call the attention of the group to an event immediately after it occurs, interrupting the group to do so. (This latter method has been found particularly effective where a demonstration group is operating before an audience.) Which method is used by the observer can depend only upon group preference. It has been found in practice that the first method, that of a short "evaluation session" at the end of a meeting, is the most used. But there is as yet no definite evidence as to which of these three methods of descriptive-level feedback is felt by groups to be the most useful.

The second level of observer-functioning is actually a wide range of functioning, rather than a level. Here the observer takes on the responsibility of advancing hypotheses or making interpretations about the reasons why certain things happened. What type or degree of interpretation is used must depend on the sensitivity, experience, and diagnostic skill of the observer, in terms of both his actual perception and understanding of persons and events and his judgment as to the timing and manner of his interpretation. Situations in which there are regular periodic meetings, for example, would seem to provide the kind of group setting suitable for gradually increasing depth of observer-interpretation. Again the sensitivity of the group to its problems and the degree of group objectivity present would determine the extent of observer-interpretations. Two examples of this range of functioning have been given [on p. 172]. The greatest potential danger in interpretive "feedback" by the observer would come if the observer pronounced judgments or appeared to think of himself as superior to the group. To the extent this occurs, the observer is seen as judge and jury and the group seems to win the "judge's" approval rather than use the observer to help the group objectively analyze its functioning.

4. Problem of Responsibility to the Group. In many group situations, then, the observer assumes in varying degree a diagnostic or interpretational function. Does such a function imply that the observer has some special professional responsibility to the group, or is his responsibility no greater than that of any other group member? Again, no definitive answer is possible: both aspects seem to operate in his role. On the one hand, because the practice of his role is more likely to provide him with more pertinent observational material than any other member, he would seem to have a greater responsibility to the group for making use of this material. Since he can use such material either as destructive or as constructive tools, he must always be keenly aware of the possible effects that his statements or questions may have on the group and on group members at certain stages of group and member development.

On the other hand, one can question whether the observer has any greater, or any different, responsibility for expressing or withholding material relevant to group and member functioning than any other group member. Perhaps one of his "professional" responsibilities is to realize that to have been assigned a specialized role by the group does not mean that he thereby acquires a higher group status or the right to play the role of God.

If we accept both points of view — that the nature of his role may provide him with more insight and sensitivity than other members concerning group and individual functioning and hence invest him with greater responsibility, but that any group member should also be aware of the same factors and exercise personal responsibility for feeding observation back to the group — we may arrive at a third observer responsibility. This is his training responsibility. It requires him to try to foster more and more insight and sensitivity to group process among the group members and to attempt to get the group to absorb more and more of the observer role, just as the chairman attempts to get the group to absorb more and more of his social control function.

Three responsibilities of the observer seem to emerge: (1) He must consider himself to be a member of the group rather than some outside person, who as an outsider has some kind of special professional relationship to the group. (2) Like any good group member, he must have a high degree of sensitivity concerning his responsibility to make contributions that will be constructive for the stage of growth the group is in at some particular time. (3) He must attempt to pass on to the group more and more of his observer functions or roles in order to free the group from any dependence on his specialized role.

Perhaps the implications of these points for the trainer of observers should be made explicit. One of the things for a trainer to do might be to try to inoculate prospective observers against the idea that in two hours, "I have become an observer, and that because I have become an observer I am a special kind of person in this group, I have a special status, and because I have a special status I can talk down to people." The trainer might further try to make his trainees aware of the fact that there are many good-member roles, that the observer role is but one of the good-member roles, that as an observer there are many of these roles which the observer is not familiar with and which he will continually want to learn.

5. *Problem of a Personal Value-System.* But it would seem that the foundation which will give the observer or any group members such an approach to his group responsibilities is some ethical and personal philosophy or system of values relating to the group. If the observer is to carry out his responsibilities in the manner suggested, he would seem to have to believe in the worth and effectiveness of the democratic group process, in the possibility of the continuing growth of the individual and in his role being shared as much as possible by other group members.

6. *Problem of Observational Objectivity.* It may be a truism to point out that essential as constructive attitudes and values may be, they must come to the level of actual expression in the form of appropriate techniques and skills in order to be effective. Just as the mechanical practice of specific skills with little understanding of their underlying rationale may be ineffective and even socially dangerous, so also the possession of the best intentions in the world can do the world little good unless they are channelled into skills and techniques which can effect the goals of these intentions.

There are several skills, or cultivated sensitivities, involved in the effective practices of the observer role as we now know it. Perhaps the primary skill is the capacity to constantly sort out what we ourselves contribute to a perception from what actually does happen. That is, we must train ourselves to distinguish between our perception of some event and what is really happening. To recognize that we cannot eliminate such personal factors from our perception is the first step. To attempt to distinguish what part subjective interpretation plays is the necessary next step for the person who has any kind of observational responsibility, group or otherwise. Suppose he notes that Mr. A was angry when his suggestion was rejected. Was the judgment of "angry" arrived at as a result of the subjective inference that Mr. A "must have" reacted with anger to the rejection of his suggestion? Actually, for all the observer knows, Mr. A may have reacted with indifference. Or was the judgment of "angry" arrived at as a result of noticing specific things Mr. A did and said: such as snapping the pencil he was holding in two, becoming very flushed, making audible comments to his neighbor about the mentality of certain people?

The basic technique question then becomes, "What kinds of things can the observer do with his eyes and ears (and his pencil) to best insure that his own needs are screened out of what he sees?" First, he would have to arrive at some objective criteria of observation: He would force himself to write down the actual things that happened, not what he thought happened — so that when he does make any generalizations or interpretations he can check back to the actual behavior and events on which his generalization was based. Merely for him to recognize the necessity of separating his own needs from the actual event in his perception [is not enough] — that is, to recognize the existence of the problem is not to solve it.

Second, he would consciously train himself to become as sensitive as possible to a widening range of clues, so that he could get more and more pertinent material for the group to look at. The cultivation of the first primary skill would seem to lead him inevitably to the second skill.

. . . WHAT SORTS OF THINGS SHOULD THE OBSERVER OBSERVE?

But what sorts of things should be observed in a group? It is necessary to select what to observe because it is impossible to notice everything that is going on. Therefore, on what bases should the selection be made for a particular stage of its development?

The answers to these problems would again seem to depend on the level of observation employed. For most individual meetings of most groups, the descriptive level is most suitable and useful. . . . The sorts of things that can be observed . . . almost exclusively [on] the descriptive level [are] group atmosphere, cohesion, leader behavior, member roles, procedures for group progress, and so on.

Which such "dimensions" to choose for a particular meeting would seem to depend on what the outstanding problem or event or focus-of-interest is for the group for that meeting. If the group seems to be continuing over-long as a collection of individuals rather than becoming a cohesive group, such dimensions as atmosphere, cohesion, communication, or perhaps leader behavior, may be helpful. If the group has decided to try out a rotating-chairman system, it may be helpful for the first one or few times a new chairman is used to observe leader behavior. If a tendency has arisen for most of the member-roles to be concentrated in the leader and two or three members, or for a number of necessary-to-good functioning member-roles to be missing from the group, it may be helpful to the group to point out member-roles played (and not played) during that meeting. Or if the group has shown discernible growth in some sore spot of its functioning, highlighting this change may ensure maintenance of change.

Once the group has become familiar with the kinds of dimensions of observation which are possible, it may specifically request its observer to observe or to feed back, or preferably both, along a particular dimension. The decision on what to observe and to feed back should be increasingly the group's decision as group life continues, rather than the observer's alone or a joint observer-leader decision. However, if the group requests the observer to feed back material which he feels convinced can be highly damaging to the group at its present stage of development, he should feel free to suggest this not be done, giving his reasons, or to suggest the substitution of some other material.

What about the interpretational range of observation? When and how should it be used? Here it may be useful to introduce what has been termed the "time-perspective" aspect or the "growth gradient" in group functioning. These terms refer on the one hand to the age or stage of development of the group members, and on the other hand to the length of time a group has been meeting. One cannot judge a group of children in kindergarten, a group of high school adolescents, and a PTA committee by the same absolute set of standards. Nor can one expect the same sort of things of a group that has worked together, meeting regularly for six months, as of a group that has come together for its second meeting. Nor can one expect the same sort of behavior of a group of school children during their first month with a progressive-methods teacher after they have had an authoritarian teacher for six years, as one can expect four months after the new teacher has been with them.

It would seem, then, that an observer functioning at the interpretational level of observation should take into account the current gradient in the group's growth. This would suggest that the interpretational level might be used most fruitfully at various strategic intervals during the group's life, utilizing the growth gradient approach: how much have we grown, in what directions have we grown, where have we not grown — during some period of group time. Some or all of the four criteria of the good group may be used as the dimensions for evaluation and interpretation. It would be preferable to have the group itself judge how well it is functioning in the various dimensions and to attempt some self-diagnosis of the reasons why it has or has not progressed in the different areas. Group self-evaluation of this nature is not only preferable, but usually possible in the case of groups meeting regularly over a period of time.

But there may be group settings in which the time factor precludes extensive self-evaluation and makes it necessary for the observer to assume the full evaluation load. Evaluation of an interpretive nature might be done most effectively by the observer at the last general meeting of a week's workshop, or of a week-end conference, utilizing the observer reports of the various group meetings held during the course of the conference as the "raw data" on which to base his evaluation. However, self-evaluation may be feasible and stimulating in such situations also. Even a one-day institute might set aside with profit part of its last meeting for a growth-gradient evaluation.

. . . What Special Techniques Should the Observer Use?

Record-Keeping. The problems of evaluation introduce the practical problem of the kinds of records an observer should keep. Observer experience during the Second National Training Laboratory in Group Development has begun to point to the necessity for close cooperation between the group's observer and recorder (secretary, keeper of minutes). In order to keep track of as much of the group interaction and process as possible, the observer can include very little actual "content" or discussion subject-matter in his notes (except, possibly, for occasional pertinent "anecdotes" — the actual interaction on which his observation is based). For instance, he may designate the participation of a particular member by noting his member role: "C.A. decision-suggester" (incidentally, this is a highly useful form of observer shorthand), but make no attempt to note just what decision C.A. suggested. It is the responsibility of the group's recorder to take note of the actual decision which C.A. suggested.

It would seem, then, that the observer and recorder should work out their respective methods of record-keeping in cooperation in order to aid the observer to integrate process with content with a minimum of delay and difficulty. Where the observer and the recorder roles are made rotating functions and the group meets regularly for some time, such a project may well be included as part of a total group "courses of training" for the observer role. The two record-structures at the end of this section are meant only for the sake of example.[1] Since these "structures" have not even been tried out in the coordinated manner suggested above, it is not known whether these examples used together have effective practical application. The example of structure for the observer's record alone has been applied and found a useful form for organizing basic observational material.

It was general observer practice during the Second National Training Laboratory in Group Development to use such a record as the basis for an "Observer Log," written up for every meeting in a narrative manner and considered the observer's permanent record. It may be, however, that with closer cooperation between observer and recorder, the narrative report should preferably be in the form of a "Recorder's Log" or "Minutes" which might be either read as a report or handed out to members of the group in duplicated form. The observer's record could then be a more coherent and legible copy of his original notes, plus a writeup of the actual feedback given to the group by the observer, including group contributions and decisions relevant to the evaluation. Observer and recorder might cooperate on these latter "memory" items to insure an accurate and reliable report.

There is no doubt that many group situations will not justify or allow time for the keeping of as careful records as has been suggested. If a choice is necessary, it may be permissible to forego the transcribing of the original observer notes into more permanent form. But the original noting-down of observational material should be considered as indispensable. . . .

. . . .

[1] [Editor's Note: These "record-structures" have not been included here. See pp. 156–159 and 166–168.]

SUMMARY, QUESTIONS, AND SUGGESTED READINGS

SUMMARY

Attainment of harmony within the group and among groups is difficult. True harmony may be a worthy goal, provided such harmony makes room for and expects creative differences. A superficial consensus does not represent real progress.

The group which encourages the greatest opportunity for growth within its members recognizes the uniqueness of the individual and supports him in his right to his point of view. The paradox is that these are the groups from which finally emerge creative decisions and action. Harmony achieved in this manner indicates progress.

Since the membership of each group consists of individuals with various points of view, each group achieves its own process which may be unique in one or more ways. Its uniqueness extends to many areas of its functioning: methods of handling conflict, expressing agreement, or reaching a consensus.

The character of the interaction within the group is contingent upon its purpose, its size, the character of the leadership, the extent and depth of the interest of the members in one another and in the problem.

The purposes of groups in the school setting may be divided broadly into two classifications: those concerned with problem solving and those concerned with counseling. In the former there is a visualized goal. This goal may be the solving of problems related to the planning of a project, the progress of the project, or its evaluation. The process used is directed toward reaching a decision and the satisfaction of one another's needs. The members endeavor to remain problem-centered, with a minimal number of ego-centered responses. Their goal is attained through high-level thinking and disciplined cooperation. Groups in this classification are known as classroom groups, group guidance classes, committees, action groups, adult education groups, government groups, or industry groups.

Group counseling does not have a visualized goal but a task. The task is self-understanding and understanding of others. The process of interaction of such a group is in relation to some of the experiences of its members — past,

181

present, or future. Reality testing is always implicit and frequently explicit. The members use ego-centered responses in their exploration of feelings and attitudes, with a minimal number of problem-centered responses.

The two processes of problem solving and counseling have some common elements such as thinking, disciplined cooperation, involvement, ego-motivation, and satisfaction. On the other hand, the processes differ widely in other respects. In the process of problem solving, the emphasis is on ways and means. Each member is focusing on the problem at hand and using one another's insights to generate a more acceptable plan, method, or solution. The leadership moves from one to another in terms of his contribution. Situational thinking is encouraged and appreciated, while ego-centered and conflict-laden responses receive minimal attention.

In group counseling there is a greater element of emotional interlock which develops from the intrapersonal and interpersonal involvement of the members. The leader helps in establishing a controlled and protected setting, in which each member is free to recognize his emotions and to reveal attitudes and compare them with those of others. The content is a means and is minimal; it serves as a foundation for the situational aspects open to discussion. The leader clarifies the basic rules by example.

To avoid the confusion which now exists between group guidance and group counseling, a distinction such as that outlined above is essential. In any concerted attempt to make such distinctions, the necessity for research concerning these processes should be emphasized rather than the more common concern with comparisons of individual and group counseling.

Frequently lacking in the research on group guidance and group counseling are control groups adequate for the purpose of comparison. The usual control is the time element. Seldom are controls exercised over the process. The counselor may have conducted the interview on the psyche-process (group counseling) level, whereas the group discussion may continue on the socio-process (group guidance) level.

The counselor and group-process leader are frequently assumed to have similar backgrounds and comparable skills. This is unlikely, however, since the standards for efficiency in group counseling have not received attention, and the training which counselors receive in that area is frequently limited to a theoretical survey course.

Comparisons are often made between a counselor working with an individual using chiefly a psyche-process, and a poorly trained group leader using principally a socio-process, or between a counselor using chiefly a psyche-process and a group therapist using an analytically oriented therapy process. Comparisons between the results obtained by a counselor and group leader, each with similar background training in counseling and group counseling and each using the same process, are rare. Little effort, if any, has been expended to control the types of problems or subjects in these cooperative studies.

The process or procedure used in group counseling determines the design and the type of results to be expected. Those who consider group counseling to be essentially a socio-process procedure for the interchange of information and problem solving will necessarily use a different design and will obtain different results from those who consider it to be a psyche-process operation. The unproved and unexplored assumption is frequently made that the same process can be carried on in group and in individual counseling.

Problems develop regardless of the process and the efforts of the leader. This is because of the complexity and threat of the interaction process. Becoming involved in group process and confronting the possibility of changing one's ideas or actions is a challenge to some and a threat to many, especially if one is expected to incorporate the outcomes of group action into his way of life.

These problems reveal themselves in the behavior of individuals and of the group as a whole. Individuals hesitate to speak and may react by silence. An individual may introduce tangential ideas, or recount a personal anecdote only distantly related to the topic. Another person may encourage the taking of a vote as a means of releasing himself and others from facing the ambiguity of the problem.

Several individuals, fearful of the force of the leader to gain what he desires or of having to accept a decision they do not favor, may form themselves into a clique or "block" in order to sway the outcome.

Group members who recognize what should be done but are reluctant to do it may support one another in forming a false consensus. They may appear to be genuinely interested in doing what they support but often fail to carry through on the decision they supported.

A group may feel so threatened by its perception of what logic demands that it becomes quite cohesive in its efforts to maintain the status quo.

Feelings of insecurity may cause a group to avoid the discussion of important issues and become quite active in the discussion of others.

From these few descriptions of possibilities within the group and the group as a whole, it is clear that the evaluation and improvement of group process is a many-faceted undertaking. The techniques which have been developed for observation and recording of the interaction are useful, and the results should provide members with many ideas for the improvement of the process.

But these techniques are limited to the overt interchange of expression. Much of the really important interaction is covert; it has to do with feelings and attitudes. Since the quality of the interaction is dependent in large measure upon the personality adjustment of members, this is an area which warrants more attention. How can the leader help to develop the kind of emotional climate which will encourage members to relate to each other in an understanding and genuine manner? Each member also should be encouraged to try to understand his feelings and responses during the discussion and to perform in such a manner as to help other members to become more understanding, accepting, and responsive. Research and evaluation in this intangible area of feelings and attitudes, though exceedingly difficult, could be expected to yield important insights which would enhance the value of group process.

QUESTIONS

1. What conditions enhance the possibilities of group counseling?
2. Why is social change difficult to attain?
3. What are the similarities and differences between group problem solving and group counseling?
4. Compare the possibilities for growth toward maturity in authoritarian and democratic groups.
5. What factors increase the probability that a group may become more than the sum of its parts?

SUGGESTED READINGS

Section A: Characteristics of the Group Process

Bales, Robert F.; Hare, A. Paul; and Borgotta, Edgar F. "Structure and Dynamics of Small Groups: A Review of Four Variables," in J. Gittler (ed.), *Review of Sociology: Analysis of a Decade.* New York: John Wiley & Sons, Inc., 1957. Chapter 12.

This chapter describes the structure and dynamics of small groups. It contains an excellent discussion of group-size communication, the nature of the group task, and personalities of the group members. Many research sources are referred to in the discussion, and there are five pages of bibliographical references at the conclusion of the chapter.

Powell, John Walker. "Process Analysis as Content: A Suggested Basis for Group Classification," *Journal of Social Issues*, VIII (1950), 54–64.

A discerning discussion of the function and kinds of relationships which are a part of the group process and their significance for individual growth and group achievement.

Section B: Special Problems in Interaction

Beeman, N. Phillip, and D'Amico, Louis A. "Effects of Cooperation and Competition on Cohesiveness of Small Face-to-Face Groups," *Journal of Educational Psychology*, XLVII (1960), 65–70.

A comparison of the influence of competition and cooperation on fourth grade children. This is one of the few studies comparing the effects of cooperation and competition. It is informative and thought-provoking.

Zander, Alvin; Stotland, Ezra; and Wolfe, Donald. "Unity of Group Identification with Group and Self-Esteem of Members," *Journal of Personality*, XXVIII (1960), 463–478.

This article explores the effect of group unity on self-esteem. Groups which were perceived to have more unity had more effect on the self-esteem of group members than those perceived to have less unity. Individual failure was more easily accepted by the individual in groups with high unity than in those with low unity.

Section C: Group Decision and Social Change

Babchuck, Nicholas; Wayne, Gordon C.; and Breeze, Jane. "Membership Characteristics of Small Groups," *Journal of Educational Sociology,* XXXII (1959), 333–343.

What are the effects of a small closed social system on its members? Such a system was studied on a university campus. Using sophomore girls, the study focused upon the social system itself, the unique characteristics of its members, and the results of interpersonal interaction in this small group. An interesting and unusual study.

Kelley, H. H., and Shapiro, M. M. "An Experiment on Conformity to Group Norms where Conformity is Detrimental to Group Achievement," *American Sociological Review,* XIX (1954), 667–677.

A study of the relationship between group acceptance and individual conformity. Eighty-two college freshmen in groups of five or six participated.

Section D: Problem Solving

Heimicke, C., and Bales, R. F. "Developmental Trends in the Structure of Small Groups," *Sociometry,* XVI (1953), 7–33.

What effect does the social status of a group have on its efficiency in solving problems? This was the focus of a study in which a comparison was made of the problem-solving efficiency of low- and high-status groups and the degree of satisfaction achieved.

Taylor, D. W., and Faust, W. L. "Twenty Questions: Efficiency in Problem Solving as a Function of Size of Group," *Journal of Experimental Psychology,* XLIV (1952), 360–368.

A comparison of the problem-solving efforts of individuals and small groups of two and four members. Using twenty separate questions and sixty subjects, comparisons were made in terms of the number of questions solved, the number of failures, and time spent per problem. The study was well designed and produced some interesting results.

Section E: Group Counseling

Bilovsky, David; McMasters, William; Shorr, Joseph E.; and Singer, Stanley L. "Individual and Group Counseling," *Personnel and Guidance Journal,* XXXI (1953), 363–368.

The purpose of this study was to compare the outcomes of individual and group counseling with reference to the realism of a chosen vocational objective. More than four hundred twelfth-grade boys participated in the study. Half of them received individual counseling, and half, group counseling. Each individual was rated on the realism of his vocational choice and each took the same pre- and post-battery of tests. Also, the same number of total hours was spent with groups as was spent with individuals. The outcomes of this study provide some evidence regarding the comparable effectiveness of individual and group counseling.

Davis, Donald. "Effect of Group Guidance and Individual Counseling on Citizenship Behavior," *Personnel and Guidance Journal,* XXVIII (1959), 142–145.

Which is superior for the improvement of citizenship behavior, individual or group counseling? Three groups of ten persons each who were lowest in a class of seventy in citizenship grades received counseling. Ten received individual counseling, ten received counseling in a group, and ten served as a control group. The same amount of time was spent in individual and group counseling. This is an interesting study, and one of the few which attacks the problem directly.

Froehlich, Clifford P. "Must Counseling Be Individual?" *Educational and Psychological Measurement*, XVIII (1958), 681–689.

A comparison of the outcomes of individual and group counseling. The criterion for improvement was the degree of agreement between self-rating and test scores. It was assumed that improvement would show a closer agreement between self-rating and tested abilities after counseling than before.

High school seniors participated voluntarily. Seventeen were counseled individually and twenty-five were counseled in small groups of four to six students. Each student rated himself before and after counseling on a five-point scale in each of the areas measured by the *Differential Aptitude Test*. Counselees in each group also rated the counselor's helpfulness.

Section F: Evaluation

Lorge, Irving. "Groupness of the Group," *Journal of Educational Psychology*, XLVI (1955), 449–456.

This stimulating article questions the validity of many assumptions concerning groups. Several hypotheses which require testing are offered, and the difficulty of establishing models capable of being used for the purpose is discussed.

PART FOUR

Leadership

Leadership is a long-standing and widespread topic of interest and concern. Few problems have received as much attention by speakers and writers. "Military men, journalists, politicians, novelists, dramatists, poets, feminists, financiers and physical scientists" have all circulated ideas on leadership.[1]

Despite this emphasis, there is little consensus concerning any aspect of the topic. It is agreed that leadership exists, but there is little agreement on its prediction or its method of development. There is, however, one perceptible movement in the field.

Formerly the leader was one who by his personality and rhetoric swayed the group to his wishes. It was assumed that the characteristics of leadership had been identified and that those who possessed them were leaders. If one was acclaimed a leader, he was considered so in all situations and with all types of groups. The quality of the productivity of the group was directly and wholly related to the quality of leadership. A leader was one who had more knowledge, more skills, and was further advanced in every way than his followers. Some thought, however, that he should not be too far advanced, or too intelligent, since he might not understand the followers. Theories thus held in the early fifties now seem inadequate or even detrimental.

Students of leadership now make assumptions which are in sharp contrast with those earlier held. They do not claim the ability to name the characteristics of a leader. Not only do they affirm that there are few characteristics in common among leaders but also that the differences far exceed the similarities. The current view of the leadership function has also shifted. The leader is generally considered now to be one who works well with the members of the group. His function is to free their creative potentialities, to help them

[1] Luigi Pretrullo and Bernard M. Bass, *Leadership and Interpersonal Behavior* (New York: Holt, Rinehart & Winston, Inc., 1961) p. xxvii.

reach a higher level of thought and better interpersonal relationships. Thus it is recognized that he may succeed better in this function with some groups than with others. The leader is expected to be intelligent, but not necessarily more intelligent than all of the members of the group. The productivity of the group is the joint responsibility of the members and the leader. They are viewed as a cooperating unity. The emphasis in leadership has moved from the leader's direct accomplishments to his personal characteristics: the leader is the kind of person who releases the potentialities of others for constructive ends.

Such an evolution in leadership theory and practice would hardly have taken place without insights from many experiments and several disciplines. Among these has been a growing emphasis on the privileges, rights, and duties of the individual. The authoritarian relationship is no longer accepted as the norm. Studies on interactions within the group, on the attitudes and outcomes of groups under different and opposing forms of leadership, have contributed to the understanding of group dynamics. Experiments on learning and change in behavior have also contributed significantly. The increasing emphasis on field theory concepts as opposed to association concepts have provided another basis for the critical examination of leadership theories.

The readings in Part Four focus on six considerations: the definition and qualities of leadership, approaches to leadership, foundations of leadership, leadership functioning, varied problems of leadership, and evaluation of leadership. They present vigorous differences of beliefs regarding the meaning of leadership and its functioning. They confront those who would lead small groups with the necessity of becoming more acutely aware of their own beliefs and of the relationship of their convictions to their actions. One inescapable fact is evident: leadership as an art cannot be separated from leadership in the person of the leader.

Section A

THE LEADER

The concept of the leader has changed during the last decade. Attention has shifted back and forth between his characteristics and his function. Some theories, such as "once a leader, always a leader," have fallen into eclipse. It is now recognized that a person may be a leader in one situation and a follower in another.

Although the emphasis has moved from the leader to the act of leadership, certain recognized qualities of the leader remain. These qualities are discussed by Cecil A. Gibb in "Definition of the Leader."

In "Qualities of the Leader," Murray Ross and Charles E. Hendry describe and discuss research relating to three critical leadership qualities: empathy, consideration, and surgency.

Of course these qualities alone are not adequate. The leader requires a high degree of cognitive accuracy. He must have an unusual acceptance of himself. He must be open to, and be challenged by, new experience. He must be able to discriminate expertly between means and ends; to have the capacity to grasp the covert meaning behind the verbal expression. He must also be an autonomous individual with a personal value system.

25

Definition of the Leader

Cecil A. Gibb

. . . .

Whenever two or more persons interact in the pursuit of a common goal, the relation of leadership and followership soon becomes evident. It is equally evident, however, that this relationship does not necessarily take, persistently and continuously, the same direction. Everybody has known friendships in which one of the friends was persistently the leader while the other willingly followed. But equally, one can recall friendships in which now one friend and then the other assumed the role of leader. This same reversibility of the leader-follower relation is frequently observable in the marital group. Indeed, every group will differ from every other in the details of this relation; and these differences will depend upon individual and relative differences in the endowment of members of the group as well as upon the cultural tradition within which the group is functioning. Thus a husband who is, by profession, an interior decorator may assume leadership in the decoration of his family home. The working wife whose income exceeds that of her husband may determine the residential location of the family. But paradoxically the culture confers the possibility of leadership, in each of these cases, upon that group member who would ordinarily be a follower. A moment's thought about the relative freedom to lead enjoyed by the American, the British, the German, and the Arabian wife will serve to illustrate clearly this fact.

The Leader as an Individual in a Given Office: The "popular" answer to the question: "Who is the leader?" suggests that whoever occupies a leader's office is a leader. Shartle and Stogdill[1] adopted this as an initial definition of the leader to guide the Ohio State University Studies in Naval Leadership. They have begun by assuming that "persons who occupy positions which are commonly presumed to demand leadership ability are proper and likely subjects for the study of leadership."[2] Such a convenient starting point for

From Cecil A. Gibb, "Leadership," Chapter 24 in Gardner Lindzey (ed.), *Handbook of Social Psychology*, Vol. 2, 1954. Addison-Wesley, Reading, Massachusetts. Pp. 880–884. Reprinted with the permission of the publisher.

[1] C. L. Shartle and R. M. Stogdill, *Studies in Naval Leadership* (Columbus, Ohio: Ohio State University Research Foundation, 1952).

[2] *Ibid.*, p. 6.

their investigations is made possible largely by the high degree of organization in the groups they proposed to study. When studies are made in less structured, traditionless groups there often is no leader office upon which attention can be focused. However naïve it may be to assert that the leader of an army is its general, of a team its captain, of a business organization its president, and so on, it cannot be denied that this is one place to start the study of leadership. As analysis proceeds, however, it becomes clear that such a definition of the leader embraces so wide a variety of relationships as to be of little scientific value. More analytic definitions of the leader must be employed.

The Leader as Focus for the Behavior of Group Members. A quite different approach, based on the work of Freud,[3] is made by Redl.[4] If leadership is regarded as a relation, then the types of leadership generally identified should be recognizable as expressions of different kinds of relationship. Redl introduces the concept of "central person" and distinguishes ten different types of emotional relationship between the central person and other group members. Redl uses the term "leader" for only one type of relation, giving different names to the other types. The term leader is restricted to that relationship which is characterized by love of the members for the central person, leading to incorporation of the personality of the central person in the ego ideal of the followers, i.e., they wish to become the kind of person he is. This definition is far removed from our usual conception of the leader, as represented by Stogdill and Shartle, and even from the analytic conceptions we shall next discuss. It is a highly restrictive definition of the leader, but it does use as its differentiating characteristic the nature of the emotional relationship between the leader and other group members and, in so doing, provides a model worthy of much more detailed attention than it has yet received.

Definition of the Leader in Terms of Sociometric Choice. Sociometry, a technique devised by Moreno[5] for revealing the feeling or preference relationships among the members of a human group, was early shown by Jennings[6] to be an effective instrument for the study of the leadership structure of small groups. This technique, and its many modern derivatives, has been described in detail elsewhere. . . . In this discussion we wish only to point to this method of identifying the leader of a group, and to indicate its applicability to all primary groups from traditionless laboratory small groups to military and business organizations. There is good evidence that members of a group can identify reliably those persons who exert most influence upon them and that leaders defined this way are closely correlated with leaders

---

[3] S. Freud, *Group Psychology and Analysis of the Ego* (London: International Psychoanalytic Library, 1922).

[4] F. Redl, "Group Emotion and Leadership," *Psychiatry*, V (1942), 573–596.

[5] J. L. Moreno, *Who Shall Survive?* (Washington, D.C. Nervous and Mental Diseases Publishing Company, 1934).

[6] Helen H. Jennings, *Leadership and Isolation*, First Edition (New York: Longmans, Green & Co., 1943).

identified by external observers and by other criteria. Gibb[7] has reported that when participants in traditionless groups of ten were asked a question implying selection of co-workers on the basis of "influence," though the word influence was not used, the correlation of these choices with observer ratings of "leadership" was approximately 0.80. And when participants were asked directly whom they regarded as having been leaders, the correlation with observer ratings was again 0.80. Furthermore, Wherry and Fryer[8] found that Signal Corps officer cadets were able, at the end of one month, to identify leadership to a degree equalled by officers only after four months of observation.

A word of warning concerning the sociometric definition of the leader is in order. There is now abundant evidence[9, 10, 11] that the sociometric question asked, or the nature of the sociometric criterion, makes a very considerable difference. For example, studying experimental groups of ten men each, and using ratings made by two trained observers as a criterion of leadership, Gibb[12] found a correlation coefficient of approximately 0.45 between this criterion and responses to a sociotelic question calling for identification of group members with whom respondents would like to participate further in similar activities. Similarly, this leadership criterion and responses to a psychetelic question asking for the identification of liked co-workers showed a correlation of approximately 0.42. Socio-centrality is not necessarily leadership.

These findings have been confirmed and extended by Bales,[13] using a somewhat similar technique. He had participants in small group discussions answer four sociometric questions relating to (a) contributing the best ideas, (b) guiding the discussion, (c) likes, and (d) dislikes. To these data Bales has added observations and analyses of initiation of interaction. And finally, participants indicated whom they regarded as "the leaders." In the first place, it is of interest that Bales finds a direct positive relation between basic initiating rank and votes for "best ideas" and "guidance" except that the second man is unaccountably low. Furthermore, this relation does not hold for basic initiating rank and "likes." Here the first man is low while the second man is best liked, thus suggesting that the man who is participating most heavily is losing likes and provoking dislike.

Secondly, the definition of the leader, in terms of sociometric choice, is further advanced by Bales' finding that the "best ideas" and "guidance" roles are most closely associated in the participants' minds with leadership, and that the "best liked" role is *least* closely associated with leadership.

[7] C. A. Gibb, "The Sociometry of Leadership in Temporary Groups," *Sociometry*, XIII (1950), 226–243.

[8] R. J. Wherry and D. H. Fryer, "Buddy Ratings: Popularity Contest or Leadership Criteria," *Personnel Psychology*, II (1949), 147–159.

[9] Gibb, *op. cit.*

[10] J. H. Carter, "Military Leadership," *Military Review*, XXXII (1952), 14–18.

[11] R. F. Bales, "The Equilibrium Problem in Small Groups," in T. Parsons, R. F. Bales, and E. A. Shils, *Working Papers in the Theory of Action* (Glencoe, Ill.: The Free Press, 1953), pp. 111–161.

[12] *Op. cit.*

[13] *Op. cit.*

Bales has also demonstrated that there is a change over time in the percentage of cases in which the best liked man plays "leader" roles. Whereas the "like" votes coincided with those for "best ideas" and "guidance" to the extent of 64 per cent and 41 per cent respectively in the first meeting, these figures had fallen to 11 per cent and 18 per cent respectively by the fourth meeting. As Bales points out,[14] this is a striking indication of incompatibility of these two roles.

The Leader as One Who Exercises Influence Over Others. The empirical investigation referred to above[15] provides strong support for the notion that a leader may be reliably defined in terms of the extent of his influence within a group. In the scientific literature this form of definition has been employed frequently. The O.S.S. Assessment Staff reports:

> There was nothing novel in our conception of leadership. We thought of it as a man's ability to take the initiative in social situations, to plan and organize action, and in so doing to evoke cooperation.[16]

Seeman and Morris in an early report of the Ohio State University leadership series say:

> One tentatively adoptable definition of leadership emphasizes its influence aspect: leadership acts are acts by persons which influence other persons in a shared direction. This definition implies a positional relationship between the "leader" and other persons. A leader position is defined in terms of relative status in an influence hierarchy (or relative degrees of influence).[17]

Pigors'[18] definition is still, however, the most satisfactory. He indicated that leadership is a concept applied to the personality–environment relation to describe the situation when a personality is so placed in the environment that his "will, feeling, and insight direct and control others in the pursuit of a common cause."

Leadership and Headship Differentiated. In order to define the leader as that group member who exercises most influence over his fellows or, even better, to define leaders (plural) as those members of a group who influence their fellows more than they are influenced by them, it is necessary to qualify "influence" by insisting that the term leadership applies only when this is voluntarily accepted or when it is in "a shared direction." The relation between master and slave, teacher and pupil, and frequently that between officer and men is characterized by a type of unidirectional influence which few people would want to call leadership. There is almost general agreement

---

[14] *Op. cit.*, p. 156.

[15] Gibb, *op. cit.*

[16] O.S.S. Staff, *Assessment of Men* (New York: Rinehart & Co., 1948), p. 301.

[17] M. Seeman and R. T. Morris, *A Status Factor Approach to Leadership* (Columbus, Ohio: Ohio State University Research Foundation, 1950), p. 1.

[18] P. Pigors, *Leadership or Domination* (Boston: Houghton Mifflin Company, 1935), p. 12.

in the literature of the last few years that leadership is to be distinguished, by definition, from domination or headship. The principal differentia are these: (1) Domination or headship is maintained through an organized system and not by the spontaneous recognition, by fellow group members, of the individual's contribution to group goals. (2) The group goal is chosen by the head man in line with his interests and is not internally determined by the group itself. (3) In the domination or headship relation there is little or no sense of shared feeling or joint action in the pursuit of the given goal. (4) There is in the dominance relation a wide social gap between the group members and the head, who strives to maintain this social distance as an aid to his coercion of the group. (5) Most basically, these two forms of influence differ with respect to the *source* of the authority which is exercised. The leader's authority is spontaneously accorded him by his fellow group members, the followers. The authority of the head derives from some extra-group power which he has over the members of the group, who cannot meaningfully be called his followers. They accept his domination, on pain of punishment, rather than follow. The business executive is an excellent example of a head exercising authority derived from his position in an organization through membership in which the workers, his subordinates, satisfy many strong needs. They obey his commands and accept his domination because this is part of their duty as organization members and to reject him would be to discontinue membership, with all the punishments that would involve.

The intragroup relations differentiated here as headship and leadership are not, of course, mutually exclusive; but neither are they coincident, as so much of popular thinking suggests. Many heads are recognized by their subordinates as making very positive contributions to group progress and are therefore accorded willing cooperation and, through it, leadership status. In fact, as Hartley and Hartley[19] have pointed out, the military forces of the United States and large industrial organizations in this country, which in the past have functioned almost exclusively on a headship basis, have expressed a need for much more leadership in intraorganization relations.

The Leader Defined in Terms of Influence Upon Syntality. It was suggested above that the essence of the leader role is to be found in voluntary conferment of authority by followers. It was also indicated that such leadership is bestowed only on persons who appear to contribute to group progress. In other words, the leader's influence upon individual group members is secondary to his influence upon total group locomotion. It is argued by Cattell[20] that the existence of a leader is detectable from an examination either of internal group relations, i.e., structure, or of the effectiveness of total performance of the group as a group, i.e., syntality. On this basis, he has proposed that we define a leader as "a person who has a demonstrable influence upon group syntality"; and that we measure leadership "by the magni-

[19] E. L. Hartley and Ruth E. Hartley, *Fundamentals of Social Psychology* (New York: Alfred A. Knopf, Inc., 1952).

[20] R. B. Cattell, "New Concepts for Measuring Leadership in Terms of Group Syntality," *Human Relations*, IV (1951), 161–184.

tude of the syntality change (from the mean) produced by that person."[21]

This definition of the leader has a number of important implications. There is a variety of independent dimensions of syntality, as we shall indicate later, and change may occur in any or all of these. Furthermore, change may be in the direction of either increase or decrease. From the point of view of over-all evaluation leader effect might be either positive or negative. We cannot talk of good or bad leadership because whether an increase or decrease along one of the syntal dimensions is to be considered good or bad will depend upon the extent and direction with which that factor weights various actual performances for which we already have values. Nevertheless, this concept of the leader will not take us in a completely different direction from that of the preceding category because, as Cattell points out:

> There are certain putative dimensions such as integration, cohesiveness, viscidity which must reach acceptable values for the group to function and survive as a group *at all*, and presumably any leader who can increase these is good . . . Apart from these possible exceptions, it is perfectly safe to speak of a leader only as being good or bad *for some specific performance.*[22]

Far more basic is the fact that this type of definition ignores the nature of the relationships between leader and followers. By such a definition our distinction between headship and leadership would disappear, except insofar as one could define these as subtypes of leadership. Similarly, patriarchy, tyranny, socio-centrality, and many other forms of interpersonal relations would have to be regarded as leadership subtypes. Within psychological and sociological literature, we have essentially two concepts which are both designated by the term leader. The one is the all-inclusive concept indicated by Cattell's definition. The other, and more frequently found, is more restricted. The group member confers leadership status only upon *some* individuals who exert influence upon group syntality, namely, those who are perceived to be moving the group in the direction of a goal which is a group goal because it has a potentially satisfying quality for some needs of all members. It is not true to say that the existence of a leader (in this more restricted sense) is detectable from, or definable in terms of, the effectiveness of group performance. On the other hand, if interpersonal relations of influence constitute leadership, then we may accept Cattell's suggestion that one important index of the quality of this leadership is derived from observations of the effectiveness of group or organization performance. And such a conception does have far-reaching research implications.

The Leader as One Who Engages in Leadership Behaviors. Because of the difficulties involved in using any of the above definitional schemes to guide research in leadership, Carter[23] and Hemphill[24] have recently proposed

---

[21] *Ibid.*, p. 175.

[22] *Ibid.*

[23] *Op. cit.*

[24] J. K. Hemphill, "Theory of Leadership," Unpublished Staff Report (Columbus, Ohio: Ohio State University Personnel Research Board, 1952).

the definition of leadership in terms of leadership acts. Of these Hemphill's proposals are the more rigorous and we may confine our attention to them. He suggests that "To lead is to engage in an act which initiates a structure in the interaction of others as part of the process of solving a mutual problem."[25] Leaders are then to be identified by the relative frequency with which they engage in such acts. This formulation recognizes the fact that groups develop leadership hierarchies and that differentiation between successive levels is in terms of frequency of leading. Only rarely, and then in highly structured organizations, can we identify "the leader." Most groups have many leaders. As Carter says: ". . . in actual behavior, the leaders or the followers fulfill their stereotyped roles only in the statistical sense."[26] And to quote Hemphill again: "A leadership role is a differentiation of structure-in-interaction in which the point of reference of the differentiation is frequent leadership acts."[27] In the case of Hemphill's definition the controversial element will probably be the differentium, "initiation of structure in the interaction of others." This concept Hemphill defines as "a consistency in the activities occurring during interaction which would permit the prediction of future interaction activity with an accuracy exceeding chance."[28] While this defines a leader in terms of his intragroup behavior, it again produces a definition which embraces a variety of relations from dominance to socio-centrality. This is simply a more restricted form of Cattell's definition insofar as "syntality" is "that which enables one to predict future performance of a group" and, therefore, structure in interaction can be but one facet of syntality.

Focused versus Distributed Leadership. There is one important advantage in conceiving the leader in terms of the frequency of his performance of leadership acts or functions. Leadership is probably best conceived as a group quality, as a set of functions which must be carried out by the group. This concept of "distributed leadership" is an important one. If there are leadership functions which must be performed in any group, and if these functions may be "focused" or "distributed," then leaders will be identifiable both in terms of the frequency and in terms of the multiplicity or pattern of functions performed. Such a precursory conception appears to accord well with the needs of contemporary research in this area. Heads may be distinguished from leaders in terms of the functions they usually or frequently assume. Similarly, differentiation between all types of influential persons may be possible in terms of the pattern of functional roles characteristic of each.

Whose behavior shall we observe in drawing up role prescriptions of leadership? If we observe all the behavior of all of the members, as seems best to do, by what criteria shall we differentiate leaders? Or perhaps the concept of the leader will be of no further value to us when we have differentiated such roles as those of the initiator, energizer, harmonizer, expediter, and the like.

25 *Ibid.*, p. 15.
26 L. Carter, "Leadership and Small Group Behavior," in M. Sherif and M. O. Wilson, *Group Relations at the Crossroads* (New York: Harper & Brothers, 1953), p. 5.
27 *Op. cit.*, p. 10.
28 *Ibid.*, p. 12.

To shift the problem of definition from that of defining the leader to that of defining leader behavior or leadership acts has advantages for particular researches and for particular systematic psychologies, but it offers no solution to the definitional problem. Whether we couch our definitions in terms of the leader or the leadership act it is, of course, leader behavior with which the psychologist is concerned.

. . . .

26

Qualities of the Leader

Murray Ross and Charles E. Hendry

. . . .

EMPATHY

It seems probable that the leader is able to identify with, and respond to, the emotional needs of the members of the group and/or to be the object of identification for group members. The leader, because of greater sensitivity, is aware of the needs of members of the group for recognition, affection, adventure, and so forth, and to some extent is able to meet these needs, or because of his personality, is perceived by the members as sensitive to their needs and active in meeting these needs. The statement is made in this way because, although research seems to suggest greater sensitivity and warmth on the part of the leader as compared with other members of the group, what is important is whether the members feel and recognize him as such a person. One study of the wide acceptance of Franklin Roosevelt among a sample of 963 respondents concluded, for example, that "Roosevelt was seen as a man who was warm, who liked people, who was personally democratic. His meeting of the people's need for approval and love from above was crucial in determining his tremendous acceptance."[1] Roosevelt could, of course, be

From Murray Ross and Charles E. Hendry, *New Understandings of Leadership* (New York: Association Press, 1957), pp. 43–44, 49–52. Reprinted with the permission of the publisher.

[1] Filmore H. Sanford, "Leadership Identification and Acceptance," in Harold Guetzkow (ed.), *Groups, Leadership and Men* (Pittsburgh: Carnegie Press, 1951), p. 174.

sensitive to the needs of millions only in general terms, or only in terms of common human needs. While he and most leaders probably tend to be warm, sensitive people, what is obviously fundamental is that their followers perceive them to be this kind of person. It is conceivable, for example, that one member of a group will be more sensitive to, and identified with, the needs of individuals in the group than will other members, and yet the group may fail to recognize this fact.

In a study of the abilities of leaders and nonleaders to estimate opinions of their own group, Chowdhry and Newcomb[2] found that leaders were significantly superior to nonleaders and isolates in their ability to judge group opinion on familiar and relevant issues. It is interesting that this capacity seems specific to the group: there is no evidence to suggest that they are good judges of others' attitudes in general (although they may possess such capacity and have not developed it). But their superiority in gauging opinions and attitudes in their *own* group *on issues relevant to the life of the group* is clearly marked and leads the authors to conclude: ". . . leaders of groups like these are chosen, in part at least, because of recognized qualities of 'sensitivity' to other members of the group."[3]

Bell and Hall[4] attempted to test the hypothesis that "the person selected as leader would have to be a person who was perceptive of the needs of group members" by administering the Dymond and Kerr tests of empathy in groups of rather different populations. The results suggest to the authors that a significant relationship exists between leadership position, as measured by ratings of fellow group members, and empathy, as measured by these tests. These tests show a significant relationship at a high level of confidence, although the size of one of the groups tested was considered inadequate. But again, the relationship of empathy and leadership is more than tentatively suggested.

. . . .

CONSIDERATION

It is quite possible that the item we are now about to discuss could well be included under the heading of empathy. We place "consideration" in a separate category because it seems to have a very practical implication not necessarily included in empathy. The "considerate leader" seems to be one who is able to help in very practical ways, to be ready to explain actions, to give detailed instruction, to improve the welfare of his followers relative to their work or activity in the group. This leader is not necessarily warm and sympathetic (although he often is) but is the type of person who is concerned and knows what to do in the practical situations which arise in the life of the group, i.e., when a soldier gets blisters on his feet, when a baseball

[2] Kamla Chowdhry and Theodore M. Newcomb, "The Relative Abilities of Leaders and Nonleaders to Estimate Opinions of Their Own Groups," *Journal of Abnormal and Social Psychology*, XLVII (January, 1952).

[3] *Ibid.*, p. 57.

[4] Graham B. Bell and Harry E. Hall, Jr., "The Relationship Between Leadership and Empathy," *Journal of Abnormal and Social Psychology*, XLIX (January, 1954), 156–157.

player's batting average begins to slip, when a committee chairman gets tied up in "red tape" and is uncertain about how to get attention for his report. While there is no evidence to support the idea, it may well be that the ward politician may demonstrate this quality to a high degree. He is the person who can help with any one of a hundred practical problems with efficiency and skill, if not warmth and sympathy.

Halpin and Winer in their study of the leadership behavior of airplane commanders[5] attempted to have air crews rate their commanders on a number of preconceived dimensions. Four factors, which it was felt might have general validity, were identified. One of these factors was *consideration*, which was interpreted as the extent to which the leader, while carrying out his leader functions, was considerate of the men who were his followers.[6] Cattell and Stice found that among elected leaders *practical concernedness* was one of the important criteria which distinguished leaders and nonleaders.[7] In their list of eleven leadership principles, the United States Army identifies an item which Gibb states as "knowing subordinates and showing consideration for them."[8] In another report of his study of airplane commanders, Halpin notes that superiors and subordinates were inclined to evaluate oppositely the dimensions of *consideration* and *initiating structure*, the subordinates rating consideration positively.[9] Apparently there are, or may be, differences in the importance of this item as judged from above and below. But there appears to be no question that for followers the "practical concernedness" of the leader is an item of major importance in their appraisal of him as a "good leader."

The importance of consideration in leader-behavior has, of course, been revealed in other studies. In the Roosevelt study, of which mention has already been made, it was found that one of the three major factors in this leader's success was that "Roosevelt's 'payoff' in material terms was very important, especially among the lower economic classes."[10] Similarly in several studies in industry and business the factor of consideration has been identified.[11] In a study of morale among railroad workers the differences in fore-

---

[5] A. W. Halpin and B. J. Winer, *The Leadership Behavior of the Airplane Commander* (Columbus: Ohio State University Research Foundation, 1952).

[6] As reported in Cecil A. Gibb, "Leadership," in Gardner Lindzey (ed.), *Handbook of Social Psychology* (Reading, Mass.: Addison-Wesley Publishing Company, Inc., 1954), Vol. II, p. 891.

[7] Raymond B. Cattell and Glen F. Stice, *The Psychodynamics of Small Groups* (Final Report on Research Project, Human Relations Branch, Office of Naval Research, University of Illinois, 1953), p. 93.

[8] Gibb, *op. cit.*, p. 889.

[9] Andrew W. Halpin, "The Leadership Behavior and Combat Performance of Airplane Commanders," *Journal of Abnormal and Social Psychology*, XLIX (January, 1954), 21–22.

[10] Sanford, *op. cit.*, p. 174.

[11] See, for example, Daniel Katz, Nathan Maccoby, Gerald Gurin, and Lucretia G. Floor, *Productivity, Supervision and Morale Among Railroad Workers*, Institute for Social Research (Ann Arbor, Mich.: University of Michigan Press, 1951), pp. 22–23; and Daniel Katz, Nathan Maccoby, and Nancy C. Morse, *Productivity, Supervision and Morale in an Office Situation*, Part I, Institute for Social Research (Ann Arbor, Mich.: University of Michigan Press, 1950), p. 62.

men attitudes in sections of high and low productivity were reported as
follows:

> Foremen of high and low sections differ in their attitudes toward their men.
> Foremen of high sections are more positive toward their men, take a more
> personalized approach to them and give more attention to problems of their
> motivation. Four findings support this conclusion:
>   a. Men in high producing sections feel that their foremen take more per-
>   sonal interest in them than do men in low producing sections.
>   b. Men in high producing sections report that their foremen are more help-
>   ful in training them for better jobs than do men in low producing
>   sections.
>   c. Men in high producing sections perceive their foremen as less punitive
>   than do men in low producing sections.
>   d. Foremen of high producing sections tend to be more "men-oriented"
>   than foremen of low producing sections. (This difference is not statis-
>   tically significant.) [12]

It seems clear, then, that when describing what the leader must be, we
must take note of the leader's ability to be considerate in ways which his
followers find practical and helpful. . . .

SURGENCY

Surgency is a factor identified by Cattell and Stice and is defined in terms
of talkativeness, cheerfulness, geniality, enthusiasm, expressiveness, alertness,
and originality. The difference between leaders and nonleaders in terms of
the factor surgency was not found by Cattell and Stice to be significant when
the leaders were identified by two observers, but when leaders were "elected
leaders," the difference on the surgency factor between leaders and nonleaders was highly significant. "The elected leader category differs from the
others . . . in the high weight it gives to surgency. In catching the limelight
and holding it, as the elected leader needs to do, the surgency factor is evidently of very great importance."[13]

This factor, then, is not one that is necessarily crucial for a variety of types
of leaders, such as the counselor, the appointed officer, the administrator, but
for the person who is elected to office it is probably of critical importance.
It suggests that the elected leader must be prominent, pleasant, positive. He
must be alert to all that is going on in the situation, able to contribute with
enthusiasm and originality, and able to verbalize, or to express his contribution in other ways, in a manner that has meaning for those who elect him.
This significant difference between the elected leader and followers suggests
that an appointed leader, or counselor, or deputy working with an elected
leader need not have surgency, but may need to contribute in the areas in
which the surgent personality is inadequate. He would, of course, need to

---

[12] Katz, Maccoby, Gurin, and Floor, *op. cit.*, p. 23.
[13] Cattell and Stice, *op. cit.*, p. 94.

recognize and accept the need, and perhaps inevitability, of surgency in the elected leader, for it is this factor, presumably, that permits him to be elected. But the elected leader may not be able to handle detail, to probe the depth and complexity of a problem, to foresee the consequences of group activity of certain kinds, to see the relationship between apparently isolated events, and so on. A role that supports and enriches the function of the elected leader is that which must be played by other types of leaders in a democracy and in a democratic organization. The factor of surgency will influence the selection of leaders, but to work with these elected officials, leaders with quite different qualifications may be required, whose contribution to the group or organizational goal is nonetheless vital.

. . . .

Section B

THEORIES OF LEADERSHIP

In the evaluation of the concept of leadership emphasis has moved from the leader to the group and then to the interaction among group members and the leader.

The earliest concept, the trait theory, perhaps the oldest and most superficially plausible of them all, is examined by A. W. Gouldner in the first reading, entitled "The Trait Theory."

A second approach places emphasis on the situation as the determinative factor in successful leadership. According to this theory, variation among groups demands that a leader have great flexibility. This point of view is discussed in the second reading, also by A. W. Gouldner, entitled "The Situationist Theory."

The leader satisfies some of his needs through his leadership. Through interaction persons vary greatly in their ability to evoke positive responses from others. This theory, in which leadership is considered to be the product of interpersonal interaction rather than attributes within the person, is the position taken by Helen Hall Jennings in "The Interaction Theory."

27

The Trait Theory

A. W. Gouldner

. . . .

LEADERSHIP TRAITS

The above account, accenting as it does relations between leaders and followers and the situational or group context of leadership, involves an approach which was not always entertained in studies of leadership. In the past, the conditions which permitted an individual to become or remain a leader were often assumed to be *qualities* of the individual. These were in some way believed to be *located in* the leader. It was postulated that leadership could be explained in terms of the "traits" possessed by the leader. Thus a multitude of studies were made which purported to characterize leaders' traits — i.e., those of their distinctive ways of acting, or personality characteristics, which tended to recur.

Since the trait approach has in many ways exercised an important influence on thinking about leadership, examination of some of its findings and assumptions will further serve to orient this work. Trait studies of leadership can be classified in many ways. Two that seem most useful from the present point of view are: (1) classification of trait analyses of leadership in terms of the method of study used; and (2) the relationship that is assumed to exist between the traits of leaders and the group or situational context.

In terms of the first method of classifying trait studies, two major categories may be found: first, the impressionistic accounts and, second, the experimental studies employing forms of controlled observation. Both kinds of studies were alike, of course, in that they were guided by their use of this concept. Each author tended to conclude his work with a list of adjectives (or trait-names) of varying length and content. Charles Bird, for example, studying some twenty trait-analyses of leadership, found about seventy-nine traits mentioned altogether.[1]

Typical of the early impressionistic analyses of leadership traits are the lists proposed by two military men, Munson and Miller. Miller[2] maintained that

"Leadership Traits" from *Studies in Leadership* by Alvin W. Gouldner. Copyright 1950 by Harper & Brothers. Reprinted by permission of Harper & Row, Publishers, Incorporated. Pp. 21–25.

[1] Charles Bird, *Social Psychology* (New York, 1940).
[2] Arthur Harrison Miller, *Leadership* (New York, 1920).

the outstanding military leaders were typified by a personality structure manifesting self-control, assiduity, common sense, judgment, justice, enthusiasm, perseverance, tact, courage, faith, loyalty, and other traits. Among the general leadership traits mentioned by Munson were: personality, manner, use of language, tact, cheerfulness, courtesy, justice, and discipline.[3] E. S. Bogardus proposed five traits allegedly universal to leadership: imagination, foresight, flexibility, versatility, and inhibition.[4]

Bertrand Russell, adding his list to the many already existing, commented: "To acquire the position of leader he (the individual) must excel in the qualities that confer authority: self-confidence, quick decision and skill in deciding the right measures."[5] Robert Michels has suggested the following traits: force of will, relatively wide knowledge, Catonian strength of conviction, self-sufficiency, and others.[6]

The *impressionistic* surveys of leadership traits were, in some respects, far surpassed by the more careful studies of Terman, Reaney, Nutting, Rohrbach, Bellingrath, Marion Brown, Bennett, Jones, and T. L. McCuen.[7] But they have been superseded mainly in the rigor of the investigational techniques by which the traits were isolated or determined. That is, they too assumed that leadership hinged on, and could be best described in terms of, the trait-qualities of individuals. Recently commenting on this, Lindesmith and Strauss have stated: "Leadership is commonly thought of in terms of leadership qualities. . . . In taking over this common-sense notion, social psychologists have been led to seek those traits of personality that are most usually associated with being a leader."[8]

Thus, as Lindesmith and Strauss suggest, many of the trait analyses of leadership have apparently been influenced by current popular conceptions of leaders as being in some way unusual beings possessed of extraordinary powers alien to the common run of mankind. As such, they are objects capable of being transformed into the "magical helpers" sought by those whose need for security is resolved by finding some powerful authority upon whom they can become dependent. Moreover, these trait analyses also conform to the popular conceptions of leadership in that, by divorcing the leader from his group and institutional setting, they do not challenge the assumption that social crises may be met without institutional changes.

INADEQUACIES OF THE TRAIT APPROACH

The inadequacies of the above type of trait studies can be only briefly summarized here. Leaving aside questions concerning their investigational technique, the following points may be raised:

[3] Edward L. Munson, *The Management of Men* (New York, 1921).

[4] E. S. Bogardus, *Fundamentals of Social Psychology* (New York, 1942), chap. 12.

[5] Bertrand Russell, *Power, A New Social Analysis* (New York, 1938).

[6] Robert Michels, *Political Parties* (Hearst International Library, 1915), p. 64ff.

[7] E. DeAlton Partridge, *Leadership Among Adolescent Boys* (Teachers College, Columbia University, No. 608 [1934]); this contains a very able summary of the work of these men up to that date.

[8] Alfred R. Lindesmith and Anselm L. Strauss, *Social Psychology* (New York, 1949), p. 274.

1. Those proposing trait lists usually do not suggest which of the traits are most important and which least. Not uncommonly, lists of more than ten traits are presented. In most such lists it seems very unlikely that each of the traits is equally important and deserves the same weighting. Bearing in mind that practical application of leadership studies (as, for example, in leadership selection or training) requires compromises due to time limitations and the number of candidates available, the failure to indicate the rank order of importance of the traits makes it difficult to know *at what points* compromises may be made. It is only within very recent years that the work of trait-analysts, like Raymond Cattell, gives promise of coping with this problem.

2. It is evident, too, that some of the traits mentioned in a single list are not mutually exclusive. For example, Miller lists tact, judgment, and common sense as leadership traits. It would seem, ordinarily, that the first two would be included in the last.[9]

3. Trait studies usually do not discriminate between traits facilitating *ascent* to leadership and those enabling it to be maintained. It seems to be assumed that all the traits which differentiate leaders from followers are functional to ongoing leadership. It appears entirely possible, however, that certain of the traits of leaders were necessary conditions for success in the *competition to become* a leader but are not needed by an *established* leadership.

4. Typically, most trait studies, and those of leadership are no exception, raise questions concerning the organization of behavior, the range of recurring behavior patterns manifested by individuals. They are largely descriptive. Usually they do not ask *how* these traits *develop*, or how the behavior *became* organized.[10] Thus, in so many of the trait studies there is the tacit assumption that the leaders' traits existed *prior* to their ascendance to leadership. It is therefore inferred that the leader's possession of these traits is to help explain how he became a leader.

Even in some of the trait studies which maintain that leadership traits are specific to the situation, that the situation makes them useful, it appears to be assumed that the individual *already possesses* the useful traits when he enters into leadership. The possibility that the reverse is true, namely, that it is the leadership position which fosters the *original* emergence of distinctive traits, is hardly ever systematically explored. In sum, one usually is not informed whether, and which, leadership traits exist before and which develop after leadership is assumed.

5. Finally, the study of the personalities of leaders, as of any other group of individuals, in terms of *traits* involves certain debatable assumptions regarding the nature of personality. It seems to be believed that the leader's personality can be, or is, described if all the traits by which it is composed are determined. Implicit is the notion that a personality is the sum of its component traits. This would seem, however, to ignore one of the fundamental properties of personality, its possession of *organization*. The same

[9] I have derived this illustration from E. Partridge, *op. cit.*

[10] Anne Anastasi, "The Nature of Psychological Traits," *Psychological Review*, (May, 1948), 127–138.

"trait" will function differently in personalities which are organized differently. To characterize the *component elements* of an entity such as personality is an insufficient description in that it omits consideration of the fact that these elements have varying *positions* or *arrangements*. It is only when attention is paid to arrangement or position that organization, as such, can be brought into account.

Most trait studies, flowing from the empiricist tradition, have approached the study of personality atomistically, and with little regard for personality as an organized whole. Not being oriented to any systematic theory of personality, they have pursued the "facts" of personality only to find that empiricism can be just as treacherous a guide as the most speculative of theoretical systems. It is, in part, because of the lack of any theoretical guide lines that the trait studies of leadership have produced relatively little convergence. Some scholars, for example, speak of two, ten, nineteen, and some of thirty, traits of leadership. Charles Bird's analysis of trait studies of leadership found that only 5 per cent of the traits mentioned were common to four or more investigations.[11]

· · · ·

[11] Bird, *op. cit.*

28

The Situationist Theory

A. W. Gouldner

· · · ·

SITUATIONS AND GROUPS: THE SITUATIONIST CRITIQUE

As already indicated, traits studies may be subdivided according to the manner in which they relate traits to the leadership *situation*. In general, a twofold subdivision may be made: (1) those implying or stating that the traits of leaders are universal: in other words, that the traits of leaders do not depend upon the situation, that leaders in any situation will possess the same traits; (2) the trait study which suggests that it is impossible to talk about leadership traits in general, but only about the traits manifested in concrete, particular situations. Leadership traits are conceived of as varying from situation to situation and group to group.

In order to understand the reasons which have fostered the emergence of the situational studies of traits, it is necessary to consider some of the implications of the proposition that leadership traits are universal and will not vary with the situation.

If this proposition were to be demonstrated, then several things should follow: (a) the traits or personal qualities which made an individual a leader in one group should also be useful for leadership in other groups; (b) a man who is a leader in one group should tend to be a leader in others.

That a leader is *involved in a network of relationships* with other individuals who, together with him, comprise a group, is a consideration, the full implications of which elude these trait-analysts. No matter how spontaneous and informal the group, its members never engage in random, continually unpatterned activities. There is a certain degree of persistence or patterning in the activities which a group undertakes, be it bowling, playing bridge, engaging in warfare, or shoplifting. These persisting or habitual group-activities, among other things, set *limitations* on the kind of individuals who become group members and, no less so, upon the kind of individuals who come to lead the group.

If by nothing else, the traits of a group's leaders are limited by the traits of the individuals who comprise the universe from which leaders are drawn. Any group functions as an attracting, repelling, and selecting mechanism. Not all individuals would wish, nor could they if they so desired, to become members of any group. As obvious examples: modern trade unions practically always exclude employers from membership; Girl Scouts exclude boys; armies, those physically or mentally ill. Similarly, pacifists would not be *interested* in joining the National Guard, nor would political conservatives be interested in obtaining membership in radical parties.

Trait studies themselves inform us that psychological traits are not distributed uniformly through all social strata. The distribution of traits differs with age, education, occupation, and sex.[1] From this it follows that members of particular groups will tend to possess certain traits both more and less than others. Since leaders tend to be members either of the group which they lead or of other limited groups, one may expect that the traits of leaders will vary with those of their group. Jenkins, in a recent summary[2] of leadership studies, concludes that "Leaders tend to exhibit certain characteristics in common with the members of their group. Two of the more obvious of these characteristics are interests and social background." The probability seems great, therefore, that the leaders of some groups possess *some* traits different from the leaders of other groups, and that "leadership traits" are not universal.

---

[1] Anne Anastasi, "The Nature of Psychological Traits," *Psychological Review* (May, 1948), 127–138.

[2] William O. Jenkins, "Review of Leadership Studies with Particular Reference to Military Problems," *Psychological Bulletin* (January, 1947), 54–79.

Not only are the traits of leaders limited by the traits of the individuals from which leadership is drawn, but they are further limited by the character of the group's *specific activities*. Even one of the earlier studies, made by Caldwell and Wellman, found that while certain traits — physical prowess, for example — were influential in the selection of school *athletic* leaders, these traits were not characteristic of leaders in *other* school activities. While height may be helpful to basketball players, its absence did not deter three rather short men — Mussolini, Hitler, and Lenin — from assuming the leadership of nations. In this vein, Cecil Gibb writes: "There is no one leadership type of personality. One man might achieve leadership status because he has superior intellectual endowments which force him consistently upon the notice of others and make them dependent upon him. A second achieves leadership because he has a quiet helpful interest in fellow group-members and because what British psychiatrists call his 'contact' is good. Leadership resides not exclusively in the individual but in his functional relationship with other members of his group."[3]

A. J. Murphy,[4] emphasizing the relative fluidity of leadership traits, points out that the "self-confidence" of a *work* leader may disappear if his group is placed in a parlor situation. Or that a leader noted for his "dominance" may become "shy" when placed in a situation in which his *skills* are not useful. Thus not only must the *group* in which the leader operates be considered, but also the *situation* which the group encounters. Both of these elements seem to affect the character of leadership traits. Jenkins' first conclusion of his summary of leadership studies emphasizes this: "Leadership is specific to the particular situation under investigation. Who becomes a leader of a given group engaging in a particular activity and what the leadership characteristics are in the given case are a function of the specific situation including the measuring instruments employed."[5]

Skills and Situations: the Situationist Critique Continued

The interaction between skills and situations, noted by Murphy above, has recently received cogent amplification by the OSS assessment staff:

> A member of an organization who cannot do what is expected of him is immediately confronted by the stress of self-criticism and of criticism, implicit or explicit, from his supervisor and from his co-workers. His self-confidence will diminish, and feelings of inferiority emerge; he is likely to become hypersensitive and defensive in his social relations, and blame others for his own shortcomings. . . . Thus, as soon as the strength of one component — in this case that of specific ability — drops below a certain minimum, other components are similarly affected. . . . Contrariwise, a man whose

[3] Cecil A. Gibb, "The Principles and Traits of Leadership," *Journal of Abnormal and Social Psychology*, XLII (1947), 231.

[4] Albert J. Murphy, "A Study of Leadership Process," *American Sociological Review* (1941), 675–676.

[5] Jenkins, *op. cit.*, 75.

talents are exactly suited to the job assigned to him and who, therefore, attains or surpasses the level of social expectation for him, will be continually encouraged by signs of approval and of respect from his associates, and under these conditions, his energy and initiative, motivation, effective intelligence, emotional stability, and social relations are likely to reach their maximum.[6]

The intricate relations between the psychological aspects or traits (skill, self-confidence, etc.) and the group aspects (respect, approval), so clearly described above, seem most likely to operate in the manner described *in a culture such as our own.* That is, in our culture great value is placed on *specialized skills* as the basis of legitimating occupancy of a great variety of roles, often including leadership roles. In consequence, the presence or absence of required *skills* may elicit a stronger group response in our society than it might in more traditional societies where skill was not such a primary basis of legitimation.

This suggests that skill may not be an open-sesame to leadership, *universally* facilitating ascent to or success in it. The situationists' emphasis on the role of skills may require trimming to more modest implications; in particular, limiting its operation to groups or societies outside the traditionalistic orbit. Formulated positively, the boundary conditions tacitly assumed by the situationists — and in terms of which their proposed interrelationship between situationally functional skills and leadership appears probable — include a relatively high division of labor and degree of specialization, an emphasis on achievement rather than ascription of certain statuses, and the use of skills as a basis of achieving and legitimating these statuses.

A second way in which the role of skills may be culturally bounded can be suggested. The OSS analysis of the *consequences* of skill-deficiencies or skill-competencies, their extraction of group deference, approval or respect, or their opposites, and their effects on the individual's traits (self-confidence, initiative, etc.) involve certain assumptions about *personality.*

Specifically, what must be assumed is that the individual has some motive or need for the high degree of responsiveness which he manifests to group judgments. The problem rests in the character of the motive or need. To find individuals responding to their groups, adapting, learning, modifying and being changed is not, in the light of modern psychology and sociology, in the least startling. Some degree of responsiveness and behavior modification must be accepted as "normal." But to find, or allege, individuals to be adaptable to the extent suggested by the situationists — that is, almost infinitely plastic — can be anticipated only under very limited psychological and, therefore, cultural conditions.

It may be hypothesized that the personality which would react as responsively or immediately to current group pressures is, perhaps, likely to manifest a weak or insecure ego and is in some measure, because of this, extremely dependent upon group judgments. Too, one might look for a heavy emotional investment in "success." Given these two psychological conditions, group judgments of individual worth may be *swiftly* responded to

[6] The OSS Assessment Staff, *The Assessment of Men* (New York, 1948), p. 456.

by the individual. Particularly so, if these judgments explicitly or implicitly involve assessments of the individual's "success," for it is with this that, in our culture, the individual's sense of worthiness is so intimately tied.

If such psychological conditions are pervasive, they must be presumed to be institutionally compelled. Possibly they emerge with the weakening of the stable traditional relations of family, neighborhood or church, and their substitution by the shifting, calculating ties of a market society. But the intent here is not to define the specific cultural boundaries yielding validity to the situationist propositions about the fluidity of traits, but only to suggest that these are *definable*.

To return to the situationist position:

"In practically every study reviewed," writes Jenkins, "leaders showed some superiority over the members of their group, in at least one of a wide variety of abilities. The only common factor appeared to be that leaders in a particular field tend to possess superior general or technical competence or knowledge in that area."[7]

Thus distinctive situations make specifically different demands for skill, and individuals failing to possess these will be limited in their chances for leadership. It is in this context that William F. Whyte's comment . . . to the effect that street-corner gang leaders tend to initiate group activities in which they excel, may be placed.

The unique experiences of the OSS assessment staff underscore the role of the situation still further. Directed to provide the OSS with personnel capable of performing *secret* missions, the assessment staff therefore only had a *general idea* of the assignment each man was to undertake. Consequently the assessment men could rate candidates only "according to their conception of *all-round men in a given field of activity*." (Our emphasis — A. W. G.) In attempting to explain why many of the men to whom they gave "high" ratings received "low" appraisals from the units to which they were assigned, the assessment staff writes: ". . . actually, the assessed man who went overseas was not called upon to deal fairly well with a multiplicity of rather general situations, but to deal very well with a limited number of specific situations . . . these men were appraised in the theater according to how effectively they performed a particular role in a particular location."[8]

Though not intended to refer to leadership alone, these conclusions of the OSS staff strongly suggest the limitations which concrete situations place upon the utility of leadership traits. It was clearly not enough to know the candidate's *general field* of activity to successfully predict his performance; a man *generally* competent in a field often would be judged incompetent to handle the *specific situation* in which he found himself. It is significant, too, that the assessment staff's prediction about the performance of the candidates was much more successful for those who "undertook the missions originally proposed for them than it was in the case of men who were given entirely different missions on arriving overseas."[9]

[7] Jenkins, *op. cit.*
[8] OSS Assessment Staff, *op. cit.*, p. 374.
[9] *Ibid.*

These, then, are some of the major lines of argument which those who consider, as Gibb states, that "leadership is relative always to the situation," have used in refutation of that branch of the trait school which held leadership qualities to be the same in all situations. By and large, the former school, characterizable as "situationists," have won the day. By now it is probably true that most social scientists would sympathize with A. H. Lloyd when he spoke even of *great* individual leadership as a "noble fiction." But uneasy rests the head that wears the crown of science.

．．．．

29

The Interaction Theory

Helen Hall Jennings

．．．．

In the little community studied in the present research, both isolation and leadership were found to be products of inter-personal interaction, and not of attributes residing *within* the persons placed in the respective choice-status by the membership. A social process of interaction involving a certain manner of behaving *by and towards* the individuals respectively so isolated or so "lifted" to leadership was found to form the very basis of the isolation and of the leadership. No simple variable, such as the length of time the individual had been in the community or his chronological age relative to other members or his intelligence or even his greater opportunity for contacting others, appears to account for the particular choice-status accorded to him. Instead, the reciprocal interplay maintaining between the individual and those in the same field *and constituting the individual's personality as the latter view him*, appears the underlying basic explanation of isolation and leadership. The personalities of such individuals, viewed by the investigator, also reveal from this "objective" standpoint (*i.e.*, that of an outsider) similar "estimates" to those given by co-participants in the field; but the more significant finding is not what kind of personality is likely to be isolated or what kind of personality is likely to be a leader (judged impartially by the investi-

From *Leadership and Isolation* by Helen Hall Jennings, pp. 211–217. Copyright 1950 by Longmans, Green and Company, Inc. Courtesy of David McKay Company, Inc.

gator in study of such individuals) — the more significant finding is that personality *per se in so far as it is reflected in social structure* is the capacity for interplay with other personalities, for responding to and for being responded to, in a reciprocal situation, the field in which the individual is in common with other individuals. Personality attributes accompanying isolation and personality attributes accompanying leader-positions, though they are found from an "objective" estimate to be widely contrasting, do not constitute a formula for either isolates or leaders; *within* either group the individuals vary in personality greatly from one another and *between* either group the individuals show also frequently personality variables in common. The urgent fact in either instance is the reaction to and the interpretation given to the respective behaviors exhibited by the individuals *and the latter's* characteristic manners of reacting to and interpreting the behaviors of fellow-members. Then it is seen that G. Murphy's[1] exposition of personality as not simply organism but as organism in a situation is further experimentally validated by the findings of this research. From situation to situation, the personality is re-defined, and the re-defining is reflected in the choice-status found for the individual from time to time.

Exploration of the simpler forms of biological organisms presents us with a picture similarly complicated. Weiss has vividly pointed out the field character of organization, biological and social, for individual cells — the fact that they "owe their fate . . . to the operation of forces and conditions to which they become subject in the course of development."[2]

Similarly, the physicist finds that a knowledge of electric charges does not provide an understanding of their action; it is the description of the electro-magnetic field between the two charges and not the charges themselves which is essential, the action being determined by the field.[3] Thus the field concept for physics is no longer merely "a means of facilitating the understanding of phenomena from the mechanical point of view."[4] In the construction of the field, *viz.* the lines of force, "our entire knowledge of the acting forces can be summarized."[5]

The field setting in the present research is the individual's *social space.* It describes the area in which the individual interacts or strives to interact with other persons and they with him. Each individual's social space is found to cover a varying area or sphere of other persons. The "evoking power"[6] of certain individuals to marshal to themselves the emotional expansiveness of those around them appears very great. In other instances, the individual appears conspicuous for the lack of positive choice expressed towards him.

The study indicates that exploration of the field in investigation of behavior can clearly reveal the significance of environmental factors in relation

[1] Gardner Murphy, "Personality and Social Adjustments," *Social Forces*, XV (1937), p. 473.
[2] Paul Weiss, *Principles of Development*, (1939), p. 289.
[3] Albert Einstein and Leopold Infeld, *The Evolution of Physics*, (1938), p. 157.
[4] *Ibid.*, p. 157.
[5] *Ibid.*, p. 135.
[6] The expression "evoking power" and one which follows, "press," are borrowed from the insightful contribution of Henry A. Murray *et al.*, *Explorations in Personality* (1938).

to individual characteristics. The choice-status of a given individual is seen to result not alone from his individual characteristics nor alone from the environmental factors to which he is subject but from the interaction of his individual characteristics *with* the individual characteristics of those about him, those *in his field, i.e.,* who have psychobiological relevance to his behavior (and for whom he has such relevance). Again, in a different sense, environmental factors are seen to play a negligible role. The individual's extent of emotional expansiveness towards others is seen to be *his individual* characteristic, a characteristic which finds consistent expression without relevance to the environmental factors which may exert "press" for or against its fulfillment.[7] It may be postulated that the concept of need comes nearer to describing emotional expansiveness than does the concept of trait. The individual is actually expressing how many persons he feels the need for in his life situation. We may judge it to be a trait, since the individual does not vary significantly from time to time in the extent of his expression towards others, but he, the individual giving the information, is himself of course not consciously displaying a "trait" nor aware of his consistency.

The field also reveals a number of psychological "laws" of another sort. By and large, it is seen that the positive attractions of individuals to one another far outweigh the rejecting or repelling feelings active between them in the test-community where they share a common life. Moreover, the interpersonal structure which comes to exist is characterized more by stability than by flux and displays a typical form, *viz.* has the same general outline at different times (regardless of the fact that different individuals may at different times be found to occupy various positions of choice-status). The balance in proportions of this structure at different times points in spite of the different positions ("upward" or "downward") of its individual carriers can thus be aptly described as an equilibrium in flux.[8] The question may be raised: Why does the field exhibit such a structure? The answer appears to lie in the different interpersonal capacity of individuals to draw choice to themselves, different capacities which maintain their respective differences in this respect *even as the group as a whole develops* in such capacity.

Within this structure, the phenomena of leadership and isolation appear as side by side phenomena that are born of the press exerted by field forces which are specific other persons acting upon the individual; in the one

---

[7] It is as if the individual must conceive of himself as "wanted," must not "see" the rebuffs which are being accorded him; he may not have to rationalize his situation for it may not be apparent to him.

[8] It should be noted that this interpretation refers to the *total structure* produced by choice behavior and not simply to constancy in number of certain positions of choice-status, e.g., number of isolates, number of leader-positions, number of reciprocations, etc. The writer has elsewhere reported that the extremes in position are consistently found to about the same extent upon re-test of the *same* population ("Structure of Leadership," *Sociometry*, I:99–143, July-October, 1937, p. 122). J. H. Criswell has also reported confirmation of such findings ("Social Structure Revealed in a Sociometric Retest," *Sociometry*, II:69–75, October, 1939, p. 74) and moreover noted that the degree of cleavage in a given group tends to remain constant. The importance of the present findings consequently lies in the fact that they do not concern only one or another aspect of structure or extremes in choice-status, but the *total structure in every respect considered as a whole.*

instance, individuals are propelled into positions of leadership through the response which greets their extraordinary capacity for inter-personal contribution *in specific situations* and, in the other instance, individuals are propelled into isolation through lack of positive response to their inter-personal contribution *in specific situations.*

Study of the behavior attributes accompanying high and low choice-status gives a view of individuals who differ respectively in capacity to contribute to the needs of others, to interact with mutual appreciation and benefit. It is seen that the individual's personality at a given moment reflects the field forces with which it is interacting and affects those field forces.

Leadership appears as a process in which not one individual has a major role but in which relatively many share. The specific avenues of rapport which bring one individual into contact with a particular "constituency" (selection of other persons) may not resemble those which relate a second individual to the persons who are drawn to him. The severalness of leadership appears related not alone to different capacities on the part of the leader-individuals but to the personality differences within the population; the latter are so wide that no one individual apparently can bridge the gap to rapport with others to a degree sufficient to earn choice from a majority of members. The superior capacity which one individual may have to recognize and respond to the needs of others does not show itself as a generalized capacity which may relate him to *any other individuals.* It appears in the special sensitivity between the individual and *specific* other persons, resulting in interaction between them. The concept of an individual being "a leader" (as contrasted with other individuals who are not "of this type") is, in this sense, without confirmation from the findings of the present research. The forces residing in a particular group and the expression they require evidently come to fruition according as the group contains within itself members through whom it can find outlets of representation; in the test-community, these forces are various and demand manifold expression. It is hardly likely that in larger communities and nations a less complex inter-personal structure of leaders is natural for their expression. Nevertheless the leader-positions judged by a stringent criterion are, in the test-population, limited in number; they appear to be so limited because the number of persons who are drawn to exert exceptional efforts in behalf of other members (in a manner which the latter recognize as constructive and representing their interests) are relatively few. It would seem that even as "standards" in this respect rise in a population, individual differences keep pace with the needs and leadership remains a many-sided process.

Section C

PSYCHOLOGICAL FOUNDATIONS OF LEADERSHIP

The group leader performs in terms of theory or assumptions regarding the behavior of people. This basis of his leadership may be unrecognized by him but is demonstrated in his performance. He performs in terms of his expectations concerning the actions and reactions of members in various situations. These he may have clarified and further developed through formal study.

The terms "authoritarian," "democratic," and "group-centered" are common in the vocabulary of most leaders. Without understanding these terms and their implications, many persons use them to describe a type of leadership they have seen or experienced.

Among the several theories of personality, those known as "association," "field theory," and "self theory" have been most influential in the operation of small groups. A clear and forceful discussion of the functioning of association and field theory in learning is provided in "Foundations of Authoritarian and Democratic Leadership," by L. Thomas Hopkins.

Since authoritarian and democratic leadership have their origin in association and field theory respectively, group-centered leadership takes its direction from self theory. The tenets of self theory, based upon Carl Rogers' Client-Centered Therapy are presented in "Foundations of Group-Centered Leadership," by C. Gratton Kemp.

Finally, the application of each of the theories to group process is described in "Differing Assumptions in Authoritarian, Democratic, and Group-Centered Leadership," also by Kemp.

30

Foundations of Authoritarian
and Democratic Leadership

L. Thomas Hopkins

. . . .

All theories of learning assume a psychological field in which the individual behaves. The fact that one group is called association theories and the other field theories does not mean that one has *no field* and the other has *a field*. Rather, the terms refer to two different meanings of field. The older association theories were organized prior to present concepts of psychological fields. The younger field theories are built on modern knowledge of behavior. The terms "authoritarian" and "cooperative" designate more or less adequately the existing field differences. Before discussing them I shall present the few points of field agreement so as to sharpen disagreements which are more important.

The fields assumed under the two theories are similar in these respects. (1) The field is the area of experience taken into account by the individual at the moment of his action. This includes himself as well as his external environment. (2) The field is composed of learning objects, nonlearning objects, and the way in which they affect each other. More specifically it is made up of people, other living organisms, the physical universe, events, customs, and a process of their relationship. (3) All behavior takes place in, is determined by, and is relevant to the psychological field of the individual. He has no behaviors which originate or are consummated outside of it. (4) The field is active at all times because it is partly composed of living organisms. A field without activity would be devoid of life and would therefore cease to exist. (5) Learning in some way remakes or reshapes the field including the learner. (6) Experts study fields in order to predict the movement of all things within them. Each individual studies his field so as to predict as accurately as possible his behavior and that of others within it. Psychologists and educators must anticipate with some accuracy the behavior of individuals in their various relationships. The associationist and the field theorist each assume the field which to them has the highest predictive value.

Each explores it with a similar purpose, although he begins with different perceptions and arrives at different conclusions.

. . . .

. . . Therefore, a pertinent question is how valid are the two theories in describing a psychological field which squares with the known conceptual and visceral experiences of growing people.

Both theories assume that learning is behaving or that learning changes behavior. To the associationist all behavior is composed of a few irreducible prior existing elements or fixed and immutable truths. Learning is acquiring these elements and truths in correct form under external controls by some form of conditioning. Improvement in learning is a change in the response system by deliberate or unconscious linkage or association of a new stimulus with old or new responses. This binding or linking of the new stimulus and response is always in the direction of some perfect achievement inherent in an anticipated goal. Thus increasing quality of behavior is a function of the quantity of responses and their probability of producing the perfect result. Novel response is merely a new and more complicated combination of prior existing simple elements. It can be produced by only a few individuals who are especially educated for this purpose. The masses are followers of the handed-down wisdom of the few.

To the field theorist behavior is the responding of the whole organism to the total confronting situation in order to control it or reduce need tension in the direction of life-fulfillment. Behavior is the organism in active inter-action with the environment, during which process both are modifying or changing each other. A situation can be defined operationally only in rela-tion to a specific organism. The organism can be defined operationally to obtain predictive power for behavior only in reference to the situation which it faces. Thus each serves to define the other, for each exists only in an organism–situation field. Learning is the product of living in mutual inter-action with others so that everyone can fulfill his inherent biological promise. Each person learns what he selects and accepts to live by. He learns it to the degree to which he accepts it or to the extent to which he acts on it as he acquires it. He learns it as he creates it in the ongoing life process. By sup-porting an organic interpersonal group, field theory develops mature people who believe in it and continue it.

Some students state frankly that they see no differences between the two psychological fields. To them, the contrasts are just another way of saying the same thing. Each field is based upon approximately the same concepts. They derive their support from three sources. (1) Psychologists and philoso-phers, especially associationists, have attempted in recent years to show that they hold field theory beliefs. (2) The long period of time during which associationism has dominated the social institutions of every culture gives it a validity which no mere upstart can claim. (3) Their own successful experi-ence is founded upon association theories of learning.

But there are two aspects of their situation which they may have inade-quately examined. First, their success may be due to learnings derived by the field theory process in uncontrolled experiences. Every person has a few of these even in a tight culture. These few may have had a marked effect upon the development of an individual with a receptive genetic pattern or a high energy potential. He may have lived in an authoritarian field loose enough to allow him to grow by a developmental process, even though he could not recognize or conceptualize it. Second, individuals may be rationalizing their association methods to protect themselves. They are unwilling to differentiate their learnings to new and different meanings which they cannot face. I try to help them by surveying briefly the historical background of each theory and suggesting that they study it further.

The association psychology with its accompanying philosophy originated in the a priori thinking which came down to us from Plato and Aristotle. Plato was deeply opposed to change. He lived in a world that was always in quest of certainty. To prevent the chaos which follows change and to insure the evenness of life which accompanies certainty, he sought a concept of man in his universe which permitted no change, but was grounded in universal immutable elements and their relationships. He reduced life to the same timeless, changeless, absolute principles which he found in mathematics. And since there were only a few men who could be educated so as to recollect and contemplate upon these timeless principles, which existed with them in their spirit world prior to their earthly existence, it followed that such persons should be the rulers of the state. Thus began the basic theory of aggregate fields which has been used continuously by all authoritarian personalities down to the present time.

Field theory psychology with its accompanying philosophy originated in the study of life as people know it, of experience as self-conscious activity, of man as a biological whole integrating his thinking and bodily movements into one continuous action, of persons examining together the life they have thus far lived in order to understand its process, of individuals interacting as groups so as to enhance the selves of all. Thus field theory grew out of a respect for people, for the process that is life, for the change that is growth, for the emerging intelligence that is direction, for the action that is the test of meanings, for the self that is the center of his universe.

• • • •

31

Foundations of Group-Centered Leadership

C. Gratton Kemp

The tenets of Carl Rogers' self theory are the basic assumptions of group-centered groups. These assumptions imply unique beliefs concerning the group members and the functioning of the leader.

Observers of democratic and group-centered groups may conclude that their differences are small and in terms of methods only, rather than in terms of principles also. This conclusion necessitates a closer scrutiny of the basic assumptions of self theory.

BASIC ASSUMPTIONS

Self theory is a composite of ideas and parts of theories drawn from many sources, with some creative and basic additions. The basic assumptions of self theory are organized under the following headings: (1) perception; (2) motivation; (3) knowledge; (4) symbolization; (5) change, therapy and growth; and (6) ego needs.

1. *Perception.* Perception takes place on both the conscious and subconscious levels, and both levels affect the resultant behavior. Reactions are not to the stimulus directly but to the experience which the perception induces. This experience is only a hypothesis, and judgment is suspended until it is put to the test. Unless the individual's subceptive perceptions inhibit him, he checks his tentative impression against other sources of information. Perception is selective. Those perceptions which are assimilated without distortion or some kind of modification are consistent with one's self image at the time.

2. *Motivation.* It is assumed that the organism has a single goal, that of realizing itself in accordance with its nature. The strength of this creative urge motivates a continuous striving against the most difficult odds. The mode is one of differentiation and expansion, the individual becoming more capable in decision-making and more autonomous.

3. *Knowledge.* Knowledge of one's self develops through interaction with the environment and especially through evaluative relationships with others. Through this interaction understanding, appreciations, and values develop.

Some of these are the result of direct experience, but some come from the values of others; they are not experienced directly but are perceived as important and therefore assimilated or introjected. Unfortunately, the latter are sometimes "perceived in distorted fashion as if they had been experienced directly."[1]

There is a dependence on knowledge in order to determine which are progressive and which are regressive ways of behaving. The choices must be "clearly perceived,"[2] and "adequately symbolized."[3] When this takes place, however, the person always chooses to grow. The individual has the potential for knowing himself better than he can be known by another even with the utilization of the best methods and instruments. His verbalizations are the symbolizations of inner experience and the means whereby the group leader may at least partially understand the member from the member's viewpoint. Also the individual's self reports are the best means of understanding his behavior.

4. *Symbolization.* The extent and character of the process of symbolization influences the character of the individual's development. "Psychological adjustment exists when the concept of the self is such that all the sensory and visceral experiences of the organism are or may be assimilated on a symbolic level into a consistent relationship with the self."[4] Experiences which are perceived as a threat or are inconsistent with the values one holds are not readily assimilated. Such experiences are generally ignored, or their existence is denied or given a distorted symbolization. Other experiences are usually perceived, symbolized, and organized into some relationship with the self.

All behavior is not dependent on the symbolization of experience. Occasionally it may result from "organic experiences and needs which have not been symbolized."[5] However, such behavior, since it is inconsistent with the self concept is disowned. How frequently we hear a friend say, "That wasn't like me," or "I never do that type of thing."

5. *Change, Therapy, and Growth.* These take place when the person is able to perceive, examine, and assimilate experiences which formerly were disowned and considered inconsistent with the structure of the self. The catalyst is the non-threatening situation in which the counselor completely accepts everything each group member says. This warm, accepting "climate" encourages each member to explore his unconscious feelings and bring them into awareness. The member moves slowly from the safe to the more threatening unsymbolized or wrongly symbolized experiences, but in time he becomes "in more unified fashion, what he organismically is, and this seems to be the essence of therapy."[6]

[1] Carl Rogers, *Client-Centered Therapy* (Boston: Houghton Mifflin Company, 1951), p. 498.
[2] *Ibid.*, p. 489.
[3] *Ibid.*, p. 490.
[4] *Ibid.*, p. 513.
[5] *Ibid.*, p. 509.
[6] *Ibid.*, p. 269.

The experience through which a person accepts and assimilates experiences previously denied greatly increases his understanding and acceptance of others. This recognition, acceptance, and assimilation of his experiences, both positive and negative, initiates "a continuing value process"[7] which replaces his former system built in large part upon introjected values.

6. *Ego Needs.* These have been described as "the need for positive regard," "the need for self-regard," and "conditions of worth." The need to be favorably regarded by others develops in accordance with the concept of self. This need may remain subordinate to the organismic valuing process, or the process may be ignored or discounted by the individual.

The need for self-regard grows out of the individual's life experiences. It functions within every kind of self-experience and is independent of interpersonal relations. Conditions of worth are the outcomes of the process of introspection. Following introspection, the individual avoids experiences which have lowered his self-regard and seeks those experiences which he considers will heighten it.

SUMMARY

The key ideas of self theory may be briefly stated as follows:

1. An experience is initiated by perception on both the conscious and subconsicous levels. Perceptions which are not in accord with a person's pre-formed value system are generally rejected, ignored, or distorted. The individual does not react to the perception directly but to his *feeling* with regard to it.

2. For constructive decision-making, the individual must perceive alternatives clearly and symbolize them adequately and correctly. Since the individual can know himself and verbalize his symbolizations, he can be assisted to perceive, accept, and symbolize those experiences which he formerly viewed as inconsistent with his concept of self. Self-actualization or constructive development results from the making of an increasing number of adequate, correct symbolizations.

3. The individual has one goal: to actualize himself. This he does in accordance with his biological mode of development and, if necessary, in a continuous striving against difficulties. In the process of self-actualization, he is further motivated by the need to regard himself and be regarded by others positively.

4. His values result from his reaction to his perception of direct experience and from introjection. The latter perceptions, despite the distortion involved, are valued as if they were perceived directly. The individual who is moving toward the goal of self-actualization constructively engages in a continual process of evaluation, instead of relying on introjected values.

These theoretical assumptions have important implications for the group leader. To operate within the framework of this theory, he must hold certain

[7] *Ibid.*, p. 522.

beliefs not essential to other leaders. Also, his performance must demonstrate his belief in these theoretical assumptions. The specific beliefs he holds and the methods he uses to implement them are discussed in the following selection.

32

Differing Assumptions in Authoritarian, Democratic, and Group-Centered Leadership

C. Gratton Kemp

Much of the discussion on leadership has centered upon process and outcomes. Little has been written to clarify the psychological and philosophical bases.

It is recognized that differences exist among types of leadership. Although the terms authoritarian, democratic, and group-centered are accepted as distinct methods, there is confusion regarding the differences in their basic assumptions.

This confusion may be partly caused by the overlap in the character of the responses elicited by the three methods. There are, however, both psychological and philosophical differences. The psychological distinctions arise from the fact that each method of group leadership originates in a different theory of personality. The philosophical differences come from their widely divergent assumptions concerning the nature of man.

BASIC DIFFERENCES

In an effort to distinguish among these methods, basic differences will be considered under the following five headings: locus of evaluation, principles of learning, process, material, and leader requirements.

Locus of Evaluation. In the early stages of the science of counseling, it was evident that the authoritarian method led to varying degrees of resistance. To reduce this resistance, group leaders became less directive.

Directive responses were replaced by suggestion, acceptance, approval, clarification, reflection, and encouragement. Interpretation, questioning, and evaluation were kept to a minimum. The group situation became more permissive, and the group member gained more freedom, but only the freedom to relate, respond, and make his own decisions within the framework established by or agreed upon by the leader. This has increased the opportunity for growth in decision-making and in the development of inner controls. The locus of evaluation, however, remains within the province of the group leader.

In groups using the group-centered approach the members select the material to be presented and evaluate it. They are gradually enabled to accept themselves as the locus of evaluation and to become responsible for the decisions.

Principles of Learning. The authoritarian group leader who expects intellectual assimilation to produce change uses the learning principles of association. He uses questions, interpretations, and explanations.

He assumes that integration results from the external explanation he adds to the internal reality of the group members. He assumes that he can correctly understand the significance of the material secured from the member and that the member will correctly understand the significance of his interpretations. Finally, he assumes that the member will intelligently and correctly accept the levels of aspiration set for him by the group leader.

The democratic leader, within the framework which he establishes, expects the response of the total organizing self of each member to produce change. He facilitates change by his questions, interpretation, acceptance, clarification, and reflection. He depends on his ability to involve the members and on their depth of insight.

He assumes that integration results from the internal clarification, synthesis, and evaluation of the ideas expressed by the group and the leader, within the previously established framework.

The group-centered leader, within the framework of the members' concerns, also expects the response of the total organizing self of each member to produce change. He facilitates this change by his acceptance, reflection, and clarification of each member's self-chosen verbalized material. He also depends on the depth of insight of each member, on the use of these insights as he feels able (safe), and on his drive to improve.

He assumes that integration results from the internal clarification, synthesis, and evaluation of the expressed ideas of the group which they have selected to reject or convert to their use.

Process. The authoritarian leader assumes that his decisions are superior to that of the group and that he is responsible for influencing the group to accept his views and plans. To achieve this result, he may use questions, suggestions, commands, interpretation, analysis, clarification, acceptance, reflection, or other methods. If necessary, he will reinforce his position by reward or punishment.

The democratic leader assumes that the members can reach a suitable solution regarding those issues which he presents, or those which he and they select for discussion. He therefore encourages their best thinking through the climate he engenders by his willingness and ability to listen and through acceptance and clarification. There is a minimal emphasis on questioning and evaluation.

The group-centered leader functions in accordance with the normal biological process. The members select the issues for discussion and reflect upon them orally or silently. Each member makes his own evaluation and converts the results of this to his use. In such a process, initiation, evaluation, and integration is within the choice and control of the members, individually and collectively.

The group-centered leader, through his respect for the ability and purposes of each member, assists him to understand, accept, and respect himself. He encourages the best thinking and responsibility for outcomes through his use of only reflection, acceptance, and clarification responses.

Material. In the authoritarian situation, the members feel little responsibility for the facilitation of the functioning of the group. They assume that it is the leader's function to initiate discussion and make decisions for improvement. The problems, ideas, and plans are those chosen and presented by the leader, not for evaluation, but for acceptance.

In the democratic situation, the members assume and accept more responsibility for decision-making and for the improvement of group functioning, but, though they may present issues for discussion, the acceptance of these issues for group consideration remains at the discretion of the leader. Usually the leader selects and presents the problems for discussion and does so after he is convinced that this procedure is conducive to better decisions and a higher level of functioning. (Note the decisions with reference to this in the selection entitled "Making Better Decisions," pages 246–247.)

In the group-centered situation the material for discussion is selected by a member or by the group. The material selected is of concern to the members and is also accepted by the leader as worthy of consideration and as a means for individual and group development. In this situation, the members gradually accept the responsibility for the improvement of group functioning and individual and group growth.

Leader Requirements. Every group leader needs a knowledge of psychodynamics. It is essential that he understand the meaning of the member's verbal responses and psychological movement. He must also know the psychological stages in individual development which are normal or abnormal.

The authoritarian leader relies upon his knowledge, skill, and performance. He becomes adept in his role and skillful in interpretation.

The democratic group leader, in addition to this, relies upon his increasing capacity to respect the abilities of the members to solve their problems and to translate their decisions into action.

Although all these abilities are important to the group-centered leader, for him, the crucial part of the group process is the relationship. He relies on the "self-organizing center" of the person and his "urge to mature." With the conviction that each group member can and will move toward a higher quality of behavior and better use of his abilities under the right therapeutic conditions, he is able to implement the environment necessary for these growth processes.

While the authoritarian leader works to become a friendly, tactful, skillful, interpretative thinker and communicant, the democratic leader endeavors to implement high-quality thinking through facilitation of the proper "climate." The group-centered leader strives to understand the member from his frame of reference, to see the situation from his viewpoint. The first two leaders think about the member; the group-centered leader thinks with the member.

The authoritarian leader applies himself to increasing his knowledge and developing his skills. In addition, the democratic leader tries to increase his respect for and acceptance of the thinking of the members. The group-centered leader endeavors to transform himself so that he may understand the growth process within the members, individually and collectively, and work in accordance with it.

Group-centered leadership is admittedly the most difficult to attain. It demands that the leader be willing and able to transform himself into a group-centered person. Unless he can believe that the group member has the potential for growth and will use it, he cannot become group-centered.

SUMMARY

Confusion has resulted from a lack of clarification of the philosophical and psychological bases of group methods. This confusion increases when distinctions are made only with regard to process.

When these bases are understood, certain distinctions become evident. In authoritarian group leadership, the locus of evaluation is centered in the leader. In democratic leadership, the locus of evaluation is centered in the group within the framework established by the leader. In group-centered leadership, the locus of evaluation is in the group member. In authoritarian leadership, the principles of learning are based chiefly on association psychology; in democratic leadership, they are based on field theory; and in group-centered leadership they are based on self theory.

The material within the authoritarian concept is selected and presented by the leader; in the democratic, it may be selected and presented either by the leader or by the group and confirmed by the leader; in the group-centered, the material is selected and presented by the group member(s).

Questioning, interpretation, analysis, suggestion, acceptance, reflection, approval, clarification, and evaluation constitute the responses of authoritarian and democratic leadership. The group-centered leadership responses are acceptance, reflection, and clarification.

Authoritarian group leaders rely upon their skill to diagnose, interpret, and explain. The democratic leader relies upon his ability to discern those issues and problems with which he believes the members can contend and his willingness to allow them to do so. The group-centered leader relies on his ability to understand the meaning of the response from the member's frame of reference, on the member's urge toward health, and his potential ability to express his ideas and feelings.

The training requirements of group leaders of different orientations are similar in many respects. Knowledge and skill are essential to all types of leadership. The authoritarian leader must believe in his ability to select, evaluate, and present material and to initiate action in relation to his decisions. The democratic leader must believe in the ability of the members to discuss and reach a solution or understanding concerning the issues which he, or he and the members, have selected. The group-centered leader must believe in the ability and motivation of the group member to select and evaluate material, to integrate ideas, and to initiate a higher quality of behavior.

It is erroneous to conclude that a certain method of leadership is superior in all situations and for all leaders. The decision to develop and use any method of leadership requires the consideration of several questions, the most significant of which are the following: (1) Is the leader now, or able to become, the kind of person who can meet the demands and be comfortable with the type of leadership under consideration? (2) Have the members had experience with the process the leader plans to use? If not, could it be introduced to them? Is the problem one which they may have some understanding of or acquaintance with? (3) Is the procedure to be used in accordance with the accepted administrative procedures of the institution?

Section D

LEADERSHIP FUNCTIONING

The effective leader functions differently in different situations. The demands of the situation and the needs of the members require that, within his accepted method, the leader cultivate a flexible approach.

In some situations he lacks the administrative freedom to engage in more than a limited use of democratic procedure. In others he may feel too insecure to be democratic. He may not accept the basic assumptions of one or more of the recognized methods of leadership. The expediency of the particular situation and the training and experience of the members are other variables which he considers in the decision which he reaches concerning his method of functioning.

Even leaders who attain an admirable degree of judgment and flexibility still perform within the framework of their personal beliefs concerning the assumptions of each method and their ability to use them. They must also consider their beliefs concerning people, their attitudes, how they perform, and how best to work with them. Therefore each leader has a preferred method of leadership which he uses whenever he can.

Within his chosen method, however, the leader exhibits complex behavior, not only because the situation may seem complex but also because he himself is complex. He has conscious and unconscious needs which must be satisfied in some manner within the particular situation. Also, the same person performs differently with different groups, although the activities may be the same in each.

There appears to be no particular manner of leadership behavior which is superior in all situations. Leadership in its entirety is exceedingly complex in structure and complicated in its varied methods, levels, and interactions. The first selection discusses the psychology of the leader as it affects leadership functioning.

For purposes of study leadership may be broadly classified and described. This is done in the second selection, "Distinctions in Leadership Functioning," by C. Gratton Kemp, which outlines the differences in functioning of three types of leadership.

Of the three types, group-centered leadership is the latest to receive attention and about which we are least intelligent. The group-centered leader is unique in his beliefs and his method of operation. He is distinguished by his belief concerning the constructive energy, perception and motivation of the individual. The distinctiveness of this approach is presented in "The Functioning of the Group-Centered Leader," by Thomas Gordon.

33

Distinctions in Leadership Functioning

C. Gratton Kemp

Leadership has been described from many perspectives. There is, however, general acceptance that the leader cannot be fully understood apart from the group; both are affected by the interaction. From the viewpoint of the member, the leader improves the social milieu and widens the field of participation. The members respect him as their leader to the extent that his leadership satisfies sufficiently their important self-perceived needs.

These needs vary greatly with groups. If the majority of the members in a group desire structure, preciseness, and pre-planning, they will be relatively more satisfied and secure if the leader plans and explains.

If, on the other hand, the majority of the members are open to experience, accept, and appreciate the challenge of the new, and tolerate ambiguity with little difficulty, they will support a leader who engages with them in this kind of experience.

Permeating all approaches to leadership is the reluctant acceptance of the fact that although certain personality characteristics do not necessarily ensure a leadership role, the person possessing certain qualities is more likely to become a leader than he would without them. But all of the characteristics and behaviors of leaders are not similar; some are so dissimilar that clarity necessitates their differentiation and description.

Types of Leadership

The following brief descriptions of each type of leadership are, of course, not comprehensive, and in point of view they must at times be extreme. Nevertheless, it is hoped that these distinctions will help to emphasize the important differences in their functioning.

Authoritarian. The authoritarian leader plans, directs, and informs. He decides on the goals to be achieved, or works toward those which have been given to him, by motivating the group to accept them and to use his suggestions, requests, or demands.

He centers control in himself through various forms of evaluation and the use of reward, praise, or fear of punishment. He assumes that his decisions are superior to those of the group and perceives his function as one of directing the group members toward the fixed goals. He exercises his authority in securing compliance to his wishes and expects a high degree of conformity. His decisions are based on his assumption that the group is inexperienced, untrained, or unintelligent about the problem.

Those who accept this point of view commend leaders who are forceful, energetic, good organizers and planners, firm, kind, and successful in getting group members to perform. A good leader influences members to vote for him, work for him, and give him token respect.

Members react to this leadership in various ways. Some welcome the security which structure establishes. Others apparently recognize that they are sacrificing their right to share in the making of decisions, and, as a consequence they may sabotage the plans, suggestions, or requirements demanded and become very restrictive in their response. Some react by passivity, conformity, withdrawal, or "apple polishing." Hostility toward other members or toward the leader will frequently occur and may produce counter-hostility; cliques or various kinds of subgroups may form and undermine the leader's authority.

The value of this kind of leadership is questionable. A large proportion of the membership remains dependent and ego-centered. There is little improvement in ability to make decisions, to cooperate, and to learn. Progress in self-understanding and understanding of others is limited. The leader may get things done quickly, but it is he and not the group who directs and controls, although he may spuriously label the decision a "group decision."

Democratic. The democratic leader engages in cooperative planning in accordance with the freedom in the situation, or the "unfixed ends," his own security and experience, and that of the group.

His function is to help the members clarify their interests and goals and select a problem of mutual concern. He then helps them to focus their highest quality of situational thinking on the problem, and, through their experience, to produce a product which may be ideational or concrete in form.

He is careful to develop and respect the evaluative abilities of the group members. The controls and direction are those cooperatively developed and accepted. He aids the members in the visualization of alternatives and the projection of themselves into ensuing situations, the result of which would be the choice of an alternative.

He assumes that the members of the group are as capable as he of making decisions in relation to their particular training and experience.

His status is an instrument used for the improvement of quality of thought and behavior. This is accomplished through listening, questioning, reacting, and, when necessary, by reflection, clarification, and synthesis. In this manner he helps the members to do situational thinking, assuming that free, thoughtful reflection and interaction among the members will produce better decisions.

Those who accept this point of view consider good leaders to be those who facilitate an environment conducive to freedom of expression, who respect the personality of each individual and understand the meaning of his verbal expression, who acts as a resource person and aids in the development of each group member.

Certain problems attend this kind of leadership. The leader may experience difficulty in the following: (1) permitting the members the right to evaluate; (2) recognizing situations with "unfixed ends" and using them for growth purposes; (3) appraising judiciously the ability and readiness of the group for democratic planning; (4) developing situational thinking as a prerequisite to democratic planning; (5) assisting members to modify their stereotypic concept of the leader's role; (6) encouraging member interaction, which is essential to cooperative planning.

His reasonable success in the accomplishment of these ends could be expected to produce the following outcomes: (1) a higher quality of thinking; (2) greater ability to cooperate; (3) more self-reliance, responsibility, and control in carrying out decisions; and (4) more understanding of self, of others, and of the democratic process.

Group-Centered. The group-centered leader has two goals: (1) the ultimate development of the group's independence and self-responsibility and (2) the release of the group's potential capacities. He holds attitudes similar to those of the client-centered therapist. He perceives his function to be that of helping the group to work out its own adjustment and by so doing to become more responsible. He is primarily interested in the growth process. He is interested in therapy to the degree possible within this setting.

He encourages the following conditions: (1) an increasing opportunity for participation, (2) the absence of barriers to free communications within and among all the members of the group, and (3) a nonthreatening, accepting psychological climate.

He functions by conveying warmth and empathy, by listening to each member in an effort to understand the meaning of his contribution. He uses reflection, creates acceptance, refrains from the evaluation of comments, encourages permissiveness within the limits of the situation, and performs the linkage function.

There are certain problems in the initiation and furthering of this kind of leadership:

1. The leader's method is a deterrent until he loses the stereotypic leader role and is accepted as a member of the group. Then, in the manner of any other member, his plan will be evaluated, accepted, or rejected.

2. Increasing member participation develops only through the accepting climate; it cannot be forced or verbally encouraged.

3. The limits set by the framework within which the leader and group perform may act as a hindrance and deterrent, impeding the possibilities of distributive leadership.

4. A proportion of the group membership may be unable to accept the leader on an equalitarian, non-authoritative basis.

5. The leader is unable to assess accurately and wisely and to prepare the group for their new experience.

To the degree that the undertaking is successful, the following outcomes can be expected:

1. The members feel that they are understood and accepted.

2. They accept responsibility for evaluation.

3. They internalize the functions of the leader.

4. They change from ego-centered to group-centered thinking and participation.

5. There is an increase in spontaneous expressions of feeling and interpretation.

6. There is a decreasing dependence on the leader and an increasing acceptance of group standards.

SUMMARY

Each method of leadership is based on different assumptions, procedures, and outcomes. The chief differences can be grouped under three headings: the locus of the problem, the locus of procedure, and the locus of evaluation.

In authoritarian leadership the locus of the problem and of evaluation is within the leader. In democratic leadership the locus is within the leader or within the group members and accepted or rejected by the leader and evaluation is made by the members within the framework previously established by the leader. In group-centered leadership the locus of both the problem and the evaluation is within the members.

The locus of procedure in the group with an authoritarian leader is in the leader. He initiates and continues the discussion. Questions are answered by him and ideas are presented directly to him. In the democratic group, the interaction is three-way from leader to members, from members to leader, and from one member to another. In the group-centered group, the procedure is initiated and continued by the members. The interaction is also three-way, with this important distinction: the group-centered leader uses only reflection, acceptance, and clarification responses.

34

The Functioning of the Group-Centered Leader

Thomas Gordon

. . . .

In addition to carrying out a different role during his first contact with a group, the group-centered leader continuously performs certain distinctive functions throughout the life of the group, but especially during the initial

From Thomas Gordon, *Group-Centered Leadership* (Boston: Houghton Mifflin Company, 1955), pp. 177–192. Reprinted with the permission of the publisher.

stages of the group's development. These functions gradually are taken over by other members of the group as the members lose their initial dependence upon the leader; but during the early stages of the group's development, these functions are often performed predominantly by the leader.

When we analyze a role as complex as that of a group leader, we do some injustice to its dynamic and personal nature. We need to keep in mind at all times that picking apart the leader's role tends to depersonalize him, making him appear as a collection of discrete and mechanical techniques rather than as a real person with attitudes and feelings, functioning in an integrated and purposeful manner. Nevertheless, it can be extremely helpful to isolate and identify some of the distinctive behaviors of the group-centered leader, in this way making it easier for others to understand how the group-centered leader differs from other kinds of leaders.

Social science can now help in making this kind of analysis, for we are now able through electrical recordings to reproduce group discussions accurately and we have systems of categorizing different kinds of verbal communication. In the present description of the role of the group-centered leader, use has been made of these methods of analyzing the verbal behavior of the leader.

LISTENING

Probably the most important single function performed by the group-centered leader is that of listening to the contributions of others in the group. This would hardly seem worth mentioning were it not for the fact that the group-centered leader practices a very special and distinctive kind of listening.

What We Mean by Listening. Psychotherapists have introduced us to a new kind of listening. They have shown that it can be a powerful agent for helping persons with emotional problems. Its therapeutic effect can be understood when we consider that the emotionally disturbed individual himself suffers from faulty communication, both within himself and with others, and listening by the therapist seems to improve his communication dramatically. Rogers expresses this idea clearly when he writes:

> The whole task of psychotherapy is the task of dealing with a failure in communications. The emotionally maladjusted person, the "neurotic," is in difficulty first because communication within himself has broken down, and second because as a result of this his communication with others has been damaged. If this sounds somewhat strange, then let me put it in other terms. In the "neurotic" individual, parts of himself which have been termed unconscious, or repressed, or denied to awareness, become blocked off so that they no longer communicate themselves to the conscious or managing part of himself. As long as this is true, there are distortions in the way he communicates himself to others, and so he suffers both within himself, and in his interpersonal relations. The task of psychotherapy is to help the person achieve, through a special relationship with a therapist, good communication within himself. Once this is achieved he can communicate more freely and more effectively with others.[1]

[1] C. R. Rogers and F. J. Roethlisberger, "Barriers and Gateways to Communication," *Harvard Business Review,* XXX (1952), 46.

What the therapist has learned to do is to enter a relationship with another in which he consistently listens with understanding. He has discovered a way of getting into the thought processes of the other person, or we might say that he has learned how to enter into the person's own unique "frame of reference." To do this requires an intent to understand how the other person is looking at the world, how he is perceiving things. The therapist puts on the spectacles of the other person so that he may view reality in the same way. This requires putting aside one's own spectacles, suspending one's own ideas, shutting out as completely as possible one's own way of looking at things.

This is precisely what the group-centered leader tries to do as he listens attentively to the expressions of his group members. Having no need to get his own idea across, having no secret intentions, having no particular goals which he expects the group to reach, he is thus more able to listen to the contributions of others without being concerned about their ultimate effect upon the group. In a sense, he "permits" himself to listen with understanding because he has freed himself from the need to influence and direct the group's discussion.

This type of listening requires certain attitudes on the part of the leader. He must *want* to understand how the speaker is looking at the world. There must be an earnest intent to "be with the other person," with respect to *his* thoughts, feelings, and attitudes. Such an attitude is quite different from one that predisposes the listener to try to change the other person's way of looking at things. Instead of listening with the feeling, "You should be seeing things differently," the leader tries to maintain an attitude of, "Let me try to understand how you *are* seeing things." This attitude is different, too, from one which leads a listener to interpret or "go beyond" what the speaker is perceiving at the moment. It is common practice, for example, for some group leaders to listen for the deeper meanings, for "the unconscious aspects of communication," for that which is not intended by the speaker. This is a different kind of listening attitude from the one we are describing. The group-centered leader tries to hear only what is present in the speaker's awareness and to read nothing additional into the communication.

The Test of Listening. Because we can never be sure that we have completely understood another person, it is important to test the accuracy of our listening. Unfortunately, in most situations involving an attempt to communicate with others, we rarely put our understanding to a test. Consequently, we often misunderstand others or distort their meanings. One of the best ways of minimizing this misunderstanding and distortion is for the listener to try to restate in his own language the expression of the speaker and then to check if the restatement is acceptable to the speaker. This is essentially what the group-centered leader is continuously doing throughout the initial stages of the group's development. He calls it "reflection of feelings or meanings," to convey that he is trying to mirror the speaker's expressions so accurately that the speaker himself is satisfied that he has been understood.

This is an extremely difficult thing to do, even momentarily. The reader who is interested enough to test out the accuracy of his own listening will find the following experiment both interesting and revealing:

> Choose a situation in which you have become involved in a controversial discussion or argument with another person. Suggest to the other that you both adopt a ground rule and follow this strictly throughout the discussion. The rule: Before either participant can make a point or express an opinion of his own he must first reflect aloud the statement of the previous speaker; he must make a restatement that is accurate enough to satisfy the speaker before he is allowed to speak for himself.[2]

This little experiment, if it is seriously carried out, will demonstrate, first, that it is very difficult to adopt another's frame of reference. Second, it will give the participants a new kind of experience in which they will find that emotions tend to drop out and differences become minimized. Furthermore, each participant will discover that his own views are changing and will admit that he has learned something new from the other.

The Element of Risk in Listening.   Not only does listening with understanding require a firm intent to understand another and a kind of rapt attention that we seldom give to speakers; it also requires a certain amount of courage and personal security. This is because there is a real risk involved in this kind of listening. We run the risk of being changed ourselves, for when we really understand another we may be exposing our own ideas and attitudes to opposing ones. To understand completely an opposing point of view means that we have at least momentarily looked at the world through our adversary's spectacles — in a sense, we have tried to become *him* for the moment. In the process we have suspended judgment and withheld evaluation. Consequently, we run the risk of actually adopting the other's point of view or of having our view altered by his. To expose ourselves to such a change requires courage, because each of us is organized to resist change. It is upsetting to discover we are wrong. Therefore it takes a good measure of personal security to enter into a relationship knowing that the stage is being set for a possible alteration of ourselves.

Perhaps it is fortunate that there is some compensation for the risk assumed by one who is willing to listen with understanding. Strangely enough, listening to another also facilitates change in him. This has been proved by the clinical experience of psychotherapists and is supported by a growing body of research findings in this area. Clients who successfully complete a series of interviews with client-centered therapists show measurable changes in their attitudes toward themselves and toward others. There is also evidence that changes may occur in their basic values and in their personal philosophy.

Listening facilitates change in the speaker in a very indirect way. If a person knows someone is listening carefully and is trying to understand, he may make more effort to express his attitudes and ideas more clearly. By so doing, he may obtain new understandings simply because he is expressing his own ideas more clearly. In trying to understand another person, then, a

---

[2] Suggested to the writer by S. I. Hayakawa, the semanticist.

listener may actually encourage that person to express himself more understandably. This is suggestive of the old saying that "we never really know something unless we can explain it clearly to someone else."

Why the Group-Centered Leader Listens. We have mentioned several of the effects of listening with an intent to understand another. There are many by-products or expected results from this type of intensive listening. . . . It may be useful at this point . . . to summarize some of the effects the group-centered leader has come to expect from his listening to the contributions of his group members:

> First, group members will feel that their contributions are of sufficient worth to merit being listened to and understood by the leader. This should greatly facilitate participation by the members through reduction of the threat of devaluation.
> Second, group members will make a greater effort to express their ideas and opinions more clearly, knowing that someone in the group is listening attentively and is going to reflect their ideas back to them for confirmation.
> Third, group members will begin to drop their defensiveness, open their minds to new understandings, think more flexibly, reason more effectively. This should not only improve the quality of contributions but increase the problem-solving ability of the group as a whole.
> Fourth, when conflicts or controversies arise in the group, each member is more likely to alter his own point of view rather than defend it vigorously and stubbornly.
> Fifth, group members observing that the leader is listening with understanding will themselves begin to listen to each other more attentively and with more understanding.
> Sixth, the leader himself will learn far more from listening to others in the group than he would through giving lectures, presentations, and other leader-centered activities.

These, then, are some of the important results the group-centered leader expects to achieve through listening with understanding and through testing his understanding by reflecting the meaning of members' verbal contributions. Each of these results will contribute significantly to the group-centered leader's long-range objectives and goals — (a) creating a nonthreatening group atmosphere conducive to creative participation by the members, and (b) facilitating communication so that the various members' contributions will be understood by the others and utilized by the group.

Although the leader who expects such results as these has probably learned to do so from his own experiences with groups, there exists fairly extensive experimental evidence for some of these outcomes. . . .

CONVEYING ACCEPTANCE

One of the barriers to creative participation by group members is their fear of being changed, influenced, evaluated, or rejected. People are not as free to give of themselves and to express their uniqueness in an atmosphere that is threatening, judgmental, evaluative, critical, or moralizing. Consequently, an important function of the group-centered leader is to create an atmosphere that is nonthreatening, nonevaluative, and nonrejecting.

Such an atmosphere cannot be created at once. It may take many sessions before people will begin to feel accepted and free from the threat of change or evaluation. The process can be accelerated, however, if the leader consistently is able to avoid certain kinds of responses and relies heavily on certain other responses.

Responses That Convey Intent to Change Others. There are ways of responding to others which most of us would agree show a fairly obvious intent to change others, to direct their behavior, or to influence them to behave in some particular way. Examples of such responses are:

Ordering, Commanding, Demanding, Requiring, Prohibiting
You must do this.
You cannot do this.
You have to be careful.
I expect you to do this.
Calm down.
Don't take these facts too seriously.

Obligating, Persuading, Warning, Cautioning
You should do this.
You ought not to say such things.
You need to improve your vocabulary.
You'd better not try that.

Appealing, Imploring, Wishing, Hoping
I wish you would do this.
Please do this.
Can't you do this for me?
I am counting on you to speak clearly.

Advising, Suggesting
You might try this.
Why not take another look?
Perhaps you would like to talk about something else.
You could do this, perhaps.

These four categories of responses frequently convey to the speaker that he is not accepted *as he is,* that he is being told to change in some way. What is being communicated to him is the other's desire for him to think, feel, or behave differently. He is likely to think, "I must change," "I ought to change," "It would be desirable to change," "It would please others for me to change."

Such attitudes are not conducive to the feeling of being accepted. Consequently, the group-centered leader tries to avoid using these four types of responses. As we have emphasized earlier, he will be more successful in doing this if he has freed himself from the need to change others and if his genuine attitude is one of accepting others as they are. It is difficult for a leader to avoid giving orders, persuading, advising, and appealing, unless his basic attitude is one of accepting people as opposed to wanting to change them.

Indirect Attempts to Change Others. There are other ways of responding to people which convey somewhat less directly a desire for them to change, but which nonetheless can be quite as threatening to them as the four types listed above. Consider, for example, responses which convey:

> *Criticizing, Condemning, Devaluating, Moralizing, Judging*
> That was a stupid thing to say.
> You are wrong.
> This is a ridiculous way to look at it.
> Your work is not up to par.
> You are not being cooperative.

To respond to another person with such statements frequently shows an intent to influence him to adopt new ways of behaving by "extinguishing" or "punishing" the old way of behaving. Unlike the four kinds of responses described previously, where the desired way of behaving is specified, this type of response relies upon getting rid of the undesired behavior. As opposed to saying, "You should do this," the person who makes evaluative statements is saying, "You should not do that." Both communicate an intent to change the other; both can convey lack of acceptance of the person as he is.

People can be threatened by evaluation more often than we generally suppose. This kind of threat can have an immediate and lasting effect on their behavior in a group, causing them to withdraw and avoid participating, or to expend their energies in persistent defense against such attacks on their ideas. Moreover, when the evaluation comes from the leader, who is frequently seen as an authority figure, they tend to place the locus of evaluation with him rather than with the group. This often results in an overdependence upon the leader for evaluating the ideas of behavior of the members. We have all observed groups in which the members rely heavily on the leader for evaluating the worth of contributions, because they are afraid to accept this responsibility themselves.

Does the group-centered leader also try to avoid making *positive* evaluations? It is easy to understand the potential threat contained in negative evaluations, but what is the effect of responses that convey:

> *Approving, Praising, Rewarding, Reassuring, Agreeing, Supporting*
> That was a good idea.
> You did well.
> That was the right thing to say.
> I think you should have done what you did.

Such statements as these can also convey to another that you want him to change. The positive evaluation is often a means of rewarding past desirable behavior in order to "reinforce" it — that is, to insure that it will occur again in the future. On the other hand, it is probably true that people feel less threatened by positive evaluations than by negative ones. This does not always hold, because an approving remark sometimes embarrasses a person and may even mildly threaten him, if he himself does not share the positive evaluation of his idea or behavior. However, there are other possible effects of positive evaluations which should be considered. They, too, tend to shift the locus of evaluation away from the speaker, perhaps even more than negative evaluations. If a leader of a group tends to make frequent positive evaluations of the contributions of members, he runs the risk of encouraging members to rely on his judgment of the worth of the contributions. Furthermore, there is the risk of influencing members to make only those contributions which they feel will be approved by the leader. Finally, the leader who frequently praises others' contributions may build up such an expectation of approval that, should he fail to respond positively to some member's response, it might easily be perceived as lack of approval.

Giving Information. A leader may convey lack of acceptance simply by giving information. This is especially true when the information has not been asked for, but may also be true when the information has been openly requested. Much depends, of course, upon the leader's own attitude and his manner of giving information. As each of us knows, a person who gives us the impression of "knowing it all" or of being "positively correct" will make us bristle up and become for the moment defensive. By his own manner of informing others, he devaluates their worth. He conveys, "I know, but you do not; my way of thinking is correct, yours is not." Lack of acceptance may be conveyed, though to a lesser degree, even when a leader's manner of giving information is not so extremely dogmatic. People tend to resent "being told," even when the informer genuinely has their interest in mind.

Making Interpretations. Another type of response that often communicates lack of acceptance is that of making inferences or interpretations of the feelings, perceptions, motives, or values of the other person. All the following responses might be considered in this category:

> You are being cynical.
> I always thought you knew better.
> You are saying this because you are angry.
> You must want us to agree with you.
> You don't really mean what you say.

Although it is not possible to say that such responses as these always are perceived by people as indicating a lack of acceptance of them, nevertheless clinical experience as well as common sense tells us that people often react defensively, or even with hostility, to attempts to interpret their motives, their intentions, or their inner thoughts. This can be said regardless of whether the interpretation is "correct" or not. To interpret a statement of another often has the effect of conveying an evaluation, a disbelief in the validity of his spoken words, or even an intention to influence his thoughts or behavior (as in the statement, "You are being cynical," which might often convey, "You should not be cynical.")

One research study has produced findings bearing on the effect of interpretations on the verbal behavior of the subjects. These findings strongly support the clinical observation that interpretations tend to discourage clients' further self-expression in therapy. In this study, Bergman[3] analyzed the verbatim protocols of therapeutic interviews in an attempt to study the effect of different types of counselor-statements on the subsequent responses of the client. He discovered that interpretations by the counselors (trained in client-centered methods) were followed *more* often by "abandonment of self-exploration" than would be expected by chance, and were followed *less* often by "self-exploration and insight" than would be expected by chance.

In a significant paper by Porter[4] on the nature of psychotherapeutic interpretation, an unpublished study by J. Rickard is described. Rickard obtained results similar to Bergman's on the effect of interpretation in Freudian, Adlerian, Horneyian, and Rogerian therapy interviews. This study indicated that counselors' interpretations were followed by "resistance" with greater than chance frequency.

While these studies do not present exhaustive or conclusive evidence, they do support the thesis that interpretation of a person's inner thoughts and feelings is an effective way to inhibit his self-expression and to produce resistance in him. It does not seem too great a generalization to suggest that these findings from individual therapy sessions would probably be duplicated in a similar study of the interaction of members of a group. At least this is the position taken by the group-centered leader, who tries always to avoid interpreting the statements of group members.

In summarizing these paragraphs, we might state that a leader conveys acceptance of the members of his group by avoiding statements which convey a direct attempt to change the members, statements which convey evaluation of their contributions, statements which convey an interpretation of members' inner thoughts and feelings, and statements which convey that the members are "being told" by the leader. We will conclude this summary by re-emphasizing the importance of the leader's attitudes in determining the impact of his verbal responses upon the members, and by pointing out that the members' own personalities will also influence their perception of the meaning of the leader's responses. To put it simply, a leader with evaluative and nonaccepting attitudes may communicate them to members regardless of the kind of verbal responses he uses. Similarly, some group members may be so insecure as to read evaluation and lack of acceptance into any response made by the leader.

The "Linking" Function

Another important function which the group-centered leader serves in the group is the "linking" function. In face-to-face discussion groups, it often happens that one person will say something, then a second person will add a new idea but without conveying the relationship of his idea to the first contribution. The thought of each member remains independent or unlinked

[3] D. V. Bergman, "Counseling Method and Client Responses," *Journal of Consulting Psychology*, XV (1951), 216–224.
[4] E. H. Porter, Jr., "On the Nature of Psychotherapeutic Interpretation," *Journal of Consulting Psychology*, XVI (1952), 343–346.

to other thoughts. Occasionally, someone may enter in and relate his thought to that of another, but usually we can observe several currents of thought in a group, each going its own way. If, however, the group-centered leader makes an effort to perceive the linkage between the separate comments and then conveys this relationship to the group, the discussion then seems to flow in one current, building up force as each new contribution is linked to it.

The "linking" function of the group-centered leader is related closely to his function of reflecting the meanings of members' statements. This is because the meaning of a member's comment often *is* the link to the main stream of thought or to the previous comments. Its actual linkage is frequently hidden by the content of the comment. Thus, by clarifying the meaning of a comment, the group-centered leader makes clear to the group how the new contribution is related to the previous discussion. An illustration from a recorded group discussion may clarify this point. In the following excerpt the group is carrying on a discussion of how one of the members, a social worker, should approach a group of young married people to get them to take social action in their community:[5]

1. *Bill:* I would like to go on record with a very serious objection here. This was the implied assumption that somehow church socials or gatherings in communities for discussion are somewhat more valuable and better and people should do these rather than go bowling. I felt this implied assumption. Why shouldn't men rather go there than to church —
2. *Don:* I don't go along with that implied assumption.
3. *Bill:* Well, I certainly wouldn't. I would like to bring in a diagnosis that my wife has made from the feminine viewpoint of our society. She, perhaps not peculiarly, much prefers the company of a group of men to a group of women. And I don't think this is necessarily a sex factor. She says you can almost predict what a group of women are going to do.
4. *Jane:* I'll say.
5. *Bill:* They're forced into a mold somehow by our society. She doesn't understand what it is. But a group of women get together and one group is pretty much like another. And very often women join groups not because they want to but because of social pressures. Where men — they seem to live in a much freer and easier society where what they do and who they join with is a function of their own choice. In —
6. *Frank:* I think Mrs. Adams [Bill's wife] overestimates considerably both the interest and the variety of men's society.
7. *Group:* (Laughter.)
8. *Leader:* Bill, your point would be what? I'm not sure I understand what —

8. The leader here is attempting to understand the meaning and intent behind Bill's last three comments. This is especially important here, since in number 2 Don interrupts to defend himself and in number 6 Frank humorously objects. The group responds to Frank with laughter, thus in a sense rejecting Bill. The leader does not understand the link between Bill's comments and the previous discussion.

---

[5] Throughout the excerpt the number in each note at the bottom of the page refers to the same numbered item in the group discussion. The writer has used this example in a previous publication ["Group-Centered Leadership and Administration," in C. R. Rogers, *Client-Centered Therapy* (Boston: Houghton Mifflin Company, 1951)].

9. *Bill:* That much of the operation of women in these social groups is not a function of choice on their part. It's not satisfying their personal needs. It is a function of the role that society kinda forces them into.

10. *Leader:* You are using that as an illustration of your original objection to the effect that we should attach certain values, positive or negative, to those interests and you object strongly to doing that — saying that one interest is of more social value than another one?

11. *Bill:* It seemed to me that what we were essentially saying is that the things that the men wanted to do were not as good for them — were not satisfying their needs — as well as the things that men didn't want to do. And I just kinda don't —

12. *Cathy:* If women get together to clean up the alleys, after all it's the women who have to sit and look at the alleys all day. The men are out working all day. They are not as concerned about the alleys as their wives. They should be. The fact that there isn't a playground for the children, by and large the mothers would be more concerned with that than the fathers. Questions of this sort wouldn't necessarily hit home to her husband. It seems to me they would be much more interested than their husbands might, who also because of our culture would say, "Why, that's the mother's job."

13. *Stu:* Well, would you carry that further and say that social action interests in general are more natural to the women?

14. *Cathy:* They aren't more natural. I'd say that the culture sort of —

15. *Stu:* Yeah, owing to our cultural situation, would you say in general that they are more politically active, and so forth?

16. *Leader:* Are we really understanding Cathy? I'm not sure that I am. You see a basic difference here, Cathy, between the interests of men and the interests of women?

17. *Cathy:* I see a great deal of difference when it comes to a group discussion, yes. That it can be that there is more interest in a neighborhood group, particularly in the working class, that the wives and mothers would have a more neighborhood interest.

18. *Leader:* In terms of leader behavior, this would — you are simply saying that this would be a better diagnosis of women's needs and that we have to be careful in diagnosing women's needs versus men's.

19. *Cathy:* I think we have to be very careful.

20. *Sam:* I would like to raise a kind of a point of order and wonder are we trying to be a sociology class in this emphasis upon diagnosing needs. To me we keep wandering from what our primary job is. I just sort of pull that out —

21. *Cathy:* You're right.

---

10. Here the leader is linking Bill's illustration to a previous objection of his, yet he does this in the tentative form of a question.

16. Again the leader is trying to understand Cathy and to link the meaning of her somewhat involved illustration to the previous comments. Stu, on the other hand, in numbers 13 and 15 is apparently trying to push Cathy to a broader generalization, which she does not accept in number 14.

18. The leader here provides the linkage between the difference Cathy sees between the interests of the sexes and the role of the leader, which was the topic under discussion prior to Bill's comment in number 1.

22. *Sam:* I'd be quite glad to pull back in my shell, but I'm wondering if we are not beyond ourselves. We have no resources in this area. We keep bringing up personal records which really don't count for much in our total assessment.
23. *Leader:* Diagnosing individual needs is not pertinent to our problem, Sam?
24. *Sam:* Well, I was about to jump in with all sorts of personal references. I work with these groups all the time and I can present some anecdotes on the other side but it occurred to me that that wouldn't be relevant.
25. *Stu:* It seems to me we are analyzing here, or raising the question, about the function of leadership. If one attitude toward leadership is accepted — in general the community center's point of view on leadership, the social worker's point of view — well, then one must know — one must be able to diagnose the needs of the people in order to function as leader. If another concept of leadership wins the day here, then we can dispense with all of this diagnosis.
26. *Sam:* Then we should discuss the two aspects of leadership and not diagnosis.
27. *Leader:* Stu, you are not willing to accept that that is the best way of leading — diagnosing the group and going out and fulfilling needs for —
28. *Sam:* Yes. That's the point I'd rather argue.

In a group there may be as many different channels of thought as there are members. This often can be seen in the early stages of group development, when each member has his particular axe to grind, when contributions are likely to be more ego-centered than group-centered, when members are responding to their own personal needs to the exclusion of what is going on outside of themselves. It is during this stage that the group-centered leader's linking function is so important. It might be said that the leader, by perceiving these linkages, helps the individual members to become aware of elements in the total perceptual field which previously were not perceived; that the leader helps the group members to enlarge the scope of the phenomenal field to which they respond, thus increasing the chances that their contributions will be more appropriate to the existing situation.

. . . .

22. Apparently Sam has not perceived any linkage between the discussion of group members' needs and leadership. He feels dissociated from the original topic.
23. Although Sam has not stated his feeling as such, the leader reflects tentatively Sam's meaning, thus even linking Sam's comments to the preceding topic of needs.
25. Stu, taking over the linking function, makes a successful attempt to tie together the ideas about needs and the earlier topic of leadership.
26. Sam's comment is not accepting of the group's exploration of the problem of diagnosing needs. Stu's linkage in number 25 was much more useful, as well as accepting to the group.
27. The leader in trying to catch Stu's meaning went beyond him a little. He might better have said, "You see the problem of diagnosis in relation to one type of leadership but not necessary for another type."

Section E

PROBLEMS OF LEADERSHIP

Among the many problems of the leader three have been chosen for emphasis: the problem of selecting the most useful method, the problem of developing a group climate conducive to learning, and the problem of assisting the members to broaden their perspective and deepen their thinking through his leadership.

One of these problems is considered in each of the following selections. How the leader may select the method to use is the focus in "Making Better Decisions," by C. Gratton Kemp. How he may assist a group through changing the group climate is discussed by L. Thomas Hopkins in "Changing the Group Climate." Nathaniel Cantor, in "Maintaining a Creative Difference," illustrates how the leader makes a creative difference by helping the members "to think in directions other than those they would take if he were not their leader."

Each reading has a distinct focus, with problems centered in the leader's personality, in the group, and in the larger environment.

35

Making Better Decisions

C. Gratton Kemp

Today we teachers are sometimes presumed to be democratic because we are teachers. Though we may spend years in authoritarian homes and schools, we are expected to become democratic the moment we sign a contract.

Simulated Democracy. This is a threatening predicament that forces many teachers to pretend to be democratic. A teacher may say to her class: "We planned to work on our social-studies project today, but we haven't much time, and most of us have math problems to finish. What do you think we should do?"

The children know that the teacher wants them to work on math problems, and a few respond in compliance with her wishes. But the teacher is aware of the pretense. She knows that her gesture was unconvincing, and the knowledge makes her feel threatened and weakens her chances of becoming genuinely democratic in her classroom approach.

At times some of us complain that we are not free to be democratic. We could do more, we tell ourselves, if we only had the chance. But how many of us recognize the opportunities that do come our way? How many of us would have seen an opportunity in the situation that faced Mr. Jones?

At the opening of school he was told that his fifth-grade class would be required to cover the program of studies and take the standardized test at the end of the term.

Some weeks later Mr. Jones realized that, although the pupils had been interested and busy, they were behind in preparation for the test. He explained the requirement and asked what they thought could be done.

The Children's Proposal. They suggested that each pupil determine for himself how much he had to learn, estimate the amount of time he would need to learn it, and apportion his study time accordingly. The teacher, they thought, could help each pupil, and those who hadn't much to learn could help others.

The children prepared for the test because the problem of how to accomplish the goal had become their own. Mr. Jones had used the opportunity to

From C. Gratton Kemp, "The Democratic Classroom," *Elementary School Journal,* LXI (November, 1960), 68–71. Copyright 1960 by the University of Chicago. Reprinted with the permission of the publisher.

provide experience in democratic planning and in working co-operatively toward a chosen goal.

Democratic co-operative planning is foreign to many pupils, teachers, and administrators. Some children feel threatened when they are expected to make decisions. Some teachers hesitate to try the approach because of their lack of understanding and experience. Some teachers and administrators feel that there is too much uncertainty about the outcomes of democratic planning and that too much time is required for what is accomplished. These difficulties did not discourage Miss Smith.

One day she was kindly but firmly told that, unless her fourth-graders could proceed quietly through the building to the swimming pool, they would have to give up their swimming period. A bit shaken by the announcement, she decided to wait till the end of the school day to think over her course of action.

When she considered the problem, she realized that there would have to be a change in the children's behavior. She had tried explanations, encouragement, and praise without success. She doubted that force or rewards would lead to improvement.

Doubts. She wondered whether she should place the problem before the group. Could the children make a good suggestion and carry it out? Was she herself secure enough to plan with them? Or was she fearful and likely to manipulate their plans to her own liking? She felt that she understood the method, but that it would not be easy to use it.

Was there any reason why the principal or others might object? She could think of none: the principal talked about democratic co-operative planning as if he thought it was in use.

There was the question of time. She would have to resign herself to the fact that the planning would be time-consuming, but the deliberations could be used as a language lesson, and surely the discussion would encourage psychological growth, which was commended by all educators.

Decision. Miss Smith finally decided to put the problem to the class.

The next day she explained the situation to the children and asked for their suggestions. The children seemed to be amazed, unable to understand. Then one boy volunteered, "Well, you could make us behave. You're the teacher." Another said, "You could send those who didn't behave back to the room." "You could make rules," said still another, "and send anyone who didn't keep them to the principal."

Miss Smith began to realize something of the effect that years of conditioning had had on the children.

After what seemed a long time, she said to them, "You seem to think that this is my problem. I think it's ours."

After a long silence one child volunteered, "Each of us could take care of himself."

"I don't think so," came the swift retort from a child across the room. "Some of us may be able to, but a lot of us can't."

Miss Smith reflected their feelings: "It seems that some of us think we can take care of ourselves, and others think we can't."

Miss Smith paused and waited. When no one spoke, she continued, "Each of us has had different experiences in taking care of himself. Some of us know that we are strong enough to control ourselves, but others perhaps haven't tried or have tried and found that we weren't strong enough. Suppose each one of us considers whether he is strong enough to take care of himself as we go to the pool. You can answer only for yourself. You alone know how you feel about it."

After a pause she asked, "Do you think you are strong enough to control yourself?" Most of the hands went up.

"Are any of you not sure you can control yourselves?" Several hands went up.

"As I see it," one pupil said, "those who can take care of themselves won't need watching, and you can watch the others."

"You are making it my problem," Miss Smith said. "I think it is our problem. We'll plan together, but it is the problem of each of us and all of us together."

Another silence. Then a boy said, "Why can't those of us who have had experience and know that we can take care of ourselves help the others?" "How could we do it?" someone asked. "Each of us could walk beside someone who wasn't sure," the first boy proposed.

The children accepted the plan.

A New Dignity. As they quietly went their way through the building, Miss Smith felt a new kind of freedom, a new feeling of adequacy in the group. Each child seemed filled with a new sense of self-respect as he demonstrated his worthiness to accept his obligation. Because the responsibility was shared, she herself felt more relaxed.

As she put away her books that afternoon, she realized the importance of the questions she had faced. Was the problem one for which the children could be expected to have practical suggestions? Could she accept the ideas of the group and work with the children in putting their ideas into effect? Did the administrative conditions permit this freedom?

More than Techniques. Three months later Miss Jones, a substitute teacher, stopped Miss Smith in the hall: "I thoroughly enjoyed your group the other day. They are most responsive and have excellent ideas."

Miss Roberts who had joined them added: "I agree, but I can't figure it out. We both use the same method; we plan with the children. When we compare notes, I feel that we have done exactly the same things. Yet my pupils act so differently."

The methods that Miss Smith and Miss Roberts used appeared to be identical, but they were not, and the results were very different. Miss Roberts has yet to learn that democratic co-operative planning is more than knowing and practicing techniques; it is a way of life.

To the School Executive. Our behavior is shaped by our basic attitudes. The teacher who has lived in a democratic environment is likely to be basically democratic in her attitude. The teacher who comes from an authoritarian home and an authoritarian school is likely to be basically authoritarian.

The co-operative planning each teacher attempts is influenced by her basic attitude.

Teachers conditioned by an authoritarian culture find co-operative planning difficult. In working with these teachers it is more realistic to respect gradual development than to expect sudden change. A climate of appreciation may well encourage the teacher to appraise her skills and her psychological maturity in this area and to develop at her own rate.

The democratic classroom cannot be produced by decree. The school executive who is genuinely interested in democratic classrooms will have to be liberally endowed with patience and understanding.

But the rewards may be well worth the difficulties, for in classrooms where the climate is truly democratic children grow in critical thinking, in self-control, and in a sense of responsibility, and teachers become more relaxed and more understanding.

The democratic classroom is our assurance of the development of respect for the integrity of the individual and a constructively creative civilization.

36

Changing the Group "Climate"

L. Thomas Hopkins

. . . .

How Does the Teacher Help a Class Become a Group?

The quality of the organic group is in the operating wholeness. This is first sensed by the internal members or outside visitors as a feeling tone. The atmosphere appears different. The human relations seem more tolerant and considerate. The sentiments of the members toward each other are freer and warmer. Each person feels at home, is relaxed and comfortable, and is inspired with purposeful vigor. There is no doubt about the wholeness. The empathic atmosphere is actually present and it is really different from that of an aggregate. But the group may be the former members of a class with a status teacher. How has the former teacher worked to bring about this change? What has each of the former individuals contributed toward this feeling tone? These are two questions universally asked by students. And here are some suggestions on what the teacher does to help create such groupness.

1. The teacher or status leader or the older, more mature person sets the atmosphere within which members work and out of which a class emerges into a group. Evidence available from studies of group dynamics in all aspects of living where the process is analyzed, support this statement as one of the common outstanding conclusions. A half century ago one frequently heard and read the statement that the teacher made the school. This is clarified to mean that the status leader sets the climate of opinion of the class and that the learning of members is encompassed by or never transcends the atmosphere which he sets. Since all status organizations have a hierarchy of positions, each status member at his level sets the atmosphere for learning of all persons below him. The teacher sets it for his class within that set by the principal for the school, who in turn reflects the emotional tone of the superintendent of schools. The key to any improvement lies not only in the teacher but in the larger atmosphere determined for the system by those of superior rank. Since each individual, whatever his rank, tends toward interpersonal relations that give him need-fulfillment, the status leader must change himself as a person, must reorganize his self-structure, must find a new direction and a different process of self-enhancement.

The interpersonal behavior of each individual has a much higher degree of correspondence with his need than does all of his intellectual theorizing. Some years ago I heard William Jennings Bryan lecture before the students and faculty of a large university on moral behavior. He pointed out dramatically the relation between professed belief and action by saying, "When an individual asserts that it is all right to steal, never argue with him, always search him." A status leader helps an aggregate become a group by setting the atmosphere in which cooperative interaction emerges, but only when he has action belief in such process. And the reorganization of himself must certainly accompany such action.

To change the atmosphere of an authoritarian competitive class into that of a cooperative interactive group, the status leader must release the miseducative tensions which classes tend to build in individuals. To do this effectively, he must understand a number of points about atmosphere.

First, the atmosphere is usually set by the leader at the very outset or during the initial stages of his relationship with members. And this crucial period is very short. For the members "size him up" or make a quick emotional guess as to the direction of his behavior toward them. Second, the most important factor in changing the initial atmosphere is to remove from members the threat which is always present in a situation with a status leader. While he may not remove the status given him by some outside power, he can reduce its psychological consequences. Both his verbal assurances and his interpersonal behaviors are necessary to bring this about. Third, an atmosphere once established tends to be more or less stable over a long period, perhaps even for the lifetime of the group. This is true whether it be competitive or cooperative, whether it restricts and exploits or whether it releases and develops individual capacity.

Fourth, the status leader must change the aggregate rules of the game into new principles of organic relationships and he must show members how to guide their emerging behavior by them. And he must work according to the new principles the moment he enters the group. By his actions he shows members that he believes in them, respects them as persons; he encourages them to express their sentiments or to share their experiences; he acknowledges individual beliefs and opinions while helping each to appraise them critically; he treats all fairly and helps everyone feel at home; he makes each member realize that he counts for something as a person or has worth to others, for without him the quality of the group would be lessened. Fifth, he shows by his behavior that everyone has security, belongingness, wantedness, status, as a basic field condition since he is both a creative individual and a member of the group. He never allows anyone to suggest by word or deed the old aggregate concept that the leader has and should use security or other interbehavioral qualities as rewards to those who do his bidding. Security and belongingness are the field conditions necessary for everyone to release creatively into the environment more and better directed past experience through more of his real self. In good group atmosphere each self is revealed; in good class atmosphere each self is heavily draped. The teacher more than any other person is responsible for initiating and continuing these self-releasing conditions.

But atmosphere is not enough. The leader shows others how to work together on their activities by the purposes which they select. He helps them understand and use the group process for satisfying their needs so that they feel better, think better, act better, until they are really more mature people. They accept him as a friend, expert in helping them resolve their needs by a superior process leading toward more reasonable action. He focuses his services *to* them and not *on* them. Each recognizes his dependence upon the other for his growth. The teacher takes into the classroom only his needs that are legitimate for the classroom. These are to help learners resolve their needs in an atmosphere and by a process which lead them continuously to higher levels of self-enhancement. While pupils recognize his professional needs, they contribute to his personal development in the same way that he contributes to theirs, thus accelerating and improving the learning of everyone. Atmosphere and process are so internally interrelated that one cannot exist without the other. Each learns the process in a cooperative atmosphere which releases the capacity necessary to make the process effective. The leader promotes each with such internal sincerity that his belief can be observed and accepted in external behavior by those with whom he works.

. . . .

Maintaining a Creative Difference

Nathaniel Cantor

The literature on the nature of group discussion and "group dynamics" is growing rapidly. In studying this literature and in observing different kinds of group discussions led by professional leaders, I have been struck by a quality of looseness in the structure of the discussions, an absence of focus, and a denial of the psychological realities which characterize a group meeting. In this writer's opinion some of the pivotal assumptions of current thinking, writing, and practice concerning group discussion are unsound.

Fortunately for the present purpose, a series of "selected readings with especial emphasis on group development" has recently been published.[1] The contributors include such writers and discussion leaders as Alex Bavelas, Leland Bradford, Charles Hendry, Ronald Lippitt, Alvin Zander, Kenneth Benne, Herbert Thelen, and Douglas McGregor. Naturally there are differences in approach by the various men. Essentially, however, one discovers in all of them a basic, common, non-functional approach to an analysis of the nature of group methods and development.

I wish to present an alternative, functional approach to group development which calls for a different kind of role for the leader and a different kind of focus for the discussion. This approach is not new. Social case workers in this country appreciate the achievements of a functional approach to casework. The contributions of faculty and graduates of the Pennsylvania School of Social Work in this area are recognized. During the past decade the functional approach has been extended to group work practice,[2] to employee counseling,[3] and to education.[4] The analysis which follows is, so far as I know, one of the first attempts to explore the possibility of extending the

From Nathaniel Cantor, "Focus and Function in Group Discussion," *Teachers College Record*, LIII (April, 1952), 375–382. Reprinted with the permission of the publisher.

[1] Kenneth D. Benne and Bozidar Muntyan (eds.), *Human Relations in Curriculum Change* (New York: The Dryden Press, 1951).

[2] Helen U. Phillips, "Social Group Work, A Functional Approach," *The Group* (March, 1948); Helen U. Phillips (ed.), *Achievement of Responsible Behavior Through Group Work Process* (Philadelphia: University of Pennsylvania School of Social Work, 1950).

[3] Nathaniel Cantor, *Employee Counseling, A New Approach to Industrial Psychology* (New York: McGraw-Hill Book Co., 1945).

[4] Nathaniel Cantor, *The Dynamics of Learning*, Second Edition (Buffalo, New York: Foster and Steward, 1950).

functional approach to group discussion and "conference" techniques. In a recently published volume the author tried, for the first time, to present the implications of a functional approach for discussion groups.[5]

FOCUS OF DISCUSSION

We shall begin with a quotation from one of the contributions by Benne, Bradford, and Lippitt.

> There are two principal dangers to group process. First, the goals of the group may not be clearly seen by either the leader or the member of the group. Second, the goals as set originally may be so rigid that they do not permit a change. This latter change usually comes when the leader is fearful of losing control of the group or when he feels that he has the sole responsibility of seeing that the group comes out with something. *Such a leader tends to suggest goals to groups in the beginning and then questions every alternative point in terms of whether it is in the direction of this original goal which is not to be questioned.* The leader gradually loses his group because they come to feel that he is trying to do their thinking for them. (Italics not in original.)[6]

The same authors state in another article,

> The responsibility of leadership is that of making a group aware of its need to set goals before proceeding further and of helping the group find such goals. *Final responsibility lies with the group as a whole.* (Italics not in original.)[7]

These two passages seem to present clearly the point of view of the authors mentioned. But suppose we raise certain fundamental questions: Why does a particular group come together? Why is a particular individual selected or appointed to be the leader of the group?

All of us will agree that it would be absurd for a number of people, say the first ten or fifteen who passed the northeast corner of Broadway at 116th Street in New York City on any day at 9 A.M., to decide they wanted to have a group meeting. It would be just as foolish to flip a coin to decide who the leader of the discussion was to be. This extreme hypothetical case sharpens the issue. There must be a common felt need prior to a group's formation. People do not come together for serious, formal discussion or activity unless they feel a mutual concern about a specific problem. The authors quoted above would, I believe, agree since they state that "the goals of the group may not be clearly seen by either the leader or the members of the group." The implication is that a goal or goals are dimly perceived by both leader and group. The members of the group sense a certain need concerning which they want clarification or help.

A leader is the professional person representing an agency, an industry, an

---

[5] Nathaniel Cantor, *Learning Through Discussion* (Buffalo, New York: Human Relations Films [443 Delaware Avenue], 1950).

[6] Benne and Muntyan (eds.), *op. cit.*, p. 76.

[7] *Op. cit.*, p. 149.

institution, or a school (or his own expertness in a specific area) which offers a specific service through the leader. Such specific service is offered to those who need and want it. A physically ill person who wants medical assistance ordinarily calls upon a physician, not a lumberjack or an ichthyologist. The community that desires its children to be educated calls upon professional educators to determine the process of educating them. School children who develop behavior difficulties are, in the more alert school systems, referred to the professional school guidance counselor or to a child guidance clinic staffed by professional workers who carry out their designated professional services.

The professional factor in the group discussion process through which desirable group decision and consequent behavior develop is the professional worker. The worker does *not* carry all of the responsibility for what happens in the group he leads nor does he permit the group members to carry the entire responsibility. The leader's job is to perform professionally in his role. His concern is with the movement and direction of the group as a whole as it deals with the external social limitations and with the psychological developments of the individuals within the group.

The discussion leader operates by defining what service he can offer which meets the needs of the group. He presents the limited alternatives within which his service operates. He carefully and cautiously *holds to the limits* established by the service he offers, and the needs are established by the group, that is, the more or less defined needs which initially bring the members of the group together.

Indeed the leader has the responsibility to suggest goals to the group in the beginning. He clarifies for members of the group their purpose in coming together, what kind of help *they think they want*, and how he might help them in that area. The leader, I submit, has the responsibility of structuring the discussion, of watching to see that the discussion remains focused in the direction of the needs and purposes of the meeting.

This is not mechanically and rigidly determined at the outset. A focused discussion is not to be naively identified with a yes-no, question-answer discussion. There is wide latitude in exploration, modification, and redirection so long as all of this occurs within the limits which structure the meeting. The leader discourages anecdotes and other discussion irrelevant to the purposes of the group.

"The leader," our authors remark, "gradually loses his group because they come to feel that he is trying to do their thinking for them." The leader, I have observed, more often loses a group because they feel he has nothing to offer them.[8] The skilled leader never does the thinking for the group and he never permits the members of the group to do their own exclusive thinking.

---

[8] This observation is supported by a recent study at Harvard University. The members of several discussion groups highly approved of the leader and liked the permissive atmosphere. They complained, however, of the lack of focus and structure of the discussions. They expressed their desire for the leader to take a more direct and active part in the discussions. (Lauren G. Wispe, "Evaluating Section Teaching Methods in the Introductory Course," *Journal of Educational Research*, November 1951, p. 161.)

He helps them to think in directions other than those they would take if he were not their leader. One is, otherwise, led to wonder what constitutes "leadership" in a group.

Function of the Leader

Final responsibility, it seems to me, does not lie with the group as a whole. Initial, developing and final responsibility is shared by leader *and* individual group members.

The function of the leader is to interpret and maintain his service, both in content of discussion and in his understanding of group process. He helps the individual members of the group to face problems and come to decisions. He does not resolve their problems or make decisions for them. He represents his *difference* to the group and encourages the group members to reveal their differences. An illustration may clarify what is meant.

A group of teachers met with the writer in a series of seminars to discuss the problem (the "need" which brings the group together) "How to Become a More Skilled Teacher." The leader was invited by the university authorities to lead this group because he is considered competent in supervising teachers and the teachers wanted to learn more about teaching skills.

The first three meetings were concerned with exploring the nature of skilled teaching — so the group of teachers declared. As a matter of recorded discussion the sessions were devoted to the teachers' complaints about parents, pupils, supervisors, principals, and members of the board of education.

Every experienced discussion leader has lived through such confused initial sessions. The group was uneasy, confused, uncertain, and afraid to speak. When encouraged to participate no one quite knew what point to talk to, so the talk was *about* something or other. There was no vital participation because no real challenge of the leader's difference, his defined service, was presented. The group was not held to the purpose of the meetings, namely, to discover how one becomes a skilled teacher.

At the start of the fourth meeting, the following took place:

LEADER: Good evening. I guess we're ready for a continuation of our discussion. (Silence) Perhaps our recorder can remind us where we were at the close of the last meeting?

RECORDER: Well, in general, we had a gripe session. Everyone was complaining about something.

MILDRED: Goodness knows, there's plenty to complain about. After a day like this (it had been a dreary day of continuous rain) I couldn't stand much more of the yak, yak, yak of those kids. (Silence)

LEADER: Mildred, I wonder whether we can make use of what you just said to help all of us explore the problem of discipline. Every teacher has certainly experienced the annoyance and irritation you speak of and we have all reacted many times the way you did. Would you mind, then, to help us all, telling us why you spoke of the kids as "yaking, yaking, yaking."

MILDRED: That's exactly what went on all day. I'm telling you, those kids are a problem.

LEADER: Does anyone want to comment on Mildred's description of her class?

DICK: You mean Mildred resented her pupils' talking?

LEADER: What do you mean, Dick? Would you care to elaborate?

DICK: Well, maybe *we* are the problem and not the pupils.

MILDRED: I'd like to see any of you stand up to keeping thirty-five little lunatics in line.

LEADER: Many of us, Mildred, I'm sure, would have had a tough time today. But isn't the problem of the teacher precisely that of trying to keep her own tensions under control? Not to use the children as an outlet for her needs?

MARY: It seems that kids are always worse when we scold them. They resent us more.

MILDRED: I didn't scold them.

LEADER: Well, Mildred, when you referred to the kids "yaking" all day, wasn't your attitude in the classroom one of impatience with them because you were tired? Just as Mary told us, when she scolds, the kids are worse.

The leader's relationship with the group and Mildred was secure enough so that he could single out Mildred without too much hurt to her. Mildred's personal tensions in her classroom and in the discussion group were not the group's problem. The problem she raised, however, is common to most primary and secondary school teachers. The leader felt justified, therefore, in using Mildred to help the group in the exploration of its problem of discipline.

The leader raises the question of the use of the term "yak." Mildred replies naturally, defensively. The leader maintains focus by returning to the issue of "yaking." Dick picks it up. Mildred resents the statement of Dick. The leader tries to convey his understanding of Mildred's hurt feelings but, nevertheless, continues with the challenge.

The leader holds fast to his function, namely, to help the members, in interaction, to do something to the *skilled* or professional opposition of the leader. The members must be given the opportunity (the time and place of offering it is of course crucial and mistakes can be made) to assimilate the differences of other group members and the leader. A balance between present organization of feeling and thinking regarding discipline and the different view presented by others may be sought. Mildred, or any other member of the group, is free to reject or criticize and the members and leader must learn to accept her rejection or criticism. However, the challenge or opportunity to achieve a new balance must be presented.

The leader, anchored in his function, his responsibility to offer help in realizing what goes into improved teaching, is protected against the tendencies of the members to trot off in all directions, seeking to run away from the conflict, fear, and pain of reorganization of feeling and attitude.

If there is no challenge, no difference against which or with which one must struggle, no genuine movement involving growth can occur. Creativity is blocked.

The leader helps the group to find balance in assimilating difference. It should be reiterated that he does not force issues or impose his will or conclusions or interpretations upon the group members. He does not *insist* that the group move only in the direction he indicates. The needs of the group he serves are paramount, but not every need. Only those needs are relevant for exploration which relate to the specific help he has been delegated to offer. Members will try to deny the very need they want satisfied. One side of them wants to change, the other side is fearful because genuine change must be accompanied by emotional disturbance.

The leader is aware of this. He, too, will want to have his way. The skilled leader, however, is more able to deal with his differences, his struggles, because he is not afraid to acknowledge his feelings. He must be and, if skilled, is aware of them and hence is in a better position than nonprofessional group members to deal with his conflicts. He can control himself because he is aware of what is happening, accepts it, and need not be defensive or seek justification for felt guilt or resentment.

In brief, the leader deliberately and professionally uses his difference for the sake of the group rather than for his own need satisfaction. By the same token he is prepared to accept the resentment or hostility of the group which often, at first, accompanies his declaration of difference. His chief concern is whether the several group members will profitably use his difference or one another's differences for their growth. The leader must be prepared to accept balance, growth, or rejection. He introduces his difference, he inquires about the direction the group has taken, he supports the differences expressed by others, or challenges likeness at such times as he deems most favorable for the growth of the individual member and the group.

The guilt or fear each of us experiences in being different and in expressing our individual difference in the presence of our peers is the basic factor in preventing group leaders from realizing the role they can play in helping others. It requires profound growth for a leader who possesses creative difference to define himself in *professional* relation to others in such manner that he places his difference at the disposal of others rather than imposing it upon them for his personal satisfactions.

The leader who makes such use of himself provides the professional factor in the group discussion. He watches the direction of the discussion with reference to the purposes or goal which brings the group together and the reactions of the individuals within the group. The leader helps by structuring the discussion and holding to the limits established by the specific need of the group and the skilled service he offers. In this limited professional relationship the leader recognizes and responds to the feelings of the group discussants, helping them to relate to him and to one another.

The individual member of the group will fight to maintain his present organization of self, but if he is to become an integrated member of the group, he must relate to the others, assume some responsibility to the group as a whole regarding its declared purpose or objective.

The individual members of the group must meet the external obstacles represented by the limited service of the leader, the latter's difference, the limitations and restrictions of the social, industrial, or educational context in which their group need arose. It is *the process* of meeting these limitations and external obstacles which provides the yeast of growth and the motivation for reorganization of self as a member of a group.

It is to be expected that new adjustments in relating to other group members, to the difference of the leader, and to outside limitations will be accompanied by feelings of discomfort, fear, and even pain. The group members will experience guilt and confusion, or resentment and hostility toward one another and toward the leader. The leader too will experience dislike and confusion toward the members of the group. These feelings are real and have to be faced in order to be controlled and used. Why should everyone like everyone else under all circumstances? This leads us to the chief difficulty I have experienced in recent writings on group dynamics.

Likeness and Difference

The majority of writers consider "consensus" the desideratum of group discussion. For example, we read,

Moreover, the group and its leader have built the expectation that *no* member (italics in original) is to be excluded from the thought and action of the group. Thus, the ideal of the group has come to be consensus in decision.

Again,

The expectation which the group is building as to successful group discussion is toward consensus as the only adequate basis for common action.[9]

Finally,

When one subjects himself to the controls and accepts the ideals of a group, he "belongs."[10]

If all members do not feel commitment to the same goal, then there will be continuous friction in working, the capacities of some members will be only partially utilized, there will be ambiguity in the evaluations of contributions . . . and there will be minorities that may induce disintegrative forces. For consensus, the alternatives must be discussed or studied or practiced with until one emerges as being clearly advantageous.[11]

If I correctly understand these statements, the writers in question believe that democratic values are enhanced and preserved by strong "we-feeling." Frustration of individual members is to be avoided. Grievances are to be forestalled.

[9] Benne, Bradford, and Lippitt, in Benne and Muntyan (eds.), *op. cit.*, p. 81.
[10] K. Lewin and P. Grabbe, in Benne and Muntyan (eds.), *op. cit.*, p. 86.
[11] H. A. Thelen, in Benne and Muntyan (eds.), *op. cit.*, p. 94.

It seems to me these attitudes imply a denial of democratic faith in people. Why must consensus be reached in order for one to join with others in an activity? So many of the group discussion analysts and leaders emphasize the need for democratic *process* and democratic *goals* in the activity of groups. They place a premium on likeness, identification, consensus. This is a denial of democracy as an ethical ideal, and a distortion of psychological reality. Consensus, that is, *genuine* agreement and like-mindedness, is certainly a desirable objective when it *is* consensus. It is a healthy, legitimate goal, but one rarely achieved by a group of people who represent considerable differences, personal biases, different backgrounds of interest, and so forth. What often passes for consensus is submission to or fear of majority opinion, unwillingness to be responsible for difference, unwillingness to assume the risks involved in an independent position. (It is after consensus has been reached, that the gossip, criticism, and frustration are released in the relative safety of the conference halls or coffee shop.)

Democracy, political or personal, thrives on difference. Indeed the acid test of respect for others is one's ability to abide difference. Respect for others means respect for difference, since "others" are not like you. Liking those who are like you requires no effort. To accept genuine difference, that is, to accept others who feel, think, or act in ways you do not approve of and in situations where *you* are involved is the test of respect for others. Compromise, adjustment, balance, accommodation, and disagreement, as well as consensus, characterize hygienic human relations both in the process of development and in the pursuit of goals.

The desire for only consensus is also psychologically unrealistic. The group is not the only reality. When a group strives solely for consensus it becomes a stumbling block, depriving the individual members or subgroups of the strength to meet outside situations and circumstances. The members of a group acting independently or in smaller groups feel lost without the support of the group to which they have become accustomed and upon which they have become too dependent. When a group becomes too like-minded the individual members cannot move easily without group support. The members, acting on their own fear, become lost.

Social living, pursuing group objectives, carrying out group purposes away from the sheltering support of like-mindedness bring individual differences into conflict. When the individual runs into difference he cannot easily find balance. He is accustomed to consensus. He cannot adjust to *partial* success or *partial* failure. He wants consensus or he won't carry on. He is blocked when he is crossed. He hasn't learned, in the group, to be responsible and comfortably accept his own differences or to accommodate himself to the differences imposed by his group.

Consensus, as the ideal, is a false and unrealistic objective. The group consisting of different individuals agrees on the one fundamental postulate of respecting one another's rights. Everyone agrees to permit anyone to disagree. Out of differences the members learn to weigh, to balance, to divide, to go along with others even if only partially satisfied, to go along without necessarily being in full agreement, and even, at times, to go along when one is in disagreement. One submerges independent difference for the sake of the group. This is living with likeness *and* difference.

Life demands continuous partialization, and the well-adjusted man must always be ready to live by a continuous partial paying off, without wanting to preserve or give out his whole ego undivided in every experience.[12]

A group needs to be functionally structured and to have its limits defined. The limits are found between the needs of the group and the services of the leader in meeting those needs. Only through such focus can confusion be narrowed and the group helped to discover how to reach its objectives. The final responsibility for determining goals lies not with the group as a whole, but with the leader and the group. The leader who is professional (and such skill is not acquired merely in a three-weeks summer workshop or by taking *a* course in "group observer" or "group dynamics") focuses the discussion, watches the movement and direction of the group, encourages both likeness *and* difference in others, and opposes the group with his own difference. He does not strive for consensus or for disagreement. He helps the members to discover their strengths and their weaknesses, their similarities and their differences, so that they may more profitably learn to relate to one another in carrying forward their professed goals in a spirit of compromise, partially satisfied, partially dissatisfied, but willing to work together.

[12] Otto Rank, *Will Therapy* (New York: Alfred A. Knopf, Inc., 1945).

Section F

EVALUATION

Evaluation of the concept of leadership with its intangible roots and inter-related skills is in its early stages. Leadership, focused or distributive, is a complicated concept surrounded by considerable confusion. Nevertheless, some of the major phenomena have been differentiated and there is an increasing consensus with reference to desired behavior of leaders.

Cartwright and Zander[1] report the following conclusions in their overview of the research presented: (1) Different patterns of leadership behavior result in different kinds of behavior among group members; (2) the good supervisor uses his technological skills to perform group tasks and to help members satisfy their important needs; (3) the effective leader maintains a "psychological distance" and has sufficient power for his behavior to make a difference to the group.

Further research could be expected to challenge our thinking concerning other concepts. Practical methods are essential to the teacher and the counselor because they must evaluate their leadership in the situations in which they have responsibility. The readings in this section suggest methods for the assessment and improvement of leadership in small groups.

The first two selections discuss evaluation. "Evaluation Through the Study of the Leader's Behavior," by Andrew W. Halpin describes a method which the leader or group may use as a guide in evaluating two important dimensions of leadership behavior. In "Evaluation Through the Leaderless Group Discussion," Bernard M. Bass discusses a second method and describes a situational test of leadership.

The third reading, "Evaluation Through Self-Evaluation," by Thomas Gordon, provides statements of leader attitudes which should provoke thought and reflection.

[1] Dorwin Cartwright and Alvin Zander, *Group Dynamics* (Evanston, Illinois: Row, Peterson & Company, 1960), p. 47.

38

Evaluation Through the Study
of the Leader's Behavior

Andrew W. Halpin

We will greatly increase our understanding of leadership phenomena if we abandon the notion of "leadership" as a trait, and concentrate instead upon an analysis of the behavior of leaders. It is not easy to accomplish this shift in viewpoint, for our ways of thinking about "leadership" have been encumbered by many beliefs not in accord with behavioral facts. The problem is further exacerbated because "leadership" is a value-laden concept charged with much emotion. To be a leader is "good"; not to lead is "bad" — so each of us fancies himself a leader. We consequently have tended to use "leadership" primarily as a slogan, not as a strictly scientific concept. But even our gains from the use of this term as a rallying cry have been short-lived and spurious because we inevitably have been plagued by the fuzziness of our definitions. Hence, in the present context we first shall examine the definitional problem, noting the strategic advantage of studying *leader behavior* as distinguished from "leadership" *per se*; and shall then describe two leader behavior skills that clearly characterize "effective" leaders and comment on their pertinence for teachers.

"Leadership" has been used in a variety of ways, most commonly in referring to the "leader" as an outstanding member of a class. Thus, radio and TV commercials proclaim that such-and-such is the leading brand of cigarettes, and that Marilyn Monroe is the leader of our current covey of actresses. Because of our American predilection for bigness, in no matter what sphere, the "leader" in this sense refers to the most popular product — or more specifically, to that item with the greatest sales-market potential. Similarly in education, we often confuse "leadership" with sheer bigness.

PROBLEM IN DEFINITION

But this use of the term applies equally to either things or people, and fails to take into account the central psychological characteristic of leader

From Andrew W. Halpin, "The Behavior of Leaders," *Educational Leadership,* XIV (December, 1956), 172–176. Reprinted with the permission of publisher and author.

behavior: that this is the behavior of a leader functioning vis-à-vis members of a group in an endeavor to facilitate the solution of group problems. The behavior of the leader and the behavior of group members are inextricably interwoven, and the behavior of both is determined to a great degree by formal requirements imposed by the institution of which the group is a part. For example, Mary Noel, fourth-grade teacher, is the formally designated leader of the children in her class. How she behaves as a leader is influenced by the behavior of the children (which includes their expectations of how a teacher *should* behave as a leader) and is conditioned, moreover, by the policies and regulations, both written and unwritten, of the particular school system in which she is employed. As a result of the year which they spend with her, the children in Mary's class are expected to show certain minimum changes in behavior, especially in respect to scholastic achievement and skill in interpersonal relations. The accomplishment of these objectives is the salient group problem to the solution of which Mary must contribute, and it is presumed that her contribution will be greater than that of any other group member in her fourth-grade class. This, of course, is why she was employed.

In accepting her assignment as teacher of the fourth grade, Mary assumes a role as leader of this group. This, however, tells us absolutely nothing about the "effectiveness" of her performance in this role, i.e., how effectively she contributes to the solution of group problems. What, then, are we to mean by "leadership"? The assumption of a leader's role? The "effectiveness" with which this role is performed? Or the capacity of the individual to perform this role effectively? And here we are confronted by the further question: "effectiveness" in respect to what criteria? for research on leader behavior shows that "effectiveness" in respect to Criterion X is not necessarily correlated with "effectiveness" in regard to Criterion Y. For example, the behavior of a leader who is "effective" in maintaining high "morale" (a sticky term that requires a much clearer definition than has as yet been accorded it) and good human relations within the group is not necessarily "effective" in accomplishing high production and goal-achievement.

This definitional dilemma emerges from the fact that we have incorporated into the term "leadership" both descriptive and evaluative components, and have thus burdened this single word (and the concept it represents) with two connotations: one refers to a role and the behavior of a person in this role, and another is a straightforward evaluation of the individual's performance in the role. We have compounded this confusion even more by conceptualizing "leadership" as an essentially innate capacity of the individual manifested with equal facility regardless of the situation in which the leader finds himself. This belief, however, is unsupported by research evidence; for as Stogdill[1] and Gibb[2] have shown in their comprehensive surveys of the research litera-

[1] Ralph M. Stogdill, "Personal Factors Associated with Leadership: A Survey of the Literature," *Journal of Psychology*, XXV (1948), 35–71.
[2] Cecil A. Gibb, "Leadership," Chapter 24 in Gardner Lindzey (ed.), *Handbook of Social Psychology*, Vol. 2 (Reading, Mass.: Addison-Wesley Publishing Company, Inc., 1954), pp. 877–920.

ture on leadership, a large share of variance in leader behavior is associated with concomitant variance in specific situational factors. Stated baldly, this means that it is possible for Mary to function "effectively" as a leader in the fourth-grade class of East Clambake Elementary School and yet operate quite "ineffectively" as a leader in the fourth-grade class of West Clambake Elementary School. In brief, much depends on the situation.

How can we circumvent this semantic tangle? The first step is to focus our attention upon the *behavior* of leaders without imputing to the individual a fixed capacity for "leadership." Note that the phrasing of our questions dictates the form of our answers. Thus, if we ask the question, "What is leadership?"[3] we assume gratuitously that such a capacity exists. This assumption violates the warning of the semanticists who have stressed the point that words are to events as maps are to territories, and that a word is useful to only such extent as it corresponds to the territory of events it purports to describe.[4] On this score the term "leadership" is of dubious value and may be likened to a map for which no corresponding territory exists in the "real" world. Granted that the word possesses some hortatory appeal, there is little place for it in strictly scientific inquiry.

What, then, do we gain by shifting our emphasis from "leadership" to the analysis of the *behavior of leaders?* There are two major methodological advantages. In the first place, we can deal directly with observable phenomena, and need make no *a priori* assumptions about the identity or structure of whatever capacities may, or may not, undergird these phenomena. Secondly, this formulation keeps at the forefront of our thinking the importance of differentiating between the *description* of how leaders behave and the *evaluation* of the "effectiveness" of their behavior in respect to specified performance criteria.

LEADER BEHAVIOR

This focus upon leadership behavior rather than upon "leadership," together with a careful differentiation between the *description* and the *evaluation* of the leader's behavior, is an outstanding characteristic of the research approach used in The Ohio State Leadership Studies, a ten-year interdisciplinary program initiated in 1946 and undertaken to study the behavior of persons assumed to be in leadership positions in business, educational and governmental organizations. This program, under the aegis of the Personnel Research Board of The Ohio State University, is directed by Carroll L. Shartle, who has described some phases of this work in his recent book, *Executive Performance and Leadership.*[5] The separate studies have been reported in Air Force and Navy technical reports, and in the professional lit-

---

[3] A question phrased like this implies a materialistic theoretical model, rather than a mathematical one. For a discussion of the difference in these models in respect to the question, "What is electricity?" see the pertinent discussion by [J. Z.] Young in his superb book, *Doubt and Certainty in Science* (Oxford: Clarendon Press, 1951, p. 109 ff.)

[4] This point was presented first by [Alfred] Korzybski (*Science and Sanity*, Lancaster, Pa.: The Science Press, 1933), but a more readable discussion may be found in [Wendell] Johnson (*People in Quandaries*, New York: Harper & Brothers, 1946).

[5] (New York: Prentice-Hall, Inc., 1956).

erature; and a series of technical monographs[6] on this research has been published this year by the Bureau of Business Research of The Ohio State University. We shall note findings about leader behavior that are especially relevant for teachers.

A Leader Behavior Description Questionnaire (LBDQ) was devised to measure the behavior of leaders as perceived by members of their work-groups and by their immediate supervisors. The 150 items incorporated into the original form of the LBDQ were selected from a pile of 1,790 items. In the course of successive revision, the number of items in this questionnaire has been reduced to forty, chosen on the basis of a factorial analysis by which we identified two major dimensions of leader behavior:[7]

> *Initiating Structure-in-Interaction*[8] refers to the leader's behavior in delineating the relationship between himself and the members of his group, and in endeavoring to establish well-defined patterns of organization, channels of communication, and ways of getting a job done. The leader establishes "Structure" in the way the group members interact with him and with each other so that whenever the group is confronted with a novel problem, the members can resort to these Structures-in-Interaction to facilitate the solution of group problems. Hence the group members are not dependent upon the leader for fresh and specific instructions on how to handle each new problem that arises.
>
> *Consideration* refers to behavior that reflects friendship, mutual trust, respect and warmth in the relationship between the leader and group members. This represents the "human relations" aspect of leader behavior.

Originally, these two dimensions of leader behavior were identified in a study of aircraft commanders; but subsequent research has shown their applicability to factory foremen,[9] school superintendents,[10,11] school principals,[12] and chairmen of college departments.[13] This LBDQ technique has not as yet

[6] The first of these, by [Ralph M.] Stogdill and [Carroll L.] Shartle (*Methods in the Study of Administrative Leadership*; Columbus, Ohio: Bureau of Business Research, The Ohio State University, 1955), describes the plan of the series and lists the separate titles.

[7] Andrew W. Halpin and B. James Winer, "A Factorial Study of Leader Behavior Descriptions," in R. M. Stogdill and A. E. Coons (eds.), *Leader Behavior: Its Description and Measurement* (Columbus, Ohio: Bureau of Business Research, The Ohio State University, 1956).

[8] This is a key concept in the theory of leadership developed by John K. Hemphill ("A Proposed Theory of Leadership in Small Groups," *Psychological Monographs*, in press).

[9] Edwin A. Fleishman and others, *Leadership and Supervision in Industry: An Evaluation of a Supervisory Training Program* (Columbus, Ohio: Bureau of Educational Research, The Ohio State University, 1955).

[10] Andrew W. Halpin, "The Leader Behavior and Leadership Ideology of Educational Administrators and Aircraft Commanders," *Harvard Educational Review*, XXV, No. 1 (Winter, 1955), 18–32.

[11] Andrew W. Halpin, *The Leadership Behavior of School Superintendents* (Columbus, Ohio: University Press, The Ohio State University, 1956).

[12] Philip Benevento, "Administrative Communication: A Study of Its Relationship to Administrative Leadership" (Unpublished Ph.D. Dissertation, Syracuse University, 1956).

[13] John K. Hemphill, "Patterns of Leadership Behavior Associated with the Administrative Reputation of the Department of a College," *Journal of Educational Psychology*, XLVI, No. 7 (November, 1955), 385–401.

been used in studies of classroom teachers, but there is strong presumptive evidence to suggest that these same two dimensions are of especial significance in the interaction between teachers and students.

Having developed a practical technique for describing how leaders behave, our next task was to determine the relationship between individuals' scores on these dimensions and their "effectiveness" as leaders. One of Halpin's[14] studies of aircraft commanders are those who score high on *both* dimensions of leader behavior. Similarly, Hemphill's study of twenty-two departments in a liberal arts college shows that the departments with the best campus reputation for being well-administered were those whose chairmen scored above the average on both leader behavior dimensions. Studies on leadership ideology[15,16] likewise indicate that "effective" leaders are characterized by high Initiation of Structure and high Consideration. These dimensions may be conceptualized according to the coordinate scheme presented in Figure 1, in which the four quadrants are designated by Roman numerals.

The leaders described in Quadrant 1 are evaluated as highly "effective," whereas those in Quadrant III, whose behavior is ordinarily accompanied by group chaos, are characterized as most "ineffective." The leaders in Quadrant IV are the martinets and the "cold fish" so intent upon getting a job done that they forget that they are dealing with human beings, not cogs in a machine. The individuals described in Quadrant II are also "ineffective"

Figure 1

A COORDINATE SCHEME FOR CONCEPTUALIZING THE INITIATING STRUCTURE
AND CONSIDERATION DIMENSIONS OF LEADER BEHAVIOR

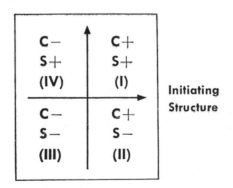

Consideration

[14] Andrew W. Halpin, *Studies in Aircrew Composition. III. The Combat Leader Behavior of B-29 Aircraft Commanders* (Bolling Air Force Base, Washington, D.C.: Human Factors Operations Research Laboratories, Sept. 1953). (HFORL Memorandum No. TN-54-7).

[15] Andrew W. Halpin, "The Leadership Ideology of Aircraft Commanders," *Journal of Applied Psychology*, XXXIX, No. 2 (1955), 82–84.

[16] Halpin, "The Leader Behavior and Leadership Ideology of Educational Administrators and Aircraft Commanders," *op. cit.*

leaders. They may ooze with the milk of human kindness, but this contributes little to "effective" performance unless their Consideration behavior is accompanied by a necessary minimum of initiating Structure behavior.

The implications of these findings for teachers are obvious. The "effectiveness" of a teacher's behavior as a leader in his classroom will be augmented only to such extent as he increases *both* his Initiation of Structure and his Consideration. The current emphasis in education upon "human relations" and upon the group dynamics approach has developed, in part, as a protest against reactionary, and often even autocratic, leadership styles that have prevailed in many school situations. But in our enthusiasm for this new approach, have we perhaps swung the pendulum too far? In applying "human relations" principles, we must be sure that we do not overlook the responsibility imposed upon every leader by the institutional realities of the formal institution of which he is a part. The designated leader has a responsibility and, in fact, a contractual obligation to accomplish specified group objectives; and judgments in respect to these goals often are beyond the decision-making purview of the immediate work-group.

At this juncture, therefore, it is imperative to re-examine our ideas about establishing a desirable balance between "human relations" (i.e., Consideration) and Initiating Structure emphases in leader behavior. In education we have properly and quite successfully stressed the importance of maintaining a "democratic" relationship between the teacher and his students. This is good. But let us remember, too, that the primary responsibility of a leader is to lead, and that by doing so he in no way becomes less "democratic." The essence of leading is to Initiate Structure-in-Interaction and to orient these structures continually toward the solution of group problems and the accomplishment of the goals prescribed for the group. Research indicates that this "Structuring" can be engaged in with no sacrifice of Consideration.

In our opinion, leader behavior characterized by high Initiation of Structure *and* high Consideration represents the ideal of democratic leadership that we all seek. The advantage of the present approach is that by identifying the components of this leadership style in behavioral terms and by focusing our efforts, as we have, upon the *behavior* of leaders, we are placed in a better position to develop dependable techniques for training teachers as more "effective" leaders.

39

Evaluation Through the Leaderless
Group Discussion

Bernard M. Bass

. . . .

At the beginning of Cameron Hawley's novel, *Executive Suite*, Avery
Bullard, President of the Tredway Corporation, could not decide whom
to choose as his successor from among his five vice-presidents.

> An idea flashed. He would get them together tonight for one last look. . . .
> He'd put some kind of proposition before them . . . anything . . . the
> possibility of building a new factory in North Carolina. It would hit them
> cold. . . . He would toss out the idea and then sit back . . . watching,
> listening, judging. Then he would pick the man who showed up best. (p. 5)

As is suggested by this passage from the recent best-seller about executive
life, the leaderless group discussion has a common-sense basis as a leadership
evaluation instrument. For the technique has high face validity.

Rationale. The rationale underlying the leaderless group discussion, and
other situational tests of leadership, can be summarized as follows: *the more
similar the problem in a new situation to one in an old situation, the more
likely [it is that] the same persons [will] attempt and be successful as leaders
in both situations.*

The hypothesis is consistent with what we know about transfer of training.
Also, when we average a series of seven test-retest studies of the leaderless
group discussion in order of the similarity between test and retest, we obtain
reliability coefficients or consistency correlations that increase from .39 to
.90 as the similarity increases in conditions during the test and retest.

What is the Leaderless Group Discussion? The basic scheme of the
leaderless group discussion (LGD) is to ask several examinees, as a group,
to carry on a discussion. No leader is appointed. Examiners do not enter
the discussion once it begins but remain free to observe and note the performance of each examinee.

From Bernard M. Bass, "The Leaderless Group Discussion as a Leadership Evaluation Instrument," *Personnel Psychology*, VII (Winter, 1954), 470–477. Reprinted
with the permission of publisher and author.

As yet, there has been no final standardization by all users of the technique of the size of the group, length of testing time, type of problem presented, directions, seating arrangement, number of raters, and rating procedure. There is considerable evidence available on the effects of many of these variations to suggest which particular aspects of the LGD are most in need of standardization and what the final standardized LGD should be like.

Unless otherwise indicated, the results we shall describe are based on observers' ratings of the *amount of successful leadership displayed* in the discussion or else are inferences about the personalities of the candidates based on observations of this behavior.

According to twelve studies involving 1,065 examinees, ranging from administrative trainee candidates to ROTC cadets, rater agreement is high, especially where standardized behavior check-lists are used. A median correlation of .82 exists between pairs of observer ratings for the twelve investigations.

What Is the Validity of the Leaderless Group Discussion? As with most other personality variables, there is no absolute or "true" criterion upon which to validate ratings based on the leaderless group discussion. Rather, we must be content to demonstrate, by experimentation, consistencies between LGD performance and other measures where these other measures are indicative, by deduction and/or induction, of the tendency to be successful as a leader.

For example, suppose we deduce or discover experimentally elsewhere that, all other things being equal, the higher an individual's verbal aptitude, the more he will display successful leadership behavior. Then, if LGD performance correlates with scores on a verbal intelligence test, we may infer that the LGD performance is, partially, at least, a sample of leadership behavior.

Various relationships concerning individual differences in successful leader behavior can be derived by definition, postulate, and deduction. The relationships are shown in Figure 1.

According to Figure 1, if the LGD is a means of measuring successful leadership behavior, then: (1) LGD scores should correlate with status as measured by rank when the LGD is among associates of different rank; (2) LGD scores should correlate with esteem as estimated by merit ratings; (3) LGD scores should correlate with leadership performance in other quasi-real situations; (4) LGD scores should correlate with success in real-life leadership situations; and (5) LGD scores should correlate with personal characteristics, as measured by psychological tests and measurements, commonly associated with success as a leader. (Status refers to the worth of a person, according to his associates, due to the position he occupies. Esteem refers to the worth of a person, as a person, regardless of his position.)[1]

Each positive correlation between an LGD rating and another of these specified measures will provide experimental evidence of the "validity" of

---

[1] A more detailed discussion of esteem, status, and the deductions mentioned is presented in B. M. Bass, "A Psychological Theory of Leadership" (Mimeographed paper, Louisiana State University, Baton Rouge, La., 1953).

Figure 1

SOME RELATIONSHIPS CONCERNING INDIVIDUAL DIFFERENCES IN SUCCESSFUL
LEADER BEHAVIOR DERIVED BY DEFINITION, POSTULATE, AND DEDUCTION

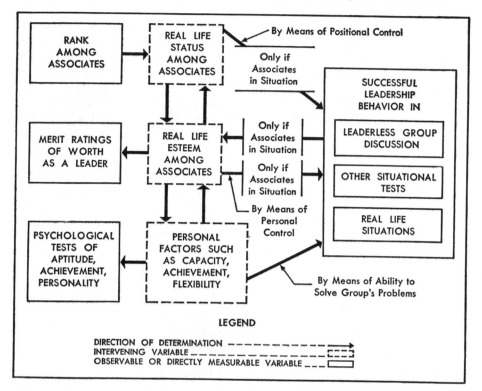

LGD performance. This rationale ignores situational variations and their important but not all-important effect on leader behavior. For we find that successful leaders in the LGD manage to exhibit success as a leader in a wide range of other situations. We therefore believe we are dealing with consistent individual differences in successful leadership behavior which are significant above and beyond the effects of situational variations.

Actually the LGD absorbs to some extent the effects of situational variations. For example, the problems on which, and the participants with whom, an individual is tested vary consistently with the problems and individuals on which and for whom the individual has high or low esteem, or on which or with whom he usually has been tested in other situations. In other words, we tend to correlate the LGD behavior of eighteen-year-old female examinees with the esteem of the examinees among adolescent girls. If we were to correlate the same LGD behavior with the examinees' esteem among thirty-five-year-old men, LGD validity would undoubtedly be altered.

We shall now consider each of the expected and obtained correlations between LGD performance and the other mentioned variables.

*What Is the Correlation Between LGD Performance and Status as Meas-
ured by Rank?* Two studies are available to answer this question. In the
first study, a correlation of .88 was found between the rank in the company
of each of 131 oil refinery supervisors and their success as LGD leaders among
their associates.

In the second study, 180 ROTC cadets were retested among their associates
a year after an original test. During the year, all cadets were promoted.
Those who were promoted from cadet "non-com" to cadet first lieutenant or
higher gained significantly more in LGD score on the retest, compared to
the test, than those who received promotions to cadet second lieutenant only.

We conclude from the results that — as expected, if the LGD is a valid
measure of successful leadership — performance in an initially leaderless discussion among associates of varying status is strongly related to status in real-
life among these associates.

*What Is the Correlation Between LGD Performance and Esteem as Esti-
mated by Merit Ratings?* Fourteen correlations are available between LGD
performance and esteem as estimated by merit ratings. They involve a total
of 1,495 cases varying from foreign service candidates to oil refinery supervisors. Only one of these published studies failed to obtain a significantly
positive correlation between LGD scores and merit ratings. (In this one
case, men of differing rank were tested together and most of the variance in
LGD success was determined by rank.) The median correlation of .44 and
the range from .29 to .68 for all these studies excepting the one where
examinees varied in rank lead us to infer (as we also deduced) that esteem
and LGD performance are moderately associated. We again conclude that
LGD performance is valid as a measure of successful leadership.

*What Is the Correlation Between LGD Performance and Personal Charac-
teristics Associated with Leadership?* According to Stogdill's[2] survey of over
one hundred empirical studies, leaders tend to surpass non-leaders in certain
traits such as capacity, achievement, responsibility, and participation. Similarly, we can deduce the existence of positive correlations between successful
leadership and capacity, achievement and participation. Therefore, if performance in the LGD is associated with these personal factors, we will have
another indirect indication of the validity of LGD performance as a measure
of successful leadership behavior.

Published studies, involving a total of 2,361 test scores, report seventeen
correlations between LGD performance and various measures of capacity and
achievement such as verbal aptitude tests, college grades, and intelligence
tests. The median correlation is .30 and the range is from .17 to .57. These
results tend to conform to expectations and lead us once more to conclude
that the LGD is valid as a measure of successful leadership.

When we examine the correlations between LGD performance and various
personality variables which approximate the "responsibility" and "participa-

2 R. M. Stogdill, "Personal Factors Associated with Leadership: A Survey of the Literature," *Journal of Psychology,* XXV (1948), 31–75.

tion" clusters of Stogdill, we infer that a consistency exists between Stogdill's conclusions concerning the relations between leadership in general and such personality traits as energy, flexibility of judgment, self-esteem, and the tendency to participate and our results concerning the relations between these traits and LGD performance. We find a median correlation of .30 and a range from .07 to .60 for the nine available correlations concerning these relationships. Some contradiction or lack of consistency appears when we consider such traits as responsibility, emotional stability, ascendency, and sociability especially when they have been measured by forced-choice rather than traditional personality inventories.

What Is the Correlation Between LGD Performance and Leadership Performance in Other Quasi-Real Situations? The median correlation is .60 and the range from .30 to .78 for the sixteen available correlations between ratings of "leadership" or "desirability for leadership positions" based on LGD performance and similar ratings based on other situational tests. These data concern over two thousand examinees varying from OSS assessees to shoe-factory management trainees. The correlations probably overestimate the relationships somewhat, for in many of the studies the same observers rated performance in the LGD and in the other situations.

However, we conclude that ratings in the LGD are associated with ratings of success as a leader in a wide variety of other situational tests and infer again that LGD ratings are valid as measures of successful leadership.

What Is the Correlation Between LGD Performance and Leadership Performance in Real-Life Situations? We find a median of .27 for seven correlations between LGD performance and real-life leadership performance. The most important result here is that while LGD ratings correlate with the tendency to hold leadership offices ($r = .27, .36$), they appear to be associated primarily with the tendency in real life to initiate structure among associates and subordinates ($r = .32$).[3] On the contrary, according to the one study available . . . a low negative correlation appears to exist between LGD performance and the tendency in real-life to be considerate of the welfare of subordinates and associates ($r = -.25$). Two factorial analyses support the hypothesis that LGD performance is a function of the tendency to initiate and to be socially bold, as well as several other factors such as esteem, intellectualism, and verbality.

What Is the Utility of the LGD as an Assessment Technique? Since 1947, the LGD has gained widespread use in the United States. In 1951, Fields[4] reported that forty-four out of 190 Civil Service agencies were using some form of the LGD. Mandell[5] has published a manual on the procedure

---

[3] A more detailed discussion of the factors of "initiation" and "consideration" is presented in E. A. Fleishman, "Leadership Climate, Human Relations Training, and Supervisory Behavior," *Personnel Psychology*, VI (1953), 205–222.

[4] H. Fields, "An Analysis of the Use of the Group Oral Interview," *Personnel*, XXVII (1951), 480–486.

[5] M. Mandell, "The Group Oral Performance Test" (Washington, D.C.: U.S. Civil Service Commission, 1952). (Multilithed.)

for use by the Federal Civil Service. The LGD is widely used by many industrial and business firms today — so widely used that it has prompted Meyer[6] to caution about the over-enthusiastic acceptance of the technique. In one West Coast city alone, the procedure has been used by a large bank, a department store, a canning and container concern, a petroleum company and an airline. According to the forty-odd published reports available the LGD has been used profitably to assess examinees ranging from officer candidates to visiting teachers.

The wide variety of situations in which the LGD has been applied with profit probably is due to the almost universal requirement that the leader adequately communicate *verbally* with those he leads. Until individuals in "real-life" groups begin communicating with each other by means of telepathy or the passing of symbols printed on cards, it is probable that the LGD will provide one general means among several others (such as individual interviews and intelligence tests) for partially assessing the leadership potential of individuals for a wide range of situations.

[6] C. A. Meyer, "The Group Interview Test: Its Weakness," *Public Personnel Review,* XI (1950), 147–154.

40

Evaluation Through Self-Evaluation

Thomas Gordon

It is not easy to become an effective discussion leader. But at least we no longer believe that leadership can be achieved only by those gifted few who happen to be born with certain leadership traits. The old adage, "Leaders are born, not made," is being replaced by the idea that leadership *can* be learned. Social science now furnishes ample evidence that people can learn new skills of leadership — particularly skills that facilitate learning and creative thinking in discussion groups.

What are these *new skills of leadership?* What does it take for one to become a more effective discussion leader? These questions are being asked by an ever increasing number of leaders from all walks of life — industrial

From Thomas Gordon, "Improving Your Leadership in Discussion Groups," *Adult Leadership,* I (March, 1953), 13–14. Reprinted with the permission of the publisher.

managers, business executives, community leaders, teachers, school administrators, ministers, social workers, politicians, and so on. Wherever people are assuming responsibility for helping groups work out their problems through discussion, there exists a need to discover and learn ways of doing this more effectively. Fortunately for such leaders, there is agreement among social scientists on some of the requirements for effective leadership. Nevertheless, because leadership has so recently become a legitimate problem for scientific study one would also expect considerable disagreement about a role as complex as the leader's. This means that to learn leadership skills one can rely upon facts and authority only up to a point. Beyond that he must depend upon his own varied experiences as he tries out different leadership methods.

Furthermore, it is a sure bet that people cannot change their patterns of leadership simply by picking up a few new techniques. Leadership is too much related to one's total personality, one's basic attitudes and values. Consequently, becoming a different kind of leader requires fundamental changes in the inner core of the person, as opposed to simply his outward behavior. Such a change will occur only through frequent exposures to new situations, through a kind of painstaking experimentation with different methods, and through honest examination and evaluation of one's attitudes toward self and others. Techniques will help, of course, but they can be effective only if they become an implementation of the leader's own philosophy and temperament. A budding Hitler would have difficulty learning some of the methods of facilitating discussion. This can be taken first as a caution against being fooled by leaders whose attitudes make it inevitable that they will employ the techniques of effective leadership to accomplish their own ends irrespective of the group's goals. There is a second reason for stressing the intimate relationship between one's patterns of leadership and his philosophy and temperament. People often get so discouraged after once trying out new methods of leadership that they give up and go back to their old ways. If, however, these leaders realized that changes in their attitudes must go hand in hand with changes in their techniques, then they might have more tolerance for their early failures and keep struggling for improvement.

The Leader's Attitudes

There is no tool more important than the leader's attitudes — attitudes toward others, toward himself, and toward groups.

Let us assume first that a leader would not even consider the use of group discussion unless he believes that its effect will in some way be better than, say, a lecture in which he alone contributes to the group. This means, then, that the discussion leader believes that *group members have something to contribute.* For some members this contribution may be a new idea; for others, an idea borrowed from someone else; for others, a fact or observation picked up from reading; for still others, an expression of their feelings, a report of their experiences or an evaluation of the discussion. All of these, the effective discussion leader considers to be worthwhile contributions.

Another way of putting this attitude stresses the *uniqueness of each individual*. The discussion leader believes that each person is unique — different from everyone else. Consequently, he has the potentiality for making some unique contribution — one that no one else could possibly make, because no one else is quite like him.

A second basic attitude of the discussion leader is that *the group exists for the achievement of the goals of its members*, not primarily for the realization of the leader's puposes. He sees the group as the vehicle for the achievement of the goals of all its members, including himself.

To hold such values as these the discussion leader needs to feel fairly secure himself. This is not to say that he needs to be perfectly well-adjusted. Rather, he must be secure enough to tolerate others having opinions different from his own. In a very real sense, he must respect his own uniqueness, else how can he respect the uniqueness of others? A strong desire to try to pattern others in our own image is usually rooted in a deep sense of insecurity, inferiority, and powerlessness. On the other hand, the willingness for others to be themselves, to have their own unique thoughts, and to see the world through their own eyes requires of any leader that he have considerable inner security and strength.

These are but a few of the basic attitudes that seem to be consistently related to the ability to foster creative participation among the members of a discussion group. Someday perhaps social scientists will be able to provide us with a more complete list. Yet even with the limited understanding existing at present, effective leadership of discussion groups seems to require all of the attitudes and values that we associate with democracy.

WHERE DO I STAND?

Leaders who wish to examine their own attitudes may find a guide in the following list of statements. Even among effective discussion leaders there will be some disagreement in their attitudes and philosophy. These are merely thought-provoking questions that other leaders have had to face and puzzle over.

The most important factor in the group's effectiveness is the wisdom of the leader.	*The most important factor in the group's effectiveness is the ability of each member to make his maximum contribution.*
Agree _____ Unsure or Neither _____ Agree _____	
Often the leader knows better than the group what goals the group should achieve.	Goals set by the total group in the long run will be best for the group.
Agree _____ Unsure or Neither _____ Agree _____	
The most effective group is the one which each member feels free to lead.	All groups need a single leader.

Agree _____ *Unsure or Neither* _____ *Agree* _____

The leader must retain some authority over the group.	Authority is rightly the property of the total group.

Agree _____ *Unsure or Neither* _____ *Agree* _____

An effective group is one whose members are always free to challenge the leader.	The leader loses his effectiveness if he allows his ideas to be challenged too often.

Agree _____ *Unsure or Neither* _____ *Agree* _____

A leader should try to minimize status differences between himself and the group.	A leader should have more status and prestige than group members.

Agree _____ *Unsure or Neither* _____ *Agree* _____

Most people are too uninformed to make a contribution to a group discussion.	Every member should be considered a potential contributor to a group discussion.

Agree _____ *Unsure or Neither* _____ *Agree* _____

A leader should welcome dependence upon him and use it to teach the group.	A leader should try to decrease dependence upon him.

Agree _____ *Unsure or Neither* _____ *Agree* _____

If the leader has power over the group, then members will not participate as freely as if he did not.	A leader should hold on to his power if he uses it wisely and justly.

Agree _____ *Unsure or Neither* _____ *Agree* _____

People are basically dependent and want their thoughts to be directed by those who know more.	People learn to be dependent, but also desire freedom from direction by others.

Agree _____ *Unsure or Neither* _____ *Agree* _____

SUMMARY, QUESTIONS, AND SUGGESTED READINGS

SUMMARY

It is now agreed that leader and group are inseparably united. If the group changes, the leader must also change in some fashion. Understanding the leader necessitates understanding the group.

A leader of one group may be a follower in another. This change in role is the result of many factors including the psychological needs within the group. The successful leader of various groups is sufficiently correct in his perceptions and flexible in his behavior to satisfy some of the important needs of these groups, but his perceptions and behavior operate within the framework of his own personality structure. If he has an authoritarian personality, his leadership is permeated with the values and methods of an authoritarian. The same process applies for those with a group-centered or democratic personality.

Since groups vary greatly in their needs to be satisfied, it is hazardous to predict the personality characteristics necessary to the success of a leader in a particular situation. He could succeed in one situation and fail in another. Certain qualities, however, seem to enhance the possibility that he will more frequently be successful. Persons who are sufficiently free of self-concern to be able to enter into the concerns of others and to identify with them are likely to gain and retain leadership.

QUESTIONS

1. Name the differentiating characteristics of the three types of leadership.
2. Why may a person be a leader in one group and a follower in the next?
3. What questions should a leader ask himself before he attempts to initiate the democratic process?
4. Choose what you think is the best theory of leadership and explain your preference.
5. Name the three personality characteristics generally common to all elected leaders.
6. Select and discuss one of the chief problems of leadership.

SUGGESTED READINGS

Section A: The Leader

Carter, Launor; Haythorn, William; Shriver, Beatrice; and Lanzetta, John. "The Behavior of Leaders and Other Group Members," *Journal of Abnormal and Social Psychology*, XLVI (1950), 589–595.

This study compares the behavior of leaders and members in groups in which a leader is appointed with those in which he is not (leaderless groups). By the use of sociometric methods, forty NROTC Junior Students were divided into eight groups, five students to a group.

It was found that some important types of behavior were performed only by the leaders and that these differed in the two kinds of groups. This selection contrasts the functioning of the status leader as opposed to the emergent leader.

Section B: Theories of Leadership

Borgotta, Edgar F.; Couch, Arthur S.; and Bales, Robert F. "Some Findings Relevant to the Great-Man Theory of Leadership," *American Sociological Review*, XIX (1954), 755–759.

This is a study of the effectiveness of the leadership in a group with "the most adequate all-round leader." Effectiveness was determined through the performance of the groups. The data is based upon 166 sessions of three-man groups in which each person participated in four sessions with the two new co-participants in each session. "Great men" were selected on the basis of their performance in the first session. Factor analysis with three orthogonal factors were used to study the rated behavior of individuals in group interaction. It was concluded that the "great men" selected on the basis of their first session continued to have an influence on the relatively superior performance of the groups in which they subsequently participated.

Carter, Launor F.; Haythorn, William; and Howell, Margaret. "A Further Investigation of the Criteria of Leadership," *Journal of Abnormal and Social Psychology*, XLV (1950), 350–358.

This study investigated five criteria of leadership. Included were the use of the leaderless-group technique, the nominating method, ratings by faculty members, ratings by friends, and the assessment of leadership in previous extracurricular and out-of-school activities. Nominations by the members of the men whom they thought would be the best and the poorest leaders were quite reliable. Nominations by faculty members and friends proved to be quite unreliable. By the use of factor analysis it was shown that there were two different tasks apparently requiring different leadership abilities. One ability was termed "an intellectual leadership factor" and the other, a "doing things with one's hands leadership factor."

Section C: Psychological Foundations of Leadership

Rinn, John L. "Group Guidance: Two Processes," *Personnel and Guidance Journal*, XXXIX (1961), 591–594.

An exploration of the functions of group guidance as perceived by graduate students is followed by the problems of the leader who recognizes a great dissimilarity in the expectations of the students. Finally, the bases of the leader's decision with reference to whether he will perform in the authoritarian role "instruction-oriented" or the democratic "development-oriented" are carefully examined and some provocative conclusions are drawn.

Section D: Leadership Functioning

Maier, Norman R. F., and Solem, Allen R. "The Contribution of a Discussion Leader to the Quality of Group Thinking," *Human Relations*, V (1952), 277–288.

For the purpose of testing the contribution of a leader to the quality of group thinking, thirty-four groups, each with five or six persons and supplied with a leader were compared with thirty-three groups, each with five or six persons and supplied with an observer. The leaders were asked to conduct a discussion, whereas the observers were asked to listen to the others while they discussed.

A mathematical problem requiring the use of simple arithmetic was presented, and all persons were asked to write their answers on a card both before and after an eight-minute discussion.

The two sets of groups gave similar answers before the discussion, but after the discussion the groups with leaders had more correct answers significant just below the 1 per cent level.

Section E: Problems of Leadership

Hamblin, Robert L. "Leadership and Crises," *Sociometry*, XXI (1958), 322–335.

This study tests two hypotheses: (1) that leaders have more influence during a crisis than in an ordinary situation and (2) that if the leader does not have a solution, he is replaced.

Before-and-after observations were made of twelve three-person groups in a crisis situation and twelve three-person groups in a control situation. The investigators involved the twelve experimental groups in what appeared to be a genuine crisis. Both hypotheses were supported.

Raven, Bertram H., and French, John R. P. "Group Support, Legitimate Power and Social Influence," *Journal of Personality*, XXVI (1958), 400–409.

It was hypothesized that a supervisor elected to the position would have greater power to influence his fellow workers than a worker who assumed the position.

Of the fifty-six participants in the study, fifty-four were volunteer female undergraduates and two were paid participants. They were organized in groups of five to eight. Each set of groups (those who had an elected supervisor and those in which a paid participant took over the leadership) was given tasks which were identical and interdependent.

The results gave clear evidence that the elected supervisor had greater power to influence the groups.

Section F: Evaluation

Bradford, Leland P.; Benne, Kenneth D.; and Lippitt, Ronald. "The Promise of Group Dynamics," *NEA Journal*, XXXVII (September, 1948), 350–352.

This article dramatically illustrates the results of teachers' meetings in which the principal is ineffective in his leadership. The description is followed by an evaluation, with suggestions for improvement.

PART FIVE

The Group Member

Kierkegaard has remarked, "the more consciousness, the more self," but we do not find it easy to become acquainted with our real selves. There is a degree of uncertainty and considerable fear connected with the process. It is not only that we may be unwilling to accept our true motives for certain actions, but in some areas of experience we may be threatened by both motives and actions.

In any case, a recognition of our motives is the beginning of any improvement in our relationships with others. The group member's knowledge of and attitude toward himself determines in large measure the character of his contribution to the group.

It is appropriate, then, that Part Five, which discusses the group member, should begin with two selections which ask him to analyze his motives and attitudes.

The increasing recognition and acceptance of various aspects of the self is only part of the story, however. The social environment in which we participate also influences our behavior, and yet we react to our unique perception of the environment. Thus no two members are actually in an identical group, since each member's perception of the group environment is unique. These perceptions, in turn, are affected by our experiences in other groups.

Efficient groups are characterized by mature and considerate action buttressed by a willing acceptance of responsibility. Individuals, however, participate in groups with varying degrees of readiness. Since we are at different stages in our advance toward "becoming a person," we all bring our needs to the group as well as our contributions. It may be possible to satisfy our needs while working with others upon a problem, but this is seldom true. More frequently we are self-oriented rather than problem-oriented and tend to divert the energies of the collective group to the satisfaction of our personal needs. Although this type of group behavior is readily expected in groups of children, it is also frequently seen in adult groups.

It is possible, however, for a member to learn to contribute to the welfare of the group without the imposition of his needs. He may indirectly satisfy certain needs or may discover that they no longer exist. The probability of this taking place is increased if the individual understands himself and the group process, and if he is dedicated to the group goal.

Although a group member can be expected to function differently in different groups, his performance in one group will in general resemble his performance in the next. This general stability has engendered the notion that to some degree the function or role of each member can be described. Thus a member may say, "You can count on John to have the information."

If the outcomes of a group process are to improve in quality, the individual member must improve his performance. This means that the member must change in performance, but this, in turn, is preceded by a change in his perception. He performs well because he perceives situations as they truly exist. He is cognitively correct. In the group, his perceptions of others is the key to his own performance.

Any change, of course, is attended by risks. Change is threatening. The familiar is more comfortable, and conformity requires less effort. Some conforming behavior, of course, is necessary to effective and productive interpersonal relationships, but the member who always conforms is in need of understanding and help.

If group members are going to help one another and themselves, each of them must fully understand the means and the outcomes of the group activity. This requires the establishment of immediate and long-range goals and criteria for the evaluation of performance, and both goals and criteria must be sufficiently flexible to correspond to the developmental growth of members and groups.

Section A

BECOMING A MEMBER

In the selection entitled "The Internal Dialogue of the Self," from his book The Self and the Dramas of History, Reinhold Niebuhr warns us against too simple an interpretation of the self. The inner dialogue, says Niebuhr, proceeds on many levels and is quite complex. Thus goals may be set by the individual which are constructive or destructive to the welfare of the group.

The degree to which the self succeeds in its relationships is in part dependent upon the breadth and correctness of its perceptions. One distorted perception may lead to others, but a correct perception leads to better understanding and the solution of problems. How perception influences our behavior is the focus of the selection, "Perception and Its Function," from the book Individual Behavior by Arthur W. Combs and Donald Snygg.

Thus the quality of the interpersonal relationships among members is a result of the correctness of their individual perceptions. The healthier the individual members, the healthier the group relationship will be. A. H. Maslow, in the selection from Motivation and Personality, entitled "Self-Actualizing People: Psychological Health," provides useful insights into the characteristics of the member who contributes to and learns from the group.

41

The Internal Dialogue of the Self

Reinhold Niebuhr

We may safely say that the human animal is the only creature which talks to itself. It maintains a rather constant internal dialogue in which it approves or disapproves its actions, or even itself. Its accusations and defences of itself are quite different from those in which it engages in its external dialogues. The self pities and glorifies itself as well as accuses and excuses itself. It could not carry on this dialogue without using its "reason"; for the dialogue means that the self in one of its aspects is making the self, in another of its aspects, its object of thought. It uses conceptual images for this procedure.

But it is important to note that the self which is doing the judging and excusing, the pitying and glorifying, is not necessarily the "rational" or the "intelligible" self in contrast to the "sensible" self. It was the primary mistake of the philosophers from classical days to this day to equate the self as subject with mind; and the self as object with either the body, or the body-soul unity, or with some other aspect of the self as creature. The fact is that there are not two distinct selves in this internal dialogue. There are merely two foci of the same self. We do, of course, know of a pathological condition in which the self becomes separated into two warring and comparatively discrete entities. This is known as "schizophrenia." There are pathological states which border on this internal division. But the healthy self is always one self, no matter how much it engages in a perpetual internal dialogue.

The dialogue within the self proceeds on many levels. Sometimes it is a dialogue between the self as engaged in its various responsibilities and affections and the self which observes these engagements. Sometimes the dialogue is between the self in the grip of its immediate necessities and biological urges, and the self as an organization of long-range purposes and ends. Sometimes the dialogue is between the self in the context of one set of loyalties and the self in the grip of contrasting claims and responsibilities.

When artists try to depict a character in a novel or drama, they frequently resort to the record of this internal dialogue because it may be more revealing than the self's external dialogue or dramatic action. With artistic license they claim to be privy to the secrets of this dialogue, though it is by its very nature secret; and the self which entertains ambitions and desires is subject to temptations and considers alternative modes of action about which even the most intimate friend may know nothing. Only the victorious, and not the vanquished, forces are known to the outside world. The self remains such a mystery even to its friends because so little is known about the stratagems which produced the victory of the one over the other force.

An interesting witness to the reality of the self's inner dialogue, and more particularly of the phenomenon of the self as spectator of its actions and attitudes, is furnished by Lucy Sprague Mitchell in her biography of her husband and her own autobiography, entitled *Two Lives*.[1] Speaking of her adolescence, she writes: "It was at this time that I became aware of the complexity of one's make-up. When I acted in our stable-theatre I seemed to be two people: one making up dramatic lines and rendering them in fine action, and the other listening, approving or disapproving. I was actor and critic at the same time. I found that this was disturbingly true, whatever I did. When I talked with father or helped mother with household arrangements, I always heard and saw myself doing these things. I must be hopelessly insincere, I always thought. But the sense of guilt did not change me one bit. So vivid this inlooker self became, that I called it 'the thing in the corner.' Among my old papers I find a curious document, written in my fourteenth year and beginning: 'Tis seldom that one personality speaks to another. Even more rare is it that one's other personality speaks to another personality. Too seldom alas, for more often than not they speak another language." Obviously this is a very significant memory of a vivid experience of childhood, and throws a bright light on the anatomy of selfhood which is superior to the analyses of many learned men.

The analyses of Freud and of subsequent "depth psychology" into the inner tensions of the human psyche have both illumined and obscured this inner dialogue. They have illumined it insofar as the analyses proved conclusively that the old "body-mind" separation was mistaken; and that the inner organization of the self is much more intricate than was supposed.

The Freudian division of the self into "id," "ego" and "super-ego" indicates at least two levels of the dialogue, that between the self in the grip of its immediate necessities and the self in its more inclusive and coherent organization; and that between the self as concerned with itself and the self in its relations to the community. It also proves that the dialogue may leave many scars. The therapeutic efficacy of depth psychology rests largely upon the discovery that a part of the "unconscious element in the ego" is but the repressed portions of a preconscious desire. Freud, in fact, denied the freedom of the will, partly because he was so preoccupied with the limiting forces upon the will by neurotic anxieties, which he attributed to the baneful effect of repression. Sometimes Freud pictured the task of analysis to be that of freeing the "ego" from the limits placed upon it by the "id" and the "super-ego." The task of psychoanalysts is, he declares, "to strengthen the ego, to make it

[1] Simon and Schuster, Inc.

more independent of the superego, to widen its vision and extend its field of organization so that it can take over portions of the id. Where the id is, there shall the ego be."[2]

For all of the therapeutic skill of Freudian psychology, and its wisdom in exploring the labyrinths of the self, it has confused the realities of the internal dialogue in some degree by obscuring the fact that the self is really in both the "id" and the "super-ego." The "id" is defined as a cauldron of "seething excitement." But it obviously has the guile of a real self in trying to evade the guard of the "ego's" "censor." Sometimes Freud pictures the tension between the "ego" and the "repressed" portions of the self. Inasmuch as neuroses are due to these repressions, it is important to bring this repressed material into the open consciousness. The tool of emancipation is the recollection of the experiences in which the repressions took place. Freud notes that the resistance to this process of recollection is offered by the conscious self. "There is no doubt," he declares, "that the conscious and preconscious ego subserves the pleasure principle. It is trying to avoid the pain which would be aroused by a release of the repressed material."[3] Thus the self is in this dialogue between the "coherent ego" and the "id" more than it would at first appear.

The presence of the self in the dialogue between the "ego" and the "super-ego" is even more mistakenly obscured. This is obviously a debate between the self as engaged and obligated to its various communities and the self concerned with its own ends. But the Freudian psychology moves within the limits of a rigid naturalism; and this second level of transcendence is not conceivable within those limits. The "super- ego" is therefore no more than the pressure of society upon the "ego"; and it does not occur to Freud that the self has both the power to defy the community for the sake of its interests and for the sake of interests more inclusive than those of a given community.

The inclination to ascribe the sense of social responsibilities to the external pressure upon the self and to imagine the self resisting these pressures makes Freudianism pessimistic about the possibility of extending any kind of social discipline to the extent required by modern society. This pessimism is expressed in Freud's *Civilization and Its Discontents*. The conviction prompts the conclusion that there is a tremendous amount of "aggression" stored up by the weight of the "super-ego" and also by the "cultural super-ego." Since there is no possibility of channeling all this aggression, Freud is sceptical about the problem of eliminating conflict in life. This curious conclusion has persuaded our social, as well as psychological, sciences to such a degree that some of them have become practically irrelevant to the serious task of dealing with conflicts of interest on every level of politics and economics. It is certainly not relevant to deal with the monumental collective egoism of nations, compounded of many genuinely historical cumulations; of illusion, and power lusts, as if they were merely the aggregate of individual "aggressiveness." Thus a discipline, which has proved itself therapeutically efficient in dealing with pathological states of individuals, has been betrayed into the

[2] *New Introductory Essays on Psychoanalysis*, p. 112.
[3] *Beyond the Pleasure Principle*, p. 20.

inanity of speculating whether the Germans, Russians and Japanese could be cured of their "aggressiveness" by a sufficiently wide application of psychotherapy.

Freud himself has had some curious evidence of the reality of the self, which he initially obscured in his analysis. He thought, for instance, that many forms of anxiety neuroses were due to traumatic experiences in youth, chiefly of a sexual nature. He was finally made suspicious by the indicated excessively high rate of incest which was confessed in these recollections; and it dawned upon him that the confessions were bogus and merely betrayed the incestuous desires of the patients in their youth.[4] In the same fashion a modern psychologist[5] reports, on the one hand, that the analysis of specific causes has banished the idea of a transcendent self from the consideration of causes as successfully as an earlier natural science had banished God; but, on the other hand, he cautions against the possibility of the banished and guileful self, manipulating the tools of analysis for its own self-justification.

Incidentally, the emphasis put by modern psychiatry upon the voluntary cooperation of the patient and the futility of forcing submission to therapy is another indication of the importance of the banished self and of the reality of the freedom which has been denied.

The inability of Freudianism to comprehend the reality of a free self prompts it to reduce the problem of guilt to the manifestation of neurotic guilt. Neurotic guilt may be defined as the sense of guilt due to fancied violations of arbitrary norms. It has little to do with the sense of guilt, arising from the self's violations of norms accepted by it as valid and validated by the experience of other men. It also tempts psychiatry to reduce all forms of egotism to vestiges of childish egocentricity which greater experience will correct. Thus an approach to the self which is therapeutically adequate for pathological aberrations of selfhood is incapable of comprehending the real problems of the self on either the political or the religious level.

The dialogue which the self carries on within itself is certainly more complex than understood in classical philosophy. Depth psychology has uncovered many of these complexities. But it has no doubt obscured many others because it failed to grasp that the same self is in the various *personae* of the dialogue.

[4] Ernst Jones, *Life and Work of Sigmund Freud.*
[5] L. F. Shaffer, *Psychology of Adjustment.*

42

Perception and Its Function

Arthur W. Combs and Donald Snygg

THE SELECTION OF PERCEPTIONS

Anyone comparing the ways in which he perceives with the perceptions of someone of the opposite sex can very quickly discover that men do not perceive in all things as women do. Nor do children perceive like adults, Americans like Russians, or schoolteachers like engineers. The self concepts we hold have a vital effect upon the ways we perceive. They determine the ways it is necessary and appropriate for us to behave and, as a result, the things we see, the ideas we note, and the objects we accept or reject.

At any instant, the things possible for us to perceive in any situation are almost limitless. Yet we do not perceive in any such chaotic fashion. What we perceive is always organized and has meaning, and that meaning derives from the phenomenal self. Men see what seems appropriate for men to see while women see what seems appropriate for them. In our society the use of taboo words is regarded a more serious offense for women than for men and this difference shows up when men and women are asked to report such words after they have seen them. Under these conditions men report more taboo words than women. People with low opinions of themselves underestimate their performance more than people with higher self concepts.

We need but to look about us to see thousands of examples of this selective effect of the phenomenal self upon perception. The same political candidate is seen quite differently by the Republican and the Democrat, and segregation is not the same seen by the Northerner or the Southerner. Professors do not see college-student behavior in the same way in which parents do, students do, or the city police do. Mr. and Mrs. Brown on the way home from the party discuss the people who were there. When Mrs. Brown asks her husband if he noticed "the dress that Helen was wearing," she may be quite annoyed to discover that her spouse did not notice Helen's dress at all. Being a man, there may have been other things about Helen more appropriate for men to perceive, however, which Mr. Brown did notice, but about which his wife does not think to ask him.

Little boys in our society are raised quite differently from little girls and come to see themselves quite differently as a result. When boys fall down and bump their noses, we are inclined to say, "Here, now! Little boys don't cry!" So little boys learn that it is not proper for boys to display their emotions. When little girls fall down and bump their noses, however, it is a very different matter! We rush to their assistance, pick them up, and comfort them as best we can. So little girls discover that crying is acceptable female behavior. In later life the results of these self concepts may make it difficult for the young wife to understand why her husband is "such an unfeeling brute" or may make it hard for a husband to understand why his wife "gets so upset over little things." The ways we see ourselves, once established, continue to select our perceptions throughout our lives.

The self even affects the relationships between the individual and other people through this selective effect upon perceptions. Harry Stack Sullivan, for example, pointed out: "If there is a valid and real attitude toward the self, that attitude will be manifest as valid and real toward others. It is not as ye judge that ye shall be judged, but as you judge yourself so shall you judge others." The principle that self acceptance is related to capacity to accept others has also been demonstrated in studies of counseling improvement. Even the individual's levels of aspiration are a function of the kinds of self concepts he holds.

We are only beginning to discover the tremendous importance of this fact in dealing with human problems. Every day brings to light some new and intriguing consequence of individual self perceptions. People behave in terms of the self concepts they possess, and this fact is tremendously important to anyone who must work with people in any capacity whatever. We are even beginning to discover that many, if not most, problems which persons bring to the psychological clinic are primarily problems brought about by unfortunate concepts of self.

. . . .

The Circular Effect of the Phenomenal Self. . . . A great many of us are the unwitting victims of our concepts of self. . . . It is even possible that some of the readers of this book may be laboring under unfortunate concepts of themselves as unable to make a speech, do mathematics, drive a car, swim, or remember people's names. Indeed, this limiting effect of our phenomenal self upon perception sometimes produces great tragedies.

As Lecky has pointed out, we perceive in ways that are consistent with our concepts of self. A given phenomenal self perpetuates itself by permitting only such perceptions as are consistent with its already existing structure. People limited by their self perceptions behave in ways that seem to corroborate the self concepts they already hold. They seem almost to be "asking for" proof of what they feel about themselves, and indeed, they often get just what they ask for. The individual who, for example, feels that he is incapable of successfully making a speech perceives so many flaws in everything he does and turns his attention so intensely upon himself, expecting himself to fail, that he may stumble and falter or become tongue-tied with

stage fright, which of course simply serves to demonstrate how right he was
in the first place!

Perceptions are selected which are consistent with the perceived self of
the behaver. Such selection occurs, furthermore, without regard to whether
such perceptions seem to be complimentary or self-damaging in the eyes of an
outside observer. It will be recalled that we have stated the fundamental
need of all human beings is the maintenance and enhancement of the
phenomenal self. Since the first need of the individual is to maintain his
perceived self, perceptions inconsistent with what he believes are unlikely to
occur because they would not fit his self structure. The girl who has a deep
feeling of her own unattractiveness may feel we are cruelly baiting her when
we tell her how pretty she looks. It seems inconceivable to her that we mean
what we say. She may believe quite genuinely that we are "just trying to
make her feel good."

There are literally millions of people in this world who are the prisoners
of their own perceptions of self. Vast numbers of people believe they are
able to do far less than they really can. As a result, they remain chained to
unhappy, unproductive, and unsatisfying ways of life. Studies with various
self concept scales at Vanderbilt University show that (1) patients are differentiated from nonpatients; (2) failures in paratroop training, from passers;
(3) alcoholics, from nonalcoholics; (4) delinquents, from nondelinquents;
(5) drop-outs, from stay-ins in school — all on the basis of self-concept. Can
one conceive the kind of world we might achieve could we but find the means
to release ourselves from the slavery of inadequate concepts of self? Here is
a waste of human resources compared with which our losses in warfare or
automobile accidents seem small indeed.

Distortion of Perception. When individuals are confronted with events
inconsistent with their self structure they may seek consistency of perception
by doing violence to the facts. They may perceive a particular event in so
distorted a fashion as to be almost unrecognizable to a disinterested outside
observer. Thus, the senator who sees himself as a professional Communist
hunter and savior of the nation may begin seeing Communists behind every
bush or discover conspiracies where none actually exist. Labor and management in the midst of a strike often see events in a manner distorted beyond
recognition by the onlooking public. Rationalizations, in which people may
be found giving *good* reasons instead of *real* reasons for their behavior, are a
form of seeking for better organization by which inconsistent events can be
brought into closer harmony with existing self concepts. This is a form of
self deception to which all of us succumb on occasion.

When it is unflattering to admit the truth, it is sometimes much easier
to distort the perception enough to make it appear in a more flattering light.
In our society the term "laboring" class carries distasteful connotations, so
most people prefer to class themselves as "workers" rather than as "laborers."
We can avoid the consequences of our mistakes by seeing them as none of our
doing. We failed to make the meeting, not because we failed to start on time,
but because the train was late, the streets were too crowded, or the clock did

not go off. What is more, we may even believe this story! We would certainly object with vigor if anyone suggested it were not true!

Inconsistent or threatening events may also be dealt with by denying their existence entirely. A person confronted with a situation highly derogatory or destructive to his concepts of self may find it possible to maintain or enhance his integrity by the simple expedient of relegating the perception to someone else or denying its existence entirely. Thus, he may really not see what he would rather not see. The scientist who has spent his life proving the truth of a particular notion may be unable to accept the possibility of another solution and protects his phenomenal self by simply denying the new fact exists. Threatening derogatory comments about self can often be effectively dealt with by assuming they really refer to others. The teacher who asked the class to keep quiet was really directing her remarks "at Jane, not me!" . . .

The Phenomenal Self and Role. The concepts of self held by the individual determine the perceptions he will have of any particular event. Out of all the perceptions possible at any moment only those which are appropriate and consistent with the phenomenal self are available to him. This selective process determines the roles people play in any life situation.

The particular roles we feel called upon to play in life are the result of the goals and techniques we have differentiated as appropriate for us in those circumstances. Such roles will be appropriate to the phenomenal self existing for the individual at the moment. The professor and student act quite differently in the classroom. The behavior of each depends upon the concepts he has of himself and of the situation. The same person in the same situation at different times might feel called upon to make a speech, keep scrupulously clean, faint, tell a story, start a fight, or powder his nose (in preparation for a TV appearance, of course).

Though we speak here of "playing a role," we are not using the term in the theatrical sense of putting on a mask or playing a part not natural or appropriate to one's self. We use the term to mean simply the selection by the individual from his perceptual field of those goals, techniques, or ways of behaving that seem to him appropriate for the kind of person he feels himself to be in the situation he sees himself in. These roles will be the kinds of behavior that seem to him appropriate to or consistent with his phenomenal self in the situation.

Whatever roles we feel called upon to play will always be a function of need satisfaction. Whenever it becomes clear to us that our roles are inconsistent with our way of regarding ourselves, we will change them to others more likely to produce results and more consistent with our perceived selves. . . .

. . . .

43

Self-Actualizing People: Psychological Health

A. H. Maslow

Interpersonal Relationships[SA]

Self-actualizing people have deeper and more profound interpersonal relationships than any other adults (although not necessarily deeper than those of children). They are capable of more fusion, greater love, more perfect identification, more obliteration of the ego boundaries than other people would consider possible. There are, however, certain special characteristics of these relationships. In the first place, it is my observation that the other members of these relationships are likely to be healthier and closer to self-actualization than the average, often *much* closer. There is high selectiveness here, considering the small proportion of such people in the general population.

One consequence of this phenomenon and of certain others as well is that self-actualizing people have these especially deep ties with rather few individuals. Their circle of friends is rather small. The ones that they love profoundly are few in number. Partly this is for the reason that being very close to someone in this self-actualizing style seems to require a good deal of time. Devotion is not a matter of a moment. One subject expressed it so: "I haven't got time for many friends. Nobody has, that is, if they are to be *real* friends." The only possible exception in my group was one woman who seemed to be especially equipped socially. It was almost as if her appointed task in life was to have close and warm and beautiful relations with all the members of her family and their families as well as all her friends and theirs. Perhaps this was because she was an uneducated woman who had no formal task or career. This exclusiveness of devotion can and does exist side by side with a widespreading *Gemeinschaftsgefühl*, benevolence, affection, and friendliness (as qualified above). These people *tend* to be kind or at least patient to almost everyone. They have an especially tender love for children and are easily touched by them. In a very real even though special sense, they love or rather have compassion for all mankind.

This love does not imply lack of discrimination. The fact is that they can and do speak realistically and harshly of those who deserve it, and especially of the hypocritical, the pretentious, the pompous, or the self-inflated. But the face-to-face relationships even with these people do not always show signs of realistically low evaluations. One explanatory statement was about as follows: "Most people, after all, do not amount to much but they *could* have. They make all sorts of foolish mistakes and wind up being miserable and not knowing how they got that way when their intentions were good. Those who are not nice are usually paying for it in deep unhappiness. They should be pitied rather than attacked."

Perhaps the briefest possible description is to say that their hostile reactions to others are (1) deserved, (2) for the good of the person attacked or for someone else's good. This is to say, with Fromm, that their hostility is not character based, but is reactive or situational.

All the subjects for whom I have data show in common another characteristic that is appropriate to mention here, namely, that they attract at least some admirers, friends or even disciples or worshippers. The relation between the individual and his train of admirers is apt to be rather one-sided. The admirers are apt to demand more than our individual is willing to give. And furthermore, these devotions are apt to be rather embarrassing, distressing, and even distasteful to the self-actualizing person, since they often go beyond ordinary bounds. The usual picture is of our subject being kind and pleasant when forced into these relationships, but ordinarily trying to avoid them as gracefully as possible.

THE DEMOCRATIC CHARACTER STRUCTURE

All my subjects without exception may be said to be democratic people in the deepest possible sense. I say this on the basis of a previous analysis of authoritarian[1] and democratic character structures that is too elaborate to present here; it is possible only to describe some aspects of this behavior in short space. These people have all the obvious or superficial democratic characteristics. They can be and are friendly with anyone of suitable character regardless of class, education, political belief, race, or color. As a matter of fact it often seems as if they are not even aware of these differences, which are for the average person so obvious and so important.

They have not only this most obvious quality but their democratic feeling goes deeper as well. For instance they find it possible to learn from anybody who has something to teach them — no matter what other characteristics he may have. In such a learning relationship they do not try to maintain any outward dignity or to maintain status or age prestige or the like. It should even be said that my subjects share a quality that could be called humility of a certain type. They are all quite well aware of how little they know in comparison with what *could* be known and what *is* known by others. Because of this it is possible for them without pose to be honestly respectful and even humble before people who can teach them something that they do not know

[1] A. H. Maslow, "The Authoritarian Character Structure," *Journal of Social Psychology*, XVIII (1943), 401–411.

or who have a skill they do not possess. They give this honest respect to a carpenter who is a good carpenter; or for that matter to anybody who is a master of his own tools or his own craft.

The careful distinction must be made between this democratic feeling and a lack of discrimination in taste, of an undiscriminating equalizing of any one human being with any other. These individuals, themselves elite, select for their friends elite, but this is an elite of character, capacity, and talent, rather than of birth, race, blood, name, family, age, youth, fame, or power.

Most profound, but also most vague is the hard-to-get-at tendency to give a certain quantum of respect to *any* human being just because he is a human individual; our subjects seem not to wish to go beyond a certain minimum point, even with scoundrels, of demeaning, of derogating, of robbing of dignity.

DISCRIMINATION BETWEEN MEANS AND ENDS

I have found none of my subjects to be chronically unsure about the difference between right and wrong in his actual living. Whether or not they could verbalize the matter, they rarely showed in their day-to-day living the chaos, the confusion, the inconsistency, or the conflict that are so common in the average person's ethical dealings. This may be phrased also in such terms as: these individuals are strongly ethical, they have definite moral standards, they do right and do not do wrong. Needless to say, their notions of right and wrong are often not the conventional ones.

One way of expressing the quality I am trying to describe was suggested by Dr. David Levy, who pointed out that a few centuries ago these would all have been described as men who walk in the path of God or as godly men. So far as religion is concerned, none of my subjects is orthodoxly religious, but on the other hand I know of only one who describes himself as an atheist (four of the total group studied). The few others for whom I have information hesitate to call themselves atheists. They say that they believe in a God, but describe this God more as a metaphysical concept than as a personal figure. Whether or not they could be called religious people as a group must then depend entirely on the concept or definition of religion that we choose to use. If religion is defined only in social-behavioral terms, then these are all religious people, the atheists included. But if more conservatively we use the term religion so as to include and stress the supernatural element and institutional orthodoxy (certainly the more common usage) then our answer must be quite different, for then almost none of them is religious.

Self-actualizing people most of the time behave as though, for them, means and ends are clearly distinguishable. In general, they are fixed on ends rather than on means, and means are quite definitely subordinated to these ends. This, however, is an over-simple statement. Our subjects make the situation more complex by often regarding as ends in themselves many experiences and activities that are, for other people, only means to ends. Our subjects are somewhat more likely to appreciate for its own sake, and in an absolute way, the doing itself; they can often enjoy for its own sake the getting **to** some place as well as the arriving. It is occasionally possible for them to make out of the most trivial and routine activity an intrinsically enjoyable game or dance or play. Wertheimer pointed out that most children are so creative that they can transform hackneyed routine, mechanical, and rote experiences, e.g., as in one of his experiments, transporting books from one set of shelves to another, into a structured and amusing game of a sort by doing this according to a certain system or with a certain rhythm.

. . . .

CREATIVENESS

This is a universal characteristic of all the people studied or observed. There is no exception. Each one shows in one way or another a special kind of creativeness or originality or inventiveness that has certain peculiar characteristics. These special characteristics can be understood more fully in the light of discussion later in this chapter. For one thing, it is different from the special-talent creativeness of the Mozart type. We may as well face the fact that the so-called geniuses display ability that we do not understand. All we can say of them is that they seem to be specially endowed with a drive and a capacity that may have rather little relationship to the rest of the personality and with which, from all evidence, the individuals seem to be born. Such talent we have no concern with here since it does not rest upon psychic health or basic satisfaction. The creativeness of the self-actualized man seems rather to be kin to the naïve and universal creativeness of unspoiled children. It seems to be more a fundamental characteristic of common human nature — a potentiality given to all human beings at birth. Most human beings lose this as they become enculturated, but some few individuals seem either to retain this fresh and naïve, direct way of looking at life, or if they have lost it, as most people do, they later in life recover it.

This creativeness appears in some of our subjects not in the usual forms of writing books, composing music, or producing artistic objects, but rather may be much more humble. It is as if this special type of creativeness, being an expression of healthy personality, is projected out upon the world or touches whatever activity the person is engaged in. In this sense there can be creative shoemakers or carpenters or clerks. Whatever one does can be done with a certain attitude, a certain spirit that arises out of the nature of the character of the person performing the act. One can even *see* creatively as the child does.

This quality is differentiated out here for the sake of discussion, as if it were something separate from the characteristics that precede it and follow it, but this is not actually the case. Perhaps when we speak of creativeness here we are simply describing from another point of view, namely, from the point of view of consequences, what we have described above as a greater freshness, penetration, and efficiency of perception. These people seem to see the true and the real more easily. It is because of this that they seem to other more limited men creative.

Furthermore, as we have seen, these individuals are less inhibited, less constricted, less bound, in a word, less enculturated. In more positive terms, they are more spontaneous, more natural, more human. This too would have as one of its consequences what would seem to other people to be creativeness. If we assume, as we may from our study of children, that all people were once spontaneous, and perhaps in their deepest roots still are, but that these people have in addition to their deep spontaneity a superficial but powerful set of inhibitions, then this spontaneity must be checked so as not to appear very often. If there were no choking-off forces, we might expect that every human being would show this special type of creativeness.

. . . .

Section B

INTERPERSONAL RELATIONSHIPS OF GROUP MEMBERS

In order to retain his position, a leader must satisfy some of the important needs of the members. These needs vary from those which support group aims to those which in their demands are clearly apart from the purposes of the group. Although in every discussion there are many member responses which are self-oriented, it is understood that unless the goal of the group is therapy such responses do not contribute to the progress of the discussion.

Self-oriented responses are the results of various psychological needs. They arise from feelings of insecurity and threat and they express themselves in disguised drives for power. Descriptions of these various needs and their influence on other members is dealt with in the two studies in this section: "Measurement of Self-Oriented Needs in Discussion Groups," by Nicholas T. Fouriezos, Max L. Hutt, and Harold Guetzkow, and "Self-Esteem, Group Interaction, and Group Influence on Performance," by Ezra Stotland and Nickolas B. Cottrell.

44

Measurement of Self-Oriented Needs
in Discussion Groups[1]

Nicholas T. Fouriezos, Max L. Hutt,
and Harold Guetzkow

In social psychology today much energy is being directed toward better understanding of group process. Social psychologists attempt to answer such questions as, "What are the determinants of participant satisfaction with a group product?" and "How is it that one group using one set of processes reaches a decision, while another group using different processes fails?"

Ingenious observational techniques — involving machines, human perceptions, and combinations of these — have been devised to investigate behaviors in groups.[2,3,4,5,6,7] These techniques aim to record and classify the more or less objective functionings of a group and its members. For example, records are often made of who says what and to whom. Category systems are set up to code specific behaviors considered relevant by particular investigators. In descriptions of problem-solving behavior, such categories as infor-

From Nicholas T. Fouriezos, Max L. Hutt, and Harold Guetzkow, "Measurement of Self-Oriented Needs in Discussion Groups," *Journal of Abnormal and Social Psychology*, XLV (October, 1950), 682–690. Reprinted with the permission of the publisher.

[1] Publication No. 7 of the Conference Research project at the University of Michigan, sponsored by the Office of Naval Research (Contract N6Onr-232, T. O. 7), under the general direction of Dr. D. G. Marquis, Chairman of the Psychology Department. Grateful acknowledgment is made to Sidney Cleveland, Maizie Gurin, Richard Sanders, and Harvey Schrier for aid in the clinical phases of the pilot study reported in this paper.

[2] H. H. Anderson, "The Measurement of Domination and of Socially Integrative Behavior in Teachers' Contacts with Children, *Child Development*, X (1939), 73–89.

[3] R. F. Bales, *Interaction Process Analysis* (Reading, Mass.: Addison-Wesley Publishing Company, Inc., 1950).

[4] K. D. Benne and P. Sheats, "Functional Roles of Group Members," *Journal of Social Issues*, IV (1948), 41–49.

[5] E. D. Chapple, "Measuring Human Relations: An Introduction to the Study of Individuals," *Genetic and Psychological Monographs*, XXII (1940), 3–147.

[6] K. Lewin, R. Lippitt, and R. K. White, "Patterns of Aggressive Behavior in Experimentally Created 'Social Climates,'" *Journal of Social Psychology*, X (1939), 271–299.

[7] Dorothy S. Thomas and Associates, *Some New Techniques for Studying Social Behavior* (New York: Bureau of Publications, Teachers College, Columbia University, 1929).

mation-giving, solution-proposing, and summarizing are used to classify the contributions of each participant.[8]

There is increasing recognition that the outcomes of a group's behavior are not merely determined by the intellective aspects of its process — by its semantic efficiency and its problem-solving ability. Lewin, Lippitt, and White[9] over ten years ago demonstrated the importance of "climates" on the functioning of groups. And more recently Cartwright[10] has sketched a general theory of group "emotionality."

Most group psychologists also admit the importance of motivation as a factor in determining the nature of the processes which go on within the group. Yet little work has been done to make it possible to study the operation of the motivational processes in the group situation. This paper adapts a common conceptualization of motivational factors and suggests a technique whereby one of these motivations may be measured in group discussion situations.

The behavior of individuals in a group may be regarded as generated from one or both of two sources. First, the behavior may be induced mainly by the requirements of the group situation, e.g., when a person accepts the chairmanship of a group because the rest of the group want him to; in this manner he feels he can serve the group. Second, the behavior may be generated mainly from within the individual, e.g., an individual moves to get himself elected chairman of a group because of certain ego-related tensions within himself; the position will give him desired prestige or an opportunity to dominate others. This motivation from within may be conscious or unconscious, while the desire to aid the group is secondary but not necessarily absent. The two-fold division of motivational factors loosely parallels the distinction between task- and ego-orientation made by Lewis.[11] Although the self-enhancing and self-defending motives may express themselves in concrete ways, the personal welfare motives *per se* (as desire for larger income because of economic wants and interest in shorter hours and longer vacations because of recreational needs) are not conceptually included in the self-oriented needs. In line with this conceptualization an empirical effort was made to evaluate the extent to which participant behavior in the group is motivated directly from the individual's self-oriented need system. This behavior is not necessarily directed toward a group goal or the satisfactory solution of a group's problems. Self-oriented need behavior is directed primarily to the satisfaction of the need itself, *regardless* of the effect on the attainment of the group goal.

This paper describes the exploratory study in which the original conceptualization was tested, the categories and procedures finally developed for mak-

[8] R. W. Heyns, "Functional Analysis of Group Problem-Solving Behavior," in *Conference Research Staff Papers, 1948–49.* (Microfilmed)

[9] *Op. cit.*

[10] D. Cartwright, "Emotional Dimensions of Group Life," in *Second International Symposium on Feelings and Emotions,* 1948.

[11] H. B. Lewis, "An Experimental Study of the Role of the Ego in Work," *Journal of Experimental Psychology,* XXXIV (1944), 113–126, 195–215.

ing self-oriented need ratings, and the reliability with which observers were able to estimate the presence of self-oriented needs. Then, relationships found between detected expression of the needs in conference-group situations and other measures of conference behaviors are discussed.

THE INITIAL EXPLORATORY STUDY

The self-oriented need rating scheme was first tested in the course of a pilot study conducted in the summer of 1948. In that study fifteen undergraduate students volunteered for four hours of clinical appraisal of their personal needs. The data were collected by means of Rorschachs, TAT's, and sentence completion tests, coupled with intensive interviews. This clinical work was done by four advanced graduate students under the supervision of Hutt. After the tests, the subjects participated in a series of five conferences throughout which they were observed by members of the research staff.

Each of the subjects was rated by three clinicians on nine items describing various aspects of their need structure. The three observers approached the rating problem in different ways. The first rated solely on the basis of the clinical data concerning the subjects, obtained before the series of conferences had begun. The second made ratings on the basis of this same clinical data plus continued observation of the participants in action during the conferences. The third observer rated solely on the basis of observation of behavior during the conferences, with no recourse to the clinical data.

Analysis of the ratings made by the three different observers is achieved by comparing the over-all self-oriented need scores obtained by each of the participants. This over-all score was computed simply by summing the scores assigned an individual on the nine items by an observer. Thus, three over-all need scores were obtained for each subject, one from each of the observers. The correlation between the over-all need scores assigned the fifteen individuals by the observer who rated solely on clinical data and the scores assigned by the conference observer who also had access to clinical data was .54.[12] The correlation between ratings based on clinical data alone and ratings based on observation alone was .44. However, a correlation of .82 was obtained between the ratings of the conference observer who had access to clinical data and the ratings of the observer who rated solely on the basis of conference behavior.

The correlation of .82 between the ratings of the two conference observers indicates that they interpreted the subjects' behavior in a similar fashion, that an observer working solely on the basis of watching individuals in a group perform could substantially agree with an observer who supplemented his observations with clinical data.

Out of this exploratory work, the following description of needs originated and the final rating techniques were adopted.

---

12 For an N of 15, a correlation of .64 is significant at the 1 per cent level, a correlation of .51 is significant at the 5 per cent level.

Description of Self-Oriented Needs

Five areas of need constitute the framework within which individuals are classified. The areas were selected by the experimenters from a large number used by observers in the pilot study mentioned earlier. The areas chosen were rated with less difficulty than other areas in which ratings were attempted. These areas are designated primarily to serve as a guide for the rater's appraisal of the over-all self-oriented need expression of an individual during a meeting. To date specific observation within each of the areas has been used only to aid the observers make an over-all estimate of self-oriented needs; neither individual nor groups have been classified according to specific need areas.[13]

Dependency. Dependency needs include indications of (a) need for dependence on authority, and (b) need for succorance.

The first of these, dependence on authority, is typified by the individual who is submissive in the face of authority and who continually relies upon authority, especially in difficult situations. For instance, a participant who demands rigid structuring of his group along the lines of parliamentary procedure when the occasion does not warrant such formalizing is taken as having need for dependence on authority. The dependent person continually looks to the chairman for support.

An example of expression of Dependence on Authority are continual references, such as, "Mr. Chairman, would you clear this up for me?"

By succorance is meant generalized dependency, as contrasted with dependence on authority alone. There is a desire to continually conform to the wishes of others, whether they are in authority or not. The individual who tends always to the supporting role is considered as exhibiting a need for succorance. He may or may not give reasons for supporting what others say. An example of Need for Succorance is a statement like, "In regard to what Mr. X has just said, I feel it is very good because he is usually right about these things."

Status. Status needs are exemplified by the individual who wants formal designations, the individual who makes bids to obtain a "title for title's sake," not because he wants primarily to serve the group. The individual with strong status needs works to obtain and maintain the status he desires. Within this area fall indications of aspiration in social situations. To differentiate between behaviors arising from the self-oriented need for status and behaviors that have a legitimate basis in the group's situation, the rater must take advantage of such cues as the individual's presentation of arguments, his reaction to criticism from other members, his emotional orientation while making contributions — in effect, the total situation. An example of the Need for Status is a statement like, "I was a member of a coordinating committee once and we did some wonderful work in this field."

---

[13] Some attempts have been made to use ratings in specific need areas to characterize individuals and groups. The schedule requirements of the research project limited the time that could be spent on training observers, and thus far reliable ratings by specific areas have not been obtained.

Dominance. In this category are included expressions of (a) intellectual dominance, and (b) dominance in social situations.

By expression of intellectual dominance is meant an individual's attempts to show intellectual superiority over one or more members of his group. The participant may attempt openly to assert this intellectual dominance, or he may do so more subtly by persistently trying to get his own ideas accepted. An example of Intellectual Dominance might be, "But the logic of the situation demands you adopt my conclusion."

Dominance in social situations includes attempts to control and direct in the social situation, as exemplified in "social bossiness." Situations with "authoritative" leadership tend to be of this kind. The leader here controls with little concern for the needs of the group, since he is mainly oriented to satisfy his need to dominate. The dominance situation, in extreme, is noted in conference process when one individual refuses to hear arguments against his own ideas and proceeds to force the group to follow his plan. An example of Dominance in Social Situations might be a dogmatic, overpowering assertion, "This is the way it must be done."

It is important for the rater to distinguish between dominance based on ego-needs and dominance which has more situational basis. In the former instance the dominant individual is motivated by his need to assert authority over others. In the latter case, an individual may legitimately move to bring about a different structuring of the group because the group has strayed from fruitful approaches to its goal or the leader may halt an argument because of time limitation.

Aggression. Here are included expressions of (a) aggression against authority, and (b) extrapunitiveness.

Indications of aggression against authority are found in the expressions of hostility and rebelliousness directed by the participant to his group leader or some outside authority. The individual who resents and protests against structuring in the group, no matter how minor, by the leader or other sources of authority, is considered as expressing aggression against authority. Comments about the inhibiting and "meddlesome" nature of authority may be verbalized, e.g., "Why are they trying to bother us with these silly rules anyway?" Another example of Aggression against Authority is, "We can't do a thing with that kind of a boss."

Extrapunitiveness refers to generalized aggression. Here the aggression is not directed solely toward authority but against the external world or the environment. The expressions of extrapunitiveness are detected in the interpersonal relationships of the individual. This individual's contributions may be entirely of the opposing kind. The participant who characteristically reacts negatively in his affective relationships, the individual who tends to "tear down" the contributions of others is taken as expressing the Need for Extrapunitiveness, e.g., "I disagree, I think that all you guys are on the wrong track!!" — and he says this with great feeling.

Catharsis. In this category fall expressions of need for personal unburdening. Indications of need for catharsis are obtained when there is continual self-reference in the contributions of the participant. This behavior is found in the individual who expresses his conflicts by acting them out. In discussion situations when an illustration of a certain type of activity is in order, the individual will exhibit need for catharsis by giving overly elaborate descriptions. This individual does not want to dominate; he just wants to talk. He usually becomes quite emotionally involved in what he is saying. A participant who continually refers to personal experiences when the situation does not require such contributions is probably indicating Need for Catharsis, e.g., "Once I was in a situation where I was forced to . . . ."

UTILIZATION OF CUES

The emphasis of this classification of needs is not on the categories *per se*, but on the categories as a stable background or framework within which the observer can estimate the extent of operation of an individual's self-oriented need system in a particular group situation. The above materials were used as a "cue manual" in training observers. The trainer emphasized that reliable ratings of self-oriented needs depends to a great extent on the development of the observer's ability to utilize the latent meaning of the many cues available in group situations. The observer makes his ratings in relation to the immediate situation with which he is concerned. He attempts to understand the frame of reference of the individual making a statement. The validity of his ratings will depend upon his ability to discriminate between what appears to be a "rational" reaction calculated primarily to aid the group and what appears to be predominantly a self-oriented need expression, despite its superficial group-centered character. The observer evaluates the whole field in which the participant's behavior occurs before the ratings can be made.

The observer's attention is directed not only to the content of the participant's contribution but also to the effect behind the contribution — the "feeling tone" that the contribution determines. For example, a participant says "you are pretty good, aren't you?" This may appear to be a statement of praise as far as the content is concerned, but it may be uttered in such a way that expresses much aggression. Ruesch and Prestwood[14] have empirically demonstrated the importance of such inflectional and timing nuances in their study on the communication of anxiety.

Full recognition must be made of the fact that the self-oriented need ratings merely estimate the extent of need expression in the particular situation under study. The technique in no way fathoms the extent to which the participants possess unexpressed needs. They probably do not represent the need level of an individual in other group situations, under quite different circumstances.

THE RATING SCALE

The rating scale used by the observers in most of the studies to be reported below was an eleven-point scale ranging from 0 (no expression of self-oriented need) to 10 (all behavior of the self-oriented type). The scale breaks down as indicated . . . [in Fig. 1 on page 302.]

The self-oriented-need observer devotes almost all his observational time to the tallying of particular instances of the expression of the five different types of needs. Then, at the conclusion of the conference, he makes a sub-

---

14 J. Ruesch and A. R. Prestwood, "Anxiety, Its Initiation, Communication, and Interpersonal Management," *Archives of Neurological Psychology* (Chicago), LXII (1949), 527–550.

Figure 1

—|— 0 —— No expression of self-oriented need.

—|— 1 ——

—|— 2 —— Some slight indication of self-oriented need behavior.

—|— 3 ——

—|— 4 —— Some self-oriented need behavior indicated but not predominant.

—|— 5 ——

—|— 6 —— Considerable self-oriented need behavior.

—|— 7 ——

—|— 8 —— Almost all behavior of self-oriented type; a great deal of expression.

—|— 9 ——

—|—10 —— All behavior of the self-oriented type.

jective, integrating appraisal of his tallies in the form of a single, over-all rating on the scale just presented. When the ratings of an observer of the over-all self-oriented needs of 671 persons from seventy-two groups[15] are plotted in a frequency distribution, the curve does not differ significantly from a normal distribution as tested by a chi-square.

Computation of Group Scores on Self-Oriented Need

Thus far self-oriented need ratings have been discussed only at the individual level. That is to say, each individual in a group is given his own ratings by the observer. For some analyses, a group's score on self-oriented needs may be obtained by averaging the scores assigned all the individuals in the group. However, direct ratings of the amount of self-oriented needs displayed by a group may also be obtained. Observers watching live groups may rate the extent to which each group's process is characterized by the expression of self-oriented needs. The scale in this case also ranges from 0 to 10; the 0 point represents an entirely objective meeting and the 10 a discussion entirely permeated by self-oriented need expression.

The group and average individual type of scores conceptually differ from each other in one basic respect. Group scores theoretically represent the extent to which each time-unit of the group's interactional process is permeated by the self-oriented needs. Conceptually, then, the group need scores represent the sum of the need intensities for each time-unit of the meeting.

[15] Extensive use of the self-oriented-need ratings was made in the Field Study of seventy-two actual decision-making conferences in government and industrial organizations. (Conference Research 1949). Many of the reliability and validity figures to be presented in this paper are taken from this study. These groups varied in size from five to seventeen, with an average of about ten persons in each.

In practice, of course, no unit-by-unit account was made of the needs. The average individual scores indicate, on the other hand, the extent to which the "average" individual in the group expresses his self-oriented needs. The essential difference between the two scores is that the group score "averages" over time, weighting each unit of process equally; the average individual score "averages" over individuals, weighting each person within the group equally.

In the Conference Research field study of seventy-two decision-making conferences, three observers simultaneously watched the meetings and then gave each discussion a "group-score," indicating the extent to which its process was permeated by self-oriented needs. The mean of these three ratings was used as the final "group-score." One special observer also made individual scores, which were averaged into the "average-individual" score. The correlation between the direct rating of the group's self-oriented needs level and the group rating obtained by averaging the scores assigned to all the individuals in the group was .67, when the two types of scores were compared over the seventy-two groups. The two techniques, therefore, give fairly similar results. A higher correlation could not very well be expected. The score calculated from the individual's score corresponds to the average self-oriented need level of the members of the group and not necessarily the extent to which the group's *process* time was characterized by self-oriented needs.

RELIABILITY STUDIES

Four different appraisals of the reliability of self-oriented-need ratings have been made thus far. These are reported below.

1. Two observers sat in on an hour's conference of nineteen graduate students discussing university affairs. On the basis of their observations, the observers rated the over-all, self-oriented-need expression of each of them. The correlation between their ratings was .67.

2. Thirty persons, observed in five decision-making groups in government and industry, were appraised by the two observers. A Pearson product-moment correlation of .73 between their over-all ratings for each individual was obtained.

3. Mishler used self-oriented-need observers as one of the observational techniques in an unpublished study ("Ascendant and Submissive Members and Leaders: Their Interaction in Group Discussion") on problem-solving groups. He found reliability rho-correlations of .96 and .86, obtained when two observers' ratings of thirty-two individuals studied in two sets of two groups (with eight participants in each group) are correlated. His observers rated on a scale using only seven points.

4. A reliability estimate of the "group score" is afforded by comparing the scores assigned a group by each of the three observers making the ratings. On a sample of thirty of the seventy-two groups studied, the average correlation among the three observers was .81. This figure represents the reliability with which three observers working at the same time rated the extent to which the group's process was characterized by expression of self-oriented needs.

On the basis of the correlations indicated above, the working reliability of the self-oriented need ratings has been established.

The Relationship of Self-Oriented Need Expression
to Other Group Measures

In the field study mentioned above, it was possible to check the usefulness of the self-oriented-needs technique in predicting the outcome of decision-making conferences, as well as to gain understanding of the nature of the needs rating by comparing it with other measures of group process.

There are various ways of measuring the result of a small face-to-face meeting of executives "in conference." A most cogent case can be made for the use of appraisals by the participants who worked together in the meeting — appraisals of the extent to which they felt satisfied with the meeting as a whole, with the decisions which were reached, and with the procedures used to reach them, and with the chairman's handling of the meeting. Ratings on each of these outcomes can be obtained from the participants and then averaged to give group scores on each facet of outcome. These four types of ratings can then be compared with the average-individual and group self-oriented need scores described above. Correlations computed between each of the two observer-estimates of need and each of the four measures of participant satisfactions indicate in every case a statistically significant (all but one at the 1 per cent level) negative relationship between the variables. In other words, those groups with the highest scores on self-oriented needs rated themselves lowest on the satisfaction measures; groups which exhibited more self-oriented-need behavior were least satisfied with the meeting in general, with the decisions reached, with the way in which the group reached its decision, and with the chairmanship of their meeting. The correlations range from $-.37$ to $-.49$[16] when the satisfaction measures are correlated with the mean of the three observers' ratings of self-oriented needs, and from $-.28$ to $-.38$ when the satisfaction measures are correlated with the average of the single observer's rating of the individuals comprising the groups.

Other measures of outcome may be obtained from indices of productivity. For example, in the field study the groups with high need ratings tended to complete fewer of the items considered at their meetings than the low groups did in their meetings ($r = -.32$ for mean of 3 observers; $r = -.15$ for special observer's average of individuals in the group). Yet their meetings tended to last longer ($r = +.32$ and $+.39$). Thus, on the basis of both the participant-satisfaction measures as well as on the objective measures of productivity, the self-oriented need rating technique provided a predictor of conference outcome.

By comparing the need estimates with other measures of group process, it is possible to delineate to some extent the meaning of the self-oriented need ratings. In the earlier part of this paper, it was indicated that moves to satisfy the self-oriented needs may be made regardless of their effect upon group process. Thus, it is not surprising to note that there is a correlation of $+.73$ between the three observers' mean need estimate and the amount of group conflict. Groups which are high in expressed self-oriented need tend to perceive themselves as less unified than do the low need groups ($r = -.55$).

[16] All correlations reported hereafter are significant with an N of 72 if $r = .30$ at the 1 per cent level, or $r = .23$ at the 5 per cent level.

In describing the nature of self-oriented needs, an attempt was made to distinguish between the self-enhancing and defending needs and those motives arising out of concern for personal welfare, as threats to personal remuneration, vacation time, etc. In light of this, it is interesting to note the correlation of +.46 between the need estimates and the extent to which the groups regarded themselves as having a stake in the way the agenda problems were settled. Yet the correlation between the way in which the participants rated the importance of the agenda and the observers' mean need estimate for the groups was +.07. This would indicate that the self-oriented needs estimates reflect personal involvement, arising from the agenda problems, but are relatively uncontaminated by situationally induced motivations which make particular agenda regarded as important to the industrial or governmental organization to which the participants belong.

These correlations are merely suggestive that there are interrelations between the self-oriented needs and the way in which the group functions. After further analysis is made of the field data, it may be possible to hypothesize more exactly how the self-oriented need expressions are mediated in their effects upon the group's satisfactions with and productivity in its discussion.

SUMMARY AND DISCUSSION

The materials presented in this paper demonstrate that the expression of self-oriented needs can be rated in the discussion-group situation without clinical background information about the need-structure of the participants. Examination of data collected on seventy-two decision-making conference groups indicates that the self-oriented needs of the participants are negatively correlated with their satisfaction with its outcomes and are related to various processes which occur during the meeting itself, such as group conflict. Thus, a rating technique has been developed to study an aspect of the motivational factor in group psychology, an area somewhat neglected because of its technical inaccessibility.

It is valuable to contrast the system of categorization proposed by Bales[17] and that suggested in this paper. From one point of view there is similarity between some of Bales' interaction categories, especially those indicating group "solidarity" (Nos. 1, 2, 3, 4, 5, 6) and "antagonism" (Nos. 42, 43, 44, 45, 46, 47, 48, 49). Yet, closer analysis of his other, more neutral categories indicates that many of them code behavior which might or might not be ladened with self-oriented need expression. For instance, even behavior as neutral as that coded in category No. 22 ("Reports about situation, gives information, repeats, summarizes") might be said to indicate strong self-oriented need. Bales' system is primarily directed at a description of group process in terms of a very explicitly stated sociological framework; it gives full recognition to the importance of certain emotionally toned behaviors. The self-oriented-need rating technique in Conference Research looks at *all* behavior acts within the interaction system to determine whether they have latent characteristics, expressing self-oriented need, in addition to their manifest meanings which are directed toward the substantive aspects of the agenda and the

[17] *Op. cit.*

procedures involved in operating the group. Bales' categorizations attempt to encompass all aspects of the group's functioning; the Conference Research schema merely attempts to isolate one aspect of the motivational processes underlying group functioning.

Worthy of future intensive study is the relation between particular self-oriented needs — like status and dominance — and group processes and outcome. To accomplish this the observation techniques would have to be refined to the point where ratings within each of the areas of need could reliably differentiate individuals and groups.

The Conference Research group has been working also on the relationship between the satisfaction of the self-oriented needs and group functioning. Thus far observational ratings of self-oriented need *satisfaction* has not been adequately reliable. There is only suggestive evidence that groups with most need *satisfaction* are most satisfied with their meetings in general and with their decisions than are groups who obtain less *satisfaction* of self-oriented needs during the discussion process.

Implied in our results is the possibility of training conference leaders to use on-the-spot appraisals of self-oriented needs as a guide in their conduct of the meeting. Training in the diagnosis of such behavior might be useful in handling persons who interfere with the functioning of the group. Exploration would be needed of the methods whereby leaders might redirect the disturbing contributions of self-oriented-need-driven individuals into channels of more direct benefit to the group.

45

Self-Esteem, Group Interaction, and Group Influence on Performance[1]

Ezra Stotland and Nickolas B. Cottrell

The present study was concerned with the conditions under which the performance on a task by one group member affects the expected and actual

From Ezra Stotland and Nickolas B. Cottrell, "Self-Esteem, Group Interaction, and Group Influence on Performance," *Journal of Personality*, XXIX (September, 1961), 273–284. Reprinted with the permission of the publisher.

[1] The research was conducted under a grant from the National Institute of Mental Health (M 2423).

performances of other group members. The first condition studied was the level of self-esteem of the members. Previous research[2, 3, 4] has shown that persons low in self-esteem are more subject to social influence than persons high in self-esteem. The underlying reason for the differential susceptibility may be that lows are less certain of their beliefs, including their beliefs about themselves. Under such conditions of uncertainty, as Festinger[5] has pointed out, the individual is highly likely to evaluate himself on the basis of his perception of others. It was therefore hypothesized that group members low in self-esteem would expect to, and actually would, perform on a task at the same level as another group member, while those high in self-esteem would not be so influenced.

The second condition studied which might influence the degree to which one group member will make himself like another in performance is the degree of interaction between them. It was hypothesized that the tendency of a group member to expect and actually to perform at the same level as another member would be more pronounced if the two persons had previously interacted than if they had not done so. In a general fashion the hypothesis can be regarded as an extension of Heider's[6] theory of cognitive balance. He maintained that individuals strive to attain balance between different sentiments involved in a social relationship. In the present case it was reasoned that the individual would be motivated to increase the similarity between himself and someone else, especially if he was involved in an interaction with him.

METHODS

Subjects. The Ss were 147 students, men and women, from a number of introductory and child psychology courses at the University of Washington. They were mostly freshmen and sophomores. These Ss participated in the study as part of a series of four sessions of research for which they were paid. The selection of the 147 was based solely on the possibility of scheduling them in groups of six for one-hour experimental sessions. In assigning Ss to groups, an effort was made to assign Ss from different classes, living groups, discussion sections, majors, etc., to minimize the possibility of previous acquaintance among the Ss. Each group consisted of like-sexed persons. The Ss were notified by mail as to the time and place of the experiment.

The sample size (147) is not evenly divisible by six, the number of Ss who served in a single experimental session, for three reasons: First, Ss

[2] I. L. Janis, "Personality Correlates of Susceptibility to Persuasion," *Journal of Personality*, XXII (1954), 504–518.

[3] C. I. Hovland and I. L. Janis (eds.), *Personality and Persuasibility* (New Haven, Conn.: Yale University Press, 1959).

[4] E. Stotland, S. Thorley, E. J. Thomas, A. R. Cohen, and A. Zander, "The Effects of Group Expectations and Self-Esteem Upon Self-Evaluation," *Journal of Abnormal and Social Psychology*, LIV (1957), 55–63.

[5] L. Festinger, "A Theory of Social Comparison Processes," *Human Relations*, VII (1954), 117–140.

[6] F. Heider, *The Psychology of Interpersonal Relations* (New York: John Wiley & Sons, Inc., 1958).

who served as the model were dropped from the analysis. Second, when all of the scheduled Ss did not appear, "stooges" were introduced to fill out the group. The data gathered from the stooges were not considered in the analysis. Third, those Ss who later indicated that they had had previous training in the Hindi language (this language was used in the behavioral dependent variable which will be described below) were discarded from the sample.

Self-Esteem Measure. During a previous session of the four in which Ss participated, they took a modification of the Q sort to measure self-esteem. The Q sort used, based on the work of Weinberger[7] consisted of giving a list of twenty-six desirable trait adjectives to the Ss for them to place into five categories by an appropriate check mark. The categories were ordered in terms of the importance of standing high in these traits. The Ss could place only five adjectives in a category, except for six in the middle category. Then, on another page, Ss repeated their procedure, this time categorizing the adjectives in terms of how high they actually were on these traits. The Ss' score was the total across adjectives of the squared discrepancies between the two categorizations of the same adjective; the higher the discrepancy, the lower the self-esteem score.

Experimental procedure. The Ss arrived in the experimental room in groups of six. They were asked to sit around a small table which had a Lazy Susan in the center with six compartments. Each S could see only the faces of the other Ss, since there were wooden separators between them. Thus, before each S was a compartment formed by the two separators on each side of him and by the Lazy Susan in front of him. In each compartment were a pack of six slips of paper with ten syllables on each one, a pack of six slips with five lines on each numbered from one to five, a sheet with two columns of fifteen letters in alphabetical order, a pencil, and a pad of scratch paper.

The Ss were told that they were to list names from different categories, each person collecting names from a different one. Each person found the name of his category at the head of the sheet with the two columns of letters and also was given a list of all the categories (animals, automobiles, cities of the United States, foreign countries, fruits and vegetables, and states of the United States). In addition, each of the compartments in the Lazy Susan was labeled with one category.

The Ss were told that they were to obtain these names by forming pairs of syllables within each of the sets of ten they found on the slips before them. Thus each S produced five names from each set. He listed these names first on one of the sheets with five lines numbered 1 to 5 (although many Ss did not obey this instruction). The S was to write any name from his own area on the sheet with the columns of letters, after the initial letter of the name he had formed. The objective was to find one name for each of the letters on his sheet. If the S formed a name from

<hr>

[7] B. Weinberger, "Achievement Motivation and the Self-Concept" (Unpublished honors thesis, University of Michigan, 1951).

a category other than his own, he would write it on a slip of scratch paper, place it in the appropriate compartment in the Lazy Susan, and then turn the Susan until the right S received it. Each S had six such sets of ten syllables.

Thus any S could complete his collection of thirty names from names he had formed himself, as well as from names he received from others. In the high-interaction condition, twenty-five of the thirty names each S formed from the syllables were from a category other than his own. He would have to send five names to each of the five other Ss. In the low-interaction condition, twenty-five of the thirty names were from each S's own category. He would send the other five to the other five Ss, one to each, receiving one from each in return. The groups were assigned alternately to one or the other condition. The group worked on this word task for twenty minutes. Of the 147 Ss, seventy-one collected all the words in their category in this length of time and 113 collected twenty-eight or more.

When the word task was completed E then told the group that there was a new task which he would like the group to try out, but that first he would like one person to work on it, to demonstrate it to the others. E then told them that the person to do the demonstrating was to be selected entirely by chance. He continued, saying the schedule called for a person who happened to have the category x to be the demonstrator. (The category varied randomly.) That person was then given the task which consisted of mentally counting the number of times that a designated syllable was repeated in a passage in Hindi.[8] The demonstrator listened to the recorded passage over a set of earphones. At the end of the passage, he went behind a screen and wrote down the mental tally he had been keeping. Thus, the other Ss neither heard the passage nor were they acquainted with the model's actual count. The demonstrating S was given two such syllables and passages. The model then returned to his seat and the E evaluated his performance. In half the cases the model was told: "You must have been paying pretty close attention because your counts were fairly close, one way or the other, to the actual number. Once your count was 25 per cent above the actual number and once it was 25 per cent below the actual number." In the other half of the cases he was given a poor evaluation, the E saying: "You must not have been paying very close attention because your counts were either way too high or way too low. Once your count was 75 per cent above the actual number, and once your count was 75 per cent below the actual number." The characteristic of paying attention or not paying attention and hence doing well or poorly served as the attribute of possible assimilation by the other Ss.

The Ss then responded to the following item on a seven-point rating scale ranging from "very well" to "very poorly." "How well do you think you will do on this task?" In addition, the Ss predicted their percentage of error by choosing one of the following percentages: 75 per cent above the correct number, 50 per cent above, 25 per cent above, right on the correct number, 25 per cent below, 50 per cent below, 75 per cent below.

---

[8] The authors wish to express their appreciation to Dr. Prem Shanker for his assistance with the Hindi material.

The Ss were then all given their own sets of earphones, and listened to the two passages, recording their counts of the appropriate syllables on individual sheets immediately after each passage. The absolute size of the discrepancy of these counts from the actual number of syllables was later calculated and is referred to below as the number of errors. The Ss then rated their performance, using the same rating scale as mentioned first in this paragraph. They then estimated the number of errors, choosing from among the same percentages as in the second item mentioned.

The syllable-counting task was chosen for three reasons. First, pretests had shown that social pressures could influence performance. Second, such a task was likely to be unfamiliar to most Ss. Third, pretests had also shown that the demonstrating S and the other Ss would find it extremely difficult to determine themselves how well they had performed and consequently difficult to question E's evaluation.

At a subsequent meeting of the Ss they were given a complete description of the methods and hypotheses and all their questions were answered.

Results

To test the hypothesis that the S's level of self-esteem influenced their degree of similarity to the model on the listening task, the sample was bifurcated at the median of self-esteem, and the means on prediction of performance, prediction of percentage of error, actual number of errors, evaluation of performance, and postdiction of percentage of errors were calculated and are shown in Table 1.

It is apparent there that the evaluation of the model had a potent effect on the prediction of performance, the ratings of performance, and the actual level of performance of persons with low self-esteem. When the model received a good evaluation, these Ss predicted performance, performed, and rated their performances at a higher level than when the model received a poor evaluation. The results are quite different for the Ss with high self-esteem. Like the Ss with low self-esteem, these Ss in the good-model condition predict better performance than do those in the poor-model condition (Table 1). However, the evaluation of the model has no influence on their actual performance; nor does the evaluation of the model influence their ratings of their performance. In short, then, the data confirm the first hypothesis that for persons of low self-esteem the evaluation of the model influenced both performance level and cognition about performance, while only predictions of performance were affected among Ss with high self-esteem.

This pattern of results suggests that there may be greater correlation between predictions and performances for Ss low in self-esteem than for those high in self-esteem. The relevant correlations are presented in Table 2. There it appears that, as expected, the Ss with low self-esteem tended to perform more consistently with their prediction about their performance than did the Ss with high self-esteem. This is manifest in the significantly greater correlations between prediction of performance and actual per-

Table 1

MEAN RATINGS AND PERFORMANCE FOR Ss HIGH AND LOW IN SELF-ESTEEM
FOR THE GOOD- AND POOR-MODEL CONDITIONS

	Ss low in self-esteem		Ss high in self-esteem	
	Good model A	Poor model B	Good model C	Poor model D
1. Prediction of level of performance[a]	3.44	3.89	3.46	3.81
2. Prediction of percentage of error	26.4%	33.6%	25.0%	34.0%
3. Number of errors	6.53	9.60	7.40	7.97
4. Evaluation of performance[a]	3.40	4.06	3.75	3.56
5. Postdiction of percentage of errors	25.0%	31.6%	27.8%	30.7%
N	36	35	37	36

[a] The lower the figure, the better the evaluation.
Note—Cells significantly different from each other:
Row 1: A vs. B ($t=2.630$, $p<.02$); C vs. D ($t=1.826$, $p<.10$);
Row 2: A vs. B ($t=2.517$, $p<.05$); C vs. D ($t=3.438$, $p<.01$);
Row 3: A vs. B ($t=2.001$, $p<.06$);
Row 4: A vs. B ($t=2.757$, $p<.01$);
Row 5: A vs. B ($t=2.208$, $p<.05$).

Table 2

CORRELATIONS BETWEEN PREDICTIONS OF PERFORMANCE AND
QUALITY OF PERFORMANCE

	Ss low in self-esteem		Ss high in self-esteem	
	Model good A	Model poor B	Model good C	Model poor D
1. Correlation with prediction of performance	.83*	.19	.05	−.26
2. Correlation with prediction of percentage of error	.36*	−.03	.20	−.17
N	36	35	38	36

* $p<.05$.
Note—Positive correlation means that good predictions are associated with good performance. Cells significantly different from each other:
Row 1: A vs. B ($p<.01$); A vs. C ($p<.01$); B vs. D ($p<.07$).
Row 2: A vs. B ($p<.05$).

formance for the lows in both the good- and poor-model conditions. The direction of difference between the correlations of performance with prediction of percentage of error is consistent with this trend, although these differences are not significant.

Another interesting trend that is suggested by the pattern of correlation is that, for both high- and low-self-esteem persons, there is more positive correlation between both prediction of performance and actual performance in the good-model than in the poor-model conditions. In fact, three of the four correlations in the poor-model condition are negative, while all four correlations in the good-model condition are positive. The joint functioning of the two trends evident in Table 2 — the difference between high and low self-esteem and good and poor models — is clearly evident in the fact the two correlations significantly different from zero occur in the low-self-esteem, good-model conditions.[9]

The second hypothesis was that in the high-interaction condition, the Ss who perceived the demonstrating S to do well on syllable counting would expect to do better themselves than Ss who perceived the demonstrating S to do poorly. No such difference was predicted in the low interaction condition. It will be recalled that the Ss had two opportunities to indicate their expectations of their own performance, rating first their expected level of performance, and, second, estimating their percentage of error. The means on these two scores for each experimental condition are presented in Tables 3 and 4. It can be seen there that for both of these scores, the Ss in the high-interaction conditions expected to do better when the demonstrating S had done better than when he had done poorly. For ratings, the difference was

[9] No significant correlations nor correlations significantly different from each other were found between performance and post-performance evaluations for any of the subgroups.

Table 3

MEAN PREDICTIONS OF LEVELS OF PERFORMANCE ON
SYLLABLE COUNTING FOR Ss IN EACH EXPERIMENTAL CONDITION
(Ns IN PARENTHESES)

		Interaction high	Interaction low	Total
Model Performance	good	A 3.51 (37)	B 3.36 (39)	E 3.43
	poor	C 3.84 (38)	D 3.85 (33)	F 3.84
Total		G 3.68	H 3.58	

Note—The lower the figure, the better the performance predicted. Significantly different by two-tail t tests: A vs. C ($t=1.946$; $p<.07$) B vs. D ($t=2.737$, $p<.01$); E vs. F ($t=3.462$, $p<.01$).

Table 4

MEAN PREDICTIONS OF PERCENTAGE OF ERROR ON
SYLLABLE COUNTING FOR SS IN EACH EXPERIMENTAL CONDITION
(NS IN PARENTHESES)

		Interaction high	Interaction low	Total
Model Performance	good	A 27.0% (37)	B 24.3% (39)	E 25.7%
	poor	C 31.5% (38)	D 36.3% (33)	F 33.8%
Total..............		G 29.3%	H 29.4%	

Note—Significantly different by two-tail t tests: A vs. C ($t=2.118$, $p<.05$); B vs. D ($t=3.876$, $p<.01$); E vs. F ($t=4.326$, $p<.01$).

significant at the .07 level, while it was at the .05 level for estimates of percentage of error. The results also show, however, that in the low-interaction condition the Ss expected their own performance to be similar to the demonstrating S's. This effect in the low-interaction conditions can be observed in Tables 1 and 2 for both the ratings and the estimates of percentage of error, both differences being significant at the .01 level. Thus, the second hypothesis was not supported.

The second hypothesis also led to the prediction that the S's actual performances on the syllable counting task would resemble that of the demonstrating S in the high interaction condition. In Table 5 are presented the

Table 5

MEAN NUMBER OF ERRORS ON SYLLABLE-COUNTING TASKS FOR
SS IN EACH EXPERIMENTAL CONDITION
(NS IN PARENTHESES)

		Interaction high	Interaction low	Total
Model Performance	good	A 7.35 (37)	B 6.33 (39)	E 6.83
	poor	C 8.24 (38)	D 9.39 (33)	F 8.78
Total..............		G 7.80	H 7.73	

Note—Significantly different by two-tail t tests: B vs. D ($t=2.03$, $p<.05$); E vs. F ($t=1.938$, $p<.07$).

error scores for Ss in the various conditions. It can be seen there that no significant difference obtained among Ss in the high-interaction conditions between those observing good and poor performances by the demonstrating S. Moreover, the data in Table 5 show that in the low-interaction condition, the Ss who perceived a good performance by the demonstrator actually performed significantly better than those who perceived a poor performance ($p<.05$). The hypothesis had led to the prediction that no such difference would obtain in the low-interaction condition. Thus, with regard to actual performance, the hypothesis was reversed by the data, those interacting less with the demonstrator performing more like him.

The original thinking about the present study led to the predictions that, when the Ss rated their performance on a scale after having counted syllables, those in the high-interaction conditions would evaluate themselves in line with the demonstrator's performance. In Tables 6 and 7 are presented the mean scores, for each experimental group of evaluation ratings of own performance and of estimates of percentage of error. It can be seen that for ratings of performance the prediction is confirmed since those Ss in the high-interaction condition with a good demonstrator rated themselves better than those with a poor demonstrator. As predicted, in the low-interaction condition, no similar difference occurs. With regard to the mean estimates of error of performance, Ss in both the high- and low-interaction conditions evaluate the percentage of errors consistently with the demonstrator's performance. It must therefore be concluded that no clear evidence can be obtained in support of the prediction that only in the high-interaction condition would Ss evaluate their own performance consistently with the demonstration.

No statistical interaction was found between self-esteem and the interaction conditions.

Table 6

MEAN EVALUATIONS OF PERFORMANCE OF SYLLABLE-COUNTING TASK
FOR Ss IN EACH EXPERIMENTAL CONDITION
(Ns IN PARENTHESES)

		Interaction high	Interaction low	Total
Model Performance	good	A 3.44 (36)	B 3.66 (38)	E 3.55
	poor	C 3.92 (37)	D 3.67 (33)	F 3.80
Total...............		G 3.69	H 3.66	

Note—The lower the figure, the better the evaluation. Significantly different by two-tail t test: A vs. C ($t=2.043$, $p<.05$).

Table 7

Mean Postdiction of Percentage of Error on Syllable-Counting
Tasks for Ss in Each Experimental Condition
(Ns in parentheses)

		Interaction high	Interaction low	Total
Model Performance	good	A 27.1% (36)	B 24.2% (38)	E 25.7%
	poor	C 32.4% (36)	D 36.3% (33)	F 34.0%
Total..............		G 29.8%	H 29.9%	

Note—Significantly different by two-tail t test: A vs. C ($t=2.172$, $p<.05$); B vs. D ($t=3.898$, $p<.01$); E vs. F ($t=4.497$, $p<.01$).

Discussion

In this study, it was found that Ss low in self-esteem tended to conform more consistently to the demonstrator's level of performance than did those with high self-esteem. This differential conformity was most evident in the actual levels of performance on the task. The lows were more accurate in their syllable counts when the demonstrator was said to be more accurate. No such difference occurred for the highs. It was also found that the lows then tended to behave more consistently with their predictions about their own performances as was partially indicated by the relative size of the correlations between predictions and performance.

This pattern of results can be extrapolated to give a considerably idealized, but suggestive, picture of the behavior of persons with low self-esteem. They appear to be quite susceptible to social forces, probably because of the low evaluation they place on their own actions, activities, etc. When presented with a new task such as syllable counting, these Ss are very unsure of any estimates they may make of their ability to perform the task. Therefore, any information they may receive with regard to an expected level of performance will have a great influence. In the present study such influential information emanates from the E's evaluation of the demonstrator's performance. The expectation that they have of their own performance then determines their own performance. It may be that their motivation to find some certainty in a situation in which they are unsure of themselves leads them to behave consistently with their expectations, even when this consistency leads to a decrement of performance. Even after they have performed they evaluate themselves in line with these expectations, which have been originally derived from the behavior of another person. This intrepretation is supported by the findings reported in Hovland and Janis[10] that persons with low self-esteem are more persuasible than those with high.

On the other hand, the high-self-esteem persons may use the information about the demonstrator's performance as a basis of predicting their own, but also may take their own ideas into consideration, since they evaluate these ideas highly. Therefore, their predictions of their own performance were not as consistent with the demonstrator's performance as were those of the Ss of low self-esteem. Moreover, the high-self-esteem Ss are not guided in their own performance by their stated expectations, since they are highly likely to be influenced by their own motivations, goals, expectations, etc., which they value more highly than the lows. By the time of the completion of the actual performance, whatever social influence did affect them was dissipated.

Another trend that was suggested by the data is that, for persons of high and low self-esteem, actual performance is more highly related to prediction of performance when the demonstrator was good than when he was poor. It may be that, when an individual's prediction of his behavior is related to a poor model, he defensively reacts by rejecting the significance of his prediction. When the demonstrator is good, there is less need to reject his influence defensively.

The other hypothesis of this study that higher interaction leads to greater conformity was not supported. Ss in both high- and low-interaction groups conformed to the evaluation of the model. A possible reason for the failure to confirm the hypothesis is that the interaction may have been too diffuse, i.e., the Ss interacted with all of the other group members and did not interact to a sufficiently high degree with the model. This equality of interaction could also have led the S to judge his "closeness" to the model relative to his degree of interaction with all the Ss, so that he did not judge himself to be closer to the model than to anyone else. Thus in both high- and low-interaction conditions, the judgment of the closeness might have been the same.

SUMMARY

College student Ss were given a Q-sort measure of self-esteem. At a later session, they were seated six at a time around a table in the center of which was a Lazy Susan with six compartments. The Ss were instructed to collect lists of words of various categories, each S collecting a different category. Each S formed words by pairing syllables within lists of ten syllables. Some of the words formed belonged in the S's own category, some in the category of another person. These latter were passed by means of the Lazy Susan to the appropriate member. The Ss kept the words from their own categories. The syllables were arranged so that in half the groups there was a great deal of interchange of words and in the other half, little interchange. After the lists of words had been completed, one of the Ss was given a task of mentally counting the number of times that a designated syllable in Hindi was repeated in a spoken passage of Hindi. In half of the cases, this S was told he had

[10] *Op. cit.*

done well, in the other half, that he had done poorly. The other Ss were then given the same task, predicted their performance levels, and rated their performances after working on the task.

It was found that the Ss expected to do better on the syllable-counting task actually performed better on it, and evaluated their performances higher when the first S performing on the task was perceived to do well than when he was perceived to do poorly. This difference obtained more for Ss of low self-esteem than for those of high. The difference did not occur significantly more under conditions of high interchange of words than under low.

Section C

PERFORMANCE OF GROUP MEMBERS

No two members of a group perform alike. Each fulfills his needs in relation to the demands of the situation, and, since different situations make different demands, each member develops a certain degree of flexibility.

His performance from one discussion to the next varies within a limited range in accordance with his personality structure. His actions within different groups and discussions, however, have sufficient likeness that he can be viewed as functioning in a particular fashion or role. The various roles of members are discussed by Kenneth D. Benne and Paul Sheats in "Functional Roles of Group Members."

A member's response in a discussion is in part influenced by his perception of the leader. On the basis of his perception, the member involves himself to the degree that he understands and accepts the leader's functioning. Also, the member is interested in using the boundaries of the situation as a guide to action.

A good leader is necessary, but the outcomes of the discussion are the result of the interaction among members and leader. If the members do not perform at a reasonable level of efficiency, the discussion is unsuccessful. L. Thomas Hopkins, in the selection, "What Does Each Member Contribute?" tells what group members may do to ensure a high quality of thinking.

46

Functional Roles of Group Members

Kenneth D. Benne and Paul Sheats

. . . .The member-roles identified in this analysis are classified into three broad groupings.

(1) *Group Task Roles.* Participant roles here are related to the task which the group is deciding to undertake or has undertaken. Their purpose is to facilitate and coordinate group effort in the selection and definition of a common problem and in the solution of that problem.

(2) *Group Building and Maintenance Roles.* The roles in this category are oriented toward the functioning of the group as a group. They are designed to alter or maintain the group way of working, to strengthen, regulate, and perpetuate the group as a group.

(3) *Individual Roles.* This category does not classify member-roles as such, since the "participations" denoted here are directed toward the satisfaction of the "participant's" individual needs. Their purpose is some individual goal which is not relevant either to the group task or to the functioning of the group as a group. Such participations are, of course, highly relevant to the problem of group training, insofar as such training is directed toward improving group maturity or group task efficiency.

GROUP TASK ROLES

The following analysis assumes that the task of the discussion group is to select, define, and solve common problems. The roles are identified in relation to functions of facilitation and coordination of group problem-solving activities. Each member may, of course, enact more than one role in any given unit of participation and a wide range of roles in successive participations. Any or all of these roles may be played at times by the group "leader" as well as by various members.

a. The *initiator-contributor* suggests or proposes to the group new ideas or a changed way of regarding the group problem or goal. The novelty proposed may take the form of suggestions of a new group goal or a new definition of the problem. It may take the form of a suggested solution or some

From Kenneth D. Benne and Paul Sheats, "Functional Roles of Group Members," *Journal of Social Issues*, IV (Spring, 1948), 42–47. Reprinted with the permission of the publisher.

way of handling a difficulty that the group has encountered. Or it may take the form of a proposed new procedure for the group, a new way of organizing the group for the task ahead.

b. The *information seeker* asks for clarification of suggestions made in terms of their factual adequacy, for authoritative information and facts pertinent to the problem being discussed.

c. The *opinion seeker* asks not primarily for the facts of the case but for a clarification of the values pertinent to what the group is undertaking or of values involved in a suggestion made or in alternative suggestions.

d. The *information given* offers facts or generalizations which are "authoritative" or relates his own experience pertinently to the group problem.

e. The *opinion giver* states his belief or opinion pertinently to a suggestion made or to alternative suggestions. The emphasis is on his proposal of what should become the group's view of pertinent values, not primarily upon relevant facts or information.

f. The *elaborator* spells out suggestions in terms of examples or developed meanings, offers a rationale for suggestions previously made, and tries to deduce how an idea or suggestion would work out if adopted by the group.

g. The *coordinator* shows or clarifies the relationships among various ideas and suggestions, tries to pull ideas and suggestions together, or tries to co-ordinate the activities of various members or sub-groups.

h. The *orienter* defines the position of the group with respect to its goals by summarizing what has occurred, points to departures from agreed upon directions or goals, or raises questions about the direction which the group discussion is taking.

i. The *evaluator-critic* subjects the accomplishment of the group to some standard or set of standards of group-functioning in the context of the group task. Thus, he may evaluate or question the "practicality," the "logic," the "facts," or the "procedure" of a suggestion or of some unit of group discussion.

j. The *energizer* prods the group to action or decision, attempts to stimulate or arouse the group to "greater" or "higher quality" activity.

k. The *procedural technician* expedites group movement by doing things for the group — performing routine tasks, distributing materials, or manipulating objects for the group, e.g., rearranging the seating or running the recording machine, etc.

l. The *recorder* writes down suggestions, makes a record of group decisions, or writes down the product of discussion. The recorder role is the "group memory."

GROUP BUILDING AND MAINTENANCE ROLES

Here the analysis of member-functions is oriented to those participations which have for their purpose the building of group-centered attitudes and orientation among the members of a group or the maintenance and perpetuation of such group-centered behavior. A given contribution may involve several roles and a member or the "leader" may perform various roles in successive contributions.

a. The *encourager* praises, agrees with, and accepts the contribution of others. He indicates warmth and solidarity in his attitude toward other group members, offers commendation and praise, and in various ways indicates understanding and acceptance of other points of view, ideas, and suggestions.

b. The *harmonizer* mediates the differences between other members, attempts to reconcile disagreements, relieves tension in conflict situations through jesting or pouring oil on the troubled waters, etc.

c. The *compromiser* operates from within a conflict in which his idea or position is involved. He may offer compromise by yielding status, admitting his error, by disciplining himself to maintain group harmony, or by "coming half-way" in moving along with the group.

d. The *gate-keeper and expediter* attempts to keep communication channels open by encouraging or facilitating the participation of others ("We haven't got the ideas of Mr. X yet," etc.) or by proposing regulation of the flow of communication ("Why don't we limit the length of our contributions so that everyone will have a chance to contribute?", etc.)

e. The *standard setter* or *ego ideal* expresses standards for the group to attempt to achieve in its functioning or applies standards in evaluating the quality of group processes.

f. The *group-observer* and *commentator* keeps records of various aspects of group process and feeds such data with proposed interpretations into the group's evaluation of its own procedures.

g. The *follower* goes along with the movement of the group, more or less passively accepting the ideas of others, serving as an audience in group discussion and decision.

"INDIVIDUAL" ROLES

Attempts by "members" of a group to satisfy individual needs which are irrelevant to the group task and which are non-oriented or negatively oriented to group building and maintenance set problems of group and member training. A high incidence of "individual-centered" as opposed to "group-centered" participation in a group always calls for self-diagnosis of the group. The diagnosis may reveal one or several of a number of conditions — low level of skill-training among members, including the group leader; the prevalence of "authoritarian" and "laissez faire" points of view toward group functioning in the group; a low level of group maturity, discipline and morale; an inappropriately chosen and inadequately defined group task, etc. Whatever the diagnosis, it is in this setting that the training needs of the group are to be discovered and group training efforts to meet these needs are to be defined. The outright "suppression" of "individual roles" will deprive the group of data needed for really adequate self-diagnosis and therapy.

(a) The *aggressor* may work in many ways — deflating the status of others, expressing disapproval of the values, acts or feelings of others, attacking the group or the problem it is working on, joking aggressively, showing envy toward another's contribution by trying to take credit for it, etc.

(b) The *blocker* tends to be negativistic and stubbornly resistant, disagreeing and opposing without or beyond "reason" and attempting to maintain or bring back an issue after the group has rejected or by-passed it.

(c) The *recognition-seeker* works in various ways to call attention to himself, whether through boasting, reporting on personal achievements, acting in unusual ways, struggling to prevent his being placed in an "inferior" position, etc.

(d) The *self-confessor* uses the audience opportunity which the group setting provides to express personal, non-group-oriented "feeling," "insight," "ideology," etc.

(e) The *playboy* makes a display of his lack of involvement in the group's processes. This may take the form of cynicism, nonchalance, horseplay and other more or less studied forms of "out of field" behavior.

(f) The *dominator* tries to assert authority or superiority in manipulating the group or certain members of the group. This domination may take the form of flattery, of asserting a superior status or right to attention, giving directions authoritatively, interrupting the contributions of others, etc.

(g) The *help-seeker* attempts to call forth "sympathy" response from other group members or from the whole group, whether through expressions of insecurity, personal confusion or depreciation of himself beyond "reason."

(h) The *special interest pleader* speaks for the "small business man," the "grass roots" community, the "housewife," "labor," etc., usually cloaking his own prejudices or biases in the stereotype which best fits his individual need.

THE PROBLEM OF MEMBER ROLE REQUIREDNESS

Identification of group task roles and of group building and maintenance roles which do actually function in processes of group discussion raises but does not answer the further question of what roles are required for "optimum" group growth and productivity. Certainly the discovery and validation of answers to this question have a high priority in any advancing science of group training and development. . . .

It may be useful in this discussion . . . to comment on two conditions which effective work on the problem of role-requiredness must meet. First, an answer to the problem of optimum task role requirements must be projected against a scheme of the process of group production. Groups in different stages of an act of problem selection and solution will have different role requirements. For example, a group early in the stages of problem selection which is attempting to lay out a range of possible problems to be worked on will probably have relatively less need for the roles of "evaluator-critic," "energizer," and "coordinator" than a group which has selected and discussed its problem and is shaping to decision. The combination and balance of task role requirements is a function of the group's stage of progress with respect to its task. Second, the group-building role requirements of a group are a function of its stage of development — its level of group maturity. For example, a "young" group will probably require less of the role of the "standard setter" than a more mature group. Too high a level of aspiration may frustrate a "young" group where a more mature group will be able to take the same level of aspiration in its stride. Again the role of "group observer and commentator" must be carefully adapted to the level of maturity of the group. Probably the distinction between "group" and "individual" roles can be drawn much more sharply in a relatively mature than in a "young" group.

Meanwhile, group trainers cannot wait for a fully developed science of group training before they undertake to diagnose the role requirements of the groups with which they work and help these groups to share in such diagnosis. Each group which is attempting to improve the quality of its functioning as a group must be helped to diagnose its role requirements and must attempt to train members to fill the required roles effectively. This describes one of the principal objectives of training of group members.

THE PROBLEM OF ROLE FLEXIBILITY

The previous group experience of members, where this experience has included little conscious attention to the variety of roles involved in effective group production and development, has frequently stereotyped the member into a limited range of roles. These he plays in all group discussions whether or not the group situation requires them. Some members see themselves primarily as "evaluator-critics" and play this role in and out of season. Others may play the roles of "encourager" or of "energizer" or of "information giver" with only small sensitivity to the role requirements of a given group situation. The development of skill and insight in diagnosing role requirements has already been mentioned as an objective of group member training. An equally important objective is the development of role flexibility, of skill and security in a wide range of member roles, on the part of all group members.

A science of group training, as it develops, must be concerned with the relationships between the personality structures of group members and the character and range of member roles which various personality structures support and permit. A science of group training must seek to discover and accept the limitations which group training per se encounters in altering personality structures in the service of greater roles flexibility on the part of all members of a group. Even though we recognize the importance of this caution, the objective of developing role flexibility remains an important objective of group member training. . . .

47

What Does Each Member Contribute?

L. Thomas Hopkins

. . . .

A class cannot be changed into a group solely by the action of the status leader, no matter how deep his interest, how high his ability, or how much he understands group process. The favorable atmosphere which he initiates will gradually vanish or revert to the competitive levels of a class unless members are willing and know how to contribute their part. For group quality emerges from the interactions of members and must be nurtured by everyone. So I shall enumerate some basic general points for members to consider.

1. Each member must recognize that group quality or atmosphere or feeling tone is made by people. It evolves through their behavioral interrelations as they try to resolve some common area of need which disturbs them.

2. Each individual must perceive himself and others as referents in the same need situation, to reach the psychological level at which a social group field may be formed. Each transcends his existing point of view by relating it to or modifying it by that of others. Such a phenomenon occurs only in the individual as a product of his released creative activity. It is not something superior to the interactive process injected by supernatural forces. It is an emergent meaning and empathy in a mutually shared field.

3. The key to an adequate resolution of a situation or need lies in the interactions of people, not in their reactions to external objects or things in their common environment. While the latter may sometimes appear to be important, the relation between a person and an external thing, a nonliving object, is never so crucial as the psychological interactions between person and person, for both are energy systems that perceive, feel, understand, and self-select their own direction of action. The qualitative atmosphere of a group is a product of the psychological interaction of person and person, both of whom are mutually modifiable.

4. Each individual must recognize that anyone who is unwilling to modify his prior perceptions through interaction structures the field in a fixed direction which tends to prevent the emergence of groupness. Since he denies

creative insight in himself, he is usually unwilling to admit or allow it in others.

5. Each individual must work to reduce in himself and others the threats arising from their earlier aggregate fields. Each will then be free to modify his perceptions of external nonhuman objects or things, thus giving them a more realistic value to the need situation. His dominance by fear, through interactive release, is modified to purposeful goals.

6. Each member must recognize that high feeling tone can be maintained only so long as there is sustained effort to manage adequately a common area of disturbance. Such working together may or may not mean that the group as a whole takes action to change external conditions. Frequently need is cleared on a higher level when the favorable climate helps each better conceptualize and differentiate himself. He then takes such overt action as he believes best within his clarified perception of his field. Thus there are action groups and discussion or clarification groups, each depending upon field atmosphere for the quality of consensus action or of individual behavior. Intimate social groups are usually not action groups but opportunities for members to feel, release, and express tensions to psychologically kindred persons who help each other reactivate their purposeful energy. The results appear in improved actions of individuals in many and varied life activities.

7. Each individual recognizes that members with heterogeneous abilities and experiences can contribute more toward emergent group quality than the same number of individuals with relatively homogeneous backgrounds and experiences. Group phenomena are both the product of and the conditions for deliberative actions of individuals. The greater the spread of ability and experience within the common need area, the greater the possibility for extending and clarifying perceptions and for remaking figure–ground relationships in individual fields. But each must be free to release his ideas, meanings, values to the group as he sees them for the interaction of others as they understand them.

To achieve this group relationship each member performs certain services or studies his behavior toward others or carries on in a direction within the moving molar experience which I shall describe here as a series of molecular observations.

1. Each member accepts a common area of disturbance on which to work even though his need which falls within it may not be his first choice or the one which is most pressing. He is willing to move along in the area in the direction formulated by the group. He allows his particular versions of the need or interpretation of the situation to become a part of the total experience, but not a dominating control. He is ready to learn that his self-discipline in the interest of the larger group quality brings greater benefit to everyone including himself.

2. He helps the group locate the center of disturbance within the area and clarifies his own individual need in relation thereto. He focuses the major difficulty and works on it until a new and better direction emerges. He holds himself to the points at issue. He does not wander afield to drag in interesting

but unrelated material that would detract from cogent thinking. He is constantly trying to refine his responsibility to the group as a whole, knowing that in the end this will give him the greatest outlet for his own creative energy.

3. He is always willing to revise his thinking in the light of the dynamics of the situation. He does not push toward a previously determined, fixed conclusion based upon limited perspective and evidence. He searches for that creative insight within the group, and that new experience from without, that merge into a new qualitative stream of endeavor flowing toward a sea of better individual satisfactions.

4. He encourages each member to express his own feeling tone, his deeper sentiments, his integrated learnings, which compose his real self. He accepts their sincerity even though he may not agree with them. He respects individual personality by giving each person confidence in himself. He encourages all to create new insights and helps to direct them constructively in the situation. He is sensitive to every opportunity for upbuilding each self into more mature action.

5. He keeps his eye constantly upon the moving situations that constitute the direction of need action. He tries to locate and examine all factors pertinent to each situation the better to deal with each succeeding one. Thus he reduces personality conflicts, releases tensions while in the making, and gives freedom to everyone for need-fulfillment.

6. He is alert to keep out all conditions operating against the high level of quality which he and the others are striving to reach. The greatest of these is fear. Individuals tend to fear people that they do not understand: people in authority who can control them, restrict their abilities, and debase their personalities; people with greater ability and more ideas than they; people with fewer ideas who achieve their ends by subversive means. They fear their own meanings will not be acceptable to the group, so they will not propose them. They look with suspicion on this creative group quality which is released by cooperative effort. They fear change of any sort, creative or regimented, as a foreign instrument designed to circumscribe and frustrate them more than do their established ways of behaving. All of these fears are not in any one person, but all are usually present in any class. They are difficult dynamics to overcome in developing group quality. Only through patient constructive effort by each member with the sympathetic leadership of an older person can they be so reduced that energy is released constructively on higher levels.

The second greatest influence against group quality is that some members will strive for and the leader will allow them to become an inner elite subgroup quietly managing the larger membership toward their preconceived ends. No alert leader will ever allow himself to be maneuvered into this technique of aggregates, and every alert member will study the signs of its formation so as to expose it promptly. The private pipeline of a few to the leader is one of the surest ways of denying group quality.

Both the status teacher and the aggregate pupils or the authoritarian parent and the managed children learn these new vital group relationships while acting deliberatively on their needs. They are first experienced as a better feeling tone, a happier place to work, a greater personal belongingness and status. As the atmosphere of at-homeness increases, the group discusses the basic dynamics and how to apply them in varied life situations. Eventually all accept interaction as the conscious guide to quality of behavior brought by every person to all new experiences. Thus do individuals mature themselves as they move from aggregates to groups.

• • • •

Section D

THE PROCESS OF CHANGE IN GROUP MEMBERS

Increasing the number of discussions does not ensure that the quality of the discussion will improve. Members do not change without effort. It is true that certain group conditions predispose the member favorably toward change, but genuine change is a re-educative process in which the member must be fully involved. To involve him sufficiently and to lower his resistance to the new is difficult. What is included in this undertaking is carefully and clearly discussed in the first selection taken from the writings of Kurt Lewin and Paul Grabbe, entitled "Conduct, Knowledge, and Acceptance of New Values."

In the process of change the member changes his perceptions of situations and of others. There is a direct relationship between change in his perceptions of his environment and change within himself as is made clear in the selection by Dorothy M. Kipnis, entitled "Changes in Self-Concepts in Relation to Perceptions of Others."

48

Conduct, Knowledge, and Acceptance
of New Values

Kurt Lewin and Paul Grabbe

. . . .

. . . The re-educative process affects the individual in three ways. It changes his *cognitive* structure, the way he sees the physical and social worlds, including all his facts, concepts, beliefs, and expectations. It modifies his *valences and values,* and these embrace both his attractions and aversions to groups and group standards, his feelings in regard to status differences, and his reactions to sources of approval or disapproval. And it affects *motoric action,* involving the degree of the individual's control over his physical and social movements.

If all three of these effects (and the processes which give rise to them) were governed by the same laws, the practical task of re-education would be much simpler. Unfortunately they are not, and the re-educator, in consequence, is confronted with certain contradictions. For instance, treatment involving the training of a thumb-sucking child in certain roundabout hand movements, designed to make the child aware of his thumb-sucking and thereby giving him more control over these movements, may set the child apart from other children and undermine his emotional security, the possession of which is a prerequisite for successful re-education.

How these inner contradictions may be avoided is one of the basic problems of re-education. A correct sequence of steps, correct timing, and a correct combination of individual and group treatments are presumably essential. Most important, however, is a thorough understanding by the re-educator of the way in which each of these psychological components — the cognitive structure, valences and values, and motoric action — are affected by any specific step in re-education.

The discussion that follows touches but two of the main problems here involved, one related to a change in cognition, the other, to the acceptance of new values.

From Kurt Lewin and Paul Grabbe, "Conduct, Knowledge, and Acceptance of New Values," *Journal of Social Issues,* I (August, 1945), 56–64. Reprinted with the permission of the publisher.

CHANGE IN THE COGNITIVE STRUCTURE

The difficulties encountered in efforts to reduce prejudices or otherwise to change the social outlook of the individual have led to a realization that re-education cannot merely be a rational process. . . . We know that lectures or other similarly abstract methods of transmitting knowledge are of little avail in changing his subsequent outlook and conduct. We might be tempted, therefore, to think that what is lacking in these methods is first-hand experience. The sad truth is that even first-hand experience will not necessarily produce the desired result. To understand the reasons, we must examine a number of premises which bear directly on the problem.

3. *Even extensive first-hand experience does not automatically create correct concepts (knowledge)*.[1]

For thousands of years man's everyday experience with falling objects did not suffice to bring him to a correct theory of gravity. A sequence of very unusual, man-made experiences, so-called experiments, which grew out of the systematic search for the truth were necessary to bring about a change from less adequate to more adequate concepts. To assume that first-hand experience in the social world would automatically lead to the formation of correct concepts or to the creation of adequate stereotypes seems therefore unjustifiable.

4. *Social action no less than physical action is steered by perception.*

In any situation we cannot help but act according to the field we perceive; and our perception extends to two different aspects of this field. One has to do with facts, the other with values.

If we grasp an object, the movement of our hand is steered by its perceived position in the perceived surroundings. Likewise, our social actions are steered by the position in which we perceive ourselves and others within the total social setting. The basic task of re-education can thus be viewed as one of changing the individual's social perception. Only by this change in social perception can change in the individual's social action be realized.

Let us assume that inadequate information (knowledge) has somehow been replaced by more adequate knowledge. Does this suffice to change our perception? In answering this question, let us again take a lead from the field of physical perception by asking: How can false physical perception, for instance, visual illusions, be rectified?

5. *As a rule the possession of correct knowledge does not suffice to rectify false perception.*

Our insight into the conditions which determine the correctness or incorrectness of perception is still very limited. It is known that some relation exists between visual perception and knowledge. However, the lines which appear curved in an optical illusion do not straighten out as soon as we "know" that they are straight. Even first-hand experience, the measuring of the distances in question, usually does not eliminate the illusion. As a rule,

---

[1] [The first two principles from this article and not reprinted in full here are: (1) *The processes governing the acquisition of the normal and abnormal are fundamentally alike.* (2) *The re-educative process has to fulfill a task which is essentially equivalent to a change in culture.*]

other types of change, such as the enlarging or the shrinking of the area perceived or a change in the visual frames of references are needed to straighten out the lines.

When we consider resistances to re-education we usually think in terms of emotional obstacles. It is important, however, not to underestimate the difficulties inherent in changing cognition. If we keep in mind that even extensive experience with physical facts does not necessarily lead to correct physical perception, we will be less surprised at the resistances encountered when we attempt to modify inadequate social stereotypes. . . .

. . . .

Only if a psychological linkage is made between the image of specific individuals and the stereotype of a certain group, only when the individuals can be perceived as "typical representatives" of that group, is the experience with individuals likely to affect the stereotype.

6. *Incorrect stereotypes (prejudices) are functionally equivalent to wrong concepts (theories)*.

We can infer, for instance, that the social experiences which are needed to change improper stereotypes have to be equivalent to those rare and specific physical experiences which cause a change in our theories and concepts about the physical world. Such experiences cannot be depended on to happen accidentally.

To understand the difficulties in the way of changing conduct, an additional point has to be considered:

7. *Changes in sentiments do not necessarily follow changes in cognitive structure*.

Even if the cognitive structure in regard to a group is modified in an individual, his sentiments toward this group may remain unchanged. The analysis of an opinion survey on the Negro problem, involving white respondents with varying educational backgrounds, . . . shows that knowledge and sentiment are independent to a marked degree. The sentiments of the individual toward a group are determined less by his knowledge about that group than by the sentiments prevalent in the social atmosphere which surrounds him. Just as the alcoholic knows that he should not drink — and doesn't want to drink so the white American soldier who observes a Negro dating a white girl in England may feel that he should not mind — and he might consciously condemn himself for his prejudices. Still he may frequently be helpless in the face of this prejudice since his perception and emotional reaction remain contrary to what he knows they ought to be.

Re-education is frequently in danger of reaching only the official system of values, the level of verbal expression and not of conduct; it may result in merely heightening the discrepancy between the super-ego (the way I ought to feel) and the ego (the way I really feel), and thus give the individual a bad conscience. Such a discrepancy leads to a state of high emotional tension but seldom to correct conduct. It may postpone transgressions but is likely to make transgressions more violent when they occur. . . .

A factor of great importance in bringing about a change in sentiment is the degree to which the individual becomes actively involved in the problem.

. . . Lacking this involvement, no objective fact is likely to reach the status of a fact for the individual concerned and therefore influence his social conduct.

The nature of this interdependence becomes somewhat more understandable if one considers the relation between change in perception, acceptance, and group belongingness.

ACCEPTANCE OF NEW VALUES AND GROUP BELONGINGNESS

Since action is ruled by perception, a change in conduct presupposes that new facts and values are perceived. These have to be accepted not merely verbally as an official ideology, but as an action-ideology, involving that particular, frequently non-conscious system of values which guides conduct. In other words,

8. *A change in action-ideology, a real acceptance of a changed set of facts and values, a change in the perceived social world — all three are but different expressions of the same process.*

By some, this process may be called a change in the culture of the individual; by others, a change of his super-ego.

It is important to note that re-education will be successful, i.e., lead to permanent change, only if this change in culture is sufficiently complete. If re-education succeeds only to the degree that the individual becomes a marginal man between the old and new system of values, nothing worth while is accomplished. . . .

One of the factors which has been shown to have a very important bearing on the success or failure of the re-educative process is the manner in which the new super-ego is introduced. The simplest solution seems to lie in outright enforcement of the new set of values and beliefs. In this case a new god is introduced who has to fight with the old god, now regarded as a devil. Two points may be made in this connection, illustrating the dilemma facing re-education in regard to the introduction of a new set of values.

a. Loyalty to the old and hostility to the new values. An individual who is forcibly moved from his own to another country, with a different culture, is likely to meet the new set of values with hostility. So it is with an individual who is made a subject of re-education against his will. Feeling threatened, he reacts with hostility. This threat is felt all the more keenly if the individual is not voluntarily exposing himself to re-education. . . . A comparison of voluntary and involuntary migration from one culture to another seems to bear out this observation.

One would expect this hostility to be the more pronounced the greater the loyalty of the individual to the old system of values. Accordingly, persons who are more socially inclined, therefore less self-centered, can be expected to offer stronger resistances to re-education, for the very reason that they are more firmly anchored in the old system.

In any event, the re-educative process will normally encounter hostility. The task of breaking down this hostility becomes a paradox if one considers the relation between acceptance of new values and freedom of choice.

b. Re-education and freedom of acceptance. . . . . Much stress is laid on the creation, as part of the re-educative process, of an atmosphere of freedom and spontaneity. Voluntary attendance, informality of meetings, freedom of expression in voicing grievances, emotional security, and avoidance of pressure, all include this element. Carl Rogers' emphasis on self-decision by the patient stresses the same point for the psychotherapy of the individual.[2]

There seems to be a paradox implied in this insistence on freedom of acceptance, and probably no other aspect of re-education brings more clearly into the open a basic difficulty of the process. Since re-education aims to change the system of values and beliefs of an individual or a group, to change it so as to bring it in line with society at large or with reality, it seems illogical to expect that this change will be made by the subjects themselves. The fact that this change has to be enforced on the individual from outside seems so obvious a necessity that it is often taken for granted. Many people assume that the creation, as part of the re-educative process, of an atmosphere of informality and freedom of choice cannot possibly mean anything else but that the re-educator must be clever enough in manipulating the subjects to have them think that they are running the show. According to such people, an approach of this kind is merely a deception and smoke-screen for what to them is the more honorable, straight-forward method of using force.

It may be pointed out, however, that if re-education means the establishment of a new super-ego, it necessarily follows that the objective sought will not be reached so long as the new set of values is not experienced by the individual as something freely chosen. If the individual complies merely from fear of punishment rather than through the dictates of his free will and conscience, the new set of values he is expected to accept does not assume in him the position of super-ego, and his re-education therefore remains unrealized.

From this we may conclude that social perception and freedom of choice are interrelated. Following one's conscience is identical with following the perceived intrinsic requirements of the situation. Only if and when the new set of values is freely accepted, only if it corresponds to one's super-ego, do those changes in social perception occur which, as we have seen, are a prerequisite for a change in conduct and therefore for a lasting effect of re-education.

We can now formulate the dilemma which re-education has to face in this way: How can free acceptance of a new system of values be brought about if the person who is to be educated is, in the nature of things, likely to be hostile to the new values and loyal to the old?

9. Acceptance of the new set of values and briefs cannot usually be brought about item by item.

Methods and procedures which seek to change convictions item by item are of little avail in bringing about the desired change of heart. This is found to be one of the most important experiences for those engaged in the field of re-education. Arguments proceeding logically from one point to another

[2] Carl Rogers, *Counseling and Psychotherapy* (Boston: Houghton Mifflin Company, 1942).

may drive the individual into a corner. But as a rule he will find some way —
if necessary a very illogical way — to retain his beliefs. . . . No change of
conviction on any specific point can be established in more than an ephemeral
way so long as the individual has not given up his hostility to the new set of
values as a whole, to the extent of having changed from hostility at least to
open-mindedness.

Step-by-step methods *are* very important in re-education. These steps,
however, have to be conceived as steps in a gradual change from hostility to
friendliness in regard to the new system as a whole, rather than as a conversion of the individual one point at a time. Of course, convictions in regard to
certain points in the total system may play an important role in the process
of conversion. It is, however, important for the over-all planning of re-education not to lose sight of the fact that efforts directed toward bringing about
a change from hostility to open-mindedness and to friendliness to the new
culture as a whole be given priority over conversion in regard to any single
item or series of items of the re-educative program.

How, then, can acceptance of the new values be established if not by an
item-by-item change in conviction?

CREATION OF AN IN-GROUP AND THE ACCEPTANCE OF A NEW VALUE SYSTEM

One of the outstanding means used today for bringing about acceptance
in re-education, as discussed above, is the establishment of what is called an
"in-group," i.e., a group in which the members feel belongingness. Under
these circumstances,

10. *The individual accepts the new system of values and beliefs by accepting
belongingness to a group.*

. . . Allport formulates this point as a general principle of teaching people
when he says, "It is an axiom that people cannot be taught who feel that they
are at the same time being attacked." . . . In other words, in spite of whatever status differences there might be between them, the teacher and the
student have to feel as members of one group in matters involving their sense
of values . . . the normal gap between teacher and student, doctor and
patient, social worker and public can be a real obstacle to acceptance of the
advocated conduct.

The chances for re-education seem to be increased whenever a strong
we-feeling is created. The establishment of this feeling that everybody is in
the same boat, has gone through the same difficulties, and speaks the same
language is stressed as one of the main conditions facilitating the re-education of the alcoholic and the delinquent. . . .

When re-education involves the relinquishment of standards which are
contrary to the standards of society at large (as in the case of delinquency,
minority prejudices, alcoholism), the feeling of group belongingness seems
to be greatly heightened if the members feel free to express openly the very
sentiments which are to be dislodgd through re-education. This might be
viewed as another example of the seeming contradictions inherent in the

process of re-education: Expression of prejudices against minorities or the breaking of rules of parliamentary procedures may in themselves be contrary to the desired goal. Yet a feeling of complete freedom and a heightened group identification are frequently more important at a particular stage of re-education than learning not to break specific rules.

This principle of in-grouping makes understandable why complete acceptance of previously rejected facts can be achieved best through the discovery of these facts by the group members themselves. . . . Then, and frequently only then, do the facts become really *their* facts (as against other people's facts). An individual will believe facts he himself has discovered in the same way that he believes in himself or in his group. The importance of this fact-finding process for the group by the group itself has been recently emphasized with reference to re-education in several fields.[3] . . . It can be surmised that the extent to which social research is translated into social action depends on the degree to which those who carry out this action are made a part of the fact-finding on which the action is to be based.

Re-education influences conduct only when the new system of values and beliefs dominates the individual's perception. The acceptance of the new system is linked with the acceptance of a specific group, a particular role, a definite source of authority as new points of reference. It is basic for re-education that this linkage between acceptance of new facts or values and acceptance of certain groups or roles is very intimate and that the second frequently is a prerequisite for the first. This explains the great difficulty of changing beliefs and values in a piecemeal fashion. This linkage is a main factor behind resistance to re-education, but it can also be made a powerful means for successful re-education.

[3] See the following reports:

Gordon Allport, "Psychology of Participation," *Psychological Review*, LIII (1945), 117–132; C. E. Hendry, R. Lippitt, and R. Hogrefe, *Camp as a Laboratory for Scoutmaster Training* (New York: Boy Scouts of America, Research and Statistical Service); Rosemary Lippitt, *Camp Fire Girls Program Study*, Part I (New York: Camp Fire Girls, Inc.); Ronald Lippitt and C. E. Hendry, "The Practicality of Democracy," in *Human Nature and Enduring Peace*, Gardner Murphy (ed.) (New York: Reynal and Hitchcock, 1945), pp. 313–319; and Alvin Zander, "Centerville Studies Itself" (Mimeographed report, Adult Education Program, University of Michigan, 1941).

49

Changes in Self-Concepts in Relation
to Perceptions of Others

Dorothy M. Kipnis[1]

The self-concept is a topic of investigation which is of interest from two points of view. Social psychologists are interested in the process through which individuals form and change their beliefs about themselves. Psychotherapists are interested in the relationship between the nature of an individual's beliefs about himself and his adjustment, and in changes in self-concepts concomitant with psychotherapy.

The present investigation concerns the relationship between interpersonal perception and the process of changing self-concepts. The theoretical basis for the study is developed from the theory of social comparison processes proposed by Festinger.[2] Festinger's theory deals with the formation of subjective evaluations of abilities and is based on the proposition that self-evaluations, as well as changes in self-evaluations, take place in situations where it is possible to compare one's own performance with the performance of others. The present study is an attempt to extend the theory from the area of self-appraisal of abilities to the area of self-appraisal of personality traits.

One component of Festinger's theory is that a person's evaluation of an ability that is unclearly defined (e.g., ability to write poetry) will depend to a large extent on the opinions which significant "others" have of his ability. This assumes that the individual receives "feedback" from others as to their opinions of his abilities. When we turn to the area of personality traits, however, it may be noted that there are strong restraints against discussing

From Dorothy M. Kipnis, "Changes in Self-Concepts in Relation to Perceptions of Others," *Journal of Personality*, XXIX (December, 1961), 449–465. Reprinted with the permission of the publisher.

[1] This study was conducted while the author was a member of the Group Effectiveness Research Laboratory at the University of Illinois. The author wishes to express her thanks to Fred E. Fiedler, Eleanor Godfrey, Melvin Manis, Charles Wrigley, and Walter Cleven for their criticisms and suggestions. In addition, she would also like to thank David Kipnis for his many contributions to the preparation of this paper. The study was supported by the Research and Development Division, Office of the Surgeon General, Department of the Army, under Contract No. DA-49-007-MD-569 and MD-2060. Dr. Fred E. Fiedler, Principal Investigator.

[2] L. Festinger, "A Theory of Social Comparison Process," *Human Relations*, VII (1954), 117–140.

one's own personality directly with others. A person rarely receives direct communication from others as to what they think about his personality traits, nor is he often able to tell others what he thinks about himself. The lack of actual exchange of opinions may then prevent a process of social influence taking place through direct communication. The present investigation assumes that this barrier to direct discussion forces the individual to rely on his own observations of others, to compare their behavior with his own, and to use such data to make subjective comparisons as a basis for self-evaluation of personality traits.

The process of changes in self-concepts will be studied in relation to individuals' perceptions of their friends.

Hypotheses

1. *Individuals will perceive their friends to be more similar to themselves than others whom they like less well.*

Festinger's theory begins by positing that individuals attempt to ascertain whether their abilities are good, adequate, or poor. One means of doing this is by comparing their own performance with that of other members of groups to which they belong. Festinger points out that such comparisons are not indiscriminate, but are much more easily made when the person judges that the other group members are at least fairly like himself. The greater opportunity for self-evaluation afforded by situations where others are judged to be relatively near one's own level should then mean that individuals find such situations more attractive than situations where they judge the others to be very divergent. Or, when the traits to be judged are relatively unclearly defined as are personality traits, individuals may tend to attribute similarities to others to whom they are attracted. In either case, in support of the assumption that friends serve in part as a basis for comparisons through which self-evaluations can be made, we should find that individuals tend to perceive their friends to be more like themselves than others whom they like less well.

2. *When individuals are attracted to others whom they view as different from themselves, they show lowered stability over time in evaluations of their own personality traits.*

A person may be strongly attracted to a group in which he sees all of the other members as quite unlike himself. It was previously postulated that very divergent others do not afford a good basis for comparison. If this is true, persons who are attracted to situations where they view others as very different should have difficulty in evaluating themselves with confidence. We should expect this lack of confidence to be manifested in changes or fluctuations in the person's self-appraisal over a period of time.

3. *Individuals change self-evaluations of personality traits over time so that they are more congruent with their perceptions of persons to whom they are attracted.*

a. *Persons who are attracted to others whose personality traits they evaluate more favorably than their own will evaluate themselves more favorably at a later date.*

b. *Persons who are attracted to others whose personality traits they evaluate less favorably than their own will evaluate themselves less favorably at a later date.*

Festinger hypothesized that the perception of differences in abilities between the self and others used as a basis for comparison should lead to attempts to reduce the differences. The present study predicts the same set of events to occur in the case of personality traits. At this point, further similarities between personality and ability traits may be noted. Festinger points out that Western society maintains values concerning abilities such that the higher a performance score, the more desirable it is. This is also true of most of the personality traits in every-day usage. Characteristics such as "maturity," "friendliness," or "cooperativeness" are certainly seen as much more desirable than their opposites. Accordingly, it is expected that personality self-ratings can be ascribed along a good–bad dimension and that the direction of changes in self-ratings may be predicted along this value dimension.

4. *Attraction to persons perceived to differ negatively from the self will be less stable over time.*

Cultural standards place a premium on doing better. Consequently, individuals not only wish to assess themselves correctly — there is also definite pressure to do better and better. The value set on high performance produces a number of phenomena which are absent when it is a matter of indifference as to what kinds of beliefs one holds, so long as that belief is correct. Festinger found that individuals compared themselves predominantly with others whose abilities were superior to their own, rather than inferior, and that there were competitive strivings to excel the other person used as a basis for comparison.

If personality traits as well as abilities are differentially valued, then it can be expected that strength of attraction will differ for persons who perceive others to be superior as compared to those who perceive others to be inferior. For the person who compares himself with someone whose behavior he judges generally more positively than his own, pressure toward conformity and desire to see himself in a favorable light operate in the same direction. Thus the combined forces operating to maintain attraction in this situation are stronger than for the individual who judges another person's behavior less positively than his own. In this latter case, pressure to be like the other person will conflict with the desire to see himself favorably. These conflicting pressures are expected to produce less stable attraction over time.

METHOD

Subjects[3]

Ss were eighty-seven male University of Illinois freshmen living in one of the university dormitories. The dormitory is divided into sections by parti-

[3] These data were collected by Melvin Manis. The results of his analysis are reported [in M. Manis, "Social Interaction and the Self-Concept," *Journal of Abnormal and Social Psychology*, LI (1955), 362–370]. The author wishes to express her thanks to Melvin Manis for allowing the use of his data for the present study.

tions, most sections being occupied by four students who lived in close proximity during the semester. In addition to their roommates, most residents of the dormitory became acquainted with students who lived in adjacent sections.

Measures

Personality Description Scale. This instrument consisted of a list of twenty-four personality traits which were to be rated by Ss on a seven-point scale. The items were pairs of adjectives of opposite meaning chosen to represent twelve personality factors given by Cattell.[4]

Samples of the items are as follows:

Cooperative . . . . Uncooperative
Mature . . . . Immature
Boastful . . . . Modest

Groups of Ss were designated as those living in two adjacent sections of the dormitory, usually eight students. Ss described each member of their groups, including themselves, on the Personality Description Scale.

Sociometric Friendship Choices. Sociometric friendship choices were made by each S from among members of his group. Ss listed in order of preference the two group members they would prefer in each of ten situations such as double dating, borrowing or lending money, as roommates, classmates, or weekend guests. A weight of two and one were assigned to first and second choices respectively. Scores were summed over all situations to give a "friendship index." A "best friend" and a "least-liked roommate" were then designated for each S. The "best friend" of any S was the group member to whom he gave most choices. As no data on rejection were available, S's least-liked roommate is the roommate to whom he gave fewest choices. The least preferred of Ss' roommates was selected in order to insure that Ss were well acquainted with the person designated as least-liked. Comparisons made by Ss between themselves and their "best friends" were expected to constitute a salient basis for self-evaluations, while comparisons between the self and "least-liked roommates" were expected either not to occur or to have little effect. Perception of differences between self and "least-liked roommates" is then used for control or comparison purposes.

The Personality Description Scale and sociometric choices were obtained twice, with a six-week period elapsing between testing sessions. At the time of the first session, Ss had lived together for about five weeks.

General Statistical Procedure

D Statistic. Measures of perceived difference between self and any other group member were obtained as a function of the difference between the rating on an item of the Personality Description Scale that S assigned himself and the rating he assigned to the other group member. The difference between an S's ratings of himself at the first and second testing sessions was

[4] R. B. Cattell, *Personality: A Systematic, Theoretical, and Factual Study* (New York: McGraw-Hill Book Co., Inc., 1950).

taken as the measure of change in his self concept. In either case, the D statistic[5] was used as an index of the distance between the two descriptions. The index is computed by taking the difference between the two descriptions on each item, squaring it, and summing over the items. D is then the square root of this sum.

This measure of difference is operationally identical with that used by Fiedler and Senior[6] and Fiedler, Warrington, and Blaisdell[7] in investigations of assumed similarity. Consequently, the hypotheses and results of this study can be translated into terms of assumed similarity rather than perceived difference. In terms of the index D, the lower the score, the smaller the perceived difference and hence the greater the assumed similarity.

Self-Esteem. In addition to measures of differences (D), a second scoring system was used for the Personality Description Scale. As mentioned previously, most personality traits can be described along a desirable–undesirable dimension. In the present study three judges were asked to designate the pole of each item on the Personality Description Scale which they felt was the more desirable attribute of personality. The results of this sorting showed almost perfect agreement, one of the judges disagreeing on only one of the twenty-four items. A measure of self-esteem was obtained by scoring each item from 1 to 7 and summing over all twenty-four items. This scoring was also applied to Ss' descriptions of others, giving a measure of esteem for friends.

RESULTS

Selection of Friends

The first hypothesis was that individuals perceive their friends to be more like themselves than others whom they like less well. This hypothesis was tested by comparing the average D score between Ss and their best friends with the average D score between Ss and their least-liked roommates. These data for both time periods are shown in Table 1.

It may be seen that Ss perceived less differences between themselves and their best friends than between themselves and their least-liked roommates ($p < .01$) by sign test) at both Time 1 and Time 2. In short, hypothesis 1 is confirmed.

This result is in agreement with results obtained in a number of previous studies.[8, 9] Although neither the present study nor previous investigations allow inference of the direction of causality, they all provide strong evidence that the greater the attraction, the greater the perception of similarity.

[5] L. J. Cronbach and Goldine C. Gleser, "Similarity Between Persons and Related Problems of Profile Analysis," *Psychological Bulletin*, L (1953), 456–473.

[6] F. E. Fiedler and Kate Senior, "An Exploratory Study of Unconscious Feeling Reactions in Fifteen Patient-Therapist Pairs," *Journal of Abnormal and Social Psychology*, XLVII (1952), 446–453.

[7] F. E. Fiedler, W. C. Warrington, and F. J. Blaisdell, "Unconscious Attitudes as Correlates of Sociometric Choice in a Social Group," *Journal of Abnormal and Social Psychology*, XLVII (1952), 790–796.

[8] J. R. Davitz, "Social Perception and Sociometric Choice of Children," *Journal of Abnormal and Social Psychology*, L (1955), 173–176.

[9] Fiedler, Warrington, and Blaisdell, *op. cit.*

Table 1

AVERAGE PERCEIVED DIFFERENCE (D) BETWEEN THE SELF AND FRIEND AND BETWEEN THE SELF AND LEAST-LIKED ROOMMATE AT TESTING SESSIONS I AND II

Testing session	Average perceived difference		Diff.	N
	Self and best friend	*Self and least liked roommate*		
Time I.......	7.4	9.5	2.1**	87
Time II.......	6.5	9.0	2.5**	86[a]

** $p < .01$ by sign test.
[a] One S failed to describe his best friend at the second testing session.

Stability of the Self Concept

It was proposed that Ss who were attracted to others whom they perceived to be different from themselves would have difficulty in using these others as a basis for comparison. As a result, it was expected that such persons would show less stability over time in their self-evaluations than would Ss who were attracted to others whom they saw as like themselves. Hypothesis 2 was tested by correlating changes in self-evaluations (D scores) from Time 1 to Time 2 with differences perceived by Ss between themselves and their best friends at the first testing session.

There is a possibility[10] that Ss with large changes in self-concepts from Time 1 to Time 2 might differ in both initial level of self-esteem and in the general variability of their ratings, compared to Ss with small changes in self-concepts from Time 1 to Time 2. In other words, a correlation between amount of change in self-concept and distance from best friend could be produced by either differences in mean level of self-esteem scores or in variability of ratings, without reference to descriptions of best friends.

To take these factors into account, two steps were taken. First, Ss' self-esteem scores at Time 1 were partialed out of the correlation between distance from best friend and amount of change in self-concept. This partial correlation allowed testing Hypothesis 2 independently of initial level of Ss' self-descriptions. Second, a parallel partial correlation was computed between the amount of change in Ss' self-concepts and perceived differences between themselves and their least liked roommates. This partial correlation was considered necessary to test whether the first partial correlation merely reflected Ss' consistent tendency to show variability.

These partial correlations are both presented in Table 2. It can be seen that Ss who perceived greater differences between themselves and their best friends did tend to change their self-concepts more than Ss who perceived smaller differences. The correlation between perceived difference from the

10 Cronbach and Gleser, *op. cit.*

Table 2

CORRELATIONS OF AMOUNT OF CHANGE IN SELF-CONCEPTS WITH
PERCEIVED DIFFERENCE BETWEEN THE SELF AND BEST FRIEND AND
PERCEIVED DIFFERENCES BETWEEN THE SELF AND LEAST-
LIKED ROOMMATE WITH TIME 1 SELF-ESTEEM (S_1)
SCORES PARTIALED OUT

	$r \cdot S_1$	N
From best friend..............	.55**	62[a]
From least-liked roommate......	.15*	53[b]

* The difference between partial correlations of .55 and .15 is significant beyond the .05 level.
** Significantly different from zero beyond the .01 level.
[a] Excludes 20 Ss who changed best friends from Time 1 to Time 2, and 5 Ss whose best friends moved out of the dormitory.
[b] Analysis based on Ss who chose the same least-liked roommate at both testing sessions.

best friend and amount of change is significant at the .01 level. This correlation is also significantly higher (at the .05 level) than the correlation between amount of change and perceived difference from S's least-liked roommate.

The perception of difference between the self and friend is then associated with a tendency to change evaluations of the self, while the perception of difference between the self and a less liked other person shows little tendency to result in change. The results then clearly corroborate our second hypothesis.

Changes in Self-Ratings

Hypothesis 3 predicted that Ss would change self-ratings of personality to be more congruent with their perceptions of the personality to persons to whom they were attracted. In terms of the current research, this prediction would lead us to expect a significant reduction in the mean D value between self-ratings and descriptions of best friends at Time 2 when compared to D values at Time 1.

The data to test this hypothesis are given in Table 3. In this table — columns (a) and (b) — are given the mean D values between Ss' self-ratings and their ratings of their best friends at Time 1 and Time 2. Analyses were performed separately for Ss who chose the same person as best friend at both time periods and for Ss who chose a different friend at Time 2 than at Time 1.

Considering first the results of Ss who maintained the same friendships through both time periods, it can be seen that they described themselves as more like their best friends at Time 2 than at Time 1. D values for Time 2 were significantly less than D values obtained at Time 1 ($p < .01$).

Before it can be concluded that the data support Hypothesis 3, it is necessary to show that the results were not due to Ss describing their best friends at Time 2 as more similar to themselves — that is, that Ss did not merely change their perceptions of their best friends while keeping their self-perceptions unaltered. Evidence on this point is provided in columns (c) and (d)

Table 3

CHANGES IN PERCEIVED DIFFERENCES BETWEEN THE SELF
AND BEST FRIEND FROM TIME 1 TO TIME 2[a]

	Mean perceived differences (distance scores)			Comparison		
	Self and best friend	*Second self-description from first description of best friend*	*Second description of best friend from first self-description*			
	Time 1 (a) D	Time 2 (b) D	(c) D	(d) D	(a) vs. (b) *t*	(a) vs. (c) *t*	(a) vs. (d) *t*
Ss who maintained the same best friend (N = 61)	7.13	6.33	6.62	7.18	3.05**	3.20**	*ns*
Ss who changed best friends between Time 1 and Time 2 (N = 20)	8.05	8.60	7.10	9.40	*ns*	3.06**	*ns*

** Significant beyond the .01 level.
a Five Ss chose persons who moved out of the dormitory as best friends the first session, while one S failed to describe his best friend at the second testing session. These Ss were omitted.

of Table 3. In column (c), the mean D value between Ss' self-ratings at Time 2 and their original descriptions of their best friends at Time 1 has been computed. This D value is significantly less than the average D value between self-ratings and descriptions of best friends, both taken at Time 1 ($t = 3.20$, $p < .01$). Thus, by Time 2, Ss perceive themselves to be more similar to their previous perceptions of their best friends. On the other hand, it is seen in column (d), that the average D value between self-ratings at Time 1 and descriptions of best friends at Time 2 is not significantly less than the original average D value computed at Time 1. These data clearly indicate that the changes that occurred from Time 1 to Time 2 can be attributed to changes in Ss' conceptions of themselves and not in their conceptions of their best friends' personalities.

Data for Ss who changed friends are also presented in Table 3. While the hypotheses of the study do not lead to specific predictions for these Ss, the analyses as applied to them gave rise to interesting and suggestive results. Two trends are apparent. First, in contrast with Ss who maintained consistent friendships, they perceived themselves as slightly less similar to their best friends at Time 2 than at Time 1 — column (b). Nevertheless, their second self-ratings have become significantly more similar to their original conception of their best friends' personalities — column (c). Thus, for these

Ss, there were changes in both their conception of themselves and their conception of their best friends' personalities. At Time 2, they described themselves as more like their original conception of their best friends, even though they no longer chose the same persons.

These Ss can also be considered in relation to the new friends they chose at Time 2. If this is done, they perceived less difference between themselves and their new best friends at Time 2 than at Time 1 ($t = 2.33$, $df = 18$, $p < .05$). This process was apparently accomplished through changes in both self-perceptions and perception of the new best friends. Neither change, however, was statistically significant when considered alone.

As a final point, it will be noted that Ss who changed best friends tended to perceive greater difference between themselves and their best friends at Time 1 than did Ss who did not change friends. The difference in D values is not significant ($t = 1.43$), but it does suggest that lack of perceived similarity might be concomitant with less stable friendships.

Changes in Self-Esteem

Hypotheses 3a and 3b predicted that Ss who evaluated their best friends more positively than themselves at Time 1 would describe themselves more favorably at Time 2 and similarly, Ss who evaluated their best friends less favorably than themselves at Time 1 would describe themselves less favorably at Time 2.

Ss were categorized according to the direction of the difference (as indicated by esteem scores) they perceived at Time 1 between themselves and their best friends. Ss who changed best friends were categorized in terms of perceived difference from their original best friend. Table 4 gives the percentages

Table 4

PERCENTAGES OF INCREASES AND DECREASES IN SELF-ESTEEM
ACCORDING TO THE DIRECTION OF THE PERCEIVED DIFFERENCE
BETWEEN THE SELF AND BEST FRIEND AT TIME 1[a]

	Ss with consistent friendship			Ss who changed best friends		
	N	Percentage increasing in self-esteem	Percentage decreasing in self-esteem	N	Percentage increasing in self-esteem	Percentage decreasing in self-esteem
Best friend described more favorably than self	40	70	23[b]	7	86	14
Best friend described less favorably than self	18	28	67[b]	11	45	55

[a] Excludes five Ss who described self and best friend equally favorably, five Ss who chose persons who moved out of dormitory, and one S who failed to describe best friend at second testing session.

[b] The residual percentages of Ss neither increased nor decreased.

of Ss in these categories who increased or decreased in self-esteem from Time 1 to Time 2.

Considering first the Ss who chose the same best friend at Time 1 and Time 2, the results show clearly that the direction of the perceived difference between the self and best friend is related to the direction of change in self-esteem. At Time 2, 70 per cent of the Ss who described their best friends more favorably than themselves increased in self-esteem while only 28 per cent of the Ss who described themselves more favorably than their best friends showed similar increases. This difference is significant at the .01 level by chi-square (chi-square $= 8.63$, corrected for continuity, $p < .01$, $df = 1$).

The possibility existed that Ss who described their friends more favorably than themselves were Ss with initial low self-esteem scores, while those who described their friends less favorably were Ss with exceptionally high self-esteem scores. Accordingly, an analysis was performed where pairs of Ss were matched on the basis of their initial self-esteem scores. The member of each pair who gave his friend the higher rating at Time 1 was then selected, and it was tested whether these Ss showed the greater subsequent increases in self-esteem at Time 2 in comparison to the matched Ss who rated their friends less highly at Time 1. This analysis gave parallel results to those reported above. Ss who described their friends more favorably showed significantly greater increases in self-esteem at Time 2 than Ss with equal initial self-esteem scores who had given their friends less positive descriptions ($t = 2.50$, $N = 30$, $p < .02$).

The results for Ss who chose different best friends at Time 2 than at Time 1 were in agreement with the results for those who chose the same best friends. Although the proportions were based on a small number of Ss, and the difference was not significant, most Ss who described their best friends less positively than themselves subsequently decreased in self-esteem, while most of the others increased.

Another way of stating Hypotheses 3a and 3b is to predict that the correlation between esteem scores of selves and friends at Time 2 will be greater than the correlation at Time 1. Table 5 shows a matrix of correlations between esteem scores for selves and best friends at Time 1 and Time 2, among

Table 5

PRODUCT-MOMENT INTERCORRELATIONS OF SELF-ESTEEM AND ESTEEM
FOR FRIENDS AT TIME 1 AND 2[a, b]

	S_2	F_1	F_2
Self-Esteem — Time 1 (S_1).........	.77	.33	.36
Self-Esteem — Time 2 (S_2).........		.47	.56
Friend Esteem — Time 1 (F_1)......			.66
Friend Esteem — Time 2 (F_2)......			

[a] Matrix based upon 62 Ss who maintained the same best friends from Time 1 to Time 2.

[b] Correlations of .33 or better are significant beyond the .01 level.

Ss who retained the same best friends. It will be seen that the correlation between selves and best friends at Time 2 ($r = .56$) is greater than at Time 1 ($r = .33$). The difference between the correlations ($.56 - .33$) is equivalent to the correlation between selves and best friends at Time 2, after removing the effects of ratings at Time 1 in each case, or r ($S_2 \cdot S_1$) ($F_2 \cdot F_1$).[11] This correlation is .29, significant at the .05 level.

That this effect was due primarily to changes in self-concepts, rather than shifts in perception of friends, is shown by comparing the correlation between selves at Time 2 with friends at Time 1 ($r = .47$) with that of selves and friends at Time 1 ($r = .33$). This difference is equivalent to the part correlation between ratings of friends at Time 1 with ratings of selves at Time 2, after removing effects of the initial self-rating, r F_1 ($S_2 \cdot S_1$). This part correlation is .33, significant at the .05 level. The analogous part correlation (comparable to the difference of $.36 - .33$ in the appropriate correlations) between ratings of selves at Time 1 and of best friends at Time 2, after removal of the effects of initial best friends ratings, r S_1 ($F_2 \cdot F_1$), is .17, which is not statistically significant.

In summary, the results of this analysis also indicate that Ss' self-concepts become more like their conceptions of their best friends.

Stability of Friendship

The last hypothesis was that less stable friendships would be formed by Ss with persons they perceived to differ from themselves in a negative direction than where the perceived difference was positive.

Of the forty-seven persons who initially described their best friends more favorably than themselves, only seven Ss (15 per cent) changed best friends from Time 1 to Time 2. Among the twenty-nine persons who described their best friends less favorably than themselves, 11 Ss (38 per cent) changed best friends from Time 1 to Time 2 (see Table 4). The difference between the two proportions was significant at the .05 level (chi-square = 4.01, corrected for continuity, $df = 1$). Thus, Ss who evaluated their best friends less positively than themselves tended to break off the relationship.

In summary, Ss who evaluated their best friends less positively than themselves at Time 1 tended to both change best friends and to decrease in self-esteem, while Ss who evaluated their best friends more positively both maintained the relationship and increased in self-esteem. It is interesting to consider these results in relation to the idea that individuals will be attracted to situations where they can maintain their self-esteem by contrasting themselves with inferior others. At least in a population of normal Ss, it would seem that individuals are neither attracted to such situations, nor is their self-esteem enhanced by them when they occur. Instead, the route to more positive self-evaluations seems to be identification with a positively valued object, even though this means that the self is considered inferior to another individual.

[11] These correlational analyses were suggested by Isaiah Guttman as an extension of the part correlation statistic. [See P. H. DuBois, *Multivariate Correlational Analysis* (New York: Harper & Brothers, 1957).]

DISCUSSION

The present investigation was based on a theory of social influence and conformity to social pressures. However, the manifestations of conformity which it predicts are somewhat different from those usually expected in investigations of social influences on self-evaluations. According to Festinger's theory, the individual's conformity is an attempt to attain or maintain comparability with others who furnish his "yardstick" for evaluating himself.

The role played by social influence in the Festinger theory can perhaps be contrasted with two other current positions. On one hand, psychologists are frequently highly suspicious of self-evaluations because they believe that social pressures mislead the individual into ascribing only socially desirable characteristics to himself. On the other, theorists such as G. H. Mead generally ignore the dimension of social desirability.[12] Instead, Mead's position is that the person accepts what he believes to be the judgments of others around him, without reference to their desirability or undesirability.

In contrast to both of these, Festinger's theory specifies that individuals are concerned with evaluating themselves favorably, but also correctly. The person's conformity is not with the opinions of others, but rather with what he perceives to be their standards of behavior, and a self-evaluation at any one point in time can furnish motivation for behavior which will allow changing the self-evaluation.

The present study has assumed that perception plays an important part in the process of conformity. If a person perceives that others' standards of behavior are higher than his own (assuming that the behavior concerned involves value judgments) the individual must either conform or continue to judge himself to be inferior. If he perceives himself to be superior, he has the task of maintaining his own level of behavior in the face of the belief that others do not maintain theirs. In terms of some of the items of the present study, he could try to be cooperative although he did not expect cooperation in return, he might try to be reliable although he did not expect his friend to be, etc. It is apparent from these examples that our theory assumed that perceived differences are based upon observations and comparisons of behavior, and that the person's perception and evaluations in turn have consequences that determine further behavior. This does not mean that the person evaluates his own behavior as an objective observer might, or that he is necessarily correct in his evaluations. It does mean that the individual's perception of others who are important to him has very real consequences for the way he behaves or attempts to behave.

One may ask why changes should occur primarily in self-perceptions rather than in perceptions of best friends. In my view this is because perceptions of friends are likely to be based upon social reality. Opinions of others are freely and frequently discussed in the absence of the person concerned. While beliefs about friends are open to continual confirmation through social interaction, the individual rarely receives similar confirmations for his views about

[12] G. H. Mead, *Mind, Self, and Society* (Chicago: University of Chicago Press, 1934).

himself and thus may be more likely to change, given discrepancies from valued others.

The relationships between Ss' perceptions of their friends and changes in self-concepts indicate strongly that interpersonal perception and self-perception are closely related. The consistency of these data on self-perception would seem to warrant further investigation of behavioral changes in a situation where more direct observation is feasible.[13]

Changes in Adjustment in Relation to Changes in Self-Concepts

A number of recent investigations of psychotherapy have been concerned with changes in self-perception as an integral part of changes in adjustment which occur during therapy. Rogers and Dymond[14] have presented evidence that self-concepts of clients changed markedly when therapy was effective. These changes in self-concepts were systematically related to progress in therapy as measured by analysis of TAT responses.

The present investigation was in part designed to test whether similar changes in self-concepts could be observed outside the formal therapeutic setting. The changes in self-concepts noted by Rogers and Dymond were such that the client changed from very negative or unfavorable opinions about himself at the beginning of therapy toward a more and more positive self-picture, so that he described himself as quite similar to the kind of person that he would ideally like to be. In the present investigation, some Ss chose friends to whom they attributed very positive personality characteristics. These Ss, like the clients in therapy, later attributed to themselves more positive personality traits.

The changes in self-perception in the present study were predicted on the basis of Ss' perceptions of their best friends, who presumably were individuals with whom Ss maintained an important interpersonal relationship. This suggests that, in the therapeutic relationship, clients' perceptions of themselves in relation to their perceptions of their therapists might be a crucial determinant of the success of therapy.

According to the hypotheses of the present investigation, one would expect that two conditions of interpersonal perception would be maximally effective in bringing about changes in self-concepts of the kind noted by Rogers and Dymond. First, the client should perceive himself to be different from the therapist. If motivation to change results from the perception of difference between the self and an important other person, then a therapeutic relationship in which the client perceived his therapist to be similar to himself would be expected to result in little change.

Secondly, a client should evaluate his therapist favorably rather than unfavorably. If perceived differences between himself and his therapist are then reduced, changes will be toward a more positive self-picture.

[13] Further work related to this problem has been conducted. See F. E. Fiedler, E. B. Hutchins, and Joan S. Dodge, "Quasi-Therapeutic Relations in Small College and Military Groups," *Psychological Monographs*, LXXIII (1959), 473.

[14] C. R. Rogers and R. F. Dymond, *Psychotherapy and Personality Change* (Chicago: University of Chicago Press, 1954).

There is some evidence that both of these conditions are true of the effective therapeutic situation. In an investigation of the interpersonal perception of therapists and their clients, Fiedler and Senior[15] obtained measures of clients' perceptions of their therapists in relation to both self-perception and descriptions of their ideal selves. Some of the therapists had been rated "good" by their colleagues while others had been rated "poor." Clients of the "good" therapists perceived greater differences between themselves and their therapists than did clients of the "poor" therapists. Clients of the "good" therapists also described their therapists to be more similar to their ideal selves than did clients of the "poor" therapists.

These results are consistent with the results which we would expect from the theory of social comparison processes. The client who does not perceive difference between himself and his therapist would be expected to show little change. Both the perception of difference and the direction of the perceived difference, on the other hand, are conditions which should be conducive to effective therapy.

SUMMARY

The purpose of the study was to investigate the effects of interpersonal perception on self-evaluations. The hypotheses tested were derived from a theory of social comparison processes which posits that self-evaluations are formulated through comparison between the self and others. If this is true, perception of the others who are used as a basis for comparison should be an important determinant of self-evaluations.

The Ss of the study were eighty-seven students living together in a university dormitory. Self-evaluations of their own personality traits were examined in relation to their perception of their best friends.

The results of the study were as follows:

1. Ss perceived smaller differences between themselves and their best friends than between themselves and a least-liked roommate.

2. Ss who perceived their best friends to be relatively unlike themselves changed their self-evaluations more in a six-week time interval than did Ss who perceived their best friends to be like themselves.

3. Ss changed their self-evaluations during the six-week time interval so that they perceived smaller differences between themselves and their best friends. This reduction in perceived difference was accomplished through a process such that at the end of the six weeks, Ss tended to evaluate themselves in the way that they had previously evaluated their best friends.

4. Ss who ascribed relatively "good" personality traits to their best friends, as compared with themselves, changed their self-evaluations so that they later ascribed more positive traits to themselves. Ss who gave their best friends relatively poor descriptions changed their self-evaluations in a negative direction.

5. Ss who ascribed more negative traits to their best friends than to themselves broke off their friendships more frequently than did Ss who ascribed more positive traits to their best friends than to themselves.

[15] *Op. cit.*

Section E

ASSISTING MEMBERS

Members vary in their ability to cooperate with others. This variability is the result of factors not the least of which is emotional stability. To be genuinely constructive in one's relationships with other members requires a level of maturity which some members find difficult to attain.

In fact, all members need assistance in understanding themselves, the requirements of group participation, and the development of the necessary skills. But a few need special assistance if they are to understand their maladjustive behaviors, feel accepted and understood, and develop the inner control necessary to constructive group participation.

In rare instances it may be impossible for a member to exercise the control necessary to engage in group participation. In these situations the leader should help the member to secure more adequate assistance.

Some descriptions of types of maladjustive behavior, with suggestions for giving assistance, are provided in the following selections, the first by Hazel Osborn, entitled "Some Factors of Resistance Which Affect Group Participation," and the second entitled "Understanding the Behavior of Problem Members in Groups," from the Horace Mann-Lincoln Institute Guide to Study and Experimentation in Cooperative Planning.

50

Some Factors of Resistance Which Affect Group Participation

Hazel Osborn

. . . .

RESISTANCE ACCOMPANIED BY DESIRE

Some time ago Dr. Karin Stephen said that trying to understand human behavior is a little like peeling an onion in that every layer is *true* but there is always another layer right underneath it that is also true. What I would like to do is to apply this "onion theory" to the matter of voluntary participation in general and then to some particular aspects of agency and group experience. To begin with, it is important for us to recognize that most people come to new experiences of *any kind* both wanting and fearing them. Just as we must remind ourselves in other situations that there are many shades of grey between black and white, so we must recognize that all voluntary affiliations are not equally fervid. In almost all instances, in fact, joining is more like a five-to-three vote than the miniature landslide that we might anticipate or prefer. However, in many of our assumptions about voluntary participation, we have concentrated on the five and have tended to overlook or forget the three. Here, the three will stand, somewhat symbolically, for the factors of resistance that the member brings with him when he comes to the agency.

As most of you know, resistance is really a psychiatric concept for the true understanding of which we would need training and experience beyond that which most of us possess. However, we are equipped to understand and use parts of the concept and to apply them to the kinds of situations with which we deal. In fact, it seems possible that such use of this and other concepts from psychiatry may be somewhat overdue. For instance, most of us know that other people, as well as ourselves, very often "feel two ways" about a variety of life situations and have a hard time choosing between alternatives.

From Hazel Osborn, "Some Factors of Resistance Which Affect Group Participation," *The Group*, II (January, 1949), 2–4, 9–11. Reprinted with the permission of the National Association of Social Workers.

We also know that in its more complicated forms this feeling is called ambivalence. I mention it here, because it is so closely related to resistance. To repeat a little; the fact that people come to our agencies voluntarily does not mean that they wholly want to come. In order to gratify some of their desires they have to deny others. These other desires (like the three in the "election" mentioned earlier) do not abdicate when they are outvoted but stay close by exercising the prerogatives of all minority groups.

There is very little in social work literature concerning resistance which relates very directly or helpfully to the kinds of situations with which group work agencies deal. Bertha Reynolds' book, *Learning and Teaching in the Practice of Social Work*, is an outstanding exception, especially because her references to resistance are focused on learning rather than on what is usually called a therapeutic relationship. The following is representative of Miss Reynolds' observations:

> Probably learning always contains some of both elements — desire and resistance to the effort, or the pain of the giving up of something else which may be involved. Perhaps it is only a matter of the relative strength of these elements that makes us think that when desire is dominant, there is no resistance, and then when avoidance is evidenced, there is no desire to learn. Our experience, which so frequently confirms the Truth of the psychological theory of ambivalence of feeling, gives weight to the hypothesis that the learning one eventually does, results from conflict of opposite motives.

WHAT RESISTANCE LOOKS LIKE

Perhaps this is as good a place as any to consider what resistance looks like. We are all familiar with the ways in which people express their not wanting of the things they have contracted to want. Perhaps it is enough to say here that there are both active and passive (direct and indirect) ways of holding new experiences at bay. Some people forget, miss the point, come late or on the wrong day, get even simple arrangements confused, postpone, or tend to be overly meticulous and submissive about hewing to the line. We are familiar with all these expressions, but may not always have recognized them as different ways of saying the same thing. . . .

. . . .

RESISTANCE BOUND TO COME WITH INTERACTION

Since it may seem discouraging to realize that resistance nests so readily in our limbs and branches, there is importance in emphasizing that it is an inevitable by-product of the interaction between people in any environment. Thus it is impossible to conceive of a club that is either so static or so dynamic that expressions of not-wanting or not-liking on the part of the members would be eliminated. In 1938 Herbert Aptekar wrote a paper entitled "The Concept of Resistance" in which he said that:

When two individuals come together in any situation, there are likenesses and differences between them. When likeness is predominant, we say that there is identification; when differences make themselves felt, we speak of resistance. This brings up the question whether the interaction of likeness with likeness, or of likeness with difference or of difference with difference leads to the creation of *force* . . .

It seems possible that some of us may have operated on a theory resembling "the melting pot" idea which was once the goal of many Americanization efforts. Basically, this approach seemed to aim at a smothering of differences in the hope of producing more amenable citizens. Although the undesirability of such a purpose was recognized long ago, the hope of "blending" has lingered on in a variety of disguises. To the extent that our point of view or even our function has been conceived in ways that resemble "the melting pot" in demanding conformity of thought, behavior, or rate of development — expressions of resistance or unwillingness are hard to tolerate. We have counted so heavily on the *force* that could be created by "the interaction of likeness with likeness" that we have wanted to ignore other (and possibly less spontaneous) possibilities. At long last then, we must face the fact that human difference is here to stay — and that we must make provision for differences as well as similarities of response in all aspects of group life.

We are no longer as concerned with classifying groups as we were when we hoped that by putting a group into a given category, we somehow derived a real understanding of the meaning of group experience to the members. However, the title "natural group" is widely used still and generally includes the ready-made groups that come to our agencies, after having ascertained our eligibility requirements, to ask for a room to meet in — and more reluctantly, for the help of a Leader. We have nourished a number of assumptions about these natural groups — in regard to their compatibility, their readiness for organized group life, the ease with which they can conform to agency mores, both as represented by the other members, as well as those that the staff secretes. Very often the "natural leader" is much more of a boss than our democratic credo makes it possible for us to tolerate and innumerable struggles have resulted from such differences in political identification. The reason that I have chosen to single out the "natural group" for attention is that in many of our agencies and organizations, we have become attached to it in a kind of mystical way and have frequently tied it to voluntary participation as though one were the subject and the other the predicate. In general, we have anticipated more hopefully than practically that groups where the members were similar in age, neighborhood, nationality, racial or religious background would be sufficiently homogeneous to prevent "engine trouble." However, these hopes have not materialized. Fritz Redl has called our attention to "the law of optimum distance" by which he means that groups should be heterogeneous in enough ways to insure their vitality and homogeneous in enough ways to insure their stability. However, he has also indicated that this is a difficult equation to determine or maintain. Consequently, we can be quite sure that in almost every group there will be ways in which the members will be and feel different from each other and that out of these feelings of difference will come a variety of suspicions and struggles of one kind and another.

We are well acquainted with the fact that the presence of an adult leader is more than many groups of boys and girls can tolerate on a "voluntary" basis. If they can take adults at all, it is only in dilution — as for instance in mass activities. Almost all young people, unless they submerge themselves in their identification with an adult, find that their leaders represent at best a mixed blessing. It is not my intention to indicate that as people grow older they find leadership easier to take. Neither do I intend to overlook the fact that at any age and in any situation the Leader is a convenient target for free-floating resistances to any and all aspects of group participation. . . .

· · · ·

51

Understanding the Behavior of "Problem Members" in Groups

Horace Mann — Lincoln Institute School of Experimentation

. . . The following suggestions and questions are not meant to be an easy course in psychiatry "in a nut shell," but rather are intended to suggest a few factors which may help as reminders that people are important — and human . . .

When your patience is tried to the utmost remember this: *There is always a reason for people behaving as they do*, and, almost without exception, *people want to be liked or respected by the group*. True, the reasons for the way an individual acts may not be clear to the group, or even to himself, but the reasons are there nevertheless. People's methods of getting liking and respect must be better understood. We must learn more about how to deal

From *Guide to Study and Experimentation in Cooperative Planning in Education* (New York: Horace Mann–Lincoln Institute of School Experimentation, Teachers College, Columbia University, 1947), pp. 15–20. Reprinted with the permission of the publisher.

with methods that interfere with the individual's effectiveness and with the group's progress.

There are aspects of liking and respect which all of us want and need. Some which frequently are evident in cooperative planning situations are: the need to establish or maintain self-respect; the need to "belong" to the group; the need to establish or maintain a role; and the need for recognition or affection. For some persons, working with the particular group at hand is a satisfying way of meeting such needs. In that case the needs may be said to operate favorably for good group relations. . . .

It is important, therefore, for the group members to try to understand the needs of one another and, when possible, to meet these needs. In fact, one of the great values of cooperative planning is that it makes it possible for the group to strengthen each of its members, in addition to leading to efficient results and being within our concept of democratic action.

MEETING UNFULFILLED NEEDS

Some of the ways people may behave when they have unfulfilled needs, and some of the things a group may do about each, are suggested below.

(Caution: Human behavior is far too complex to be analyzed as simply as the following statements may imply. Keep in mind that these statements are merely suggestions for further study.)

1. *Need to Establish or Maintain Self-Respect.* Each of us has a mental picture of a minimum pattern for himself, a sort of personal "height-weight" chart by which he measures himself and which indicates whether he is above or below par. Many and various things may go into the making of this pattern. For some, it is a religious creed; for others, it may be a personal philosophy, or a picture of what makes a "good" person; for still others, it may be a picture of "success" — in areas ranging from sports to professional skill; for many, it is a combination of all of these. But if anyone falls below par in his own estimation, watch out! He will fight, consciously or unconsciously, to get up to that point he considers normal for himself. (And don't forget that this may be quite different from what others may consider normal.) The way the individual fights to get up to par may not always be acceptable to the group. He may talk too much. He may be sullen and not talk at all. He may oppose what someone else suggests just to show himself that he had the strength to oppose the other fellow. For whatever reason he behaves as he does to get "up to par" with himself, it is not going to do any good to argue with him. Argument may just make him feel worse about himself, and therefore make him fight the harder. The best approach is for the rest to show him they respect his ideas, even though they may not agree with him. Sometimes this requires considerable tolerance and self-control, but it will further group processes in the long run.

2. *The Need to "Belong."* In almost every group there are people who cannot say: "I belong in this group. I am wanted. I can make a contribution here." But those people *want* to belong. If they do not think they belong

and are wanted, watch out! It is probable that the individual who does not belong will act in ways not conducive to good group action. He may "go with the crowd" even though he doesn't agree with the proposition, just to show he is a good guy and *ought* to be accepted. The result is that the group is not able to make use of his possible contributions because his own thinking never emerges. Or he may resist what others suggest, just to show that if they do not accept him (as he thinks) he will not accept them. The more one argues with him, the more he has to argue back, and the group gets nowhere. The best approach is to help him feel that he *does belong* and that he *is wanted*, whether or not his ideas are similar to those of the group. Give him a "we" feeling if possible, and avoid any "you vs. us" attitude by word or gesture. Sometimes these feelings of not belonging can be forestalled by making everyone feel welcome and wanted from the very beginning. The leader of a group has a special responsibility here, though every group member should help. The leader protects the right of every member to contribute to the group and sees that all suggestions are considered by the group. It is his special responsibility to help the group grow as a group without the exclusion of any member, physically or psychologically.

3. *The Need to Establish or Maintain a Role.* This need may be thought of as a combination of needs 1 and 2. Everyone wants to belong, and everyone strives to find a place in the group which is consistent with his idea of what his role in the group should be. Some people seem to feel they should always be "boss" and others feel they should always be "followers." Cooperative planning discards, to a large extent, this leader–follower concept and implies that all get together on an equal basis. This is difficult for some people to take. It asks them to rearrange that mental picture mentioned earlier, and this is never easy. For some people, it takes considerable time and extended experience in a cooperative planning atmosphere. They may resist strongly being thrown out of role. The person who feels he ought to be boss may try to grab the reins. He may talk too much, act aggressive, be autocratic in his actions and suggestions. In other words, he tries to act like the boss he thinks he should be. The person who feels he ought to be a follower may try to be inconspicuous, refuse to enter into discussion, claim that group planning is inefficient and wasteful. In other words, he tries to act like the follower he thinks he should be. In either case, the person is not operating on the group-equality basis which is best for group planning. Probably the best antidotes are time and experience in an atmosphere of group planning, but some special helps may be given as well. The "boss" may be given some assurance that his ideas are important to the group (as he feels only a boss's ideas can be), and the "follower" may be reassured that if he expresses an idea he is not being presumptuous.

4. *The Need for Recognition and Affection.* This need, too, is closely allied with others mentioned above. Perhaps the most satisfying sign of recognition and affection is for a person to be made to feel that he "belongs" and that his ideas are respected. If he does not have this reassurance, the individual may react negatively. Some persons become more bossy, more loqua-

cious, more autocratic. Some become more silent, more servile, more mousy. Some let their feelings out in crabbing. These persons seem to feel that the way to become respected is to be feared. They may make cutting remarks, they may gossip, they may boast about their "pull" or other forms of power they think they have.

Each individual hopes through his actions to be liked or recognized — according to *his* mental picture of a likable or respected person! Where, in a group of thirty-five people, there are thirty-five different mental pictures of how a likable or respected person should behave, it becomes a bit difficult to keep up with all of them, but there *are* things to do. As mentioned before, helping people feel wanted, that they belong, is perhaps the most important. All can try to understand the mental picture of each and give the kind of recognition which will fit the picture and at the same time further group action. As group planning progresses and each understands the purpose of group action, how it operates and how each individual can find his place in it, the diversity of "mental pictures" becomes less, and the group will very likely become more unified.

To make things more complicated, the source of any one need may be quite outside the group in which the individual finds himself. The teacher in a cooperative planning group may feel that he does not belong to the teacher group because he feels he has not been accepted by the community. The youngster who needs affection and recognition in the classroom may feel as he does because he believes his mother does not love him. It is best to recognize that the *cause* of the feeling cannot always be corrected within the group, but the group can go a long way toward correcting the feeling itself. In fact, the group *must* find ways to meet unfulfilled needs of individuals if there are to be satisfactory group experiences.

How to Deal with People Who Are Problems

So far, we have talked in terms of the *reasons* people behave as they do in cooperative planning situations. Trying to understand reasons is of major importance. Until we recognize these, we have little hope of permanently effecting change for better group living. However, it often happens that certain types of behavior must be dealt with before there is time to know people well enough to understand basic reasons. In such situations one must probably operate on the basis of hunches. Perhaps it will be helpful to have some suggestions of things to try with different type members who are problems to the group.

First, the member who *just does not contribute.* Perhaps he is scared to talk before a group. Many of us were scared out of talking rather early in the game by some rather severe teacher or parent. Try to find out in what size group this person will contribute. See if he will contribute if asked a question about something that is his specialty.

Perhaps this person has found that whenever he speaks up he get squelched, or gets put on a committee! Maybe he is just playing it saf and easy. Will he begin to contribute if he discovers that suggestions are no

jumped on as they are being given? Will it help if he sees that jobs are assigned later on the basis of interest and ability and not to the person who happened to bring in an idea for the group to consider?

Perhaps this non-contributive member is new to the group and feels that his contributions will not be welcome until he has been around a little longer. Will it help if the "old" people make a point of asking how a given problem was handled where the new person was before? Will it help to learn the new person's interests and special experiences through individual contact so that he will not be embarrassed by being asked in a group for an opinion he is unprepared to give?

Second, the member who *talks too much.* Perhaps he is only trying to be helpful. Maybe he belongs to that large group of people who, for some unfathomable reason, are scared to death of silences in a group discussion and feel compelled to rush in and fill a gap. Maybe he really knows more than anyone else about the topic under discussion, and, knowing that he knows, is making his contribution (in which case he may not be talking too much after all). Maybe he just *thinks* he knows more than the others, and that's another matter. Maybe it is all just a habit. Some people seem to have a "gift of gab." Perhaps he feels a need to exert his influence on the group in order to seem important. Maybe he feels very strongly about the matter under discussion.

In any case, great tact is required in helping the talkative member to share the floor with others. One thing that may help is for the chairman not to set an example by monopolizing the discussion himself. Might the leader or someone in the group help to make the "talker" aware that he is monopolizing time by suggesting that *everyone* should have an opportunity to express his opinion; that others of particular competence in this area should be heard from? Could the talkative one be given the feeling of importance he may need by expressing gratitude for his contributions, then turning to other people for their ideas? Can he be helped to feel he belongs by calling on his "we" feeling, by suggesting to the group as a whole, "Now we have heard from ———; we want to know what the rest of us think"? Can we offer the talker a particular responsibility to help him feel important and wanted so he need not put all his energies into talking?

Third, there is the *wanderer.* He does not seem to be able to stick to the point of the discussion. Is it because the purpose of the present discussion is not clear? Has the group shifted to another phase of the discussion without a definite statement to that effect? Is the wanderer less mature or less intelligent than others in the group? Is he being expected to deal with abstract things when he can understand only the more concrete situations? Is he wandering because his attention is tied up with how to be important, how to get the approval of the group, rather than with the point under discussion?

Will it help to have the jobs to be done in this meeting listed on a blackboard and checked off as they are taken care of? Will it help to have the chairman summarize frequently: "We have decided this and this. Now let us get ideas on our third item." Are there things we can do to help him feel at home, to feel that he belongs to the group?

Fourth, there is the individual who is *slow to learn* cooperative techniques. All of his experience may have been to the contrary. He may have been brought up on a diet of being told what to do. Perhaps he does not yet see the values in the new way of working. Maybe he has always seen himself in the role of boss or follower.

Will it help to focus on group processes once in a while, attempting to point out how the group is trying to operate? Will it be easier for the "slow-learner" to understand if it is made quite clear that everyone has a place in the group process?

Fifth, there is the *out-and-out scrapper.* This individual seems to enjoy a fight. Against whom are the fighting remarks usually directed? Are there personal antagonisms in the group? Does this individual tend to stereotype others, reacting to what he thinks others ought to be saying to fit his stereotype rather than being a genuine listener? Do others in the group stereotype the scrapper, always expecting him to have a chip on his shoulder and failing to give him credit when he is reasonable?

To what extent will soft voices, patient reasoned statements disarm the scrapper? Will it help to preface answers to the scrapper by such remarks as, "I see your point, Miss Smith. I don't blame you for feeling strongly about it because it is very important. Perhaps we could think of several ways of handling this." Or might the leader urge Miss Smith to go ahead and map out a rather complete program of caring for her complaint?

Does the scrapper appear more reasonable when dealt with in small groups or individually? Is he seeking prestige in a non-constructive way? Can this desire be met by giving him definite responsibility that is most congenial to him? . . .

Section F

EVALUATION

Improvement of the group member's understanding and participation is unlikely to take place by chance. Establishment of goals individually and collectively are necessary, and criteria of evaluation must be defined for appraising progress. Without the use of these methods it is quite possible to assume improvement when there is little evidence for such a conclusion. It is easy to engage in "wishful thinking," to believe that something happened just because you wanted it to happen.

On the other hand pre- and post-evaluation could indicate problems requiring more attention as well as areas in which progress had been made. This information would assist in the intelligent resetting of goals and of planning their accomplishment.

Suggestions of the types of instruments which may be used and illustrations of their possibilities are provided in the following selections, "Evaluating the Performance of Individuals as Members of Small Groups," by Launor F. Carter, and "A Group Studies Itself," by Alice Miel.

52

Evaluating the Performance of Individuals as Members of Small Groups

Launor F. Carter[1]

The many techniques for assessing individuals range from the simplest paper-and-pencil devices to intensive clinical appraisal. In the past few years there has been increasing interest in evaluating individuals in small group situations. Such assessment is thought to allow an exceptional opportunity to evaluate certain characteristics which are uniquely prominent in group interaction.

The major problem to be discussed in this paper attempts to answer one question, namely: What are the characteristics which can be evaluated by observing people interact? In the use of small group observational techniques it seems probable that some such process as the following often occurs. The experimenter has a hypothesis he wishes to investigate. He desires to test this hypothesis in terms of variables he thinks observable in group behavior, and proceeds to develop a list of rating categories. Thus, in a study of leaders' behavior, Carter, et al.[2] attempted to rate nineteen variables such as the individual's cooperation, efficiency, confidence, prestige, insight, initiative, and leadership. During the last war the OSS Assessment Staff[3] tried to rate ten variables such as effective intelligence, leadership, interest, motivation, energy, and initiative. Recently, Hemphill and Coons[4] described leaders' behavior in terms of nine dimensions. Wherry[5] has described Army Officers' behavior in terms of thirteen dimensions. Each group of investigators has attempted

From Launor F. Carter, "Evaluating the Performance of Individuals as Members of Small Groups," *Personnel Psychology*, VII (1954), 477–484. Reprinted with the permission of the publisher.

[1] The opinions expressed are those of the author and do not necessarily reflect the position of the Human Resources Research Office or The Department of the Army.

[2] L. F. Carter, W. Haythorn, B. Meirowitz, and J. Lanzetta, "The Relation of Categorizations and Ratings in the Observations of Group Behavior," *Human Relations*, IV (1951), 239–254.

[3] Office of Strategic Services Assessment Staff, *Assessment of Men* (New York: Rinehart & Co., 1948).

[4] J. Hemphill and A. Coons, *Leader Behavior Description* (Columbus, Ohio: Personnel Research Board, Ohio State University, undated).

[5] R. J. Wherry, *Factor Analysis of Officer Qualification Form QCL-2B* (Columbus, Ohio: Ohio State University Research Foundation, 1950).

to examine "logically" the dimensions of behavior which might be observed, and then to build some instruments for recording this behavior. While good semantic distinctions can be made among quite a large number of supposed dimensions of behavior, the major theme of this paper will be that the actual number of dimensions which can be assessed is quite small. It will be contended that in assessing the behavior of individuals participating in small groups or situational tests, probably only three or at most four independent dimensions of behavior can be evaluated.

There are a number of empirical studies which support such a view. Couch and Carter[6] have some evidence suggesting that only three factors are needed to account for the variance obtained in ratings made on nineteen variables. They asked observers to make ratings on aggressiveness, cooperativeness, sociability, leadership, submissiveness, authoritarianism, task orientation, talkativeness, and many other logically distinguishable characteristics. It soon became apparent that the observers could not clearly distinguish nineteen independent characteristics in the subjects' behavior, although a logically sound case could be made that each variable represented a somewhat different way of behaving. The problem was to discover how many psychologically independent factors need be defined to account for the variance in the nineteen ratings.

College men were formed into groups of eight or four members, and run on three different tasks: a reasoning task, a mechanical assembly task, and a discussion task. Some of the groups were run in emergent situations, and others in situations where the leader was appointed. At the end of each task, two independent observers rated the subject on the nineteen variables. Tables of intercorrelations of the trait characteristics for groups run under these conditions were obtained and factor-analyzed. The main question to be answered was: How many factors are needed to account for most of the variance contained in the nineteen ratings?

In spite of considerable variation in group size, kind of task, and leadership practice, essentially the same factorial structure was found in each analysis. In all the analyses, three factors emerged. Table 1 shows the higher loadings for each factor. The name given each factor is in capital letters, while the ratings identifying the factor appear under the factor name. This factorial composition came out essentially the same for eight independent analyses of group situations which differed in size, kind of task, and leadership structure. From an inspection of the factor loadings and their structure, the factors were identified as follows:

Factor I: Individual Prominence — the dimension of behavior which is interpreted as indicating the prominence of that individual as he stands out from the group. The behavior associated with the traits of aggressiveness, leadership, confidence, and striving for individual recognition seems to have a common element which is interpreted as the member's attempting to achieve individual recognition from the group.

[6] A. Couch and L. F. Carter, "A Factorial Study of the Rated Behavior of Group Members" (Paper read at meeting of Eastern Psychological Association, March, 1952).

Table 1

DIMENSIONS OF INDIVIDUAL BEHAVIOR OBSERVABLE IN SMALL GROUPS

Investigator	Factor I	Factor II	Factor III
Couch and Carter (Small groups ratings.)	*Individual Prominence* Authoritarianism Confidence Aggressiveness Leadership Striving for recognition	*Group Goal Facilitation* Efficiency Cooperation Adaptability Pointed toward group solution	*Group Sociability* Sociability Adaptability Pointed toward group acceptance
Sakoda (OSS data. Various situations. Over-all ratings.)	*Physical Energy* Energy and initiative Physical ability Leadership	*Intelligence* Effective intelligence Observing and reporting Propaganda skills	*Social Adjustment* Social relations Emotional stability "Security"
Hemphill and Coons (Leader's behavior described by group members and leaders.)	*Objective Attainment* "Related to output" "Initiation and organization"	*Group Interaction Facilitation* "Enable group members to recognize their function"	*Maintenance of Membership* "Behavior which is socially agreeable to group members"
Wherry (Items describing Army officers' behavior completed by other officers.)	*Forceful Leadership and Initiative* Bold Forceful Not timid Quick to take the lead	*Proper Attitude Toward Job* Sincere Helpful Cooperative *Job Competence and Performance* Competent Alert Persevering	*Successful Interpersonal Relations* Genial Cordial Well liked
Clark (Sociometric items from combat squads.)	*Individual Performance* Work with Squad leader Knows job	*Group Orientation* Patrol with Fire-fight with Helpful	*Social Relations* Share bunker with Go on pass with Cheerful
Summary Description	*Individual Prominence and Achievement*	*Aiding Attainment by Group*	*Sociability*

Factor II: Group Goal Facilitation — the dimension of behavior which is interpreted as being effective in achieving the goal toward which the group is oriented. Efficiency, adaptability, cooperation, etc., all seem to have a common element which facilitates group action in solving the group's task.

Factor III: Group Sociability — the dimension of behavior which is interpreted as indicating the positive social interaction of an individual in the group. The traits heavily loaded in this factor — sociability, striving for group acceptance, and adaptability — all have a common element which represents a friendly interpersonal behavior pattern of the individual toward the other group members.

The work of other investigators supports such a three-dimensional interpretation. A short review of several relevant reports follows. The OSS Assessment Staff rated each participant on ten different variables. When Sakoda[7] factor-analyzed the table of intercorrelations for these ratings, he also found that three factors accounted for the ten rating variables. His results are indicated on the table. While Sakoda has named these dimensions somewhat differently than Couch and Carter did, they seem to be similar in composition.

Hemphill and Coons[8] have recently published a monograph in which they describe the behavior of leaders. First they constructed a large number of items and had various group members rate the behavior of their group leaders. They also had leaders rate their own behavior. Members of the research staff then sorted the behavior descriptions into ten *a priori* dimensions. These dimensions were factor-analyzed, and again three factors were obtained as indicated in the table.

Likewise in a study by Wherry,[9] a limited number of dimensions were found. Several hundred Army officers each rated an immediate subordinate on 292 items describing the characteristics of the subordinate. The items were then sorted into thirteen logically distinct categories. The relationship of the items in these thirteen categories was analyzed by the Wherry–Gaylord Iterative Process. Wherry says, "After approximately four iterations in each case, the staff was surprised to discover that the items selected on the thirteen scales fell roughly into three groups or patterns." Feeling that more dimensions should be found, Wherry performed additional analyses. He reports, "Iteration of the (new) group of items resulted in a subtest which contained several new items. It was also tending to iterate toward one of the three groups, but iteration was stopped before it reached that stage. . . ." Here again, as can be seen in the table, three factors were found while a weak fourth one may have emerged.

Clark[10] studied rifle squads on the main line of resistance in Korea. As a part of the study, each squad member made sociometric choices relative to ten different activities. The choices were tabulated by item and the intercorrelation between types of activities obtained. As shown in the table three factors were obtained.

These studies point forcefully to the conclusion that descriptions of the behavior of individuals working in groups can be categorized into three dimensions. These same dimensions seem to be found whether the descriptions are made from the immediate observation of people working together, or from sociometric material, or from one individual describing the past behavior of another. It is quite possible to logically distingiush among a large number of disparate categories describing such behavior, but when reports of actual observations are obtained they can all be adequately included in three dimensions. It seems that these three dimensions can be described as follows:

[7] J. M. Sakoda, "Factor Analysis of OSS Situational Tests," *Journal of Abnormal and Social Psychology*, XLVII (1952), 843–852.

[8] *Op. cit.*

[9] *Op. cit.*

[10] R. A. Clark, "Analyzing the Group Structure of Combat Rifle Squads," *American Psychology*, VIII (1953), 333.

Factor I: Individual Prominence and Achievement. These are behaviors of the individual related to his efforts to stand out from others and individually achieve various personal goals.

Factor II: Aiding Attainment by the Group. These are behaviors of the individual related to his efforts to assist the group in achieving goals toward which the group is oriented.

Factor III: Sociability. These are behaviors of the individual related to efforts to establish and maintain cordial and socially satisfying relations with other group members.

The implication of these conclusions for the rating of individuals in situational tests seems clear. Whatever system of rating is to be used, it should be designed to obtain a reliable estimate of each individual's behavior relative to these three factors. A large number of techniques have been employed to describe individuals' behavior in small groups. These techniques include subjective descriptions, rating scales, descriptive items, and recordings of the minutia of behavior. No general statement regarding the best methods can be made since the technique to be used depends upon the purpose for which the assessment is made and the degree of training and competence of the observers. A discussion of the advantages and limitations of the different systems requires a separate paper.

There will be objection that, if assessment is to be made on the basis of the three factors proposed, it will not be possible to make statements regarding many customarily rated qualities, such as leadership, for example. Yet, the impetus for situational testing has largely developed from leadership assessment. The results cited indicate that leadership is not a unitary trait; rather the behaviors usually subsumed under the term leadership seem to involve loadings on both Factor I, Individual Prominence, and Factor II, Group Goal Facilitation. In the Couch and Carter study the largest leadership loading was on Factor I, with a smaller loading on Factor II. In Sakoda's study, leadership was about equally loaded on these two factors, as it was in Clark's study. Leadership did not show a significant loading on the third factor, Group Sociability, on any of these studies. Thus it appears that leadership is not a single basic dimension but a composite of behaviors related to individual prominence and achievement, and of behaviors related to assisting the group in achieving group goals.

In attempting to determine the advisability of using situational tests an analysis must be made of the criterion of success employed relative to the three factors described. In measuring an individual's performance in the criterion situation it is necessary to determine the extent to which his success reflects (a) individual prominence, (b) aiding attainment by the group, and (c) sociability. If the criterion does not reflect performance in these three areas it is not useful to employ small group procedures or situational tests. The low validities found for situational tests in evaluating the performance of clinical trainees reported by Kelly in this journal issue are to be expected. An examination of the criteria used in evaluating these trainees' success will show that the criteria do not significantly reflect performance in the areas mentioned above.

In conclusion, it seems apparent that the interaction behavior of indi-

viduals involved in small group situations can be adequately described by
three factors. Using these three factors simplifies the conceptual problem
of describing individual behavior, and may also clarify thinking regarding
such concepts as leadership.

53

A Group Studies Itself

Alice Miel

. . . .

Chaos or Continuity: An Analysis of Running Records.   Perhaps the equilibrium of the three recorders who spontaneously took to describing the
group's discussions had been disturbed most by a fluidity in the discussion
which gave the impression that there was no central tendency in the palaver.
There seemed to be too many digressions; too often points were made and
then not discussed; the seminar did not seem to arrive at conclusions or decisions that the group would abide by.

At the initial meeting covered by the reporters, the plan for the day was
presented first, calling for reports from committees that had met previously.
A report on structure in group process was made, and discussion followed.
Attention was devoted to "weasel words" which had been mentioned in the
report. The purpose of the discussion was questioned; relation of the report
to the ultimate goal then took the focus, and definition of structure was
accepted as the next step. Convinced that structure was inextricably tied up
with status and role-playing, the seminar now turned its attention to those
aspects of the problem. Intermission followed, after which plans were made
for the next session, including setting up the committee to discuss process-in-
process, and listing problems for study in preparation for the next meeting.

At the second meeting the plan was stated as study of types of groups.
Emergent, nebulous, structured, pre-structured, and fluid groups were described. Some members discussed the need for some individual's taking the
initiative to transform the aggregate into the group, and discussion turned
to the role of the leader. This discussion was concerned with appointment
or election, with the fact that the manner of the leader's operation was perhaps more significant than the manner of his selection, with getting things
done, with the confusion of leadership and administration. The effect of pre-

From Alice Miel, "A Group Studies Itself," *Teachers College Record*, XLIX (October, 1947), pp. 33–43. Reprinted with the permission of publisher and author.

existing and informal groups in any situation was mentioned. The problem was then defined as discovering methods to keep both pre-structured and emergent groups operating with fluidity. Intermission was taken, and subsequent discussion was limited to future goals of the group and re-evaluation of original purposes.

Summarized in this manner, the two-day discussions seem to be well disciplined, admirably directed, focused sharply on goals; yet the class as a whole received an impression of chaos. The many tangential or completely unrelated remarks made may be one reason for this impression. Such remarks were deliberately omitted in the summaries in the preceding paragraph. In the graphical presentation on page 35 they stand out in sharp relief.

A *Group Process "Seismogram."*   The success factor in group endeavor is a powerful force in cementing groupness and motivating continuing group activity. Groups which have met for the purpose of dealing with common problems are often evaluated by their members by such comments as: "We are not getting anywhere," or "We are really doing things."

These evaluations are of fundamental importance. While dissatisfactions concerning group progress may be voiced consciously by the leadership to facilitate a group's structuring itself during its formative period, these dissatisfactions continued over too long a period of time inevitably lead to disintegration of structure.

A basic operating principle for the "problem–action" type of group is: *The group members must feel a sense of forward movement.* The desired sense of forward movement has to do with two aspects of the group's *thought process* — direction and tempo.

The necessity that all members of the group clearly perceive group purpose need hardly be elaborated. Not so evident is the fact that it is possible to proceed in a given direction at too fast or too slow a rate. Tempo not in keeping with varying requirements of subjects of discussion and composition of groups may be a basic hindrance to the group members' sense of forward movement.

Based on the above premises, an attempt was made to evolve a diagnostic device which, in some manner, would graphically portray the pattern of forward movement in the discussions of the class. The first step was to determine the possible spread of direction and tempo which might be identified in the discussions. It was seen that contributions made during a discussion might be one of three types: (1) pertinent to the subject being discussed and sensitive to the tempo of group thinking; (2) pertinent to the subject being discussed but pushing ahead too fast or trudging along too slowly — showing lack of sensitivity to the tempo of group thinking; (3) off the subject — introduction of a new topic.

The device was then constructed in the form of a running graph to be plotted as the discussion proceeded. Three horizontal lines represented the three types of contribution listed above. Double vertical lines were used to represent change in *group* subject of discussion. Each comment made was plotted on the appropriate horizontal line, numbered in order, and the same number, with the comment itself, was recorded below the graph in the space provided. Contributions made by the discussion leader were starred (*). The first comment to the right of each double vertical line gave the key to the new *group* subject.

Below is presented an illustrative portion of a "seismogram" worked out during one hour of group discussion. The reader will detect the extent to which forward movement was achieved.

GROUP PROCESS "SEISMOGRAM"

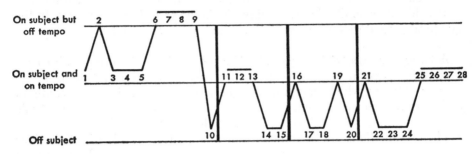

INDIVIDUAL CONTRIBUTIONS

* 1. What gets an emergent group started?
   2. What gets the group going depends on existing pre-structured groups.
   3. Will the group ever come together without a rallying point — a person?
* 4. Formation depends on emergent leadership.
* 5. Group leadership is not fixed.
   6. A nebulous group could turn out to be pre-structured as well as emergent.
   7. In the ideal group every member is a potential leader.
   8. We have three types of groups now: nebulous, emergent, and fluid.
   9. I don't understand what the emergent group is.
 10. The emergent group is not a group without outside recognition.
 11. Now we are pushing back to "what *is* a group — conditions of group-ness."
 12. Status, role, time, purpose, sustained forces.
 13. Mr. G. would add consciousness.
 14. How do you distinguish good from bad?
*15. Moving from this we want to move to an analysis of types of groups. At least, that is where we were last.
*16. Do we want to push back to what *is* an emergent group?
 17. Any superintendent, at times, uses emergent groups.
 18. I wonder if this word "emergent" is the right word? A group that keeps shifting never gets anything done. The distinction is between "fluid" and "fixed."
*19. Probably "fluid" is a subdivision of "emergent." I am still concerned with the sharp distinctions between "emergent" and "pre-structured."
 20. Some members of the group need special training in group process.
*21. Now we are seeing different types of groups.
 22. Emergent groups may become fixed.
 23. The important thing is how the leadership operates after it gets there.
 24. The status and roles of the members are the determinants of emergence.
*25. We may have rigid groups *vs.* fluid groups, dependent upon leadership.

26. Maybe this is the predetermined status and role of members.
27. How the curriculum director operates depends upon (1) how he got the job; (2) the people in the situation, if he works on a fluid base.
*28. Perhaps all this discussion of distinction is fruitless. What we want to discuss is "how do we work from pre-structured to emergent," if we agree that emergent is desirable.

A Vocalization Chart. In this experiment the committee attempted to chart the amount of vocalization of each member of the group in the second meeting covered. Employing graph paper and a watch, the recorder drew a jagged line (horizontal) beside the speaker's name in the corresponding time unit in which he spoke. Solid vertical lines were used to connect the remarks of succeeding speakers, the speakers being arranged on the vertical axis of the graph. This pictured graphically both the time taken by silent periods and who spoke to whom. Slanting lines showed by degree of slant the length of silent periods, while perpendicular lines denoted quick questions or responses.

The completed work was a graph of the group meeting which correlated with the discussion recorded by the running notes.

The tabulation of vocalization was merely a summary of the number of minutes and seconds each member had spoken. From that was drawn the total amount of time which each individual had spoken and also the percentage of total group time which each had consumed.

A glance at the tabulation reveals that out of twenty-five persons present nine did not participate vocally, and of the sixteen who did participate two persons used more group time than all the other fourteen participants combined. Perhaps significantly, both of these very vocal members were "status persons," members of the faculty, and one of the two was chairman of the meeting.

From the graph it could not be ascertained who was over-participating vocally or who was under-participating. Individual members have varying contributions to bring to varying topics. However, a series of graphs representing a number of meetings might point out any undesirable trend toward either extreme.

. . . a thirteen-minute excerpt from the graph [is shown below.]

VOCALIZATION GRAPH

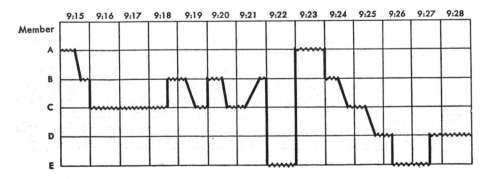

STATISTICAL TABULATION OF VOCAL PARTICIPATION

Contributor	No. of times speaking	Amount of time used		Per cent of total time used	Per cent of lines in report of previous meeting*
		Minutes	Seconds		
Chairman	76	45	0	30.0	10.5[1]
Second faculty member	33	30	40	20.4	20.4[2]
Student					
A	24	10	30	7.0	8.7
B	13	8	0	5.3	5.7
C	11	6	50	4.5	0.2
D	8	6	0	4.0	13.8
E	13	5	10	3.8	12.3[3]
F	8		30	3.0	0.6
G	12	4	30	3.0	1.2
H	5	2	20	1.5	0.6
I	3	2	10	1.4	2.4
J	3	1	30	1.0	0.9
K	2	1	30	1.0	0.0
L	1	0	30	0.3	0.0
M	1	0	30	0.3	2.1
N	1	0	20	0.2	0.3
O to W (9 students)	0	0	0	0.0	
Members absent at second meeting but present at first:					
X					9.6[4]
Y					3.3
Z					3.9

* Of 333 lines reported in the running notes of the meeting prior to the one where the more accurate statistical record was kept, the last column indicates the percentage of lines attributed to each member. This record was highly subjective, but similarities to the more objective record are of interest. Members O to W were represented in the earlier meeting by vocalization on the part of S (1.5%) and T (1.5%) only.
[1] Not chairman at the earlier meeting.
[2] Chairman for one-third of earlier session.
[3] Presented somewhat lengthy report of subcommittee.
[4] Chairman for two-thirds of meeting.

Sociometric Approach. The committee felt that interpersonal relationships have an important bearing on the group process. In order to get some insight into the relationships among the members of the group it was decided to use the sociographic technique. A simple question was prepared and presented to the members of the group at the next meeting. It was: "With what three members of the group would you prefer to work in committees?"

From these lists of names a chart was prepared. The names of the people making choices were listed down the left-hand side of a large sheet of paper.

The names of all the members chosen were placed along the top edge of the paper. The choices were then plotted in the columns below. A very sketchy illustration of the technique [is shown below.] Numbers are substituted for names.

	1	2	3	4
1		x		
2			x	
3		x		
4	x			

From this chart it was possible to see who were the ones chosen many times and who were the ones chosen not at all. For example, one individual was chosen ten times, six were chosen not at all. Though some people thought the terms were inappropriate for our use, the former were called "stars" and the latter "isolates."

The chart was examined for cross-sex choices. It was discovered that of the thirty-six choices made by the twelve women, twenty were women and sixteen men; of the thirty choices made by the ten men, eighteen were men and twelve women.

After some discussion preliminary conclusions were reached as follows:

1. As far as it was possible to ascertain, there were no definite cliques in the group.

2. Sex had little effect on choices.

3. The so-called "isolates" seemed to talk little in group discussions, while the "stars" varied in amount of talking from very little to a great deal.

A Study of Roles Taken During Group Discussion. The material presented thus far has given some idea of continuity and chaos in the discussion, of vocal participation, of personal preferences and animation in the group. The committee was interested in the individual and the role he played as well as in the group and its general welfare. Here the effort was to analyze each member's contributions. Obviously the committee was limited to what had been expressed vocally.

The contributions that each member made were assembled on separate sheets for each individual. Keeping the general discussion in mind, the analyst looked for repetitions of thought or attitude, for a general orientation, for a hobby horse that the speaker might be riding.

The variety of interests and concerns and the tendency to play consistent roles explain the difficulty in keeping so large a group together in any discussion. For example, the analysis pointed to some such conclusions as the following.

One member is firmly convinced of the value of group discussion, *per se*. She feels that general, uninhibited talk is necessary and that the time consumed is well spent.

A second member feels that the discussion must *get* some place. She is concerned with proving the efficiency of the group process. This same member wants clear analyses of all points, a rigorous intellectual approach to the best that has been written in the field.

A third member wants to work inductively, proceeding to generalization from specific cases which are not to be considered merely as examples. She wants to use experience, not books, as the background and she is concerned that the results be intelligible to the average teacher.

An administrator in the group continually refers to the place of the leader in group process.

A director of teacher education in a small college is concerned with pre-existing groups and their influence on group process.

The two members of the class most instrumental in acceptance of the topic of group structure by the class continually try to bring discussion back to structure.

A third member, who opposed this orientation, takes every opportunity to stress function and the danger of bogging down in a sterile and static approach.

One man is concerned with psychological bases.

A woman is concerned with sociological bases.

One member plays the role of purpose-questioner: Where are we going? What does this mean?

Another tries to act as conciliator and to bring opposing points into synthesis.

It becomes fairly clear that various considerations outside the group continually impinge upon the group's process. A member's occupational status and the nature of his job are probably most significant; intellectual bent and emotional attitudes reveal themselves; previous courses show definite influence. Personality structure in the sense of moving toward, against, or away from people (*cf.* Karen Horney) may be seen as an effective agent. Needs for security, intellectually, emotionally, and socially, may assert themselves. All of these factors influence the role that an individual takes in the group process; it would seem futile to attempt to analyze or conduct discussion without taking these into account.

OTHER STUDIES CARRIED ON

These, then, were the devices employed in describing and analyzing participation in the group. When this material was presented on the appointed day keen interest was aroused and many questions were asked. The group recognized that both quantitative and qualitative analyses had been made by their Process-in-Process Committee. However, they were eager for further analyses of a qualitative nature.

Accordingly, a second volunteer committee was charged with the job of making additional qualitative analyses of the group's procedures.

Paralleling the work of the Process-in-Process Committee and the Qualitative Committee, a third group, known as the Principles Committee, was at work also.

Owing to limitations of space it is impossible to include the records of these committees in full, but one device for analyzing group discussion as developed by the Qualitative Committee can be described.

A *Study of Persistence of Interest.* The purpose of this study was to show how many times a different topic was mentioned during a class period and to discover how well members of the class stayed with the particular topics under discussion. In the tabulations below, the letters A, B, C, and D represent the topics which the class decided should be of major concern. The numbers indicate the various other topics that arose during the discussion, most of which were related to the major topics. The number of people who talked about each topic is indicated: twenty-one people discussed Topic A, while Topic 1 was mentioned once.

FREQUENCY TABLE

Topic	Stated Purpose	Number Talking on Topic
A	To discuss kinds of groups in education	21
B	To discuss the validity of each kind of group for its purpose	8
C	To discover how to move toward the more desirable kinds	3
D	Plans for next discussion	20

OTHER TOPICS ARISING DURING DISCUSSION

1.	Organization around problem	1
2.	Hypothesis as a beginning point	1
3.	Definition of emergent groups	23
4.	Differentiation between structure and function	2
5.	Elements in groupness	3
6.	Leadership role	8
7.	Importance of how group works	3

These data were also presented to the class in graphic form.

It is interesting to note that Topic A was considered important and received a great deal of attention. Topic C was touched upon slightly because of the time element. Topic D was not neglected because time was reserved for it. Topic 3 received much attention because of the desire for clarification. These efforts finally resulted in a satisfying definition. Topic 1 was dropped because it would have changed the course of the discussion.

A study of this type serves the purpose of showing where individuals failed to stick to a particular topic. However, its weakness lies in its failure to show the progressiveness of the discussion, and the quality or relationships of the various topics.

EVALUATING THE EXPERIENCE

Since there was universal acceptance in the group of the principle that learning is evidenced by a change in behavior, it was a logical next step to determine whether any changes in the behavior of the individuals making up the group, or any change in the way the group carried out the group process had resulted as a consequence of the study. Were they any more skilled either as individuals or as a group in achieving their purposes through group process? Finally, after having determined what changes had taken place, the group should also consider what had caused the changes, and then try to draw some implications and make general evaluations of the things done.

Throughout the study, questionnaires, interviews with staff members, and other resources were used to gather reactions to various procedures and devices being employed. Two sets of results as reported by the students are included here. The first is based on individual judgments of changes that had or had not taken place; the second is based on reactions to instruments used in the group study.

The Individual Looks at Himself and Others. In order to obtain the reactions of the members of the group to the changes that had taken place two questionnaires were used. In the first of these the members of the large group were asked to answer two questions:

1. What has been the nature of your contribution to the group?

2. If you feel that your behavior with reference to your contribution to the group has in any way changed recently as a result of our study of ourselves, please indicate and, if possible, note evaluating techniques which you think helped bring about the change.

In the second questionnaire two members of each small committee were asked to list, first, the types of contribution to group activity and, second, the changes in behavior resulting from evaluating techniques, which they could observe for the other members of their committee.

After all the results of the questionnaires had been received, each member of the committee working on this questionnaire was asked to study them and to tabulate the various changes which had been listed. At a later meeting of the committee, certain general areas of change were selected and the more specific ones were then included under them. These general areas of change, with some representative quotations from the questionnaire, are given below.

1. *Growth in Responsibility to the Group*

> The discussion of evaluating techniques strengthened my sense of personal responsibility to the group.

> The use of the techniques has made me aware of the responsibility an individual owes to the group. My reaction before their use was to a great extent selfish. I was interested only in what I could get from the group. I felt that I could gain much more from the discussions by being an observer.

My time participation record has led me to try to speak less and to evaluate a proposed contribution in terms not of "getting it off my chest" but
of the value of my thought to the group.

2. *Increased Understanding of Self and Others*

I have become aware of undercurrents operative in groups working on a
problem. Result in behavior is a willingness to consider these undercurrents as significant factors in making group attack on problems. This
awareness has led to self-analysis — consideration of my own strengths
and weaknesses in relation to group process.

Matching running notes against criteria made me more sensitive to real
meanings behind remarks, and increased my understanding of myself and
others.

Insights into group relationship through sociogram and devices for measuring participation changed my behavior toward those who have not had
opportunity to participate in accordance with their competencies. I have
consciously tried to recognize them, value their contributions, and draw
them into discussions.

Increased toleration and care in understanding and trying to see that the
group uses the contributions of others have resulted from consideration of
this study.

I think the techniques of evaluating against criteria helped me to be more
critical of my contributions and to extend the kind of evaluation one can
do of his contributions.

3. *Growth in Security, Belongingness, and Rapport*

I would like to say that I was pleasantly aware of the absence of "flut-
tering butterflies" in my stomach when I gave my report to the group last
week.

A feeling of satisfaction has resulted from making a contribution that
seemed worth while.

A certain definite feeling of "groupness" has developed. Members are
concerned about each other — as group members and as persons.

An identification with the group and individual members as they function
in the group which causes me to evaluate continuously what is being said
in terms of observable reactions as well as in terms of my intellectual
concept of the manner in which the group activity is progressing.

Greater personal expansiveness, security, "belonging," etc.

Greater willingness to accept criticism and understand opposing viewpoints.

4. *Loss of Security, Belongingness*

The only change in behavior I can detect is a loss of confidence in my
ability to follow this type of discussion.

I used to consider a statement twice before uttering it, but as a result of reviewing the running notes and discovering two personal remarks that sounded inane in retrospect, I consider my contribution so many times now that I finally discard it as unworthy, because of the time lapse that enters.

5. *Growth in Interest*

I have been more interested since I have been trying to evaluate "us." The difficulties of getting valid measures have served as a challenge and have provided me with a specific purpose toward which to direct my attention.

Because of our study of ourselves I now feel a much keener interest in observing and trying to analyze group process.

As a result of the use of the evaluating techniques, I have become much more interested in the work of the group.

6. *Purpose*

Greater identification with group purposes.

I feel that I am a little more ready to merge my purposes with those of the group and perhaps a little less inclined to place responsibility for the lack of noticeable progress on others rather than on myself.

7. *No Change*

It is my belief that the techniques have not yet been employed long enough to lend themselves to full evaluation; thus my behavior, in my opinion, has not yet changed as a result of this study.

I am not conscious of having made any changes as a result of our study of ourselves.

After examining the results of the second questionnaire in which two members of each committee were to list the changes they had observed in the other members of their respective committees, it was thought that the sampling had been too thin to yield significant observations. There seemed to be little agreement concerning the changes that had taken place. In fact, one observer might list some significant change which had taken place in an individual's behavior, but the other observer commenting about the same individual would state that there was no noticeable change. In most cases in which the two observers agreed, both stated that there was no observable change in the behavior of the individual.

Conclusions. In its discussions concerning the findings of the questionnaires the committee thought that certain implications and conclusions might be drawn. These were as follows.

There was a wide difference of opinion regarding the amount of change taking place in an individual when the person analyzed himself as compared with the analysis of that person by another.

Attempts at self-analysis are highly subjective. In some instances too little may be seen and in others too much credit may be given. Members of a group often see changes in themselves which are not observed by others, and sometimes distinctive changes are not recognized.

It is difficult to analyze or observe changes in others over a short period of time with insufficient data.

The changes that were listed by persons as having taken place in themselves were for the most part changes in attitude and not in outward behavior.

The change in attitude was the first type of change to take place in an individual, and possibly over a longer period of time the overt behavior would be modified.

There is indication of a need for clearly defined criteria at the beginning of the evaluation activities.

The Individual Looks at the Diagnostic Devices Used. After the trial of various ways of studying the groups' process, the Process-in-Process Committee attempted to lure the entire seminar into participation in its project through evaluation of the material gathered and drawing inferences from the descriptive reports. Informal comment along these lines was solicited, and the following outline indicates the seminar's reactions.

A. *Value of the Devices Used*

1. There was not too much agreement concerning the most valuable of these devices. Each was mentioned by some members as being of value, and vice versa.
2. The sociogram was most often cited as the least valuable. Some members felt that it failed to show various interests and cliques which they felt existed. Others feared that it might lead to undue amounts of introspection and develop self-consciousness.
3. It was agreed, generally, that the value of all these devices would be increased with attempts at more qualitative interpretation.
4. The time chart was felt to be of particular value in revealing the participation patterns of the group, and the place of the status leaders in guiding the group discussion.

B. *Generalizations*

1. Although it is not felt nor too apparent, there does seem to be progress in the group discussions. This fact implies the need for a more effective process of summarization.
2. The group needs to become informed concerning what other techniques can be used to keep the members aware of progress.

Summarization by one member should serve as a fitting conclusion to this study: "It seems basic to effective group process that every individual make deliberate and conscious effort to fulfill his responsibilities to the group by merging his purposes with those of the group, by exercising his capacities toward achieving the group purpose, and by assisting in drawing out the capacities of others."

SUMMARY, QUESTIONS, AND SUGGESTED READINGS

Summary

Although there are many groups, there are, comparatively speaking, few group members. To become a group member requires not only a high degree of skill but a kind of maturity which develops slowly. This "becoming" may be described as a process having several aspects, all of which are present in any group activity.

One of these dimensions of the process is the group member's perception of self, his attempt to analyze and understand his motives, his self-doubts, his fears, and his reactions. Such an endeavor is difficult but essential if a group member is to set goals and progress toward them.

A closely related aspect is the member's perception of the interrelationships among group members, with himself as the focus of introspection. With such perception comes the recognition of the times when he and others use the situation for the satisfaction of personal needs rather than for concentration on the group problem. But it may also include a study of the degree of congruence attained in the understanding of one another's meaning.

Another factor is the degree of acceptance and encouragement of one member for another in the expression of his ideas and feelings. Research studies have shown these and other factors to be worthy of attention in the development of better, more productive interpersonal relationships.

Still another aspect is the matter of performance. Each member performs certain functions in the group. The more flexibility members show in their reactions to one another, the greater the possibilities for their improvement in understanding one another. Each member should study his behavior in order to recognize its usual pattern and the ways in which he can be more useful in the group process.

Each member's study of his own behavior, as well as that of other members and of the group as a whole, can lead to the reduction of tangential statements, over-elaboration of ideas, reluctance to offer ideas, poor listening, and uncalled-for negative or positive statements.

Research findings emphasize that each member brings to the group his past experiences, his attitudes toward problems, and his established methods of working. Especially important is the member's degree of self-esteem and his ability to tolerate ambiguity and to examine issues on the basis of their intrinsic merits. Changes in behavior are preceded by changes in an individual's perception of self; a genuine change requires a total involvement and it takes place more readily when the individual is in a group than when he is alone. However, recognizing the special needs of individuals, the members may endeavor to extend the degree of permissive understanding in their interpersonal relationships, to locate the center of evaluation in each member, and to encourage one another in the symbolization of feelings and incongruities of thought.

Such an endeavor will do much to increase the competence of each member and the productivity of the group. One important key to the development of the individual as a useful group member is mutual trust and acceptance.

QUESTIONS

1. What is the contribution of self-examination in becoming more adequate as a group member?
2. In what specific ways does a member's status and self-esteem affect his group performance?
3. Compare the positive and negative outcomes of self-oriented needs in socio-process discussions and in psyche-process discussions.
4. Indicate the reasons why members may function differently in various groups.
5. Discuss those behaviors which indicate that a member may not have reached the maturity required for participation in a socio-process group.
6. Select and discuss the criteria for the evaluation of individual behavior in the group process.

SUGGESTED READINGS

Section A: Becoming a Member

Loomis, Earl A., Jr., M.D. *The Self in Pilgrimage.* New York: Harper & Brothers, 1960. Chapter 4, "The Self in Communication."

Healthy development requires communication with others on both the verbal and the nonverbal levels. The growth potential of the communication is increased to the degree that each participant is interested in what the other has to say, sees him as a real person in his own right, and offers him the understanding of which he is capable. This chapter invites careful reading.

Section B: Interpersonal Relationships of Group Members

Hochbaum, Godfrey M. "The Relation Between Group Members' Self Confidence and Their Reactions to Group Pressures to Conformity," *American Sociological Review,* XIX (1954), 678–687.

An excellent source of information for an understanding of the reaction of the member to group pressures.

Leavitt, Harold J., and Mueller, Ronald A., "Some Effects of Feedback on Communication," *Human Relations*, IV (1951), 401–410.

Feedback within narrow limits increases the accuracy of the information transmitted. It also raises the confidence of both sender and receiver. Zero feedback is accompanied by low confidence and hostility between sender and receiver. The explanation offered in this article is that uncertainty is frustrating and that lack of feedback results in great uncertainty. This is a useful article for understanding the several implications of the use of feedback and the manner in which interpersonal communication can be improved.

Section C: Performance of Group Members

Hamblin, Robert L. "Group Integration During a Crisis," *Human Relations*, XI (1958), 67–76.

The effect of a crisis on a group is chiefly dependent upon the ability of the group to find a solution. If the solution it generates is inferior to that of a competitive group, then the group apparently loses confidence in itself and degenerates. This study suggests several new approaches in understanding the meaning of crisis. It forces the reader to look at group crisis, not in terms of the seriousness of the crisis itself, but rather from the viewpoint of the group's ability to overcome it.

Kirscht, John P.; Lodable, Thomas M.; and Haire, Mason. "Some Factors in the Selection of Leaders by Members of Small Groups," *Journal of Abnormal and Social Psychology*, LVIII (1959), 406–408.

In a group with an authoritarian structure the member who talks a great deal is perceived as an appropriate representative, but in a group with a democratic structure group-centered and integrative behavior is relatively more important. In this situation the members elect one who increases cooperation in the group. This study illumines new aspects in the member–leader relationship.

Slater, Philip E. "Role Differentiation in Small Groups," *American Sociological Review*, XX (1955), 300–310.

Differentiation of roles is the result of psychological and sociological pressures, and the choice of roles is influenced significantly by both personality and situational factors. In a group with high positive perception the most active participant receives the highest rating on task ability. If a single leader performs all functions, differentiation does not occur. In a group with low positive perception the most active participant is less frequently rated high, and the differentiation of roles springs from an "overdetermined response to inner needs rather than a flexible response to the needs of others." This study clarifies the manner in which groups are differently influenced by sociological and psychological pressures.

Section D: The Process of Change in the Group Member

Festinger, Leon, and Thibaut, John. "Interpersonal Communication in Small Groups," *Journal of Abnormal and Social Psychology*, XLVI (1951), 92–99.

As the members perceive their group becoming more homogeneous and also feel some pressure toward uniformity there is an increased tendency to communicate with those who have extreme opinions. This is followed by an actual change toward uniformity of the group as a whole.

Jackson, Jay M., and Saltzstein, Herbert D. "The Effect of Person–Group Relationships on Conformity Processes," *Journal of Abnormal and Social Psychology,* LVII (1958), 17–24.

Conformity behavior of both members and marginals was found to be greater in a real-life situation than in an experimental one. It was concluded that in a goal-oriented group of interdependent persons forces to conform are induced and are perceived by all persons who are accepted as members. This is a good explanation of the dynamics of conformity.

Stock, Dorothy, and Thelen, Herbert A., *Emotional Dynamics and Group Culture.* New York: New York University Press, 1958. Chapter 16, "Readiness for and Characteristics of Individual Change."

A discussion of the dynamics of change in the group member. Change is viewed as the result of the interplay of three factors: the member's values and attitude patterns, the group culture, and the interaction between them. This chapter provides a basis for the thoughtful consideration of the problem of change and non-change in groups.

Section E: Assisting Members

Miller, Horace G., M.D. "The Psychic Trauma of Becoming Part of a Group," *Diseases of the Nervous System,* VI (September, 1945), 280–282.

The author of this article believes that the child will be less threatened in entering a new group if his parents have respect and feeling for "something larger," of which they are a part. Several provocative ideas confront the reader with the problem of what can be done to help children to face new experiences realistically and with an open mind.

Section F: Evaluation

Dymond, Rosalind F. "A Scale for the Measurement of Empathic Ability," *Journal of Counseling Psychology,* XIII (1949), 127–133.

A six-item scale was developed for the measurement of empathic ability. A re-test six weeks later indicated that although the female subjects in general did not have an initial advantage, they learned to understand other group members better than did the males. This study clarifies a number of the problems involved in the study of empathy and demonstrates the use of one of the better empathy scales.

Index

Academic achievement, group size and, 99–100
Adegbite, Joe, 111n.
Adjustment, changes in, 348–349
Adolescents, and group counseling, 151–152
Adult education, 47
Aggregate, differentiated from "group," 23–24
Aggression, 300
Allee, Walter C., 6–7
Allport, Gordon, 66, 335n.
Anastasi, Anne, 2–5n., 207n.
Anderson, H. H., 296n.
Angel, Ernest, 14n.
Aptekar, Herbert, 352
Aristotle, 218
Asch, Solomon E., 23, 85, 86–90
Authority, philosophy of, 3

Bailey, Bruce, 147
Bales, Robert F., 96n., 192–193, 296n., 305
Bass, Bernard M., 187n., 260, 267–272
Bavelas, Alex, 132, 133, 251
Baxter, Bernice, 67, 76–78
Behavior, learning as, 217; leader's, 261–266; of "problem members," 354–359
Bell, Graham B., 198
Belonging, need for feeling of, 355–356
Benevento, Philip, 264n.
Benne, Kenneth D., 137n., 251, 252, 257n., 296n., 318, 319–323
Bennett, Margaret E., 41n., 143, 149n., 204
Bergman, D. V., 240
Berkeley, George, 4
Bernard, Claude, 4
Berry, Isabel, 111n.
Bird, Charles, 203, 206
Blaisdell, F. J., 340
Blum, Milton L., 145n.
Bogardus, E. S., 204
Bordin, Edward S., 146n.
Borgatta, Edgar F., 96n.
Bos, Maria C., 126
Bradford, Leland P., 47, 53, 67, 68–76, 121, 135–140, 251, 252, 257n.
Brammer, Lawrence M., 146n.
Broedel, J. W., 154n.
Brooklyn College, 100n.
Brown, Marion, 204
Bryan, William Jennings, 249

Cantor, Nathaniel, 244, 251–259
Caplan, Stanley William, 143, 147, 152

Carter, J. H., 192n.
Carter, Launor F., 195, 196, 360, 361–366
Cartwright, Dorwin, 260, 297
Cassidy, Rosalind, 67, 76–70
Catharsis, 300–301
Cattell, Raymond B., 25, 194, 195, 196, 199, 200, 205, 339
Change: educational, social engineering in, 114–120; planning for, 117; stabilizing results of, 120; self theory and, 220; in cognitive structure, 330–332
Chapple, E. D., 296n.
Character structure, democratic, 291–292
Chowdhry, Kamla, 198
Clark, R. A., 363, 364
Class: as a group, 68; individual learning as goal of, 68–70; mental health and climate, 70–71; teacher-student relationships, 72–73
Cleveland, Sidney, 296n.
Cleven, Walter, 336n.
Climate, group: and learning, 136; changing, 248–250
Coch, L., 133
Coffey, Hubert Stanley, 9, 22, 40, 46–54, 141
Cognitive structure, change in, 330–332
Cohen, A. R., 307n.
Cohesiveness, group, 77, 135–136
Collection, differentiated from group, 23–24
Columbia University Teachers College, 110, 157
Combs, Arthur W., 281, 286–289
Comte, Auguste, 4
Conference Research field study, 302n., 303, 305, 306
Congruence, 34–36; and communication in interpersonal relationships, 36–38; general law concerning, 38; and the therapeutic relationship, 39
Consensus in group discussion, 257–259
Content: and group guidance, 41–42; and process, interaction of, 43–44
Coons, A., 361, 363, 364
Cooperation: as basis of group development, 6–7; group, 350. See also Planning, democratic cooperative
Cottrell, Nickolas B., 306–317
Couch, Arthur S., 362, 363, 364
Counseling, group (multiple), 22, 141, 142; methods of, 41–46, 152–153; characteristics, 143–144; benefits of, 144–145; growth of, 145–147; research with, 147–148; when to use, 148; how to do, 148–

149; used for, 149; versus individual, 150–151; clients for, 151–152; for adolescents, 151–152; selection of subjects for, 153–154, 157; study results, 154–155; group-centered, 156–160; problems of evaluating, 160–161
Cozort, William, 97n.
Creativeness, 293–294
Criswell, J. H., 213n.
Cronbach, L. J., 340n., 341n.
Crookston, Burns, 111n.
Crutchfield, Richard S., 24, 62, 145
Culver, Jayne, 111n.

Darwin, Charles R., 4, 6
Dashiell, J. F., 124n.
Davitz, Joel, 109, 110–114
Decision-making, group difficulties in, 110–114
Democracy in the classroom, simulated, 245; cooperative, 245–248
Dependency, 299
Descartes, René, 4
Dewey, John, 8, 49
Dickerman, Watson, 171n.
Discussion, focus of, 252–254; and leader's function, 254–257; likeness and difference of opinion in, 257–259; leaderless group, 267–272
Drasgow, James, 152
Driver, Helen I., 147
DuBois, P. H., 346n.
Dymond, Rosalind F., 348

Education, adult, 47. *See also* Learning
"Ego-involvement," 63
Einstein, Albert, 4, 212n.
Ellenberger, Henri F., 14n.
Emotional problems, learning and, 75, 137–138
Empathy, 197–198
Evaluation, 162; of group therapy, problems of, 160–161; self-, by group, 163–171; problem of yardstick for, 173–174; of leadership, 260; through study of leader's behavior, 261–266; through leaderless group discussion, 267–272; through self-evaluation, 272–275; of individual member performance, 360–366; locus of, and leadership, 222–223
Evolution, dependence upon cooperation, 6–7
Executive Suite, Hawley, 267
Experience, philosophy of, 3–4; defined, 91

Faraday, Michael, 4
Faust, W. L., 96n.
"Feedback," 164, 169, 175
Festinger, Leon, 123, 125, 127–128, 307, 336, 337, 347

Fiedler, Fred E., 336n., 340, 349
Fields, H., 271
Fleishman, Edwin A., 264n., 271
Floor, Lucretia G., 199n.
Force field, 115–116
Forces, driving and restraining, 115; examples of different, 116–117; ways of changing, 118; selection for modification, 118–119; modifying, 119; affecting learning, 135–139
Forrester, Gertrude, 41n.
Fouriezos, Nicholas T., 295, 296–306
Fox, David, 109, 110–114
French, J. R. P., Jr., 27, 64, 133
Freud, Sigmund, 65, 191, 283–285
Froehlich, Clifford P., 142, 143, 146n., 147
Fromm, Erich, 291
Fryer, D. H., 192

Galileo, 4
Galton, Sir Francis, 4
Gaskill, Evelyn R., 146n., 149n.
Gersten, Charles, 152
Gibb, Cecil A., 23–28, 189, 190–197, 199, 208, 211, 262
Gibb, J. R., 96n.
Gibson, Jack, 97n.
Gillin, J. L., and J. P., 25
Gleser, Goldine C., 340n., 341n.
Godfrey, Eleanor, 336n.
Goldman, Leo, 40, 41–46
Gordon, Thomas, 55, 61–66, 233–243, 260, 272–275
Gouldner, A. W., 202, 203–206, 206–211
Gowan, John C., 151
Grabbe, Paul, 108n., 257n., 328, 329–335
Grinnell College, 100n.
Group(s): historical development, 3–5; and unresolved issues, 5–6; basis of relationship in, 6–7; functioning, determinants of, 9–13; challenges to leader of, 10–13, 14; operation, patterns of, 20; laissez-faire, 20; work versus group counseling, 20; authoritarian or aggregate, 20–21, 55, 56–58; democratic or organic, 21, 55, 58–61; having retrogressive effect, 21; three types of relation denoted by term, 23–24; definition of, 23–28; interdependence of members, 24–25; as instrument of satisfaction to individual members, 25–26; functional, defined, 25–27; unitary versus segmentary, 26; as a quantitative concept, 27; as organization, 27–28; foundations of, 29; guidance, 41–46 (*see also* Counseling); psyche versus socio, 49–50 (*see also* Group process); therapy, and psyche group process, 51–52; training, 52; therapeutic, 53; adult education, 53; patterns, 55; group-centered, 55, 61–66; propositions regarding adjustive ca-

pacity of, 61–66; class, 68–76; experience in democratic behavior, 76–78; differing cohesiveness, 77; size, 96–101, 102; "small," 102–105; change in, 108–109; and problem solving, 121–133; educational, developing and maintaining, 139; self-evaluation of, 163–171; and situations, 206–208; measurement of self-oriented needs in, 296–306; interaction, 307–317; self study by, 366–377. *See also* entries immediately following, as well as Counseling *and* Participation

Group member(s), 279–280; becoming a, 281; interpersonal relationships of, 295; performance of, 318; functional roles of, 319–323; individual contributions of, 324–327; process of change in, 328–335; assisting, 350; "problem," 354–359; evaluating performance of, 361–366

Group process: socio and psyche, 4, 49–51; needed depth in, 14–17; distinctions based on historical development of, 47–48; confusions resulting from lack of theory in, 48–49; group differentiation, 49–50; psyche, of therapy groups, 51; theoretical framework as source of distinctions, 52–53; theoretical framework, implications of, 54; defined, 91–93; the silent period in, 94, 106–107; self theory and, 220

Grubb, J., 151, 152
Grunwald, Hanna, 145n.
Guetzkow, Harold, 101n., 134, 295, 296–306
Guidance, group methods of, 41–46. *See also* Counseling
Gurin, Gerald, 199n.
Gurin, Maizie, 296n.
Gustad, John W., 146n.
Guttman, Isaiah, 346n.

Hall, Harry E., Jr., 198
Hall, Lydia, 111n.
Halpin, Andrew W., 199, 260, 261–266
Hare, A. Paul, 96n.
Hartley, E. L. and Ruth E., 194
Harvard University study, 253n.
Haug, William, 111n.
Hawley, Cameron, *Executive Suite*, 267
Hayakawa, S. I., 235n.
Haythorn, William, 361n.
Health, psychological, 290–293
Heider, F., 86, 87, 88, 307
Hemphill, John K., 195–196, 264n., 265, 361, 363, 364
Hendry, Charles E., 189, 197–201, 251, 335n.
Herrold, Kenneth F., 109, 110–114, 146n.
Hertz, Heinrich R., 4
Heyns, R. W., 134, 297n.

Hobbes, Thomas, 4
Hobbs, Nicholas, 141, 156–161
Hogrefe, R., 335n.
Hood, Bruce, 97n.
Hopkins, L. Thomas, 55, 56–61, 85, 91–93, 215, 216–218, 244, 248–250, 318, 324–327
Hoppock, Robert, 41n.
Horace Mann-Lincoln Institute Guide to Study and Experimentation in Cooperative Planning, 350, 354–359
Horn, H. Francis, 16
Horney, Karen, 372
Hovland, C. I., 125n., 307n.
Hughes, D. Patrick, 95, 106–107
Hume, David, 4
Hutt, Max L., 295, 296–306

Imagination, productive, 14–15
Individuality, 30–33
Individuals, evaluating performance of, 361–366
Infeld, Leopold, 212n.
In-group, creation of, 334–335
Interaction, problems in, 94–95
Interaction theory of leadership, 211–214
Interest, study of persistence of, 373
Interpersonal relationships, 290–291, 295; new insights into, 13–14
Isolates, group consultation of, 104

Jacob, Philip E., 101n.
Janis, I. L., 125n., 307n.
Jenkins, David H., 109, 114–120, 162, 163–171, 208, 210
Jenkins, William O., 207
Jennings, Helen Hall, 49, 191, 202, 211–214
Johnson, Wendell, 263n.
Jones, Ernst, 285n.
Jung, C. C., 15, 16
Juvenile delinquents, 152

Kallegian, Vern J., 146n.
Kant, Immanuel, 15
Katz, Daniel, 199n.
Katz, Elihu, 144, 145
Kelley, Harold H., 96n., 121, 122–133
Kelly, E. Lowell, 101n.
Kelman, H. C., 125n.
Kemp, C. Gratton, 215, 219–226, 228 229–232, 244, 245–248
Kierkegaard, Søren, 13n., 14, 279
King, B. T., 125n.
Kipnis, David, 336n.
Kipnis, Dorothy M., 328, 336–349
Kirk, Barbara, 151
Klems, Marvin A., 146n.
Knowles, 47, 53
Kornhauser, A., 64
Korzybski, Alfred, 263n.

Krech, David, 24, 62
Kroner, Richard, 15
Kropotkin, Prince Peter, 6
Kunkel, Fritz, 31n.

Lanzetta, John, 361n.
La Rosa, Julius, 105
Laughlin, Henry P., 145n.
"Law of optimum distance," 353
Lazarsfeld, Paul F., 144, 145
Leader Behavior Description Questionnaire
  (LBDQ), 264–266
Leader(s): challenges to, 10–13, 14; methods, 20; role in group-centered method,
  21; of the "small group," 103; therapy
  group's reaction to, 158; concept of, 189;
  as individual in given office, 190–191; as
  focus for group behavior, 191; definition
  of, in terms of sociometric choice, 191–
  193; as influence over others, 193; defined in terms of influence upon syntality, 195–196; as one who engages in
  leadership behaviors, 195–196; qualities
  of, 197–201; empathy, 197–198; consideration, 198–200; surgency, 200–201;
  requirements, 224–225; authoritarian,
  229–230; democratic, 230–231; group-
  centered, 231–232; group-centered, functioning of, 232–243; and change of group
  climate, 249–250; role in focusing discussion, 252–254; function of, 254–257;
  evaluation of, 261–266; self-evaluation of,
  272–275; attitudes, 273–274; "natural,"
  353. *See also* Teacher
Leaderless Group Discussion, 267–272
Leadership, 187–188; effective social, 74;
  and headship differentiated, 193–194;
  focused versus distributed, 196–197;
  theories of, 202; trait theory of, 203–206;
  situationist theory of, 206–211; traits,
  208; interaction theory of, 211–214; psychological foundations of, 215–226; authoritarian and democratic, foundations
  of, 216–218; group-centered, foundations
  of, 219–221; differing assumptions in
  three types of, 222–226; functioning,
  227–243; types of, 229–232; problems of,
  244; in making better decisions, 245–
  248; in changing the group climate, 248–
  250; in maintaining a creative difference,
  251–259; problem of defining, 261–263;
  and leader behavior, 263–266
Learning: as goal of class group, 68–70;
  social, emotional and value areas, 73–76;
  group forces affecting, 135–139; motivation for, 138; and teacher's requirements,
  139–140; and behavior, 217; principles
  of, and leadership, 223
Lerner, Arthur, 145n.
Levy, Dr. David, 292

Lewin, Kurt, 24, 50, 108n., 116n., 132,
  257n., 296n., 297, 328, 329-335
Lewis, H. B., 297
Lindesmith, Alfred R., 204
"Linking" function of group-centered leader,
  240–243
Lippitt, Ronald, 251, 252, 257n., 296n.,
  297, 335n.
Lippitt, Rosemary, 335n.
Listening: and the group-centered leader,
  233–234; test of, 234–235; element of
  risk in, 235–236; reasons for, 236
Lloyd, A. H., 211
Locke, John, 4
Locke, Norman, 146
Lorge, Irving, 109, 110–114
Lynd, Robert S. and Helen Merrell, 6

Maccoby, Nathan, 199n.
McCorkle, Lloyd W., 145n.
McCuen, T. L., 204
McGregor, Douglas, 66, 251
McKeachie, Wilbert J., 100n., 101n.
Maier, Norman R. F., 132
Malthus, Thomas Robert, 6
Man, nature of, 7–9; as individual, 31–33
Mandell, M., 271
Manis, Melvin, 336n., 338n.
Marquis, D. G., 134, 296n.
Marrow, A., 64
Maslow, A. H., 281, 290–293
Maxwell, James Clerk, 4
May, Rollo, 14
Mead, George H., 32n., 347
Means and ends, discrimination between,
  292–293
Metler, Jack, 111n.
Meyer, C. A., 272
Michels, Robert, 204
Michotte, A., 86–87
Middletown study, 6
Miel, Alice, 360, 366–367
Miller, Arthur Harrison, 203, 205
Mitchell, Lucy Sprague, 283
Moreno, J. L., 191
Morgenstern, O., 130
Morris, R. T., 193
Morse, Nancy C., 199n.
Motivation: for learning, 138; and self
  theory, 219
Mowrer, O. H., 7
Mudd, Emily Hartshorne, 146n., 149n.
Munson, Edward L., 203, 204
Muntyan, Bozidar, 251n.
Murphy, Albert J., 208
Murphy, Gardner, 212
Murray, Henry A., 212n.

National Training Laboratory in Group
  Development, 171–180

Needs: ego, and self theory, 221; self-oriented, measurement of, 296–306; unfulfilled, 355–357
Neumann, J. von, 130
Newcomb, Theodore M., 198
Newton, Isaac, 4
Niebuhr, Reinhold, 29, 30–33, 281, 282–285

Observer, group, 166–168, 171–172; problems faced by, 172; problem of evaluation yardstick, 173–174; problem of purposes and functions, 174–175; problem of responsibility to group, 176; problem of personal value system, 177; problem of observational objectivity, 177; sorts of things to be observed by, 178–179; special techniques, 179–180; self-oriented-need, 298, 301–302
Oersted, Hans Christian, 4
Office of Strategic Services Assessment Staff, 209, 210, 361, 364
Ohio State Leadership Studies, 263
Ohio State University, Bureau of Business Research, 264
Ohlsen, Merle M., 141, 150–155
Organicism, 4
Organization, 27–28
Osborn, Hazel, 350, 351–354

Participation, value of, 63–64; in learning activities, 136–137; resistance factors affecting, 351–354; vocal, statistical tabulation of, 369–370
Partridge, E. De Alton, 204n.
Paster, S., 152
Patterns, group, 55
Patton, John D., 145n.
Peirce, Charles, 4
Pennsylvania School of Social Work, 251
Perception(s): and self theory, 219; selection of, 286–289
Personality: problems, 102; for leadership, 211–212; theories of, 215
Personality Description Scale, 339, 340
Phillips, Helen U., 251n.
Pigors, P., 193
Planning, democratic cooperative, 245–248
Plato, 218; symbol of the cave, 16
Plummer, Mark, 97n.
Porter, E. H., Jr., 240
Prejudices, 331
President's Committee on Civil Rights, 63
"Press," 212n., 213
Preston, Burman H., 145n.
Prestwood, A. R., 301
Pretrullo, Luigi, 187
Problem solving, group, 121–133; and the individual, 123–126, 129–130

Process: and group guidance, 41–43; and content, interaction of, 43–44; psyche group, 51–52; defined as life movement, 91–93; and leadership, 223–224
Productivity observer, 166–168; feedback of information from, 169–170
Proff, F., 154n.
Psyche group process, as focus of therapy groups, 51–52
Psychology: and group goals, 7; existential, contributions of, 13–14; field theory, 216–218

Rank, Otto, 259n.
Recognition, need for, 356–357
Record-keeping, observer's, 179–180
Redl, Fritz, 191, 353
Re-education, process of, 329–335
Reik, Theodore, 83
Relationships: interpersonal, new insights into, 13–14; general law of, 33–39; teacher-student, 72-73; intra-group, and learning, 137; interpersonal, 290–291; interpersonal, of group members, 295; group, sociometric approach to, 370–371
Resistance, factors of, 351–354
Responses implying intent to change, 237–239
Reynolds, Bertha, 352
Rickard, J., 240
Roethlisberger, F. J., 233n.
Rogers, Carl R., 8, 29, 33–39, 55, 146n., 215, 220n., 233, 241n., 333, 348; self theory, 109, 219
Role(s): of leader in group-centered method, 21; of leader in focusing discussion, 252–254; group task, 319–320; group building and maintenance, 320–321; "individual," 321–322; problem of requiredness, 322–323; problem of flexibility, 323; need to establish or maintain, 356
Roosevelt, Franklin D., 197–198, 199
Ross, Murray, 189, 197–201
Ruesch, J., 301
Rugg, Harold, quoted, 3, 4
Russell, Bertrand, 204

Sanders, Richard, 296n.
Sanford, Filmore H., 197n., 199n.
Schellenberg, James A., 95, 96–101
Schrier, Harvey, 296n.
Seeman, M., 193
"Seismogram," group process, 368
Self, internal dialogue of, 282–285; concepts of, 286–287 (see also Self concepts); phenomenal, circular effect of, 287–288; and distortion of perception, 288–289; phenomenal, and role, 289
Self-actualizing people, 290–293

Self-concepts, 286–287; changes in, in relation to perceptions of others, 336–349; stability of, 341–342; changes in adjustment in relation to changes in, 348–349

Self-esteem, study of, 306–317; measuring, 340; changes in, 344–346

Self-evaluation, group, 163–171; of leadership, 272–275

Self-knowledge, 219–220

Self-ratings, changes in, 342–344

Self-respect, need to establish or maintain, 355

Self theory, 219–221

Self-transcendence, human capacity for, 31–32

Senior, Kate, 340, 349

Shaffer, L. F., 285n.

Shanker, Dr. Prem, 309n.

Shartle, Carroll L., 190, 263, 264n.

Shaw, M. C., 151, 152

Shaw, M. E., 128n.

Sheats, Paul, 54, 137n., 296n., 318, 319–323

Sherif, M., 28

Shostrom, Everett L., 146n.

Sign versus symbol, 16

Silent period, 94, 106–107

Simmel, E., 87

Situations, groups and, 206–208; skills and, 208–210

Skills, and situationist theory, 208–210

Skinner, B. F., 7n., 8

Slater, Philip, 96n.

Slavson, S. R., 149n.

Social: change, inducement of, 108–109; engineering, 114–120; leadership, 74; organization, creative, 74–75

Sociometric friendship choices, 339

Southard, C., 154n.

Spencer, Herbert, 4, 6

Stephen, Dr. Karin, 351

Stice, Glen F., 26, 199, 200

Stogdill, Ralph M., 27, 190, 262, 264n., 270, 271

Stotland, Ezra, 295, 306–317

Strauss, Anselm L., 204

Structure-in-interaction, 25

Students, mental health and climate, 70–71; and teacher relationships, 72–73; group size and satisfaction of, 98–99, 101

Super, Donald E., 146n., 149n.

Surgency, leader's, 200–201

Symbolization and self theory, 220

Symbols, 15–17

Snygg, Donald, 281, 286–289

Syntality, defined, 196

Taylor, D. W., 96n.

Teachers, guidance problems of, 44–46; relationships with students, 72–73; satisfaction with group sizes, 99, 101; requirements for, 139–140; and democratic cooperative planning, 245–248; role in helping class become group, 248–50

Teachers College, Columbia University, pilot study at, 110; research in group therapy, 157

Thelen, Herbert A., 251, 257n.

Therapy, group size in, 22; group versus individual, 47; group, abortive venture in, 48; self theory and, 220. *See also* Counseling

Thibaut, John W., 96n., 121, 122–133

Thomas, Dorothy S., 296n.

Thomas, E. J., 307n.

Thorley, E. J., 307n.

Thorndike, R. L., 124n., 126

Tillich, Paul, 15n.

Timmons, W. M., 123

Tonsor, Charles A., 95, 102–105

Tournier, Paul, 83

Traits, distribution of, 207

Underachievers and group counseling, 151–152, 154

University of Kansas, Western Civilization Program, 97–98, 100

Values, learning of, 75–76; new, acceptance of, 332–334; new, and creation of an ingroup, 334–335

Vanderbilt University, 288

Vocal participation, graph of, 369; statistical tabulation of, 370

Ward, Lester Frank, 4

Warrington, W. C., 340

Warters, Jane, 41n.

Weighting: of individual problem solutions, 126–127; by direct social pressure, 127–128; self-, 129–130

Weinberger, B., 308

Weiss, Paul, 212

Western Civilization Program, University of Kansas, 97–98, 100

Wheeler, W. H., 6

Wherry, R. J., 192, 361, 363, 364

Wherry-Gaylord Iterative Process, 364

White, R. K., 296n., 297

Whitehead, Alfred North, 8, 53

Whyte, William F., 210

Willerman, B., 134

Winer, B. James, 199, 264n.

Wispe, Lauren G., 253n.

Worley, Betty, 111n.

Wrenn, C. Gilbert, 146

Wright, Chauncey, 4

Wright, E. Wayne, 141, 142–149

Wrigley, Charles, 336n.

Zander, Alvin, 251, 260, 307n., 335n.

Znaniecki, F., 26, 27, 28